Genealogy and the Librarian

Genealogy and the Librarian

Perspectives on Research, Instruction, Outreach and Management

Edited by CAROL SMALLWOOD
and VERA GUBNITSKAIA

Foreword by D. Joshua Taylor

McFarland & Company, Inc., Publishers
Jefferson, North Carolina

RECENT McFARLAND WORKS WITH CAROL SMALLWOOD:
Teaching Technology in Libraries, edited by Carol Smallwood
and Lura Sanborn (2017)
Library Partnerships with Writers and Poets, edited by Carol Smallwood
and Vera Gubnitskaia (2017)
Library Volunteers Welcome!, edited by Carol Smallwood
and Lura Sanborn (2016)
Continuing Education for Librarians, edited by Carol Smallwood,
Kerol Harrod and Vera Gubnitskaia (2013)
Job Stress and the Librarian, edited by Carol Smallwood
and Linda Burkey Wade (2013)
Marketing Your Library, edited by Carol Smallwood,
Vera Gubnitskaia and Kerol Harrod (2012)
Mentoring in Librarianship, edited by Carol Smallwood
and Rebecca Tolley-Stokes (2012);
Women on Poetry, edited by Carol Smallwood,
S. Harris and Cynthia Brackett-Vincent (2012)

ISBN (print) 978-1-4766-7087-4
ISBN (ebook) 978-1-4766-3322-0

LIBRARY OF CONGRESS CATALOGUING DATA ARE AVAILABLE

BRITISH LIBRARY CATALOGUING DATA ARE AVAILABLE

© 2018 Carol Smallwood and Vera Gubnitskaia. All rights reserved

*No part of this book may be reproduced or transmitted in any form
or by any means, electronic or mechanical, including photocopying
or recording, or by any information storage and retrieval system,
without permission in writing from the publisher.*

Front cover image © 2018 CharlieAJA/iStock

Printed in the United States of America

*McFarland & Company, Inc., Publishers
Box 611, Jefferson, North Carolina 28640
www.mcfarlandpub.com*

Table of Contents

Foreword
    D. Joshua Taylor — 1

Preface
    Carol Smallwood *and* Vera Gubnitskaia — 3

Part I: Overview

Trends in Genealogy
    Charlene Garcia Simms — 5

The Future of the Past: How Chronicling America Can Impact Genealogical Stories
    Robin C. Pike, Anna J. Kephart *and* Douglas McElrath — 12

Something Old, Something New: Reviving Traditional Editing Tools in the Digital Age
    Debra Carrier Bloom — 21

The Rest Is History: Using Historical Resources to Enrich Genealogy Results
    Tracy Carr — 29

The Affective Nature of Genealogy Collections: New Narratives Through the Altered Book
    Anastasia Varnalis Weigle *and* Renée L. DesRoberts — 36

Part II: Collaboration

A Genealogy Digitization Collaboration
    Ben Walker *and* Chelsea S. Dinsmore — 45

Destined for the Dumpster: A Collaboration Between Librarians and Genealogists to Make 79,000 At-Risk Records Available for Research
    Joanne M. Riley, Jessica Holden *and* Susan Steele — 52

Community Engagement Stimulates Collaboration and Innovation for Local History and Genealogy Programming to Public Housing Residents
    Roland Barksdale-Hall — 60

Building a Collaborative Partnership Between a Genealogical Society
    and a Public Library
    Anastasia Varnalis Weigle, Wendy Lombard Bossie
       and Brenda Jackson Bourgoine   69

Part III: Case Studies

Making the Case for Genealogy Reference Instruction
    Lisa A. Oberg   77

Introducing Genealogy to the Academic Library in the 21st Century
    Thomas McFarland and Joan M. Barnes   85

Part IV: Research

Finding Military and Court Records: Strategies for Research
    Rosemary L. Meszaros and Katherine Pennavaria   95

Contemporary Chinese Genealogy: Value and Status in Academic
    Research and Library Collection
    Hong Cheng   104

Supporting Genealogists in Oral History Research: The Role
    of the Library
    Noah Lenstra   112

Preparing for Genealogical Reference Work
    Beth Stahr   120

Part V: Instruction

Education Techniques for Genealogy Instruction
    Carmen Nigro   129

Instructing Patrons on Using Free Online Genealogical Resources
    Andrew Hart   138

Special Collections Librarians Assisting Patrons in Finding and Preserving
    Family History
    Nancy Richey   146

Beyond Names and Dates on a Tree: How Librarians Can Help Explore
    Family Heritage and Preservation
    Barry L. Stiefel   156

Finding Death-Related Records: Strategies for Research
    Katherine Pennavaria and Rosemary L. Meszaros   164

Genealogy Literacy: Helping Patrons Build Stable Trees Through Information
    Literacy Standards
    Cheri J. Daniels   173

Part VI: Family

Finding Family, Friends, Neighbors and Community in Patent Records
  BARBARA J. HAMPTON — 183

Putting Family History on the Map: Creating Visual Representations of Family Migration, Settlement and Encounters
  LESLIE A. WAGNER — 193

Part VII: Outreach

Genealogy Behind Bars: Professional Development Through Prisoner Requests, a Case Study
  KATHRINE C. AYDELOTT — 203

Community Outreach: Making Your Collection Known and Used
  LARRY NAUKAM — 210

Crowdsourcing Genealogy with Tea and Sympathy: Outreach Approaches That Instruct and Engage
  CHERI J. DANIELS — 218

Part VIII: Management

Accessing and Creating Local Digital Services for Genealogy
  RHONDA L. CLARK — 227

Genealogy for Academics: Utilizing Genealogy Resources for More Than Family History
  NANCY A. BUNKER *and* JENNY L. PRESNELL — 235

The Butler County Obituary and Newspaper Index: An Example of Genealogy Database Creation and Ongoing Management
  MARGARET E. HEWITT — 242

Digitize Your Old Media: A Self-Service Station for Public Library Patrons
  KIRSTEN CANFIELD — 250

Crowdsourcing Genealogy: Evaluating Sources in the Age of Ancestry.com
  KATHRINE C. AYDELOTT — 258

Doing Your Data Digitally—Why and How
  LARRY NAUKAM — 264

Part IX: Finances

Grants: Finding, Writing and Following Through
  NATALIE BAZAN STAROSTA — 271

Developing Materials and Instruction on a Budget for Local Patrons
  JANET CURTISS — 278

About the Contributors — 285
Index — 289

Foreword

D. Joshua Taylor

It is no secret that I have a deep love for genealogical librarianship. My first experiences as a librarian were spent behind the reference desk, where I was consistently in awe of the knowledge of my colleagues, and the array of questions that came my way. Today, whether working on personal genealogical research, a *Genealogy Roadshow* segment, or with a project of the New York Genealogical and Biographical Society, the relationship between genealogists and librarians is more diverse and vibrant than ever before. For many librarians, the genealogical customer is one of the most challenging. We tell stories, we arrive unprepared, we fail to heed your advice, and we expect that every experience should be as simple and easy as clicking on the "shaky leaf" or the recent episode of *Genealogy Roadshow* we viewed the evening before. The reality is—genealogy and family history is a complex and diverse topic for librarians, one that requires careful navigation, constant development, and an ever-growing range of skills and patron services.

Fortunately, coeditors Carol Smallwood and Vera Gubnitskaia have expertly represented the complex world of genealogy and librarianship. *Genealogy and the Librarian* soundly demystifies elements of the research process and suggests diverse, multi-faceted approaches libraries can take to harness the needs of their customers. From its opening pages, this essential resource outlines the important shifts and trends within the field, providing invaluable insight for any librarian (and their administrators) who find themselves seeking to understand their patrons. Digital resources and television programs have set new expectations—and created new opportunities—for librarians and genealogists. The transition from a traditional library setting with rows of microfilm readers to one that includes daily reference questions covering topics ranging from DNA testing to searching Ancestry.com is the reality of any librarian serving genealogists today.

Expertly organized, the pages that follow move beyond serving the essential needs of the genealogical customer. These carefully crafted sections provide the tools for public, academic, and special libraries to harness the strengths of their respective institutions to meet (and often exceed) the expectations of genealogical customers. Perhaps most importantly, the range of topics covers areas of the world often forgotten by professional genealogical organizations, while also offering a variety of practical ideas for providing tools for underserved populations. Regardless of your library's size, collection, structure or budget, *Genealogy and the Librarian* provides new ways to harness the worldwide interest in genealogy to grow and expand your library's services.

More than 30 individual experts move their conversations beyond theoretical discussions, offering practical case studies that provide unique, realistic, and insightful viewpoints on methods libraries undertake to develop services that expand their genealogical offerings beyond the reference desk. These real-life examples show the endless opportunities for libraries and genealogists: working with local schools, advocating for records at risk of closure or destruction, and becoming an epicenter for crowd-sourced projects. The discussions of how libraries can (and should) leverage their own unique collections—both onsite and online—are essential for any library seeking to increase visibility and support for their institution. This practical guidance has the ability to transform any library's genealogical services, increase patron satisfaction, and solidify the role of your library in serving genealogists.

The diverse group of talented librarians whose words fill the pages of *Genealogy and the Librarian* offers a rare—and unparalleled—insight into the diverse and expansive opportunities available to libraries and librarians who aid genealogists. The authors of each section, each practicing professionals themselves, carefully explain the myriad of opportunities libraries have to expand their genealogical services: creating unique digital resources, developing unique collections based on specific localities and subjects, and guiding patrons to publicly available projects, such as mapping tools, that are often overlooked by customers. For those seeking to understand the modern-day genealogical patron and the role a librarian can play in their experience, the authors of the following pages are indispensable.

It must be said that genealogists owe a tremendous debt of gratitude to librarians. As *Genealogy and the Librarian* so eloquently illustrates, librarians can serve as guardians over priceless collections, gateways to unforetold knowledge, voices for records preservation and access, and provide immeasurable resources for customers seeking to find out more about their past. The role of a librarian serving genealogists is certainly not easy—as rapid changes in available tools, new diverse populations, and the increasing popularity of the topic require that any librarian who encounters genealogical customers remain on the forefront of new developments in the field. This reality makes the following pages fundamental and essential reading for any librarian who interacts with genealogists. The exceptional work of Carol Smallwood and Vera Gubnitskaia and the more than 30 authors they have gathered is a groundbreaking and fundamental resource.

D. Joshua Taylor is a nationally known genealogical author, speaker and researcher. He is president of the New York Genealogical and Biographical Society (NYG&B). He holds an MLS (in archival management) from Simmons College in Boston. He has been featured on Who Do You Think You Are? *on NBC and TLC and is a host of* Genealogy Roadshow *on PBS.*

Preface

CAROL SMALLWOOD *and* VERA GUBNITSKAIA

Genealogy is no longer a hobby of a few, a "something-to-do-with-my-time" thing for retired people. Neither is it an occupation that involves mostly genealogy specialists and archivists. Genealogy has been gaining popularity among diverse multicultural American society as people want to learn more about their roots, the history of their families, and the past of their communities. This interest exploded in the last decade or so with the development of a seemingly easy online access to recorded ancestry and proliferation of businesses offering DNA analysis. Consequently, more and more library professionals find themselves becoming "accidental genealogists" and assisting their communities with heritage research, which is why we consider this volume to be timely and needed.

The 34 essays of *Genealogy and the Librarian: Perspectives on Research, Instruction, Outreach and Management* are grouped into nine parts: Overview, Collaboration, Case Studies, Research, Instruction, Family, Outreach, Management and Finances. The essays are written by experts across the United States who are actively engaged in helping patrons with genealogical research. We are immensely grateful to the contributors for sharing their genealogy experience with fellow librarians.

Part I. Overview

Trends in Genealogy

Charlene Garcia Simms

The Study of Genealogy and Family History Today

I recently had a two-day opportunity to be with 20 scholars from all over the country who were brought to my city to help construct a Borderland history exhibit. I was apprehensive about spending two days with them because I am not a scholar, although I do hold two master's degrees, and as a librarian and genealogist, I consider myself well rounded in knowledge. My apprehension came because up to about twenty years ago when I told scholars I was a genealogist, many treated me as inferior to them. After all, genealogy was thought of as more of a pastime or hobby even though it emerged as a science since the 1930s. This time around when I said I was a genealogy and special collections librarian, I was treated with utmost respect and I discovered that many of these scholars greatly value family and oral histories and have done their own family research. We had several discussions about the importance of family history.

I was asked by several of these scholars what got me started in genealogy research. I always told the same story when asked: I was the curious one in the family. There is someone like me in most families, wanting to know everything about everyone. I wanted to know who the parents of my great-grandmother were and who their parents were and so on. I felt that there was something greater than my present. I also had a past and a future. I started writing poems and stories about my childhood memories as I got older, especially when my elders started passing away. I felt that there was something important about remembering and capturing in images or words the essence of people who once walked on this earth who were part of my biological and cultural makeup. Several other genealogists share the same beliefs.

People who were not scholars could not understand my obsession with researching my family tree. Some members of my own family made fun of me and others just dismissed me. Although many of my elder relatives enjoyed answering my questions and without some of them I would not have the photo collections I have accumulated nor the family information I have acquired. Today, ironically, a week does not go by without me getting an inquiry from family members about the family genealogy and others who dismissed me are now asking for my help with their genealogy. I feel I was born to be a genealogist and to add on librarianship to what I do is a great honor and responsibility.

Paradigm Shift

When did the paradigm shift take place about perceptions of genealogy? Alex Haley's book and made for television movie, *Roots,* was a beginning. But technology and the ease of finding information on the Internet, I believe, has had the greatest influence for the growing interest, along with television shows such as *Who Do You Think You Are?* and *Finding your Roots* with Dr. Henry Lewis Gates, Jr. More recently, commercials about finding out where you come from through DNA testing are adding to the allure because today DNA testing is more available and affordable to the common person. Nevertheless, the gates of genealogy have been opened wide and they aren't going to close. The easiest and most affordable place to go through these genealogy gates is the local library. The trends on one hand are going to make it easier for librarianship, but on the other hand it is going to increase the responsibility of information providers such as librarians.

As librarians today are not the librarians of yesterday, the modern study of genealogy is not the genealogy of yesterday. We must give credit to those who came before us and undertook genealogy in a paper world where you had to organize it and store hard copies. We depend on the genealogists of the past who researched primary sources for verifying the research we do online and for doing research beyond five generations.

In the past, genealogy was a paper world of charts and notes and documents in folders stored in file cabinets or boxes tucked away in the basement. Today, technology and the digital world have made it so much easier by making it possible to save online, in your computer software, a flash drive, or share in the cloud. Technology is here to stay, and librarianship must keep up with the trends and make available what is needed to keep up with the ever-changing technology. More important is that training is provided so that the patrons can confidently use the technology.

There is a greater demand by patrons for librarians to have expertise in the tools and resources that they need to do their genealogy research in the 21st century. As the trends continue, it is expected that libraries have experts on not only basic genealogy research but methodologies and standards. Training and support for librarians are very important. In 2015, Federation of Genealogical Societies (FGS) and Roots Tech had a joint conference in Salt Lake City. There were over 20,000 professional people in attendance. This is a testimony to the support that is out there to train and educate information providers about the trends in genealogy research.

Genealogy Trends in the 21st Century

In the evolution of genealogy, the Internet and the number of technology tools that are available to the 21st century genealogist is overwhelming. There are: hundreds of websites, databases, software packages, storage options, search engines, Facebook, Wikis, podcasts and so much more that it becomes confusing as to what is the best method to use in researching and in sharing that research. The speed of that research is faster than ever. You can purchase vital records online and don't have to travel to get them. You would think that you no longer need to visit the library or archives to find information because research is as close as your fingertips. Nothing could be farther from the truth. People still need to be guided and trained in methodology and standards of genealogical research.

Our library has kept up with the trends of technology. Our highest used genealogy database subscription is Ancestry. We have 24 useful websites listed on our webpage, such as Cindy's List, Ellis Island, Family Search and so on. Patrons can use our search engines for free and we encourage using Facebook for genealogy connections. Some people can't afford the Internet so they rely on the library for connectivity. We offer classes on software packages to use for organizing your research, or learning and improving your computer skills. Not everyone has a computer at home and many people, especially older ones, fear technology. We offer the tools of technology and training for free. There are other trends that we have started or followed examples of others. Here are some of them.

We have started digitizing our photo collection and have uploaded thousands of historical photos that people can find on our website, and we continue to increase our numbers. We have 2,000 interviews that were recorded in the 60s and 70s with people who were pioneers of our city or children of pioneers. The interviews were on cassettes which were deteriorating. We have started the process of converting them to DVD format but we have also put many of them online and in a cloud. We are also digitizing funeral records that are getting so brittle that we are afraid to touch them and they are no longer available to the patrons. Soon, we will be able to let our patrons use them digitally and the originals will be put safely away. Preservation of old records digitally is one of our priorities.

Forming partnerships with schools is a trend that is increasing every year. Last year, we were contacted by one of our middle school history teachers who wanted to do a class on genealogy. We decided to make it interdisciplinary with history, geography, mathematics, science, anthropology, and writing. We constructed a one-hour long lesson that would do this. We conducted six classes in two days and ended up with 99 students attending.

One week prior to the classes, the students were given a questionnaire to take home to ask their parents questions about the names of their family members, and when (approximately) and where they were born. Other questions included more personal things, such as the name of their first dog, their best friend as a child, favorite subject in school, etc. These questions made the process more humanistic and required interview skills. Within the first few minutes of the class we explained that genealogy was more than names on a chart, it was giving ancestors more depth. We started talking about memories of the students' childhoods, their grandparents, food that was traditional to them, and traditions they celebrated. These questions were attention getters because they were personal; by the time kids started using ancestry.com, they were hooked, especially since most of them found at least one family member. There was a feeling of pride in the students, even the ones who started with an uncaring attitude. One student even brought his family bible; many of the students had charts with a lot of information. This will be a yearly lesson for 8-graders at a middle school that is just across the street from one of our branch libraries and where we are able to provide computers for every student.

We are doing outreach not only with the schools but with senior citizen centers where we go to them and use two computer labs with ten computers. We do classes on genealogy research using computers. Some seniors adapt easily; when they have field days they choose to come to the library to do more genealogy research.

One of the trends that has grown tremendously is family history research among diverse ethnic groups. This calls for the library to have a collection of relevant historical records for the different ethnic groups and unique primary source materials. Years ago, it was hard to get resources for a variety of ethnic groups, but today there are hundreds of books available and our collection reflects this.

The Hispanic population in our city is almost 50 percent. The migration pattern of our Hispanic patrons consists of ancestors who arrived in New Mexico since 1598 from Mexico with a Spanish and Indigenous heritage. We now have over 500 books called the New Mexico Collection. Many of these books are primary sources that three genealogical societies transcribed and translated from the Spanish Archives in Santa Fe, New Mexico. We focused on this group because of the vast amount of material that was being published and the demand. We try to focus on different ethnic groups every quarter. Two years ago, we had a large German exhibit and the German Club participated by lending us photos, artifacts, and genealogy charts. We had several programs on German history, culture and music. We increased our German resources because we were given several donations.

Another trend that we have become involved in is self-publishing of family history books by our patrons. In the last two years we helped our patrons publish at least ten genealogy books. We have helped them do the research and offered classes on how to scan images and insert them into their text. We have also conducted classes on citing sources and publishing, and those who have been serious about it have been successful.

The last trend is DNA testing. The interest in DNA testing has become so popular, we started a DNA interest group that meets every three months. We have brought several DNA experts to conduct workshops. Many people have had their DNA tested. Some people have had good experiences and some have not.

Having your DNA tested or someone in your family tested should come with a disclaimer of "Beware." In comparing the paper trail and the DNA trail, the paper trail is a traditional genealogy research which gives you an idea of who your ancestors were. The DNA trail shows your genetic makeup and can prove who your ancestors were or weren't. Before you decide to go this route, you must be sure that you and other family members can take the truth if the DNA proves that you are not who you think you are. This may not affect you but it might be hurtful to other family members. There is a NPE (not the parent expected) estimate between 1 and 3 percent or higher. By the sixth generation, many of ancestors in your family tree may not be who you think they should be. This possibility should be understood and patrons should not be discouraged because DNA testing can open new worlds in your research.

An example: A group of the same surnamed people took DNA tests on the paternal side at separate times. Through a DNA project where almost 2,000 people have been tested, comparisons are made so that when the results come back connections are made. In this example six people had matching DNA. However, it was not through the surname they thought they were testing. This caused quite a stir. How could this not be their surname? It was difficult and caused many hurt feelings and created more questions than answers. Fortunately, in this case there was a simple explanation. The error occurred five generations prior to the generation that was being tested. Five generations prior, a child was left an orphan when his parents died. He was raised by his maternal grandfather and took his mother's maiden name instead of his father's which carried into the present. For the generation that was tested, they had another surname and family line to research. This ended up as a good thing but it doesn't always turn out this way.

Librarians need to guide people to the facts, and libraries must have workshops given by DNA experts who can explain issues such as this one. There are two kinds of people who want their DNA tested. Some just want to discover their ethnic mix. This is an easy test and does not involve much interpretation. Others want to discover distant relatives and find further details about their unique family history. It's important to figure out which category a person falls into so the right information is given. In 2015, when FGS and Roots Tech had their conference in Salt Lake City, they covered many aspects of DNA testing including legalities and ethics. Information providers should be sent to these kinds of conferences to keep their patrons informed responsibly.

Patron and Librarian Interaction

Librarians have to be able to keep up with the latest trends and also must understand the behavior of researchers who are studying their roots. Some genealogists remained hobbyists, while others take their methodology and evidence of proof to a very high level. Librarians must understand what kind and category of genealogist they are dealing with so they can give them the best service possible. The following are the most common researchers I deal with.

1. The experienced genealogists who have been doing research for years, who come from a paper world trying to avoid the digital world. They no longer must handle tons of paper but refuse to change their methodology, often because they can't afford computers or are afraid of technology. Their records are most often accurate because they have done their research using original documents. They continue using a physical collection of books and other bound resources. Sad to say, many of these people are dying, and unless you have a caring genealogist in the family these records are tossed out and years of research are destroyed.

2. The second type consists of experienced genealogists who want to get away from the paper world and are willing to learn the digital world. They are hybrid genealogists who bring the best of both worlds to their research. They go to workshops and classes and they join organizations that will help them further their research. They are willing to spend money on software programs and learn to use them. They use the library the most, the physical collection and free databases. They save their work digitally for generations to come. This is what librarians should encourage in their genealogy curriculum.

3. Many patrons are just starting to get interested in genealogy and want to learn how to do a family tree. They may have a lot of information or very little. They are given a pedigree chart to fill out on their own or with the help of other family members. If they return with more information they are serious about getting started and the work begins. These patrons enter the digital world of genealogy right away with databases such as Ancestry.com (library edition), which is free to use in the library. Some get serious enough and purchase a subscription to use at home or we give them other choices to use at home for free such as Family Search. As they progress, especially if they go back more than five generations, they must use the physical collection, and the library is there with the resources they need. We partner with our E Resources and digital collections librarian to teach patrons computer skills, from basics to saving pictures to a cloud. For two years now we have had a Super Seniors computer class where seniors who have no experience with

computers meet up weekly to learn the world of technology. We schedule at least one genealogy class per session and many follow up and become our new genealogists. Their work will more than likely be preserved for many generations.

    4. Some patrons have they want to verify, or they may have reached a road block and need help. These are hard cases to work with because the information they are seeking may not exist or it may take hours to help them. We have two nights a month set aside for these patrons where experienced genealogist can assist them.

    5. Patrons may have special goals, such as finding their birth parents; lost family members, Native American Roots (which is a study all on its own), etc.

    6. Patrons may be interested in doing their DNA test to confirm their paper trail. Or, they are just interested in doing a DNA test and they need information on how to get it done. We have books, pamphlets and DNA workshops given by experts.

Issues That Come Up When We Are Dealing with the 21st Century Genealogy Researcher

Introduction of the Internet to the genealogist opens new worlds. The interconnectivity is wonderful, but it is also dangerous. One has to be careful and know where the information is coming from. As librarians, we need to tell people that they need to source their information. With the Internet we have to emphasize this task because most often you do not know the source of the information. Sometimes people get impatient and make assumptions or don't have time to verify facts.

When we train people to use databases such as Ancestry.com we use a qualifier that this type of database is only a tool in genealogy research. Information was put into this database by people and people may make mistakes. If you take everything that is entered as truth without verifying the information or using other vital documents, then the mistake can be perpetuated for many generations. I share a rule of thumb: don't write anything in ink until you have three verified sources.

An example is my grandfather. There are several names that are similar, especially in Hispanic Genealogy. I found his name in Ancestry.com several times and narrowed it down to the man who was born in southern Colorado in 1882. The information about him by others looked accurate until his death date showed up as 1940. I knew he died in 1958 because I had his death certificate. There is a feature in Ancestry.com where you can see what other families are researching the same family. There were six other families who were researching my family and they had all perpetuated the error that the man who was born in 1882 died in 1940. This is only one example of the errors that can be picked up on databases and need correction. There is still no better evidence of proof than a primary document such as a birth record, baptismal record, marriage record, death record, and having more than one source is crucial.

The Responsibility of Librarians

Librarians must inform patrons that when collecting personal information on living relatives, one must be careful how and who they share this information with. Dates of birth, home addresses, and other data on living relatives can be used by criminals for identity theft. You need permission of the relative who provided the information if you are going to publish it in any format. When a living relative gives you information, it belongs to them, and you have a duty and care to protect it.

Genealogy is complicated with many layers. There are legal and ethical issues but as a librarian you cannot give legal advice and you cannot be judgmental. You cannot recommend a DNA company, but you can offer as much good and thorough information as possible Then it is up to the patron to decide what is best for them.

Genealogy is no longer just a hobby. It is a process of discovering, interpreting, and providing evidence. It is an important research, and user satisfaction is greater when the resources are available to facilitate it. Genealogy communities are forming their own social networks and going outside the library and archives in search of information. The technology available to genealogists is increasing the availability of documents online. However, it is still the library that provides free access because genealogy research can be costly. The library remains a center for genealogy research and librarians remain creators of knowledge and accessibility.

The Future of the Past

How Chronicling America Can Impact Genealogical Stories

Robin C. Pike, Anna J. Kephart *and* Douglas McElrath

Introduction

The U.S. Newspaper Program (USNP), a National Endowment for the Humanities grant-funded initiative, facilitated newspaper preservation and access across all 50 states through the creation and circulation of microfilm copies of newspapers ("U.S. Newspaper Program" 2017). Each state in the program designated a repository for the microfilm, and in Maryland, it was the Maryland State Archives, with use copies sent to many state public libraries and historical societies. This project greatly facilitated genealogists' free access to newspapers, although it still presented accessibility issues. Genealogists value the information in historic newspapers, but many did not use them because of the well-known technical and physical limitations posed by microfilm. Instead, most genealogists preferred published newspaper abstracts. The indexes to birth, marriage, and death announcements were essential; particularly when identifying ancestors before 1850 when the census and vital records are incomplete; however, most indexing projects focused on large dailies and county newspapers of record and neglected many titles from smaller towns. For many librarians, genealogy represents both the past and the future of library services. Genealogical researchers can account for 50 to 90 percent of users in typical archives and special collections across the country. The digitization of genealogical source material, particularly newspapers, is a primary contributor to the growth in genealogical research (Haddad 2014).

National Digital Newspaper Program and Chronicling America

Modeled after the access provided by licensed newspaper databases, free newspaper access in the 21st century has evolved from microfilm to a new, freely accessible database of digitized newspapers. Established in 2005 and growing out of the USNP, "The National

Digital Newspaper Program (NDNP), a partnership between the National Endowment for the Humanities (NEH) and the Library of Congress (LC), is a long-term effort to develop an Internet-based, searchable database of U.S. newspapers with descriptive information and select digitization of historic pages" ("National Digital Newspaper Program" 2016). The project focused on newspapers from 1836 to 1922, from 2005 to 2016, and then expanded to include newspapers from 1690 to 1963. The database, Chronicling America, "will be developed and permanently maintained at the Library of Congress" ("About Chronicling America" 2017). The NDNP NEH award program funds digitization with the goal of funding the content contribution from all U.S. states and territories; as of the 2016 award cycle, 43 states, the District of Columbia, and Puerto Rico contributed newspapers. The corpus of nearly 12 million pages is word-searchable and browsable in multiple ways. Chronicling America also facilitates a second point of access to the Newspaper Title Directory, the catalog records created during the USNP; historical essays about the titles digitized and available on Chronicling America; bulk data downloads via an Application Program Interface (API); and NDNP Extras, projects and resources expanding building on the newspaper data ("National Digital Newspaper Program" 2016).

Historic Maryland Newspapers Project

The Historic Maryland Newspapers Project (HMNP) began in 2012 as the Maryland State newspaper digitization project ("The Historic Maryland Newspapers Project" 2017). From 2012 to 2016 during the first two two-year grant cycles, the project digitized 211,866 pages across 15 families of newspaper titles from 11 cities or regions from 1840 to 1922 ("Awardee: University of Maryland, College Park, MD" 2016). The project team and Advisory Board, a group comprised of archivists, librarians, educators, and historians, received proposals from researchers and proposed Maryland newspaper titles for all three grant awards, and prioritized these titles based on NEH content selection criteria and potential use by researchers, including genealogists, building a body of newspapers representing the people, businesses, and culture of Maryland ("Content Selection" 2017). Because the project is not permitted to digitize newspapers previously digitized and available through other resources, such as commercial databases, the HMNP focused on digitizing community-based and small-town newspapers, which feature a wealth of information about local life.

During the 2016 fall Advisory Board meeting, members discussed opportunities for project outreach to increase knowledge and use of Maryland papers in Chronicling America (Pike and McElrath 2016). Members agreed that genealogists could benefit from training on how to use this newspaper database to create family narratives to expand their research beyond naming family members found in birth and death notices. For example, the newspapers document the rise of local industries, such as railroads, which affected family-owned businesses (and in turn, the families). Social events, such as parades, dances, religious gatherings, and social visitations, are well documented in these smaller papers, and provide insight into family life. Newspapers also document larger regional, national, and international events, such as the Civil War and World War I, which tie families into a larger narrative. By providing additional awareness of Chronicling America and educational resources customized to this patron group, genealogists would be able

14 Part I: Overview

to create compelling family narratives from newspapers and get to know their ancestors in ways previously lost to time.

Methodologies and Approaches

In designing Maryland's outreach to genealogists, members of the project team and Board first researched similar initiatives and resources created by other statewide NDNP projects, including informational handouts and web guides of compiled resources and search tips, instructional videos, and hands-on interactive sessions led by project team members. The Library of Congress's webpage of NDNP extras links to many of the established outreach projects and the project awardees' internal wiki ("Extra! Extra! NDNP Extras!" 2017). Vermont, Connecticut, Washington, and Wisconsin state projects created extensive libguides, blogs, or web pages dedicated to genealogical research search tips, or explanations on how to use Chronicling America for genealogical research ("For Genealogists" 2017; "Resources for Genealogists" 2017; "Genealogy at the Washington State Library 2017; "Getting Started Researching Your Family History" 2017). Florida and Puerto Rico's joint state project developed an excellent video tutorial on how to use Chronicling America ("Chronicling America Tutorial" 2016).

As a first step, the Maryland team decided to create an informational brochure that could also be posted online. Distributed to local libraries, historical societies, and other organizations that attract genealogical researchers, the brochure also targeted events such as in-person demonstrations and workshops for different communities. Robin Pike, HMNP Co-Principal Investigator, based the brochure information, including search and browse tips, on the Vermont Digital Newspaper Project resources, with some additional insight from the Washington Historical Society's web page, and added Maryland-specific information, such as the titles and regions represented in the 2012–2016 digitization projects, and a search diagram using Maryland-specific search tips.

The brochure links to the Florida and Puerto Rico video tutorial on how to use Chronicling America, which provides a helpful systematic guide for non-native technologists. Many genealogists are accustomed to the simple search and viewer interfaces at sites like Newspapers.com; hence, the Chronicling America interface can be intimidating because they contain more elements. The video tutorial alleviated this issue, as did hands-on workshops, which assisted genealogists during Maryland's outreach program.

The team experienced other issues beyond the challenges of helping genealogists overcome a new and complex platform. Though Chronicling America has nearly 12 million pages of newsprint from across the country and a substantial subset from Maryland, the collection is not exhaustive. It excludes specific papers of record because the NDNP will not digitize newspapers available elsewhere, including commercial database products like ProQuest, Readex, or Newspapers.com. In addition, many of these commercial vendors have obtained publication rights through licensing or publisher acquisition and have ingested copyrighted materials into these databases, whereas Chronicling America contains public domain content from 1836 to 1922, soon to be expanded to 1690–1963. For example, the archive of the *Afro-American*, the premiere African American title in Maryland, is available via ProQuest, and Readex, another vendor, holds limited runs of four additional African American newspaper titles ("The Afro Black History Archives" 2017). These titles form the known, extant copies of African American newspapers in

Maryland, and are not included in the Maryland corpus on Chronicling America, creating a knowledge gap for those who lack access to these databases. The HMNP has created geographical diversity in coverage by targeting a substantial portion of newspapers from Western Maryland, Southern Maryland, and the Eastern Shore.

Genealogical Reference in the Public Library

Mary Mannix has managed the Maryland Room of the C. Burr Artz Library in Frederick, MD, for more than 20 years. Mannix's insights into the changing needs of genealogists and her membership on the HMNP Advisory Board have helped guide the outreach project. Mannix and her staff oversee a rich collection of special materials documenting the history and people of the region, and they regularly provide reference services to in-person and virtual patrons. For Mannix, the advent of digitized newspapers and other online content "has changed the face of genealogy.... Genealogy is no longer a retirement pastime, now anyone can do it from home at any time." Her observation is echoed in the 2016 Pew Internet and American Life Study, which found that 27 percent of those surveyed had used a library website to find resources, and the 2003 study in which 24 percent of those surveyed had used library online tools to research their family history ("Datasets" 2017).

Mannix noted that genealogists are increasingly interested in building upon the stories of their ancestors by exploring the history of localities and finding details about living in the past. To accomplish this, genealogists document important local institutions such as churches, organizations, and businesses. Genealogical researchers also reconstruct the social networks of friends, family, neighbors, business partners, and other relationships that were as important in the past as they are today. Using digitized newspapers made these goals more achievable. Abstractors rarely noted the contents of society columns, reports of vacation visits, and other gossipy updates, but they contain clues to relationships when an out-of-town person visited. Descriptions of social events such as parades, dances, or concerts inform researchers by identifying community leaders and interactions among families. By assisting genealogists using newspaper databases to locate these types of articles and trace relationships, Mannix has seen genealogy supporting the work of local historians. Similarly, historians often seek genealogical information in online newspapers, as their research creates a snapshot of the people and events of significance to a place.

Digitized resources imparted greater independence to researchers, but also led to confusion. One of Mannix's complaints is that searching the newspaper database provides inconsistent results, and that the quality of scanning and OCR reliability can dramatically affect search results. Mannix coaches researchers "not to trust the technology," because keyword searching historic data is not as reliable as keyword searching in Google. She continues to educate patrons on how editors organized the information in historic newspapers, as a way to navigate a complex communications system.

Beyond Chronicling America, whose selection standards advise using "sufficient image quality on microfilm to yield satisfactory digital images and automated text conversion output," some of the commercially-produced products relied on poor quality microfilm that is neither readable nor keyword-searchable, resulting in frequent failed searches for information that exists on the printed pages ("Content Selection" 2016).

Mannix has also encountered serious problems with vendors' inconsistency in filming morning or evening editions, and not accounting for missing issues or pages. She noted that these problems are not as apparent with the Chronicling America database, because the NDNP program has high quality standards. Mannix also confirmed that for researchers, "Chronicling America has filled some content gaps by selecting a more diverse range of titles." Even though digitized newspapers pose unique challenges, Mannix found that most genealogists were able to develop sophisticated searching methods for digitized newspapers. In this, she echoes Curt Witcher, who stated that the most valuable skills for genealogists are "Analytical ability. Creative analytical ability. Being a historical detective" (Zuber 2016).

Genealogical Research in the University Classroom

Traditionally, genealogical research involved establishing family lines of descent, but there are other important uses for genealogy. At the University of Maryland's (UMD) School of Architecture, Planning, and Preservation, students learn to use genealogical source records, such as historic newspapers, as an essential tool for documenting historic places. All historic preservation students take the HISP 611 Historical Research Methods class, taught by librarian Doug McElrath (HMNP Co-Principal Investigator), whose responsibilities include curating the National Trust for Historic Preservation collection held by UMD Libraries. Historic preservation is primarily concerned with understanding the significance of sites using multiple criteria: qualities inherent in a structure (e.g., noteworthy architectural features and physical integrity), and whether the site is associated with significant historical events or persons. The process of nominating a site for inclusion in the National Register of Historic Places or similar processes at the state and local levels involves a complete "genealogy" of both the chain of title ownership and the people associated with the site.

McElrath's class taught students how to perform research that would place a structure within its historical context through a semester-long sequence of readings, lectures, discussions, hands-on exercises, and a final project. Part of learning how to establish historical context was to focus on the people associated with a site. McElrath asked the students to consider: "Who was associated with the site you are studying?," "What can you tell me about their lives?," and "How do these people inform our understanding of the structure?" Each student was assigned a residential property in an historic district near the University, and McElrath worked with the students to create comprehensive dossiers to present to the community at the end of the semester. The research began with property-centric public land records, but these deeds and tax records soon led the students to individuals associated with the property, whose stories provided historic context for understanding the structure, neighborhood, and community.

Once students established custodial ownership, they turned to historic newspapers in online repositories, such as Chronicling America, to develop deeper insights into the lives of the individuals and family members associated with the property, creating genealogies of individuals and the community. Students also used historic newspapers to reconstruct the broader context for the house they were researching to better understand the community, its major institutions, businesses, and events of importance. As explained in one of the principal texts the students read, *Nearby History, Exploring the*

Past Around You, "Careful newspaper research can pay rich rewards for the historian ... not only for reports of specific news events but also for many other traces" (Kyvig and Marty 2010). By understanding the people, their origins, and relationships, the students established the human context for the structure. Genealogical information about individuals explained what type of person occupied the dwelling, and information on occupations and income levels provided insight into the person's class and how this changed over time. By exploring real estate advertisements in digitized newspapers, one student discovered a sales advertisement for a nearly identical house to her assigned address in the same community. The newly-built structure was described as "A Little Villa of One's Own"—an indication that the by the 1920s, home ownership was a more common housing option for even the lower middle class, inferring the status of the owning family. Historic newspapers were essential in documenting the economic dynamics of the community during the Great Depression between 1929 and 1939. Another student used newspaper articles to show that her family had been community leaders who figured prominently on the 1920s social scene, but by the mid–1930s they had lost their house in a foreclosure auction. If genealogy is the study of relationships, then genealogical research by historic preservationists expands this concept to reconstructing the relationship of people to places.

Genealogical Reference and Outreach in the Local History Archive

Anna J. Kephart, Coordinator of the Southern Maryland Studies Center (SMSC), a small local history archive at the College of Southern Maryland in La Plata, MD, collects, preserves, and provides access to materials that document the culture and development of this historically important region. Kephart is also a member of the HMNP Advisory Board. In these roles, she has used Chronicling America as a genealogy reference and outreach tool for individual patrons and local organizations, including a genealogical society and a hereditary society, as well as for exhibit research.

In November 2016, a small group from the local Daughters of the American Revolution (DAR) chapter visited the SMSC to perform research on historic merchants in Port Tobacco, MD. While the researchers had used nineteenth century census data to develop a list of dozens of individuals who had lived in Port Tobacco and whose listed occupations identified them as being employed in trade, the researchers were unsure how to efficiently and effectively conduct additional research on the many individuals they had found. Trying to find information about each person in the paper-based archival collections would have been like finding a needle in a haystack, Kephart explained, as the SMSC's finding aids typically do not describe materials at the item level, and do not contain an exhaustive list of every name found in the collection. Wendy M. Duff and Catherine A. Johnson identified this challenge in the title of their article on genealogical research strategies, "Where Is the List with All the Names? Information-Seeking Behavior of Genealogists." In this article, Duff and Johnson wrote, "[t]he genealogists in this study wanted lists of names, or name indexes, or search engines that retrieved by name to facilitate their research…" as well as "geographic area, and a range of dates…" and "digitized images of the original documents" (Duff and Johnson 2003).

Chronicling America met these criteria, as the *Port Tobacco Times* historic newspaper was recently digitized through the HMNP, so the patrons would be able to limit their search results to this newspaper. Additionally, the researchers would be able to search within the specific period they were looking for. Upon learning about this resource, the DAR researchers decided to devote their entire research session to exploring Chronicling America, with Kephart's guidance.

All four DAR members brought a laptop, so Kephart tailored each researcher's instruction to the researcher's level of computer skills. A few of the researchers initially expressed trepidation, but soon caught on. One user enthusiastically exclaimed that Chronicling America was "like Google, but for genealogy!" The researchers were excited by their ability to make real-time discoveries, and particularly enjoyed finding advertising images associated with certain merchants, as well as information about the merchants' personal lives. They were surprised by how much rich information they could find about many individuals in such a short time period, and stated that Chronicling America was a great starting place for their very specific research questions that would otherwise take an extraordinary amount of time to answer, if they were able to answer them at all.

The researchers also appreciated that Chronicling America was a free resource that they would not need to physically visit a library to use. Genealogists often prefer to "cut out the middleman" as much as possible, and ideally seek out information independently, on their own schedule, without guidance/gatekeeping, for free, and from home. In a 2006 study, 71 percent of genealogists surveyed stated that they most commonly accessed the Internet for research from home rather than from a library or other access point (Tucker 2006, 139). While researchers found Chronicling America less user-friendly than Newspapers.com, which has integrated clipping and email-to-self tools, Kephart overcame these challenges by demonstrating use of the Windows accessory snipping tool to create images from screenshots, which researchers found very helpful.

The DAR researchers did encounter some obstacles using Chronicling America, particularly in trying to differentiate different people with the same name, or looking for names that were also commonly used words (such as the last name Short, which also returned every use of the word "short" as an adjective). Inconsistently spelled names also posed a challenge, as did abbreviations, such as Jno. for John, and printing errors. As Duff and Johnson noted, the genealogists in their study "provided a number of examples of using a record's dates to help them determine whether the information in a record related to their person or someone else with the same name" (Duff and Johnson 2003, 85). The DAR researchers found it very helpful to be able to limit their search results by year to pinpoint specific merchants once they determined the years that they were active. They also found it frustrating to repeat the laborious process of limiting search results to the *Port Tobacco Times* every time they initiated a new search.

The small size of the DAR group was crucial to the research session's success, as it allowed Kephart to work one-on-one with the researchers to help them overcome obstacles related to uneven computer skills and the limitations of Chronicling America. With a group much larger than 5–6, this would have been very challenging. For example, following the success of the DAR research session, Kephart gave a PowerPoint presentation about Chronicling America to a group of about 25 members at a meeting of a county genealogical society. This was a more challenging format for outreach because while the attendees were very interested in the program, they were not able to directly interact with the resource while learning about it. Kephart answered the members' questions, and performed several demonstrations using names suggested by the audience, but overall the session was not as effective as the small group session. As a result of these events, Kephart will explore the possibility of offering future limited-registration events, tailored to the sponsoring organization's research needs, where each user would bring his or her own laptop.

Kephart also used Chronicling America to perform genealogy research while developing an exhibit on the history of World War I in southern Maryland. She was able to find compelling details about the individual soldiers documented in photographs in her collection, and background information about the soldiers from southern Maryland who died during the war, including obituaries and memorials written by friends and family members, which made the exhibit more personal and impactful. Genealogists could undertake similar research to tie their family history to larger regional, national, and international historic events.

Future Opportunities

Genealogists are pleased to discover Chronicling America's free access and sophisticated searching. Outreach initiatives and training have demonstrated to genealogists that librarians are an important resource that maximizes the potential of Chronicling America. Overall, the project team members concluded that the most effective experiences teaching genealogists to use Chronicling America were either in one-on-one reference inquiries or small groups, such as with the DAR group or the class, and that giving presentations to larger groups, like the genealogical society, wasn't as impactful because attendees did not immediately use the database. Using the practices established in the successful events, the team members would explore teaching a how-to workshop to librarians at a state conference, so they can in turn teach their patrons how to use the database. In addition to providing search tips, the workshop will educate librarians on quality-based OCR limitations and searchability of the resource, and some of the less visible tools in the viewing interface, such as the clipping and download tools. The project team will continue to add new resources to the project webpage, focusing on the types of search tips and interface assistance for which patrons experienced the most challenges. The members may also explore the use of Chronicling America's API for data mining across newspaper titles, creating a greater newspaper index or abstract for many of the families' names, creating new access points and further assisting genealogists, as was done by indexers in the past. "The technological advances of recent years have revolutionized the way family historians discover and use records ... only the genealogist's imagination and resourcefulness limit the newspaper's usefulness" (Szucs and Luebking 2006, 561). A decade after its establishment, Chronicling America has vastly expanded the landscape for digitized newspaper research.

WORKS CITED

"About Chronicling America." *Library of Congress.* Last modified 2017. http://chroniclingamerica.loc.gov/about/.

"The Afro Black History Archives." *Afro.* Last modified 2016. https://www.afro.com/archives/.

"Awardee: University of Maryland, College Park, MD." *Library of Congress.* Last modified 2016. http://chroniclingamerica.loc.gov/awardees/mdu/.

"Chronicling America Tutorial." *Florida and Puerto Rico Digital Newspaper Project: Expanding Access to Historical News.* Last modified August 15, 2016. https://ufndnp.wordpress.com/2016/08/15/chronicling-america-tutorial-ufndnp/.

"Content Selection." *Library of Congress*. Last modified August 4, 2016. http://www.loc.gov/ndnp/guidelines/selection.html.

"Datasets." *Pew Research Center*. Last modified February 6, 2017. http://www.pewinternet.org/datasets/.

Duff, Wendy M., and Catherine A. Johnson. 2003. "Where Is the List with All the Names? Information-Seeking Behavior of Genealogists." *American Archivist* 66: 79–95.

"Extra! Extra! NDNP Extras!" *Library of Congress*. Last modified February 9, 2017. https://www.loc.gov/ndnp/extras/.

"For Genealogists: How to Use Chronicling America for Genealogy." *Vermont Digital Newspaper Project*. Last modified 2017. http://library.uvm.edu/vtnp/?page_id=1961.

"Genealogy at the Washington State Library." *Washington State Library*. Last modified 2017. https://www.sos.wa.gov/library/genealogy.aspx#newspapers.

"Getting Started Researching Your Family History." *Wisconsin Historical Society*. Last modified 2017. http://www.wisconsinhistory.org/Content.aspx?dsNav=N:4294963828–4294963805&dsRecordDetails=R:CS 156.

Haddad, Diane. 2014. "An Interview with ACPL Genealogy Center Director Curt Witcher." *Genealogy Insider*. Last modified June 23. http://blog.familytreemagazine.com/insider/2014/06/23/AnInterviewWithACPLGenealogyCenterDirectorCurtWitcher.aspx.

"The Historic Maryland Newspapers Project." *University of Maryland Libraries*. Last modified January 24, 2017. http://www.lib.umd.edu/digital/newspapers/home.

Kyvig, David E., and Myron A. Marty. 2010. *Nearby History: Exploring the Past Around You*. Lanham, MD: Rowman & Littlefield.

"National Digital Newspaper Program." *Library of Congress*. Last modified November 3, 2016. http://www.loc.gov/ndnp/.

Pike, Robin C., and Douglas P. McElrath. "Historic Maryland Newspapers Project Advisory Board Meeting." *Digital Repository at the University of Maryland* (DRUM). doi: http://hdl.handle.net/1903/18919.

"Resources for Genealogists." *Connecticut Digital Newspaper Project*. Last modified 2017. http://ctdigitalnewspaperproject.org/resources-for-genealogists/.

Szucs, Loretto Dennis, and Sandra Hargreaves Luebking. 2006. *The Source: A Guidebook to American Genealogy*. Provo, UT: Ancestry Publishing.

Tucker, Susan. 2006. "Doors Opening Wider: Library and Archival Services to Family History." *Archivaria* 62: 127–158.

"U.S. Newspaper Program." *National Endowment for the Humanities*. Last modified 2017. https://www.neh.gov/us-newspaper-program.

Zuber, Connie Hass. 2016. "20 Questions with Curt Witcher." *Fort Wayne*. Last modified October 17. http://www.fortwayne.com/20questionswith/curt-witcher/.

Something Old, Something New
Reviving Traditional Editing Tools in the Digital Age

Debra Carrier Bloom

Transcribing and abstracting are traditional editing tools used to help researchers easily access information. Without these vital skills, historical records would not be keyword searchable through an online database. At Richland Library in Columbia, SC, local history librarians are refocusing collection management strategies and seeking out hyperlocal primary documents that need documentary editing to improve accessibility. Popular with genealogists and local history researchers, these enhanced records provide easy access into historical resources.

Documentary Editing Options

Transcription

Historians Michael Stevens and Steven Burg define transcription as, "the process of converting textual and nontextual elements of original documents into readable, publishable, typescript form" (Stevens and Burg 1997, 71). A transcription allows the document to be searchable and easily read. Style guides designed for large documentary editing projects, like the *Women's Diaries and Letters of the South: A Guide for Editors,* provide a manual of streamlined editing standards that can be borrowed for smaller projects. Selecting a few standards to identify errors and illegible words can keep the transcribing process simple but still provide consistency in the final product.

Annotation

Annotation is described as "the information added by editors to improve readers' understanding of historical documents" (Stevens and Burg 1997, 157). Annotations can be shared through footnotes, endnotes, cross references, etc. The documentary editor decides the annotation rules for an editing project. The decision can range from many well-researched annotations to minimal annotating. *A Guide to Documentary Editing* wisely reminds editors that, "Documentary editions should be the beginning of research, not its culmination." (Kline and Purdue 2008, 240).

Indexing

An index organizes information using "headings describing the names, places, and major subjects contained within an edition" in ascending or descending order (Stevens and Burg 1997, 199). Indexing is the process of organizing the historical data found in a book or document. Another form of indexing, sorting, allows information to be sorted alphabetically within different fields of data. Computer software programs make sorting and alphabetizing simple jobs.

Abstracting

When an entire document cannot be made available either due to size or copyright limits providing an abstract of the document, summarizing the key points of information, is another option. Abstracts also include the complete citation needed to locate the original document for further research.

Selecting an Editing Project

Established in 1785, Richland County surrounds the state capitol, the University of South Carolina, Fort Jackson, and city of Columbia. There are more than 400,000 Richland County residents, half of whom are library card holders. The Main Library of the Richland Library system is in Columbia's newly renovated downtown, and the Walker Local and Family History Center sits neatly on the first floor. Simply referred to as the "Local History Room," it employs the small staff who serve genealogists, local history researchers, businesses, and city, county, and state government agencies researching historic properties, events, and people. While the Local History Room print resources include a selection of statewide materials, the collection management policy focuses on materials about Richland and the surrounding counties. Five years ago, the library system acquired a digital content management system to support the expansion of historic digital resources. Online resources include photographs, pamphlets, books, maps, and other historic materials from the Civil War to present day Columbia and Richland County.

Our staff often research historic record groups that long for some type of editing to save the user from tediously reading every page to find a name, or a business or maybe an event. At Richland Library, the available time staff can spend on an editing project receives the highest consideration. There may be a document or record group with amazing information, but if it is too large and the project will never be finished then staff time is wasted. Selecting a project often includes the following "time" considerations:

1. Identify a document or record group that consist mostly of names.
    a. Not only do genealogists love lists of names but public service staff can easily get back on track if they are interrupted while editing a list of names.
2. Edit documents or record groups that are easily accessed.
    a. We look for record groups that are located at other institutions in formats, like microfilm, that allow editing projects to be completed in-house.
3. Identify available viewing formats for wide accessibility of the final edited project.

a. Will the project be available as an in-house print resource or available through a website or a digital platform? Maybe it will be published in a genealogy society newsletter. The more researchers have access to the edited document, the greater the value of your project time.
4. Identify small indexing projects.
  a. Short runs of magazines, for example, are comfortably doable in the framework of a public service schedule and are available on-site.

Dusting Off the Editing Tools at Richland Library

Hidden behind the scenes in many local history rooms are old catalog cards used to record magazine articles and newspaper obituary abstracts. Abstracting projects faded as public domain periodicals became digitized and searchable online. Online databases also provide full-text access to current articles and obituaries further reducing the need for abstracting projects. However, this has left an accessibility gap between digitized historic and present-day online periodicals. Mid-century magazines, newspapers, and journals cannot be digitized because of copyright restrictions and their material is not available in the electronic format needed to upload the files into online databases. Without improved access their information is invisible to researchers. Richland Library has two projects underway to address this information gap.

Obituary Indexing

Our library is the public depository for *The State* newspaper. Beginning in 1891, *The State* newspaper continues today reporting on local and statewide news. Obituary requests from *The State* are among the most common questions received in the Local History Room so, using volunteers, an obituary indexing project was started many years ago. Now online, the obituary index boasts over one million records from several Columbia-based newspapers from 1875 to the present. Every record includes a name, publication date, newspaper title, page number, and place of death.

Although *The State* newspaper is now digitized, the online index is still our most valuable tool for finding published obituaries. For example, the obituary index gives complete citations so customers with fuzzy dates or wrong dates can quickly eye the correct citation. Also, online newspaper searching sometimes becomes a guessing game. Early obituaries were published with abbreviated first names, with or without middle names, or without first names at all. Obituary abstracting eliminates the guessing game with simple search results that can be easily scanned. Another benefit is the index's browse feature. It helps locate misspelled names published in the newspaper. Despite digitized content, the obituary index saves staff search time and so the abstracting project continues.

Records are still transcribed by hand from microfilm into a standardized form and then inputted into an Excel spreadsheet. Records receive minimal standardizations; for example, name omissions or illegible names are represented with the [--?--] symbol, state abbreviations are uniform and dates are all numeric. The updated spreadsheet is saved as a tab-delimited text file and, using MarcEdit software, the text file is transferred to a machine readable (MARC) record. Batch files, including thousands of records, are uploaded into the obituary index silo attached to the online catalog where they become keyword searchable.

Outcomes:

- Popular resource for genealogists.
- Newspaper research simplified.
- Productive use of volunteer time.

Magazine Indexing

The Walker Local and Family History Center print collection houses extensive bound volumes of local magazines that have deep historical and local information but are underused because the content is not easily discovered. Over the years' Richland County librarians attempted to organize magazine content with article title indexes and occasional attempts to add subject headings and abstracts. However, their efforts were loosely organized and inconsistent making the resulting index unreliable.

Using our online catalog system, we minimized these problems with standardized electronic workforms that provide a place to collect and make abstracted information, or metadata, accessible in one step. The records are kept in a module that sits next to the online book catalog. Initially, we began using this community records module as a database for the obituary index but expanded the module to include data from abstracted magazine articles. The module allows library staff creates online workforms that label fields like title, author, abstract, subjects, etc., into MARC records. Each librarian is responsible for inputting article information from an assigned local magazine series into the workform. After it is saved, the data is immediately available in a keyword-searchable database that sits separately from the online catalog.

There were some surprising benefits to magazine indexing assignments. Besides greater access to the historical information found in local magazines the indexing project also provided a measurable appraisal tool for employee evaluations. The module can supply managers with monthly reports numbering the records made by individual staff members.

This is a valuable learning engagement project for local history staff. Indexing local magazine articles helps staff develop areas of expertise and gives them opportunities to improve their knowledge of local history. It is also a project that can be used to engage staff from other library departments. Someone in another department may love gardening and would enjoy indexing local garden magazines. Anyone with access to the staff side of the online catalog can participate.

Outcomes:

- In-house materials rediscovered and easier to access.
- Output can be monitored for employee evaluations.
- Uses existing ILS technology.
- Helps staff develop specialized expertise.
- Assignments can be shared with other departments.

Thanks to demanding public service schedules, librarians seldom have time to undertake complex transcription projects. Local history staff, however, are a valuable, and yet, untapped resource for transcribing hyperlocal historic documents. As experts in local family names, street names, businesses, neighborhoods, etc., they can easily read and decipher local handwritten documents. Searching census records in Ancestry is a good example of the importance of correctly reading names. Most of the spelling errors in the census index do not result from the original census enumerator but from the twenty first century person transcribing the written words. They are not familiar with local names and, therefore, make mistakes. Missing from the librarian's expertise, however, are the editing standards that historians use in large documentary editing projects.

The complex standards that historians use to manage document editing projects shouldn't deter smaller transcription projects. These editing standards can be simply applied to local historical documents. Stevens and Burg encourage any level of editing to improve access to the information in historic documents if the effort is well planned, "The usefulness of published historical documents depends not on the format or the budget but rather on the care with which the documents are presented to the potential audience." (Stevens and Burg 1997, 17). At Richland Library, we have been exploring how we fit in the field of documentary editing through two projects.

Columbia City Council Minutes Project

The Columbia City Council Minutes (CCCM) provide a glimpse into the economic development of South Carolina, through the eyes of Columbia, from an antebellum agricultural commercial system into a middle-class manufacturing economy. Even seemingly simple examples of urban growth are documented in the minutes. For example, the development of street lights from gas to carbon arc lights to electric incandescent lights, demonstrate the municipal development of post-war Columbia. Available from 1883, the minutes are under lock and key in the Columbia city office building making them inaccessible to researchers. Even with access, the large ledgers cannot be accommodated on office copiers or scanners leaving the only option to read all the ledgers for information.

A project to digitize the CCCM resulted from collaboration between Richland Library, the city of Columbia and the South Carolina Digital Library (SCDL). As South Carolina's statewide digital library, SCDL welcomes partnerships to digitize and make freely available South Carolina historic documents. Each CCCM partner brought something unique to the project. The city of Columbia owned the materials and they transported the ledgers to the University of South Carolina, home to the SCDL. Using a large format scanner SCDL staff digitized the ledgers, created the metadata and hosted the collection. The project eventually entailed processing ten 2-foot-long ledgers spanning the years 1883–1919.

Besides connecting all the partners, the Walker Local and Family History Center managed the project to transcribe all the handwritten ledgers. Six thousand pages were digitized and half of those, 1883–1901, were handwritten and needed transcriptions for online searching. After the ledgers were digitized and uploaded to a digital content management system the handwritten pages could be read from any computer with internet access then transcribed into a Word document.

This was a simple transcription project. The handwritten ledgers were generally clear and easy to read. Complex text formatting was eliminated because the transcriptions were uploaded as a block of text into the metadata. Annotation was kept to a minimum using only Columbia city directories to confirm name spellings. Each completed Word file was uploaded into the metadata associated with the online image.

One staff member was assigned to manage the project. Assignments generally covered a six-month period so when one section was transcribed, e.g., January-June 1891, the project manager marked that section complete and assigned a new section. The project manager prepared the files for electronic delivery to the SCDL. The result became a searchable database of primary documents covering the growth of a war-torn southern city into a city of the New South.

Volunteers from the local genealogy society were initially used to transcribe the minutes as a crowdsourcing experiment. Although they did excellent work, we stopped using volunteers for two reasons. First, the transcribing was moving too slowly. We would need to locate and manage more volunteers to bring the project to a timely conclusion. Secondly, we soon realized that the minutes provided rare insight into Columbia history. It was a unique opportunity to help staff become more familiar with local historic events. If additional staff time would be needed to manage more volunteers then, we decided, our time would be better spent transcribing the minutes as a team and immersing ourselves into the city's turn of the century history.

Here again the project was used as an employee appraisal tool. Employee development goals were built around their productivity in the transcription project. As a time-sensitive project tying development goals to the completion of the project helped to ensure assignments were completed on time. Even so, it took us four years to transcribe the 3,000 pages. In the end, however, our efforts paid off. The Optical Character Recognition software, used to transcribe the typed pages, had an accuracy rate of 60 percent. The hand-written pages transcribed by the local history room staff was 99 percent accurate. Hooray for the people!

Outcomes:

- Tool for staff development goals.
- Promoted collaboration and local partnerships.
- The team effort encouraged discussion about the Columbia historical events.
- Offered leadership opportunities for staff.

1868 Voter Registration Census

History itself also helped determine the types of editing projects undertaken at Richland Library. At the close of the Civil War General Sherman marched through Columbia and many of our antebellum records were destroyed, however, in the Reconstruction government that followed the Civil War many record groups were created. In 1868 the federal military government conducted a survey of South Carolina voters as a prelude to new elections. This census, called *Voter Registrations Reported to the Military Government 1868* (South Carolina Secretary of State 1868, S 213103), provides the name, race, county and voter precinct of voting age males and is only available at the South Carolina Department of Archives and History.

Consistently, the 1870 census has presented itself as the final stop for African American family historians researching slave ancestors. Squeezing information about pre–1870 emancipated slaves has restrained many researchers as prior to the 1870 census slaves were enumerated without names. The 1868 voter registration series turns out to be a valuable record group for conquering the 1870 divide in South Carolina. However, it is a little used resource since it is only available at one location and is not indexed. The

Richland County portion of the survey covers 140 pages leaving researchers the unenviable task of looking through each page to locate a name.

On the other hand, as a quick editing project, this was a perfect series to transcribe. The cursive handwriting was consistent and clear and the microfilm copy was in good condition. By transcribing just Richland County it was also a brief record group to tackle. Since the information collected in the voter registration record group was minimal, all the data could be captured in the transcription.

We scanned the 1868 voter registration microfilm pages and saved them to a flash drive so the transcription could take place at any computer station. The scanned material was transcribed and entered directly into an electronic spreadsheet. The power of the spreadsheet allowed the transcribed voter names to be indexed alphabetically and sorted alphabetically within their geographic location. The final product included 450 names on 112 Excel pages. The two transcribed files were then added to an online collection called *Indexes of Local History and Genealogy* located on our digital management platform.

The transcriber conducted a basic level of annotation for this project. Questionable names were compared to the 1870 Columbia city directory for correct spellings. The Columbia city directories are digitized and searchable from 1859–1927 (with gaps) so this digital content could be simultaneously opened and names easily checked for improved accuracy.

Outcomes:

- Creating easy access to underused historical resources available off-site.
- Individual project quickly completed.
- Excellent introductory project for a first-time transcriber.

Conclusion

Googling information about documentary editing will deliver scores of documentary film editing tips but few results for tips on textual documentary editing. However, historic documentary editing is not a lonely world. The Association for Documentary Editing (ADE) was created in 1978 to promote documentary editing through the cooperation and exchange of ideas among the community of editors. The ADE professionals welcome opportunities to advise amateur editors on documentary standards and the application of standards to small projects. The organization offers a yearly conference and intense workshops like the Institute for the Editing of Historic Documents.

Cyndi's List, the popular online resource for all things genealogical, also offers a subject guide called *Transcribing, Abstracting, Extracting & Indexing* with easy to understand advice and standards for consistent editing.

Librarians assisting genealogists and local history researchers are often called upon to justify serving a small segment of the community. Documentary editing projects provide opportunities for measurable standards of engagement with historic researchers. More importantly, these projects bring underused resources closer to the genealogical and historical research community and, in return, bring those communities closer to the institutions who undertake documentary editing projects.

Works Cited

Association for Documentary Editing. 2017. "About." Last modified April 17. http://www.documentaryediting.org/wordpress/.

Cyndi's List. 2017. "Transcribing, Abstracting, Extracting & Indexing—Guidelines, Standards and How-To." Last modified April 17. http://www.cyndislist.com/transcribing/guidelines/.

Kline, Mary-Jo, and Susan Holbrook Perdue. 2008. *A Guide to Documentary Editing*. Charlottesville, VA: University of Virginia Press.

Richland Library. 2017. "Indexes of Local History and Genealogy." Last modified April 17. http://localhistory.richlandlibrary.com/.

Roberts, Giselle, and Melissa Walker. 2015. *Women's Diaries and Letters of the South: A Guide to Editors*. Columbia: University of South Carolina Press.

Secretary of State. South Carolina. 1868. "*Abstracts of Voter Registrations Reported to the Military Government, 1868.*" South Carolina Department of Archives and History: Columbia, SC.

South Carolina Digital Library. 2017. "Minutes of City Council, City of Columbia, S.C." Last modified April 17. http://library.sc.edu/digital/collections/citymin.html.

Stevens, Michael E., and Steven B. Burg. 1997. *Editing Historical Documents: A Handbook of Practice*. Lanham, MD: Rowman & Littlefield.

The Rest Is History

*Using Historical Resources
to Enrich Genealogy Results*

Tracy Carr

Librarians who do genealogy work are often found hunched over their desks, bleary-eyed after squinting at tiny census records or seasick from scrolling through microfilm. While the process is rewarding, sometimes we forgot the fact that the names and dates we're trying to make sense of belong to people: actual, human people who walked around, laughed and cried, ate dinner, went to stores, and went to work. People, in other words, who had lives outside of their birth and death dates.

Historical resources can provide contextual details that can upgrade names on a census list and turn them into family members. While some resources can pinpoint specifics, most of the time these resources will provide Technicolor to the known black and white facts, which isn't an exact science. While it may feel uncomfortable at first for those of us committed to facts, it's entirely appropriate for librarians to use a little magical thinking in order to fill in the details of a long-ago person's life.

Mapping the History of a Place: Sanborn Maps

You know what city your ancestor lived in, but want to know more: why did she move there? Where did he shop? How did they live? A central location to start answering these questions, depending on the city, is Sanborn Fire Insurance Maps.

Sanborn Maps are historical fire insurance maps that range in availability from 1867 forward. Kind of like Google Street View for the past, the maps detail the structures in a town or city for insurance purposes: what the structures are made of, what their purposes are, what size they are, and so on. Since they were not designed as historical research tools, there is a lot of data not captured, but examining a place from the map's perspective adds a level of personal understanding to genealogy work.

The maps are available electronically, through ProQuest, and some libraries may have them on microfilm as well. The Library of Congress has an online collection that includes at least a few maps for most states, though their collection is still growing. The collection is in color, which is helpful because the maps are color coded (the microfilm, obviously, and the ProQuest versions are not in color, and I didn't realize there even was color coding until I browsed the Library of Congress' collection).

Fire insurance maps may not immediately spring to mind as a genealogy research tool, but they can give clues to chronological events, such as when a cotton gin or lumberyard opened. Seeing what commerce or employment opportunities are located in a place can explain why an ancestor might have settled there. Sometimes, genealogy is matching up a story you heard someone tell ("Old Granddaddy moved to town when his Paw got a job at the brick yard") with a hard fact, and a map does this well.

The maps show the structures in the downtown or business districts of the cities, and use an abbreviation system to indicate what type of structures each box or rectangle represents. There's D for dwelling, S for store, A for automobile garage, and about a hundred other abbreviations (a list is available online), most of which refer to the building material.

Some years' maps may just have a lot of the letter S along Main Street, but if you're lucky, the type of S is indicated, which brings the city or town to life (as much as one's imagination will allow, that is). Routinely found places like banks, post offices, barber shops, and restaurants are also indicated.

It also can't be overlooked that an old map, despite its purpose in gathering information for insurance purposes, is incredibly charming. The 1909 Biloxi, Mississippi, map shows that there's a popcorn stand, a candy store, and an "air theatre" all together. If it's too far to walk, one can get one's bicycle repaired on the next block, then cruise to the newsstand to see what's going on in the world. These maps allow us to easily imagine how a person would have navigated through the town, from where the train station is, to how many restaurants they had to choose from, to where they shopped for dry goods. And while maybe we don't care quite as much, we can also note which structures have wooden posts, which are iron-clad, and which have metal roofs.

We can also see how a town or city changes through time, as most of the places have maps from multiple years, usually about five to ten years apart. Most often the place expands: more stores, more dwellings, more commerce, and as times change, opera houses become movie houses and stables become garages.

Case Study: Arlington, Texas, 1920

A patron is looking for information on the Davis family, who lived in the Dallas/Fort Worth area in the early 1900s. His great-grandparents are named Daniel and Mary, he knows Daniel did something at a lumber yard, and he wants to know more.

The first place to check, of course, is the U.S. Census, preferably the electronic version, available through both Ancestry or Heritage Quest. (Microfilm is a wonderful backup but lacks that essential search box to take us where we want to go immediately.)

In searching for Daniel and Mary Baker of Arlington, Texas, in the 1920 Census, we find them living on North Center Street. Daniel, 64, is a bookkeeper at a lumber yard. Mary, 63, is a homemaker, and their daughter Ruth Viola is 24. She is a "saleslady" (the Census worker's term) at a candy store.

Other searches for Daniel and Mary Baker in Texas do find some, even with a daughter named Ruth around Ruth's age, but Daniel and Mary's ages are way off. Ruth is presumably married by the time 1930 rolls around and is virtually unfindable without her husband's name, an additional city to search, or some other key information. This may be the only Daniel Baker who did something at a lumber yard that can be confirmed.

However, we can turn to the Sanborn Maps to see if, instead of hard facts, we can add context to this family's life.

Luckily, there are four Arlington, Texas, Sanborn Maps available through the Library of Congress' collection: 1900, 1905, 1911, and 1917. Each year the maps, like the town itself, expand a bit. However, it's clear that Arlington was a bit hardscrabble at the beginning: a couple of lumber yards, a ginning company, several blacksmiths' shops, and plenty of saloons (though perhaps the presence of Arlington College contributed to the number of saloons on that earliest map). By 1920, the map collection has grown from one sheet to five, and the town has filled out.

We can guess at which of the lumber yards Daniel was a bookkeeper. Maybe W.C. Bowman, right off of Center Street, as the map indicates an office (for once, the insurance/building information collected by Sanborn is useful). The family, according to the Census, also lives on Center Street. Down three storefronts is a confectionary store (Conf'y in Sanborn code), where Ruth may have worked. We can imagine her and her dad going to work together in the morning, or perhaps getting lunch at the lunch counter across the street from both their workplaces.

There is another confectionary store on Main Street, with which Center Street connects, but the notation says Meat/Conf'y. (Somehow the patron and I don't want Ruth to work at a meat and candy store as that combination is a little unsettling.)

Seeing the layout of the town, we can imagine Mary doing the shopping at a grocery, maybe not the one next to the pool hall (but who knows? Mary could be a pool shark!), Daniel going to the barber two doors down from Ruth's shop, and Ruth going to the moving pictures next to the bank.

Of course, we don't know what Daniel, Mary, and Ruth did for sure. Inserting a Sanborn Map into a genealogical pursuit isn't lab science, and results are mostly speculative. If the ancestor is a druggist and there is only one druggist in town, the leap is not as far. But in regards to how it might have *felt* to live in a place in a long-ago time, a Sanborn Map can definitely assist.

Using Historical Timelines for Context

Understanding what was happening in a place at a certain time can help us understand the people who lived there without delving too deep. Knowing that there was a famine or tornado can help you understand why a family moved or why someone changed careers.

Wikipedia has huge lists of historical events arranged by year. You can check out what was going on the date an ancestor was born to find out what her parents might have been talking about. Two days before my grandmother and her twin sister were born on July 11, 1918, the Great Train Wreck of 1918 happened in Nashville. With the way news traveled, they might have just heard about it on the 11th.

Some cities or states have their own chronological timelines in book form, but there is also *History for Genealogists: Using Chronological Time Lines to Find and Understand Your Ancestors* by Judy Jacobson. This no-frills approach to history contains general historical timelines that include major events (tornados, fires, boll weevils) and include a timeline for each U.S. state. These won't be a day by day tour through, say, 1800s Kansas, but you will find out when the grasshopper plague consumed fields (1874), when most of the town of Leonardville burned (1883), and when the Dalton Gang killed several in Coffeyville (1892).

Unfold History: Digital Newspapers

Digitized historical newspapers, especially those available for free online, are a true gift to the modern researcher. Plenty of the research I do is still on (unsearchable) microfilm, but when the stars align and the thing I'm looking for could possibly be in a digitized newspaper, my life is so much easier.

Many libraries have subscriptions to electronic versions of their local newspapers. These electronic subscriptions usually only go back so far, and since they're text only, researchers miss out on browsing as they would a paper, microfilmed, or scanned page.

The Library of Congress' *Chronicling America: Historic American Newspapers* is a great resource that is online and free. The collection contains over 12,000,000 pages of over 2,000 newspapers with dates ranges from 1789 to 1924. The availability of titles and the number of pages varies from title to title: for example, there are 8,034 pages of *The Ocala Express*, 1895–1922 (Ocala, FL), and only five pages of *The Idaho Labor Herald*, November-December 1914 (Boise, ID).

There's a decent chance of finding solid information about an ancestor here, such as an obituary, as the whole collection is searchable, thanks to Optical Character Recognition (OCR), and results are in JPEG files that are easy to zoom in and out of.

With a tool like *Chronicling America*, even if you can't find a newspaper for the place you want, you can certainly find a newspaper in a nearby place in that 100+ year span. You could find out what daily life was like for your ancestor: what was the local news? What were the styles and fashions? How much was butter or a can of peas? Browsing a paper from a certain time can provide a lot of information through both the articles and the advertisements.

You can also confirm some family myths. Often, stories that have passed down through generations have been misheard or details have been added. I'm not saying that the story your patron has heard her whole life isn't true; I'm just giving you a tool to help her confirm it.

Case Study: Indianapolis, Indiana

A patron is looking for information about her great-grandmother, Jessie Ragdale, who was from Indianapolis. The family lore that she is trying to confirm is that Jessie's father, who was a mortician, was accused of murder but was acquitted. We don't know Jessie's parents' names.

Starting with the Census, we easily find some Jessie Ragsdales in the 1910 Census, one of whom has a father named Alonzo Ragsdale who is listed as an undertaker. We then try *Chronicling America*. I prefer to do a general search in most databases first and narrow it down later; often things from one state may appear in another's paper and a too-specific search makes us miss some details. We try *alonzo ragsdale undertaker* and get 25 results. And those results are something.

We get the basics from *Chronicling America*, and then fill in the gaps with the *New York Times* archive. The full story:

Dr. Helene Knabe was found dead in October of 1911. Her throat had been cut from ear to ear in a style known to slaughter sheep and her head was almost severed. A weapon was never found, and despite the coroner's determination of murder, the police clung to the belief that it was a suicide. (Perhaps they can be forgiven for this small oversight, as this was pre–*Law and Order*.)

The patron and I are not the only ones who think this "cut your own head off and then toss the knife" idea is pretty dumb. The local women's club in Indianapolis, led by Dr. Knabe's friend Dr. Amelia Keller, hired a detective agency to investigate the murder.

In April of 1912, a man named Seth Nichols confessed to killing Dr. Knabe for money, but his aunt said he had fallen down and hit his head as a child, and had not been the same since. No charges were filed.

Eventually, Dr. William Craig, a veterinarian who was romantically linked to Dr. Knabe, was charged with murder, along with an undertaker, Alonzo Ragsdale, who was charged for being an accessory after the fact. Apparently Ragsdale, who was the administrator of Dr. Knabe's estate, was accused of going to the apartment where she was killed and removing evidence. On the stand, a cousin testified that she'd given Dr. Knabe a vibrant red and blue kimono for Christmas, which Knabe had been wearing at the time of the murder. The next time the cousin saw it, apparently at Ragsdale's establishment, it was faded, as though one had washed it with harsh chemicals to remove bloodstains.

Dr. Craig was acquitted when the judge abruptly instructed the jury to do so. Ragsdale's indictment was also dismissed. The patron now has a clearer, more detailed story about her ancestor, and at least knows that his part didn't involve the actual murder.

WPA County Files

In 1935, Franklin Delano Roosevelt's Works Progress Administration created the Federal Arts Projects, which housed four departments. One of these, the Federal Writers Project, had one massive collaborative effort: The American Guide Series. Each state, and some cities, would produce a guide to itself as a whole, including folkways, archaeology, history, transportation, religion, the arts, and agriculture. The guides would also include driving tours of notable places to encourage tourism in the state. These guides were published between 1937 and 1939 and are charming from today's vantage point.

However, there is a resource related to these state guides that is much more valuable to the researcher: the individual county files. Each county's history was researched by those hired by the WPA as fieldworkers, who interviewed locals and wrote copy before it was edited and shaped into the book form by someone at the state level. The WPA County Files are the source material, notes, and drafts created by those WPA fieldworkers. Much of what they collected and submitted did not make it into the state books due to space limitations, but their attention to detail means these files are invaluable.

The reason the WPA files are so important to researchers is that they contain pages of raw copy that have not been edited and often are very detailed. Not every county is even mentioned in the final product of the guidebook, so to have pages devoted to a county's most famous tree, favorite folk songs, ethnic heritage, and important historical sites is remarkable.

34 Part I: Overview

The WPA County Files are on microfilm, which makes searching them a little more difficult than other resources, especially since they are not indexed (but at least in Mississippi's case, each county has its own reel of microfilm). The Library of Congress has several thousand pages of the raw manuscripts of the WPA's Folklore Project in its *American Life Histories: Manuscripts from the Federal Writers' Project, 1936 to 1940* collection. There, you can browse around and find Rose Wilder Lane's autobiography, which includes tidbits on communism, buttered popcorn, and her mother, Laura Ingalls Wilder. This collection is very similar in format to the WPA County Files.

WPA County Files, and even the digitized pieces of the Folklore Project online, are definitely not the first place you'd turn in doing research. They probably wouldn't be second. Or third. In fact, I have only used them when I have been completely desperate and out of options because they are cumbersome and a bit disorganized. However, I wouldn't include them here as a valuable way to understand the past if I didn't think that despite being inconvenient, they hold treasures.

Historically, what did people do for fun in this county? Is there a hospital? What kind of wildflowers bloomed there, and when? How did wars affect this area? In a rural state like Mississippi, you can learn a lot from the files about partridge berries, who was a moonshiner, how roaches were common in Lafayette County, and traditional corn husking songs. There are interviews with local characters, lists of notable houses and natural springs and minerals, and matter of fact information on local folk customs. Because this is source material that was gathered and submitted to an editor, sometimes we see the editor's handwritten notations, most often one word: "Source?"

The files contain the counties' histories, but from the perspective of the mid–1930s. There is as much of note to be found in the style the information is reported as in the information itself. Customs that seem to us to be painfully out of date, racist, or sexist are cheerily reported by those who joined the Federal Writers Project, though like us, reading about the past, they in turn offer their opinions on the customs of their past (like log rolling: it was almost out of style).

Case Study: WPA County Histories

A patron wanted confirmation that a story his grandmother told him was true. She had grown up in Vicksburg, Mississippi, but lived in a town with a name that started with a K as young child in the early 1920s. In this K town lived a six-toed Native American man named Nancy. Apparently he stole women's dresses and bonnets from clotheslines, had huge feet, and always went barefoot (hence the detail about having six toes on one foot—his footprint was distinctive). He lived in the woods in a cave, and if you opened your back door and yelled, "Nancy, throw me a rock," a few seconds later a rock would hit your house. One day Nancy attacked the patron's father, leaving deep gash marks from his fingernails. The men of the town hunted Nancy, but only found some lizard skeletons in his cave.

I generally believe that patrons mean well, but a lot of times, people's memories are wrong. There are also a lot of tall tales thrown around in Mississippi, as well as a long tradition of storytelling. With all this in mind, it doesn't mean that I don't try my best, but I will admit I was very skeptical about this one. I started by narrowing down the K town, and after hearing a few possibilities, the patron remembered that it was Kilmichael, which put the action in Montgomery County. I researched Native American fables about having six toes and feats of throwing strength. I read bound histories of Montgomery County, I searched through neighboring counties' histories, and I read about Native Americans in Mississippi. It should not be a shock that I found nothing to back up any of this.

As a last resort, I tried the WPA County File for Montgomery County, and came upon the section on Native Americans (Indians) with information on the Indian Mounds in the county, and crafts the men and women made for trade. The Choctaws had mostly been removed from the area, but there was a section on *Remaining Indians*:

> When the Indians were moved to their new territory in the west, a few would not leave their old homes, and in accordance with the terms of the treaty these Indians were allowed to remain and were granted lands within the county. They were compelled, however, to become American citizens and to obey the laws of the state and county. Five Indians chose to remain here at this time. Che-ha-ka claimed the northeast quarter of section 26, town 18, range 6, and was granted a land patent. Abe-took-chege, Opan-homa, Deavenport, and Nancy also were granted patents, May 23, 1846 [WPA].

Imagine my shock: Nancy was real!

While I was never able to confirm the rest of the story, the fact that there was, in fact, a Native American man named Nancy in this county at all was fairly remarkable. I'm confident that there is no other place I would've found this information.

Conclusion

Using historical resources like WPA County Files, historical timelines, digital newspapers, and Sanborn Maps can help add life to names on a family tree. Sometimes they can help confirm or deny a story, but most of the times they will help add real-life details to a person's long-ago life. Using these resources requires patience, creativity, and a lot of imagination. Those librarians who like to start a sentence with the word "maybe…" will have the most fun painting a clearer picture for their patrons.

Works Cited

The Day Book. 1913. "Indianapolis College Dean Goes to Trial for Murder of Helene Knabe." November 28. *Chronicling America: Historic American Newspapers.*
"Deserter Got $1,500 for Killing Woman." 1912. *New York Times.* April 2.
Jacobson, Judy. 2016. *History for Genealogists: Using Chronological Time Lines to Find and Understand Your Ancestors.* Baltimore: Clearfield Company.
"Knabe Kimono as Evidence." 1913. *New York Times.* December 7.*The Lake County Times.* 1913. "Acquits Dr. Craig of Knabe Slaying." December 10. *Chronicling America: Historic American Newspapers.*
Mississippi State-Wide Historical Research Project. 1936–1938. "Source Material for Mississippi History." Volume XLIX: Montgomery County. WPA Federal Writers Project.
"No Trace of Knife." 1911. *New York Times.* October 26.
"Sleuths on Knabe Case." 1912. *New York Times.* February 11.
"Two Indictments in Knabe Murder." 1913. *New York Times.* January 1.

The Affective Nature of Genealogy Collections
New Narratives Through the Altered Book

ANASTASIA VARNALIS WEIGLE
and RENÉE L. DESROBERTS

What makes archives special is their collections-based arrangement, as opposed to the item-level arrangement in a standard library. Those collections, when viewed together, along with the contextual information so carefully gathered in the collection documents, tell a big picture story rather than just supplying a singular piece of information.

To many genealogists, the "story" is the big, magical thing for which they doggedly search in archives near and far. Conversely, genealogists who have done extensive research and who are willing to share their amassed collections and materials with repositories add to the richness of the narratives found in archives. It is truly a symbiotic relationship. As underscored by Jan Zastrow: "Libraries and archives can provide the cultural and historical context to bring those dry facts and figures to life (Zastrow, 2015, 16)."

Add to the mix works created about and inspired by archival collections, such as the altered book, and you have brought the expression of "the story" to a whole new level. What happens when you bring genealogical collections and book artists together? What do genealogists have to gain through these book works? They get to experience the story in a way they may not have before, or from the point of view they had not considered. This art form can be a great way to gain new perspectives, which can help open up new avenues of research, and as all genealogists know, the greatest days are the ones when they figure out finally how to climb over (or around or under) those brick walls.

Archivists' see firsthand the connection users make with archival collections based on their interests, hobbies, education, personal views, or life experiences connecting us to history, people, cultures, and events. For the book artist, the stories are hidden inside genealogical collections; those serendipitous finds they come across during research can have a profound affect. What is the affective nature of genealogical collections? How do book artists use genealogical collections to create, communicate, and express information as an art form? How do book artists find their voice between the pages? What forms of information do book artists use to create new narratives? Lastly, what new information can be created in support of genealogical collections? In this essay, we will discuss how one such project involving book artists' user experience with genealogy collections offered insights to the affective nature of genealogy collections.

The Affective Nature of Genealogy Collections

In 2014, the Affect and the Archive Conference was presented at the University of California, Los Angeles (UCLA) and sponsored by the Archival Education and Research Initiative (AERI); and the UCLA Center–sponsored conference for Information as Evidence, UCLA Department of Information Studies, the UCLA Department of English, and the UCLA Library (Cifor and Gilliland 2016, 2). Affect can "encompass a variety of concepts such as passions, moods, sensations, feelings and emotions" (Paszkiewicx 2016, 1). The conference was in response to the affective turn in scholarship—human emotions, and how they are influenced by the world around them. Although this is a very simple definition, archivists recognize the complex and holistic nature of people's engagement with information, which may explain why the archival world is interested in participating in this type of discourse.

Genealogical collections contain narratives about a person, a family, a place, or an event. Librarians, archivists, and genealogists may come across information serendipitously, which can tell us something more than we expected. In 2016 Renée L. DesRoberts, special collections librarian, McArthur Public Library and Anastasia Vernalis Weigle, book artist and part-time faculty for the University of Maine at Augusta, collaborated in a small pilot study to investigate the affective nature of special collections—in this case, personal papers. The study investigated how book artists use these papers as a source of inspiration to create, communicate, and express their works of art while offering archivists a different perspective on the use of genealogy collections used.

Participants

A call for book artists was made using a list of book art student emails taken from past classes taught by Anastasia Vernalis Weigle. From this list, six book artists responded with interest to participate in a 3-day workshop on altered book techniques, which included a two-and-a-half-hour visit to the McArthur Library Archives and Special Collections. All six participants were college-educated professional people who have taken courses in the arts. All were females, ages 50 or over, and have used archival collections for both research and recreation purposes. Of the six, five had created various types of book construction. However, all participants have never constructed an altered book.

Workshop and Materials

Arrangements were made in advance with the special collections librarian to set aside a two-hour time slot. The archivist had selected six collections based on their content such as a scrapbook, correspondence, photographs, ephemera and artifacts and had them ready in advance for participants to study on the first day of their workshop. Because the participants would be retelling narratives using family papers, all of the collections were dated late 19th and early 20th century to avoid any privacy issues.

On day one of the workshop, participants spent the first half of the day working on altered book construction techniques in a studio; the second half of the day was spent in the library archives and special collections where participants studied the collections. Participants had permission to handle artifacts without white gloves so as not to hinder the tactile experience. If desired, participants could take photographs of any items of interest. All participants brought a pencil and notebook to write down any information they gathered for their ideas. Some participants took photographs that could later be used in their altered books. The special collections librarian was in attendance during the two-hour visit answering any questions participants had about the collections.

On the days two and three of the workshop, participants formulated their ideas into narratives to incorporate into the altered books with assistance from the book arts instructor. Participants also brought in their own materials such as art papers, personal photographs, and letters to add to their books.

Research Method, Data Gathering and Analysis

Now it is time to find out through the participants' own voice what the experience was like working with family papers. The method of data gathering was a written "self-report." The advantage of self-reports is that it gives us the person's own perspective of the experience; it may also have disadvantages such as validity problems as users can deceive themselves or others (Paulhus and Vzaire, 2007, 229). Participants were provided with a list of open-ended semi-structured interview questions after the workshop was over. The questions were a starting point for the participants' self-report—something similar to an essay, so to speak:

- What form of information did you draw upon for your inspiration?
- Did any of the collections offer you information that helped you in the creative process?
- Tell me how you came to your decision on what story or narrative you wanted to create?
- How did you build your narrative and why?
- Did you seek out additional information other than in the collections?

The written self-reports were analyzed using a two-step open coding method. This method helps develop codes to name and describe attributes for particular phenomena and is based on grounded theory methodologies developed by Anselm Strauss and Juliet Corbin. The first step involves reading self-reports to identify various forms of information users experienced called *themes*. The second step identifies specific attributes within each *theme* of information experience by assigning of a word, phrase, or sentence. Four themes of information experience were identified with specific attributes: external, internal, social-cultural, and new information (see Table 1).

Table 1: Forms of Information and Their Attributes

Forms	Description	Attributes
External	Independent existence derived from documentary sources and objects	1. Documentary: Contained in collections (diaries, journals, letters, receipts, medical illustrations) 2. Information journey (outside collections): books, articles, clippings, information seeking through internet 3. Knowledge sharing between student/student or archivist/student
Internal	Perception, cognition, affect, emotions, numinous qualities	1. Feelings of emotion and intellect, reflection 2. Objects as links to past (tangible/symbolic) 3. Numinous (loss, mortality, death)
Socio-cultural	Rules/theory in a particular practice (ex. book constr., art theory)	1. Rules of book construction 2. Rules of composition abstract art
Creating	New information through creative process	1. Creating Pseudo collections 2. Creative writing, nonfiction/fiction, memoirs 3. Abstract symbolism

The Participants' Own Voice

External Information

External information is defined as something tangible, such as letters, diaries, journals, books, invoices, receipts, photographs, and illustrations:

> I found it to be an interesting glimpse into history. The archive I spent most of my time [had] on hand many individual documents that all came together to make a story" [Par_04].
> The world of archives felt like finding hidden treasure and now I know that those gems of information and life experience exist and I can explore them any time I choose [Par_06].

External information can be taken from other sources outside the archives, thus continuing their information journey. This would include reading books, articles, newspaper clippings, and seeking and retrieving information from online sources:

> [the] mill worker named Lucy Larcom. When I realized I could get her book at the Portsmouth Library I decided to read it. She led me down the path I was looking for. All of a sudden, the story found me—and I found the girls [Par_01]
> I did a lot of research on the Brewster family going back three generations on both sides, on the families of other children who died in similar circumstances, Mary Baker Eddy founded the Christian Scientist church, legal reform regarding religious exemption regarding medical care, etc. [Par_05].

External information also comes from knowledge-sharing—information gathered through inquiry and discussion between students:

> I found myself wondering about Alice, and I talked about her with my commuting partner every day—her story shifted and evolved with each incarnation [Par_01].
> Hearing the stories, the other students shared, while watching them select materials and work. It means learning about book repair and conservation, about valuing historical materials and ephemera [Par_02].

Internal Information

Participants use internal information such as emotional connections, feelings, perception, cognition, memories, and emotions. Numinous qualities, defined as profound feelings, such of awe, sacredness, or fascination were also experienced (Latham 2013, 11).

> The ideas have shifted and changed over time, allowing me to understand just how an author might feel as he/she moves their protagonist along the plot/setting of the story [Par_01].
>
> Mixture of love and war, the image already pre-conditioned by the fact that I'm the daughter of a veteran, but also because the book I was altering was red with dark, brownish-black tones. To me, black and red always signify conflict and passion, death and love [Par_02]
>
> This obit touched my heart and fired up feelings of anger and sadness. My father and I collect obituaries of friends as well as strangers, with compelling stories, etc., mostly lost, abandoned, alone or needy. In fact, this interest … this desire to preserve, to save was inculcated in us as a result of our own troubled family history of abandonment, and tragedy. Rescuing was how we attempted to heal ourselves I suppose [Par_05].

Socio-Cultural Information

Socio-cultural information pertains to the rules or theories in a particular practice (book construction, art theory, and so forth). It is another form of codified information. Here, the participants have pre-knowledge of book-making practices, abstract art theory, and writing constructions. These are known as discipline-specific information:

Altered book titled "Lucy Larcom and the Mill Girl" by Tess Hall, inspired by history of Biddeford Mill workers (photograph by A.S. Weigle).

I am a writer and literary critic by profession, so am obviously conditioned to process narrative, but with words, not with images, materials, or textures [Par_02].

The challenges and frustrations I met were mostly technical—what was the best way to manage the bulk of adding elements to a text block, how could I sandwich a transparency in a signature effectively, how could I adhere pages together to provide a space for a cut out, where I could then place an object with some dimension.... I managed these challenges [Par_04].

I experienced a number of challenges as my knowledge of the mechanics of altering books was limited thus I made a lot of mistakes and had to learn how to undo them and redo them often [Par_05].

Being a rookie in the world of art-making, much less altered book making, I learned about tools and techniques that were completely unknown to me [Par_06].

Creating New Information

Putting together external, internal, and socio-cultural information brought about a fourth theme—new information. The altered books with their new narratives were created using information gathered through external, internal, and socio-cultural means. This is two-step process. The first process is building the narrative, which then feeds the second process—constructing the altered book to represent the visual narrative, resulting in a final product:

Each page had to flow into the next while I also interposed some actual history of the Biddeford Mills alongside my fictional friendship between "Alice" and Lucy Larcom. This piece of "historical fiction" if you will, is a unique rethinking of the genre—why does a book have to be only words on a page? Watching the pages come together, I was amazed at how much I had learned along the way [Par_01].

I was able to imagine the scenarios that took place at the time, the people, places and things coming together to make an historical time come to life. By tapping into my own archive, my art journals, the collections of images, quotes, printed and painted papers, I reflected on other points in my life, pulled words and visual imagery together to create a document which honestly, sometimes painfully, reflects this critical moment in my life [Par_04].

At this point my single original vision of a book about Nancy became a book about children who have and continue to die because they are refused medical care by parent or guardian yet I did not want to demonize the caretakers ... messages written in a child's handwriting (my 6yo great niece) in an effort to evoke her

Altered book by Elizabeth Berkana. Book artist narrative makes a link between her ancestors and the Civil War. Inspired by the Mark Prime Papers (1862–1873), McArthur Public Library Archive, Biddeford, Maine (photograph by A.S. Weigle).

life by her hand, a kind of scrapbook. This book engendered many discussions with peers and family. I shared this story with others about Nancy and the other children and about this book … to remember Nancy [Par_05].

Summary

What was amazing was to observe how each participant took the information from various family papers and worked their narrative into these stories. For example, one participant created a historical fiction around the American writer and poet, Lucy Larcom, known as the "mill girl." The participant created a make-believe childhood friend named "Alice" who "worked" at the Biddeford Mills and wrote letters to Ms. Larcom sharing her mill experiences. This pseudo-collection included the book and a box of various textile materials, photographs, needles, correspondence, and other ephemera.

Another participant instantly is drawn into the papers of a somewhat famous comedic actor in his day. For the participant, this was the driving force in her narrative because it was in line with her passion for theatre—acting, action, dreaming, following those dreams is the feel of the book she created and aptly titled "Acting on Dreams."

For the third participant the process was a personal and emotional journey. Going through all the collections and reading about the past lives of people encouraged her to tell her story. The participant was experiencing a major life change due to the death of a spouse. The memoir was an opportunity to document private thoughts and feelings surrounding this event.

The vision to write the "narrative" of a deceased child became a realization for one participant. The narrative was inspired by a collection belonging to a medical doctor. The narrative from this collection energized the participant to create an altered book about Nancy Brewster, a child who died because of the lack of medical care. The death of the child was erased from the memory of this particular family until an obituary was written 40 years after the death of this child. The book became a memorial for this child and all other children who have died because their parent's religious beliefs did not allow them to seek medical care.

Conclusion

Introducing genealogy collections to book artists can bring stories to life in unexpected ways. The starting point for the participants was the physical engagement with the materials. Wright, McCarthy, and Meekison (2005) believed physical/tangible materials could affect users intellectually, spiritually, and emotionally which translate into attributes of emotions and feelings constructed through our personal interests and ideologies (Wright, McCarthy, and Meekison 2005, 44).

Mandy Lupton's research on information-as-it-is-experience in the creative arts investigated how artists "create, communicate and express information as an art form" (Lupton 2014, 70). Librarians and archivists recognize the importance of documentary or codified information, yet subjective and affective information is rarely studied at in the information science world (Lupton, 2014). The participants in this small study experienced various forms of information as starting points for inspiration offering archivists and genealogists a new perspective on their collections as sources of inspiration for book artists, giving archivists an interesting take on how a particular group uses that information. For the artist, information is both objective and subjective, tangible and intangible and transcends documentary sources to include sociocultural and internal information.

Genealogy collection can inspire artists to continue an old narrative in a creative way or create new narratives with their own voice, adding new information on historical events in a person's life.

WORKS CITED

Cifor, Marika, and Anne J. Gilliland. 2017. "Affect and the Archive, Archives and Their Affects: An Introduction to the Special Issue." *Archival Science* 16, no. 1 (2016): 1–6. Accessed April 21. http://link.springer.com/article/10.1007%2Fs10502-015-9263-3.
Latham, Kiersten F. 2013. "Numinous Experiences with Museum Objects." *Visitor Studies* 16:3–20.
Lupton, Mandy. 2014. "Creating and Expressing: Information-as-it-is-Experienced." In *Information Experience: Approaches to Theory and Practice*, 69–84. Emerald Group Publishing Limited.
Paszkiewicz, Katarzyna. 2016. "Thinking About Affect in Culture and Art." *452[deg]F: Journal of Literary Theory and Comparative Literature*, 14:1–4. Accessed April 17, 2017. http://www.raco.cat/index.php/452F/article/download/305129/394963
Paulhus, Delroy L., and Simine Vazire. 2007. "The Self-Report Method." *Handbook of Research Methods in Personality Psychology* 1: 224–239.
Wright, Peter, John McCarthy, and Lisa Meekison. 2005. "Making Sense of Experience." In *Funology: From Usability to Enjoyment*, edited by Peter Wright, John McCarthy, and Lisa Meekison, 43–54. New York: Springer.
Zastrow, Jan. 2015. "Genealogy: A Cheat Sheet for the Unsuspecting Librarian." *Computers in Libraries* 35: 16–20.

PART II: COLLABORATION

A Genealogy Digitization Collaboration

BEN WALKER *and* CHELSEA S. DINSMORE

Introduction

This essay will describe the collaboration between the University of Florida Libraries, Internet Archive, and FamilySearch to digitize genealogy–related materials in the University of Florida collections. This cooperative relies on Internet Archive to supply the equipment, FamilySearch to supply volunteers to scan the material, and the University of Florida to supply a location for the scanning as well as material to be scanned. This project has been in place since 2015, and to date has scanned more than 6,700 items and more than 1.28 million images. These items are added to the FamilySearch library, a free resource for genealogy enthusiasts. Select titles are added to the University of Florida Digital Collections (UFDC). Internet Archive also provides open access to these materials and provides additional preservation services. Plans for expanding the program, which includes outreach to museums, historical societies, public libraries and other organizations in Florida are underway and will be discussed in more detail. This project is unique because the University of Florida is the only public university that is currently participating in this program. Topics of discussion will include lessons learned from this project, as well as future directions for expanding the program.

Background

Genealogy is an extremely popular area of research. A quick analysis of Google Trends for the term "genealogy" (as a search term, field of study, or topic) reveals that this type of search has had a stable interest in the last five years and has broad interest around the world (Google 2017). While not as popular as searches for "YouTube" it shows similar interest to a term like "realtor." The value of one of the biggest players in this arena, Ancestry.com, was estimated at $2.6 billion dollars in 2016 (Goodman 2016). For comparison, meal delivery companies like Blue Apron and HelloFresh are valued around $2 billion, while the transportation company Lyft is valued at $7.5 billion (Austin, Canipe, and Slobin 2015). Additionally, there are numerous online services that cater to those interested in genealogy (Ancestry.com, 23andme.com, GenealogyBank.com,

MyHeritage.com, FamilySearch.org, etc.), and the development of genetic testing is increasing the interest in these services (Helft 2017). Attendance at RootsTech, the largest genealogical focused conference in the world, topped 30,000 attendees in 2017 (Stahle 2016). As a point of comparison, peak attendance at the American Library Association's Annual Conference has never exceeded 27,000 attendees and has averaged a little over 20,000 attendees in the last five years (American Library Association 2017). Comparing all of these numbers (financials, web traffic, and conference attendance), one begins to get a sense of the overall interest and commitment to genealogy.

Background of Partners

The University of Florida (UF) Libraries consists of seven libraries, more than 6 million print and electronic resources, and nearly 600 staff (George A. Smathers Libraries 2017c). The libraries serve as a core resource for the research and educational activities of the more than 30,000 staff and 54,000 students at UF (Office of Institutional Planning and Research 2017a, 2017b). Given that scope, the libraries have to serve a broad cross-section of users. However, we have generally paid less attention to genealogy. Although there is genealogical crossover in some of the Special Collections held by the libraries (P.K. Yonge Library of Florida History, Isser and Rae Price Library of Judaica, Latin American and Caribbean Collection, etc.), it is typically not the focus. Further, the amount of staff dedicated to this subject area is small, with only one staff member, who also has multiple other duties, assigned to this subject area. The libraries do collect in this broad subject area, as a quick search of the libraries' catalog shows that there are over 5,700 items with the subject term "genealogy" held at UF. However, of those less than 1 percent were published in the last five years. As further evidence, with a print and electronic book collection that exceeds 6 million volumes, that represents less than .1 percent of the total library print and electronic books. Clearly, it is not an area to which we have historically chosen to devote significant resources.

Digitization, though, has been a strong point for the UF Libraries. The UF Digital Library began in 1994 as a project to convert microfilmed Caribbean newspapers into digital format (Digital Support Services 2013). Since that time, it has expanded and is the largest digitization operation in the Southeast, with more than 12 million pages of open access materials (George A. Smathers Libraries 2017a). The content in the digital library covers a wide span, from historical children's literature to newspapers to Florida-specific material. However, as with our other collection activities, genealogy has rarely been the focus.

Beginning in 1995, the UF Libraries began storing books off campus in a variety of buildings. These eventually became the Auxiliary Storage Facility (ALF) and the Interim Storage Facility (ILF). The bulk of material stored in these buildings came from UF Libraries. They were books, periodicals, microforms, and other formats that were rarely used but determined to still be of value. Typically, the materials in these buildings rarely get requested, but it has been added to over time until it now houses more than 2.2 million volumes (George A. Smathers 2017b). The majority of the material scanned in this initial collaboration between UF, Internet Archive, and FamilySearch was drawn from these storage buildings.

Internet Archive is a non-profit organization, with a focus on "Provid[ing] universal access to all knowledge" (Internet Archive n.d.). This organization is involved in a broad array of projects, including digitization of books, archiving of web pages through the Wayback Machine, archiving of television programming, and developing tools to maintain access to video games. The University of Florida has been working with Internet Archive for about four years as a vendor for outsourcing various scanning projects. The current partnership grew from that experience.

FamilySearch.org is a non-profit organization dedicated to family history (FamilySearch.org 2017). It is the largest genealogy organization in the world (FamilySearch.org 2017), with a focus on image scanning, preservation, and online access to records. These may be records held in the Family History Library in Salt Lake City or records that they host on their web platform for other individuals and organizations. The FamilySearch site provides a variety of free and paid services to assist genealogists. While UF had never previously worked with FamilySearch, both Internet Archive and FamilySearch had been participating in an innovative cost-sharing model for digitizing genealogical printed books.

Description of the Project

In 2014, UF was exploring a way to establish a joint UF–Internet Archive scanning center in Gainesville. The goal was for this center to serve as a hub for other institutions in the Southeast. At that time, the closest hub that could handle large-scale projects was in Princeton, New Jersey. If UF could establish a hub in Gainesville, it would potentially decrease the costs of outsourcing scanning projects both for us and for universities proximal to UF. This would allow us to begin digitizing materials in the storage collections, both as a means to provide better access to those materials and to preserve them by preventing loss and/or damage through circulation. We could also maintain our other digital initiatives, undertaken by our Digital Library, which were focused on our Special Collections. This led to initial discussions with staff from Internet Archive. Initially, we wanted Internet Archive to provide scanning equipment and share in the costs for staffing those machines. UF would provide space for the equipment and the necessary Internet access. One of the initial challenges was guaranteeing enough volume to make the center profitable. While UF might be able to provide enough material in the first year, we did not know that we could maintain that beyond that point.

During these discussions, Internet Archive proposed an alternative solution. They suggested a collaborative between UF, Internet Archive, and FamilySearch. UF would provide the space, Internet access, and books for scanning. Internet Archive would provide the equipment and staff to do quality control checks and deposit scanned content into Internet Archive's online library. FamilySearch would provide volunteers to scan the material in Gainesville using Internet Archive's equipment. In return, FamilySearch would also add any new digital content to their online library. Similar projects had been run at a handful of public libraries around the country, but this would be the first partnership with a public university. These initial discussions were promising and we scheduled a follow-up call with representatives from FamilySearch to confirm this concept. After those calls, an onsite visit from a FamilySearch representative was scheduled. It was important to determine if we had enough content that would be valuable to FamilySearch and to discuss the required space and processes to get the program started.

Further conversations with Internet Archive about equipment led us to two free scanners that were currently housed at Clemson University. The scanning project at Clemson was grant funded and funding expired. Rather than shipping the equipment back to Princeton, Internet Archive agreed to send it to Gainesville. While this would not provide enough equipment to establish a large-scale scanning center, it would allow us to begin digitizing our storage collection, while still allowing us to focus our Digital Library Center on grant-funded projects and digitization of our Special Collections.

The onsite visit from FamilySearch was very promising. In August 2014, we discussed the process of finding and training volunteers, expectations for all participants, visited the space where the scanning would talk place, and evaluated the storage collections. The FamilySearch representative spent half a day in the storage collection, checking titles against the FamilySearch Library holdings. He discovered over 1,500 new items just from that initial review. This encouraged us that there were many more items in the collection that would be appropriate. Another exciting aspect of the project was that FamilySearch was happy to scan other items as needed. The goal was for 75 percent of the material to be genealogical, and the remaining 25 percent could be anything else that we wanted to be scanned. This gave us latitude to get more content scanned from this collection. We agreed that FamilySearch would begin looking for volunteers to send to Florida and that we would get the scanners delivered and installed. During this visit, we also arranged for a dinner with representatives from local museums and historical societies. One of the goals was to expand the availability of scanning services to these local organizations, many of whom did not have the funding to digitize materials. This would provide greater access to these materials for any researchers interested, while also digitally preserving them. This dinner was very successful, and we knew there were opportunities to expand this program significantly by including more organizations around Florida.

Volunteers were scheduled to arrive in February 2015. The equipment from Clemson was scheduled to arrive in September 2014. This allowed us time to work through the complexities of UF's information technology requirements. Access to the Internet, via UF's network, was restricted and required an internal review before approval. This was necessary, however, so that the scans could be shared electronically between UF, Internet Archive, and FamilySearch. The lead time also allowed us to ensure that the books identified during the FamilySearch visit had appropriate identifying information (metadata) prior to scanning. Other activities that were occurring simultaneously included coordinating access to FamilySearch's database to ensure scans at UF did not duplicate material already scanned, training our own staff, and developing a new position to coordinate the outreach to other potential partners in Florida.

The FamilySearch volunteers arrived in February 2015. We got them settled into the new space, which had previously been a large storage closet. It did not have windows, which was a bonus for the scanning operations, as it reduced the light pollution and ensured more accurate scans. Internet Archive hired a part-time employee to oversee the operations (quality control reviews after scanning, electronic transfer of digitized material, and overall supervision of the volunteers). The first week was spent orienting the volunteers to the facility and to the processes, which were slightly different than what they had trained on in Utah. This was mainly due to equipment differences, but also there were initial challenges. Accessing the UF network and transferring data did not happen smoothly. There were still problems encountered in those first few weeks. The first item was scanned and uploaded to Internet Archive on February 26, 2015. To date, we have had three volunteer couples work for us. During that time, they have accomplished the following:

- Total images scanned: 1,280,596
- Most images scanned in a month: 88,786
- Total number of items scanned: 6,727
- Most items scanned in a single month: 1,161
- Total views of items scanned: 92,829

Both the number of materials scanned but also the usage indicate that this project was successful. We accomplished our goal of making significant strides in digitizing material in the storage collection without impacting our other digital projects. We have also begun receiving material from other organizations, which was another goal. While this project was not without hurdles, the strides made in the first two years are significant. We anticipate continuing the project and expanding our list of partners around the state.

Lessons Learned

There were several challenges encountered during this project. Coordinating communication and workflows between three very different organizations is obviously a big hurdle. A large public university is inherently less nimble than smaller non-profit organizations. This was especially evident with the information technology challenges. Ensuring that the equipment could connect via UF's network and troubleshooting unexpected problems was a challenge. Also, because the equipment was different than what the volunteers trained on, there were additional delays to get up and running. Coordinating efforts from geographically distant locations, especially when it was difficult to explain the exact problem, made for challenges for all of the organizations. Meetings to involve all parties were sometimes unwieldy, which meant we did not meet as often. Our first volunteer couple stayed in Gainesville for 18 months. This meant that during the course of their stay, they encountered nearly every problem discussed in this list of challenges. However, it also meant that they were very experienced and adaptable, and could eventually figure out a solution to the problem. Since then we have had two other volunteer couples. Because neither couple stayed for as long, it meant that the training time took longer. Integrating into the culture, workflows, and equipment takes time. Learning to resolve the problems encountered also takes time. Having a stable volunteer couple makes these challenges easier to manage.

Another challenge that we were not prepared for was the amount of staff required to keep up with the volunteers. We relied on the initial review to scan the first 1,500 items. However, it required UF staff to identify new items, check the identifying information (metadata) and correct it as needed, check the FamilySearch Library to ensure the content had not already been scanned, transfer the material between buildings, and then re-shelve the material when it was completed. In total, we were using more than 40 hours per week of labor to maintain those processes. This was an unexpected cost, but over time, the FamilySearch volunteers took on more of those duties. They assisted with checking the shelves for new material and reviewing the records, which freed our staff to return to other projects. Identifying new material was always the weakest link in the entire process. Because the storage collection is a mixture of disciplines, it does not have one subject specialist assigned to it. We relied on catalog searches using subject terms to find materials. The flow of materials from other library collections was also slow. This was because many of those materials needed additional cataloging before they could be scanned. Our cataloging department was already working beyond capacity and any new projects had to be prioritized. Hiring additional skilled catalogers may have been a solution, but those are not always readily available nor affordable. Outsourcing could have helped with that, but again we were trying to keep our costs manageable.

The physical space was another limitation. Because many of our spaces are already operating at or close to capacity, we had to carve out space where we could to accommodate this new initiative. Reclaiming a closet for three people, even if the closet was large (approximately 140 square feet), was challenging. Ensuring adequate power, networking, lighting, and ventilation required effort and planning. The heat created by two large scanners and the associated computer equipment in such a small space can be overcome, but sometimes it could be uncomfortable in the office. Further, both the equipment and the space are not necessarily ergonomically ideal, creating challenges for the volunteers to operate, especially given that the tasks were very routinized and repetitive. Even considerations of where to store books to be scanned and where to house them after they were scanned had to be addressed.

One of the original goals was to bring in other organizations, such as museums and local historical societies. We had some success with this, but the process of establishing new relationships can be time consuming. Trust takes time to build, especially given the delicate and unique nature of some of the materials that were under consideration. The quality of the identifying information (metadata) for that material was also highly variable, which meant that more time was required of our cataloging department. Again, we kept coming back to the problem of competing priorities. Certainly, there are some successes, but there is more room to grow.

Overall, we feel that this is an example of a unique collaborative. Because nearly all libraries are dealing with similar challenges around limited budgets, personnel, and space, this makes this project an opportunity to think outside the box. Aligning with partners that we may not have previously considered was an excellent way to expand our capacity. Without this partnership, we would not have made as much progress as we did. Whether there is capacity for Internet Archive and FamilySearch to expand is a question better directed to those organizations, but the main lesson from this project is that there are potential partners available, and they are probably partners that we as libraries have not previously considered.

Works Cited

American Library Association. 2017. "Past Annual Conferences, 1876–present." Accessed April 22. http://www.ala.org/conferencesevents/past/pastannualconferences.

Austin, Scott, Chris Canipe, and Sarah Slobin. 2015. "The Billion Dollar Start-Up Club." *The Wall Street Journal*. February 18. http://graphics.wsj.com/billion-dollar-club/.

Digital Support Services. 2017. "Recognition: Selected Articles and Publications Featuring UFDC." Accessed April 22. http://digital.uflib.ufl.edu/history/recognition.htm.

FamilySearch.org. 2017. "About FamilySearch." Accessed April 22. https://familysearch.org/about.

George A. Smathers Libraries. 2017a. "Digital Support Services Department." Last modified February 21. http://www.digital.uflib.ufl.edu/.

_____. 2017b. "Florida Academic Repository Projects and Statistics." Accessed April 22. http://cms.uflib.ufl.edu/flare/ProjectsandStatisticsPage/TotalStatistics.aspx.

_____. 2017c. "The George A. Smathers Libraries at the University of Florida at a Glance." Accessed April 22. http://cms.uflib.ufl.edu/Communications/Libraries_glance.

Goodman, Wes. 2016. "GIC and Silver Lake Invest in US Genealogy Company Ancestry." *Bloomberg*. April 1. https://www.bloomberg.com/news/articles/2016-04-02/gic-and-silver-lake-invest-in-u-s-genealogy-company-ancestry.

Google. 2017. "Google Trends." Accessed April 22. https://trends.google.com/trends/explore?q=genealogy,%2Fm%2F0353s,%2Fm%2F04ld343,realtor.

Helft, Miguel. 2017. "Ancestry.com DNA Database Tops 3M, Sales Rise to $850M Ahead of Likely 2017 IPO." *Forbes*. January 10. https://www.forbes.com/sites/miguelhelft/2017/01/10/ancestry-com-dna-database-tops-3m-sales-rise-to-850m-ahead-of-likely-2017-ipo/#1ba677d113b3.

Internet Archive. 2017. "About the Internet Archive." Accessed April 22. https://archive.org/about/.

Office of Institutional Planning and Research. 2017a. "Enrollment & Demographics." Last modified February 9. http://ir.aa.ufl.edu/enrollment-1.

_____. 2017b. "Workforce." Last modified February 14. http://ir.aa.ufl.edu/workforce.

Stahle, Tyler S. 2016. "7 Reasons to Attend RootsTech 2017." *FamilySearch Blog* (blog). September 14. https://familysearch.org/blog/en/7-reasons-attend-rootstech-2017/

University of Florida Digital Collections. 2017. "UFDC: University of Florida Digital Collections." Accessed April 22. http://ufdc.ufl.edu//.

Destined for the Dumpster

*A Collaboration Between Librarians
and Genealogists to Make 79,000 At-Risk Records
Available for Research*

JOANNE M. RILEY, JESSICA HOLDEN
and SUSAN STEELE

Introduction

In some ways it's a familiar story: the odyssey of a group of records from the organization that created them to a community curator, and then eventually to a professionally run archives. But in other ways our story is perhaps not so typical, since two of those organizations, the community curators and the university archives, have created an unusual long-term partnership around those records. It's been an odyssey for us as humans, too.

Acquisition

The three organizations involved in this odyssey were:

1. Catholic Association of Foresters (CAF): An active business/fraternal organization
2. The Irish Ancestral Research Association (TIARA): a volunteer-driven organization focusing on Irish genealogical and historical research and education
3. University Archives and Special Collections in the Joseph P. Healey Library at the University of Massachusetts Boston (UASC/UMass Boston): a university archives with a collection policy that includes social welfare agencies and interest in community archives

The Catholic Order of Foresters

At the end of the nineteenth century, many Irish Catholic immigrants lived in the urban areas of the northeastern United States. Most of these immigrants were poor and had limited or no access to life insurance, even though the loss of a wage earner often spelled disaster for families at the margins of the economy. In response to this need, a small group of Irish Catholic Bostonians formed the Massachusetts Catholic Order of Foresters in 1879. MCOF was the first Catholic fraternal insurance organization in Massachusetts and was the first to provide life insurance benefits to Catholic families across the economic spectrum.

In addition to providing insurance benefits, MCOF established local lodges, or courts, which served as social gathering places for Foresters members. By the turn of the twentieth century, membership was booming and subordinate courts were organizing across Massachusetts. In 1961, MCOF expanded into the other New England states and Florida and changed its name to the Catholic Association of Foresters. CAF still operates today as a society whose members hold insurance policies and serve as community benefactors (Catholic Order of Foresters 2017).

As with so many organizations, MCOF/CAF quietly went about its business for many decades, generating thousands of documents yearly and storing inactive membership, mortuary, and payout records in the basement of the association's headquarters in Boston, records largely unknown to archivists or researchers. A single MCOF insurance policy record, one per member, contains an extraordinary range of material including a multi-page application and medical exam report, a death certificate, a cancelled check, and additional materials related to beneficiaries, sometimes including correspondence with relatives abroad. Obviously, such a wealth of information would be of enormous value for genealogists and academic researchers.

The Irish Ancestral Research Association

In 2002–2003, members of The Irish Ancestral Research Association (TIARA) learned of this huge cache of hitherto unknown nineteenth- and twentieth-century records stored in the basement of CAF. TIARA member Janis Duffy described the collection as comprising many rows of filing cabinets that held thousands of policies, each with a story to tell.

Soon after the discovery, however, CAF informed TIARA that the Foresters were selling their building on Commonwealth Avenue and moving to smaller headquarters, and that once the building was sold the older, inactive policies would be shredded—unless TIARA could find a way to move and preserve them. TIARA immediately put out a call to its membership soliciting office space, archival and legal guidance, and volunteers, all of which were answered. In 2005, more than thirty volunteers showed up one Saturday per month for more than six months, hauling filing cabinet drawers up two flights of stairs, placing records in archival boxes and loading the boxes into vans to be transported from Boston to newly arranged office space in a nearby town. The end result was approximately 400 boxes of original historic records in storage.

Once the records had been rescued from the threat of the shredder, several TIARA members who were active in the packing process formed a steering committee to map out the next steps in what was now referred to as "The Foresters Project." The steering committee's goal was to address access and preservation issues. The steering committee consulted archivists about preservation practices, and consulted a lawyer about privacy restrictions. They were advised that they could reasonably make the records available if they followed federal privacy laws related to the release of census data, which at that point meant releasing information for deaths from 1880 to 1930.

TIARA became familiar with two sets of index cards that the MCOF/CAF had maintained to look up policyholders, and began to enter identifying data into an Excel spreadsheet program with guidance from TIARA members skilled in data management. During the initial sampling of policies, the volunteers realized that scanning was a time-consuming process. They needed to find a more efficient way to approach preserving the more than 26,000 policies that would be made available to the public. After receiving costly estimates from several companies the TIARA Board of Directors voted to allow the Genealogical Society of Utah to digitize policies of Foresters members who died between 1880 and 1930. The Genealogical Society of Utah would eventually place copies of the digital images on the Internet, which would give a much larger audience access to the collection. According to the terms of the agreement, GSU scanned the documents free-of-charge and promised to deliver to TIARA a copy of all the scanned images, while TIARA promised to supply a spreadsheet with all of the index card data that they were entering.

By April 2007 data related to records of all members who had died before 1930 had been entered into the spreadsheet and the index was placed on the TIARA website. At that time, TIARA began a pilot program for fulfilling requests from other TIARA members for copies of Foresters records.

From the beginning, TIARA knew that preserving thousands upon thousands of original historic records was not part of their organization's mission, and thus an early Foresters Project goal was to find a permanent repository for the original paper records. TIARA's budget did not allow for ongoing payment of rent for storage in the U–Haul facility, and the basement storage area in the TIARA office had experienced several close calls with the risk of water damage. At this time, several TIARA members began additional outreach for the collection, writing newsletter articles, staffing information tables at genealogy events, and giving presentations. Through all of this, TIARA continued exploring possibilities for a permanent home for the collection within a university archives, a goal which was advanced when a staff member in the Healey Library at UMass Boston who was also an MLS candidate proposed an internship, which TIARA gladly accepted, to develop a finding aid that TIARA could use in pitching the collection to university archives.

University of Massachusetts Boston

In the fall of 2010, with the completed finding aid in hand, TIARA leadership visited UMass Boston to explore the possibility of the Foresters records coming to the university. In attendance at this first meeting were TIARA staff and UMass Boston's University Archivist, University Librarian, and two Associate University Librarians. TIARA gave an overview of the collection: roughly 400 cartons containing mortuary records, non-mortuary records, commemorative books, hand-written ledgers, and institutional publications created by MCOF and spanning the years 1879–1986. TIARA described their active volunteer program and their hope that the eventual home for the records would allow the volunteer program to continue. They also explained their strong desire to donate the records to an institution that would keep them on-site rather than in off-site storage, so that they and other researchers could have ready access to the collection.

After hearing TIARA's presentation, UMass Boston representatives were enthusiastic about the excellent fit of this collection for the university's collection areas of social welfare organizations and local history, and were impressed by the value for researchers in genealogy, history of medicine, sociology, labor history, immigration history, and more. UMass Boston assured TIARA that the University Archives and Special Collections department would welcome TIARA's continued involvement with the collection, given UMass Boston's commitment to fostering community involvement with its programs and collections, and that every effort would be made to keep the collection on-site should it come to UMass Boston.

In December 2010, TIARA and UMass Boston representatives met again and agreed that the next step would be to present the TIARA Board of Directors with information about UMass Boston's archival mission, resources, and services, along with a draft of a donor agreement. In March 2011, the Healey Library hosted TIARA's monthly membership meeting, which included a tour of the University Archives and Special Collections department and presentations about UASC's collections. Meanwhile, TIARA members continued the conversations with the TIARA Board, and in late spring 2011 the Board approved the transfer, pending a mutually acceptable deed of gift. The deed of gift went back and forth a number of times, and ended up following the usual straightforward template, with the additions of a Right of First Refusal and provision that requests for records that fell outside the NARA "72-Year Rule" (U.S. Census Bureau, 2017) would only be released with permission of the current administration of the Catholic Association of Foresters. The deed of gift was signed at UMass Boston on May 4, 2011, with many TIARA members present, and delivery of the collection was scheduled for August 2011.

On Saturday, August 13, 2011, the transfer took place. The president of TIARA organized the logistics of the move, and enlisted the help of two staff members from a local auction house. Their van stopped first in the early morning at the U-Haul facility where some of the records were stored, then proceeded to the TIARA offices to load the bulk of the records, and finally on to UMass Boston to unload—a process that took a full day and a lot of physical effort on everyone's part.

By mid-afternoon, roughly 400 boxes of the Massachusetts Catholic Order of the Foresters records had arrived at the loading dock at UMass Boston. Two library work-study students and two UASC staff members were ready to receive and assist in moving the boxes to the fifth floor of the Healey Library. After multiple trips between the loading dock and the library, down corridors, through numerous doors, and up and down two elevators in two different buildings, the move was completed by the end of the day. Thanks to clear communications, collaboration, and willingness to work out mutually beneficial agreements, TIARA and UMass Boston successfully negotiated the transfer of the historic Foresters records to their permanent home at UASC.

Ongoing Partnership and Collaboration

The Foresters records arrived at UMass Boston with 29,000 records already processed and indexed, an alphabetical index online at TIARA's website, a highly-organized and efficient group of volunteer processors, and an active research request service. Integrating all of this into the workflow of the University Archives and Special Collections department posed a new set of challenges and raised some issues that required thoughtful attention.

The TIARA volunteers were eager to jump right in to continue processing records and entering data into the online index. To that end, the Healey Library's applications programmer created a web application to accept input for the index, and UASC staff arranged suitable workspace and laptops to accommodate between four and six volunteers who were accustomed to socializing a bit while they worked. UASC introduced a revised workflow—for instance using one folder per mortuary record instead of organizing five records per folder, which was cost-effective but too time- and labor-intensive for UMass Boston's process. The TIARA volunteers worked in the back processing area of UASC, an area usually only accessible to Archives staff and trained graduate student workers. UASC tracked TIARA volunteer presence via a special sign-in procedure and required coats and bags to be left in the Archives lobby area. Cartons to be worked on were delivered by staff to the work table, and the volunteers were given special access as needed to the stacks where the Foresters collection was in temporary storage. This arrangement carried some risks, but those were mitigated by the proven care that TIARA volunteers had exercised for years in rescuing and working with the collection. To preserve that safety margin, no new volunteers were accepted for this project, just those who had been working for several years with the collection.

This period of onsite volunteer activity ceased when campus construction and parking issues made it more and more difficult for the volunteers to come to the Archives. Instead, TIARA and UASC worked out another unusual arrangement, where the TIARA volunteer coordinator is allowed to check out sets of index cards for the volunteers to work on at TIARA headquarters off-campus, entering data into an online system created by UASC staff which adds the records to the searchable index now housed on UMass Boston's servers (University Archives and Special Collections, 2017). Again, the risks were far outweighed by the confidence that UASC management felt in TIARA's proven commitment to preserve and enhance access to these important records.

Since October 2014, more than sixty TIARA volunteers have indexed more than 6,300 records, an average of 200 records per month. Through their careful work—and only because of their work—UASC is on target towards its goal of opening a new year's worth of records to the public every year. Meanwhile, UASC has enlisted student workers and classes from UMass Boston's history department's archives track to take over the processing of the physical records, rehousing them in archivally safe, acid-free folders and boxes. This provides students with valuable hands-on experience working with archival materials. Enlisting students to help process archival materials is a win-win situation: the students gain experience not typically possible within the boundaries of the classroom, and much-needed help is provided for often understaffed archives. UMass Boston's archival reference staff now respond to Foresters research requests, scanning to PDF and emailing rather than photocopying and postal mailing as TIARA had done. UASC has fulfilled requests for copies of more than 350 records as of July 2017. TIARA members had used NARA's "72-Year Rule" to govern access to records, and UASC continued that practice, along with TIARA's practice of charging a fee for copies of records. TIARA had provided access to Foresters records as a benefit of membership; UASC made the records available to the world but does not charge reproduction fees to members of

TIARA and CAF as an expression of gratitude for their respective roles in saving these records from the dumpster.

In March 2012, to celebrate the accession of this collection and the collaboration with TIARA, UMass Boston threw a party that was open to the public. There were exhibits including photographs contributed by TIARA members of their Foresters ancestors, and an exhibit curated by TIARA members detailing the records' odyssey from the Catholic Association of Foresters. There were current Foresters in attendance, and refreshments, Irish music, and a storyteller—a real celebration. As part of the evening, UMass Boston awarded its first Joseph P. Healey Community Archives Award to TIARA for its heroic work in rescuing and processing the historic Foresters records. The Healey Library now invites TIARA members to all of its events and activities, and this ongoing connection led to collaboration in 2013 on a public history project to digitize family photographs and memories (Mass. Memories Road Show) called "The Irish Immigrant Experience." Although collaborating across professional lines seemed a bit intimidating and rather difficult at first, our working together toward a common goal yielded benefits that greatly outweighed any challenges.

Challenges and Successes of Processing and Indexing

The TIARA Steering Committee researched methods to make the records contents available to the genealogical community. They explored options for microfilming and digitizing the records. They received several estimates from private companies and realized the cost was well beyond TIARA budget restrictions and it was unlikely that they could raise that amount in donations. TIARA contacted the Genealogical Society of Utah and arranged for a meeting. GSU, a division of the Church of Jesus Christ of Latter-day Saints, offered to digitize the Foresters records at no cost in exchange for a digital copy for their own files. TIARA eventually signed an agreement with GSU. Deaths through 1935 would be digitized.

TIARA researched options for a legal review regarding privacy restrictions. This was necessary because the records contained medical exams. A lawyer who specialized in HIPAA and other privacy law issues was located. He advised TIARA to follow U.S. Census release protocol. The 1930 census had been released in 2002. TIARA could release an additional year of records for every year after a census release. Before signing the agreement with GSU, TIARA reviewed these findings with a different lawyer and found the original advice still applicable.

Before TIARA could release the records to their members and to the general public they needed to become familiar with finding aids to the collection which were provided by CAF. The most important aids were two sets of index cards with information about death claims (when a claim for payment was made after death). One set of cards was arranged by surname and one was arranged by court (a member's local chapter). These surname cards would be the basis for TIARA's spreadsheet index of the mortuary records.

Archival Instruction and Biographical Research Projects

The Foresters records have become a mainstay of UMass Boston's archival instruction program, in which we bring undergraduate and graduate students into our Archives Research Room and explore the value of archival research. Introductory sessions typically cover the differences and similarities between libraries and archives, the definitions of primary and secondary sources, and how archives can benefit academic research. After presenting students with that overview, we then guide them through a hands-on exercise with archival materials. One such exercise involves passing out the records of Foresters members who died in 1919, one record per student. The students fill out worksheets with basic questions about the records (e.g., What was the member's name? When were they born? What was their occupation? How and when did they die?). Almost without fail, we see a spark of excitement in the students as they work with primary source records and find documentation of a real person's life, with often dramatic causes of death (given the preselected death year of 1919) including combat fatalities from World War I, deaths from pneumonia or "the Grippe" due to the influenza epidemic, and gruesome deaths from the 1919 "Great Molasses Flood" in Boston's North End. We use these causes of death to encourage the students to think about what the records tell us about their place in time. What kinds of histories do they reveal—social, medical, military, and personal?

The Foresters records will also tie into another large-scale collaborative project between University Archives and Special Collections and the Boston Police Department's Archives. Starting with duty roster cards held by the BPD Archives, project volunteers (which include TIARA members, UMass Boston students and staff, and community volunteers) are culling information to create biographical essays about police officers who were involved in the Boston Police Strike of 1919. Because the Boston Police Department at the time contained many Irish men, there are inevitable connections to be made between the strikers and the Foresters records in developing the biographical portraits of the officers. The Foresters records demonstrate how archival records provide connections between many people, issues, and places, and can enhance genealogical and scholarly projects by providing researchers with information not easily found elsewhere.

Lessons Learned/Conclusion

Throughout our long-term collaboration, TIARA and UASC have learned much from each other in the course of moving through the stages of archival work, from acquisition to preservation to processing to providing access and promoting use of this record collection. In the process, which was complex due to the deep involvement of two very different organizations, we found that it was critically important that we be honest about our respective organizations' goals, desires, and limitations; that we engage each organization's higher-ups in the process from the very beginning and keep them informed throughout; that we aim for an equal, collegial relationship at all times; that we remember to express gratitude and awe as it arises when observing each other's accomplishments; that we plan on commitment over the long haul; and finally, that we remain always aware of each other's passionate commitment to our respective missions and goals, and our mutual sense of responsibility for the archival records. In our case, stretching to accommodate the principles and needs of each organization resulted in a synergistic collaboration that we hope will continue for many years.

WORKS CITED

Catholic Order of Foresters. 2017. *History*. Accessed July 26. http://catholicforesters.org/about/history/.
United States Census Bureau. 2017. *The "72-Year Rule."* Last modified June 7. https://www.census.gov/history/www/genealogy/decennial_census_records/the_72_year_rule_1.html.
University Archives and Special Collections, Joseph P. Healey Library, University of Massachusetts Boston. 2017. *Foresters Mortuary Records*. Accessed July 26. http://blogs.umb.edu/archives/collections/foresters/.

Community Engagement Stimulates Collaboration and Innovation for Local History and Genealogy Programming to Public Housing Residents

Roland Barksdale-Hall

Quinby Street Resource Center, located at the Mercer County Housing Authority's Malleable Heights site in Sharon, Pennsylvania, markets the following information services:

- Employment—find a better job, plan an exciting career
- Career planning—help in applying to college or technical schools
- Computer training—assistance in using computers, writing letters
- Community—various enrichment options, from courses about cooking to workshops about tracing your roots

Survey results indicated building trust was a factor for empowerment of residents in public housing; therefore, program strived to identify employment opportunities, promote job skills, cultural enrichment, and life skills. Since 2012 the Quinby Street Resource Center held employment workshops and popular six-week program "Celebrating Multiethnic Heritage: Searching Our Roots." Participants responded favorably to recognition of "culture," "important role of extended family network," role of "family reunions," and "life lessons learned from elders" (Barksdale-Hall, 2016, 233).

In 2016, an administrator of local senior employment program sent a last minute request for computer class to offset participants' loss of hours due to host sites closure between Christmas and New Year. This request required a combination of immediate attention and opportunity sensing. Mercer County Housing Authority was one out of four senior employment sites. To schedule a "computer class" "next week… on Tuesday, Wednesday and Thursday" for Senior Employment participants posed planning challenges. The Quinby Street Resource Center planned to be open between Christmas and New Year. I was perplexed with the short notice before Christmas yet there was a need for senior participants to not lose valuable pay.

Questions existed about budgeting for speakers, marketing, programming, and staffing. Who would teach the class? Where would class be held? How was the word going to get out about the program on such a short notice? How would the program be financed? When would the class be held? Who would the target audience be? What format would computer classes and program take? What computer skill levels did the participants have?

Following a phone call to the senior employment administrator I agreed to put together an "instant computer class" based upon prior programming successes and became the teacher by default. Site selection was the Mercer County Housing Authority's Centennial Place with computer laboratory, large meeting room, and parking in a safe residential Farrell neighborhood near a senior host site closed for the holiday. The following program goals were finalized, with a combination of technology, planning family reunions, and tracing our roots:

- Increase understanding of technology for the senior community
- Strengthen an existing partnership with senior employment agency
- Create a relaxed, comfortable, computer-friendly learning environment

The workshop was designed to teach adult learners about computers. Four-hour sessions included a combination of computer instruction and lectures on topics, including Tracing Enslaved Ancestry, Planning Our Family Reunion, Creating a Family Newsletter and Blog. Two-hour morning sessions held in the computer laboratory, provided computer instruction and hands-on applications. Two-hour afternoon sessions provided programs with prior positive results. Adult learners used FamilySearch, talked about their family reunions, and highly rated the program.

Background on Community Engagement

Outreach with a technology, local history and genealogy component was developed differently to be culture-, neighborhood-, sex-, and age-appropriate. A session, "Struggles in Steel: Community-Based Programming" at the 8th National Conference of African American Librarians, Cincinnati, Ohio (2013), focused on implementation, evaluation, and recommendations for outreach. It included the following age groups:

- Preschool
- Elementary
- Middle School
- High School
- Adults

A partnership between FamilySearch and Afro-American Historical and Genealogical Society (AAHGS) to index the Freedmen's Bureau Records attracted attention in 2014. As mentioned in "Reconnecting Friends and Family, Rediscovering African American Heritage," myriad benefits to the AAHGS' National Genealogy Conference included the following:

- FamilySearch and AAHGS Partnership Freedmen's Bureau Indexing Project
- Thirty concurrent sessions
- Author luncheons
- Cultural tours, vendors, and exhibits [Barksdale-Hall 2015, 20].

Jean Elizabeth Brumfield, distance services librarian at John B. Coleman Library, served as a panelist for a general session on publishing, identified resources available, and addressed "research tools, search engines, and technologies in libraries and other places" (Brumfield 2013, 34). I served as organizer of the general session "Getting Stories Published and Broadcast" at the 34th National Genealogy Conference, held in Nashville, Tennessee in 2013. I then was the editor of the *Journal of the Afro-American Historical and Genealogical Society*.

As mentioned in "From Genealogy to History: An Interview with Author and Historian Roland Barksdale-Hall," community engagement combined with "genealogical pursuits," begun in Pittsburgh, led to "wider pursuits" in organizing, researching and chronicling a history in Farrell, Pennsylvania (Ham, 2010, 128). A school/community partnership between the Pittsburgh Public School and Pittsburgh Chapter of AAHGS provided development of modules and school visits. Students at Peabody High School presented research on the Enty family at Society meeting at the Allegheny Branch of the Carnegie Library of Pittsburgh. Fifth graders at the Martin Luther King Elementary School learned about their neighborhood and genealogy. I was then a librarian at the Carnegie Library of Pittsburgh and executive director for Pittsburgh Chapter of AAHGS. *Farrell* (Arcadia Publishing 2012) was a result of the partnership with the local Urban League, Mercer County Historical Society, and Stey-Nevant Public Library in Farrell. It traced two to three generations and promoted critical multiculturalism. I then was head librarian at Penn State Shenango in 1994. *Farrell* received recognition for "counter-narrative," photographs, and representational "cross-section" of community (Mitchell, 2010, 129). A session, "The ABC's of Inspiring Children: Skills from a Teaching Artist," presented at the 2014 University of Pittsburgh at Greenburg Children's Literature Conference, sponsored by University of Pittsburgh at Greensburg Millstein Library, discussed storytelling and youth programming in Farrell.

Elementary School, Fourth Through Six Graders

Collaboration with the Farrell Area School District begun with an eight-session literacy and family oral history project in 2007. Students in fourth and fifth grade classes read Christopher Paul Curtis' *The Watsons Go to Birmingham—1963* (Delacorte Press, 1995), listened to audiotaped oral histories, and completed interviews with grandparents and other older family members. Students were captivated by stories about children riding in wagons to church, frightened horses seeing first cars and running off.

Interview questions about family history, migration, and the Civil Rights included the following:

- What is your full name?
- When were you born?
- Do you have a nickname, and if so, how did you get this name? What do you think of your nickname?
- What are the names of your mother and father?
- Where was your mother raised?
- Where was your father raised?
- Do you remember your grandparents, if so what were their names?

- Where did you go to school, and what was your favorite subject?
- What was your favorite book?
- Who was your favorite teacher?
- What's the name of the oldest ethnic club in your community?
- What was Farrell like when you were my age?
- Did your family migrate to Pennsylvania, if so why?
- Tell me a favorite childhood memory?

Over the years the program was developed with technology, graded writing, and PowerPoint assignment and presentation, and received recognition. Students interviewed family, and then published and presented their work at a community multi-ethnic celebration in the meeting room at the public library. Fourth graders presented, published an essay, and received a trophy for their research from a local service organization. "An Interview with My Grandmother Carrie Rose Howell" provided names of great-grandparents and their parents, places of residency, military service, and reasons for migration (McCormick, 2007, 9). The genealogical programming was funded by a 2012 Black Caucus of the American Library Association (BCALA) Family Literacy Initiative Reading. It built trust relationships, increased outreach, and received BCALA recognition for "impact … literally and figuratively" on "grandparents, grandchildren, and other community people" (Lemmons 2012, 5). Teaching partner Vernon Scott, Farrell elementary school teacher, received the 2015 AAHGS Debra Newman Ham Educator Award.

Middle School

At Farrell Junior/High School I was one of over twenty presenters to bring "truth" and "wisdom" during the School and Life All Day (SaLAD) workshop. Tracy Hood, Farrell School District Librarian/SaLAD Coordinator, who recognized that perseverance was required to write *Farrell*, assigned four groups of boys to speak about perseverance, education, relationships, and respect of self and others in 2012. I talked about the importance of goal-setting for research, how perseverance was par for a writer's success, provided comparison to sports, and developed an acrostic ASKS:

- A=Achieve a goal, set your goal
- S=Setbacks, hurdles on the path
- K=Knowledge comes through identification of resources
- S=Seek mentors and stay the course

Comments from teacher evaluations included "high level of student engagement… connected with the positive message." I invited youth to learn more about local history and genealogy. Three of them attended a *Farrell* book signing at the Stey-Nevant Public Library on Saturday morning. I presented to girls in alternate years.

Dual High School/College

Farrell Honor students in the eleventh and twelfth grade participated in an introduction to United States history course through a dual high school/college program.

"Struggles in Steel: Documenting Our Historic Past" discusses development of genealogy, oral history and publication modules, provides syllabus, sample interview and course evaluation. Student learners completed the following:

    1. Compared and contrasted historical developments; examined conflicts faced by racial and ethnic groups that shaped their unique experiences in America;

    2. Explored how to combine the information gathered from oral recollections of family elders, data from local resources, and findings from Ancestry.com in order to arrive with meaningful social history;

    3. Shared the results through both oral presentations and written publications [Barksdale-Hall 2012, 94].

Class met in the newly renovated middle school/high school library. Presentations took place at a community multi-ethnic celebration at the local public library. Students published "The Robinson Family of Farrell, Pennsylvania," and "Race and Ethnic Relations in the United States during World War II." They received three credits upon completion of the course (Avery 2011, 41).

Senior Computer Classes

Comments on the first morning of computer class for seniors ranged from "nobody takes time to teach us" to "when we touch these things something always goes wrong." Seniors were ducks out of water. Some participants did not know how to turn on the computer. Adults responded to a relaxed environment, applications about family projects, and camaraderie of not being alone. They gained practical knowledge about creating word documents, setting up email accounts, scanning documents, old family photos to share with other family members, making attachments for email. They together searched FamilySearch, received printout with names of parents, expressed excitement about going home and calling family. Participants valued the detailed instruction received, followed by hands-on activities with modules. On the morning of the last computer class participants returned with more information, requested reference assistance with finding information, and expressed the desire to know more about computers.

Best Picks

The afternoon session on the first day began with discussion about Kwanzaa display, seven principles known as the Nuguzo Saba, and healthy eating selection in the meeting room. Twenty-minute PowerPoint presentation on Tracing Enslaved Ancestry was based upon extensive genealogical academic research over 30 years that appeared in journals, encyclopedias, and exhibitions across the country. It was taught as a partial requirement for the course Researching African American Ancestors during the 2012 Institute of Genealogy and Historical Research.

My interest in genealogy began with undergraduate coursework, membership in the AAHGS, and library school at the University of Pittsburgh in 1985. The acquisition of library skills formulated search strategies, provided ability to interpret findings for academic purposes, and contributed to my reputation as a genealogist. Research on enslaved ancestor Wilson Stevenson was recognized as an "excellent example." It combined newspaper sources, public records, and church records. It provided opportunity for lecture at the 1988 National Council of Negro Women: Black Family Reunion, publication in genealogical society magazine, encyclopedia entry on black family, exhibition of enslaved ancestors, and dramatic presentation "Wilson's Ashes" for the 1998 International Sons and Daughters of Slave Ancestry Juneteenth at the DuSable Museum, Chicago (Beasley 1997, 76). *African-American Family Guide to Tracing Our Roots: Healing, Understanding and Restoring Our Families* (Amber Books 2005) publication aided to secure election to 2010 class of Senior Fellows in the American Society of Freedmen Descendants, editorship of *Journal of the Afro-American Historical and Genealogical Society* from 2013 to 2015, and 2015 James Dent AAHGS Award.

Tracing Enslaved Ancestry presentation examined a case study of a family in freedom and slavery, showed photographs and documents, focused on research methodology, scholarly publication record, and nomination process to a scholarly lineage society, American Society of Freedmen Descendants. Talk based on an essay "Inheritance and Slave Status" in *Encyclopedia of African American History 1695–1895: From the Colonial Period to the Age of Frederick Douglass* provided an introduction to regional variation in the interpretation of slave status and legal requirements among state assemblies (Barksdale-Hall 2006, 196). The course rationale was that many genealogists did not understand the social, economic, and cultural development of slavery in America and the political history shaped by these changes with an emphasis on slave communities. A satirical dramatic presentation, "Wilson's Ashes," performed at genealogical societies, libraries, and museums across the country offered insight into slave status and the institution.

Outcomes included:

- Acquire basic knowledge of American social, economic, cultural, and political changes during slavery
- Integrate primary and secondary sources into research methodology
- Submit material for consideration to a scholarly lineage society

Discussion about identities, family surname naming practices in freedom, and the significance of the research process followed. There was a reception and photograph session at a Kwanzaa table.

On the second day participants enjoyed a 20-minute PowerPoint "Beginning Genealogy: Researching Your Roots: Ten Tips," previously presented for the Tenth Annual Juneteenth Seminar at the North Forestville Community Center in Forestville, Maryland on June 13, 2015. Ten tips included the following:

- Choose a family member to research and join a genealogical society.
- Record nicknames, first names, last names and various spellings.
- Let go of preconceived ideas. Interview everyone (relatives and non-relatives) you can.
- Search around the house for items.
- Be organized and work from the present to the past.
- Remember life timeline and records produced.
- Search for communities, note neighbors and record multiethnic relationships.
- Use a combination of vital records, census schedules, city directories, maps, newspapers, DNA analysis and other public records.

- Compare and contrast all records with histories, various online and other public records.
- Package genealogy (narrative, storytelling, play).

Discussion about planning a family reunion in Eufaula, Alabama, involved a community program entitled Cousins Coming Together held at the Eufaula Carnegie Public Library, collaboration between a public library, county genealogical society and African American genealogical society. Program included storytelling, preventative care presentation on prostate, breast cancer, and diabetes by a local physician, seminars on tracing family tree, and tips on planning a family reunion. Goals of the Cousins Coming Together Celebration included:

- Bringing together families, public library, and majority and minority genealogical societies
- Strengthening families
- Promoting healthy living
- Restoring communities

"The Library as a Cultural Center, Advocating African American History and Genealogy" reported findings of a survey of over one hundred African American cultural institutions in Canada and the United States, examined partnerships, programming in the public library, and outreach within communities. Survey participants discussed satisfaction with resource sharing, listed obstacles such as "hidden agendas" and identified "spinoffs from collaborative programming" (Barksdale-Hall 1995, 392). Libraries' past culture and history of exclusionary practices limited trust and comfort level and attendance in genealogical activities.

During the sharing portion participants talked about their family values, reunion activities, time and place, length and location. Participants showed an interest in the 40-page *Cousins Coming Together* souvenir book with vintage family photos, census sheets and funeral home programs. A story of how a host on WFMJ-Television 21 in Youngstown, Ohio, saw a photo of my grandmother Camilla Barksdale with a bandanna tied on her head, exclaimed "Your family was poor" caught the attention of the audience. A discussion followed on identities, teaching about ancestors, and counter-narrative; how my family members, like so many others, contrary to popular opinion, indeed were rich with love of family, strong work ethic, and spirituality (Barksdale-Hall 2016, 82). Participants shared photos, research, documentation of families' military service records, which resulted in "And We Served: Military Service Records in Pottsville, Pennsylvania," United States Colored Troops Institute pin (Muhammad 2012, 109).

On the third day, the librarian discussed newsletter and blog publishing. "210 Years Later From Georgia Slavery to Atlanta Braves and Globetrotters," presented for the Metro Atlanta Chapter of AAHGS meeting at the Georgia State Archives, Morrow, Georgia in 2014, examined stories about genealogy, music, sports, and popular culture in the newsletter, and showed blog "Illusions of Freedom on Every Now." I covered scanning, importing digital images, creating a family newsletter, and presented "Getting the Word Out: Newsletter Publication" from the 2010 Writing Success Conference. Discussion topics included the following:

- How do you increase youth involvement?
- Asking questions—Who, What, Where, How, and Why

- Keeping a conversational tone
- Presenting timely news of interest to readers
- Identifying features to wow readers
- Including reviews, member news, calendar

Stimulating brain teasers, word searches and puzzles

Evaluation

Marketing generated results in the form of telephone calls, registrations, and walk-ins.

Yet the program planning presented a challenge due to the time of request and holiday schedule. A flyer with the heading "Family Reunion Planning, Tracing Our Roots & Getting the Word Out" included images of a tree and a person on a computer, provided contact information, meeting site, dates, and time. Phone calls, posting to social media, distribution door to door at the Farrell site, and mailing to individuals who attended Tracing Our Roots class in the past were employed to get the word out.

The Herald's Community News on Christmas Eve ran the following:

> A program, Family Reunion Planning & Getting the Word Out, will be presented from 1 to 3 p.m. Tuesday, Wednesday and Thursday at Centennial Place, Farrell. Come and pick up tips on how to plan your family reunions, use Word and make a newsletter for your church, class or family reunion. Plan to discuss creative ideas. Now is the time to start making your plans for summer fun. Registration, call Roland Barksdale-Hall, Mercer County Housing Authority resident service coordinator at 724–342–4048.

The newspaper announcement unfortunately dropped "Tracing Our Roots" from the program title and narrative in the press release. Social media received credit for any buzz and walk-ins about Tracing Our Roots.

Attendees to the family reunion planning, tracing our roots and getting the word out ranged from parents with children to 71 and older. More than half of the respondents were 51 and older; they thought that the program was too short, but still enjoyed it. Respondents highly rated the information on how to trace our roots, plan a reunion, and make a. Four out of five respondents reported that they received a very high value from the workshop. They highly rated the instructor.

Computer class attendees ranged from 51 to 71 and older with minimal to no computer skills. Three out of four respondents enjoyed the computer workshop. They highly rated the value of the course. Three out of four respondents gave high ratings to the instructor. Respondents valued learning objectives of Microsoft Word and Microsoft Publisher. Comments ranged from "vital information" to "continue with more learning."

Conclusion

Since 2017, the Mercer County Housing Authority has become a training center for the senior employment program. The partnership between the senior employment program and Quinby Street Resource Center strengthened existing collaboration, built trust relationship, increased employment and computer skills. Senior computer classes witnessed increase of participation at the Centennial Place computer laboratory. The librarian developed a senior peer mentor computer teaching program, identified the senior employment participant with a high level of computer skills, and provided supervision and training for a peer teacher. The peer teacher received opportunities to learn about computers, improve public speaking skills, and build confidence. Senior learners are becoming more comfortable with the computer, learning about math, reading, genealogy, and creating valuable job skills.

A combination of genealogical pursuits and technology provided residents of public housing and neighbors with valuable computer skills, increased community engagement, supported important role of library as a culture keeper, and sparked innovation in library service delivery. Seniors now engage in a computer culture-friendly environment, pick up valuable job skills, and enjoy card making and movie making along with pleasant conversation about family. Thank you for support and encouragement to Shenango Valley Foundation, Nannette Livadas, Fran McKenna, Renea Ingram, Holly Campbell, Sheila White, and Nicole Dora.

WORKS CITED

AAHGS Metro Atlanta website. Accessed April 14, 2017.
Avery, Leon Alexander, III. 2011. "The Robinson Family of Farrell, Pennsylvania." *Journal of the Afro-American Historical and Genealogical Society* 29, 41–49.
Barksdale-Hall, Roland. 2005. *African-American Family Guide to Tracing Our Roots: Healing, Understanding and Restoring Our Families*. Phoenix, AR: Amber Books.
_____. 2016. "Collaboration Fits the Bill for Best Practices in Programming for Public Housing Residents." In *The Libraries Role in Supporting Financial Literacy*. Ed. Carol Smallwood. Lanham, MD: Rowman and Littlefield.
_____. 2012. *Farrell*. Charleston, SC: Arcadia Publishing.
_____. 2006. "Inheritance and Slave Status." In *Encyclopedia of African American History 1695–1895: From the Colonial Period to The Age of Frederick Douglass*. Ed. Paul Finkelman. Oxford: Oxford University Press, 196–199.
_____. 2016. *Leadership Under Fire: Advancing Progress, Communicating, Teaching and Setting Communities at Liberty*. Phoenix, AR: Amber Books.
_____. 1995. "The Library as a Cultural Center, Advocating African American History and Genealogy." In *Culture Keepers II: Unity Through Diversity: Proceedings of the Second National Conference of African American Librarians*. Ed. Stanton F. Biddle. Newark, NJ: Black Caucus of the American Library Association.
_____. 2015. "Reconnecting Friends and Family, Rediscovering African American Heritage." *BCALA News*, 42, no. 4, 19–25.
_____. 2012. "Struggles in Steel: Documenting Our Historic Past." *Journal of the Afro-American Historical and Genealogical Society* 30, 94–105.
Beasley, Donna. 1997. *Family Pride: The Complete Guide to Tracing African-American Genealogy*. New York: Macmillan.
Brumfield, Jean Elizabeth. 2013. "Getting Family Stories Published and Broadcast." *Journal of the Afro-American Historical and Genealogical Society* 31, 34–35.
Curtis, Christopher Paul. 1995. *The Watsons Go to Birmingham—1963*. New York: Delacorte Press.
Douglas County History blog. "Illusions of Freedom." Accessed April 12, 2017.
Harbuck, Anastasia. July 18, 2008. "African Cultural Program Tapped for Library." *Dothan Eagle*. Accessed July 28, 2008.
Lemmons, Karen. "Reading Is Grand! Reading Is Great!" *BCALA News*, 40, no. 1, 5.
McCormick, Trevon. 2007. "An Interview with My Grandmother Carrie Rose Howell." *Health Reporter* 1, no. 1, 9.
Mitchell, Anthony B., Sr. 2010. Review of *Farrell*. *Journal of the Afro-American Historical and Genealogical Society* 28, 129–35.
Muhammad, Gail. 2012. "And We Served: Military Service Records in Pottsville, Pennsylvania." *Journal of the Afro-American Historical and Genealogical Society* 28, 109–112.
Newman Ham, Debra. 2010. "From Genealogy to History: An Interview with Author and Historian, Roland Barksdale-Hall." *Journal of the Afro-American Historical and Genealogical Society* 28, 128.
Sparrow, Alicia. 2009. "Race and Ethnic Relations in the United States during World War II." *Journal of the Afro-American Historical and Genealogical Society* 27, 49–56.

Building a Collaborative Partnership Between a Genealogical Society and a Public Library

Anastasia Varnalis Weigle,
Wendy Lombard Bossie
and Brenda Jackson Bourgoine

Genealogical societies and libraries share a common ground as they both offer resource materials and assistance to their users and it is no surprise that the genealogist is a heavy user of libraries and archives, historical societies, and museums. Family history research continues to grow and is the "second most popular use of the internet" (Barnwell 2013, 261). For the archivist, understanding user needs and the behavior of genealogists was of interest back in 2003 when a study was conducted involving the in-depth interview of 10 genealogists (Duff and Johnson 2003, 79). The study found that many more relied heavily on colleagues and an informal network of researchers than on archivists. In an era of tight budgets, finding ways to maximize resources through partnerships and collaborations can prove to be advantageous for some libraries and genealogical societies. Combined resources can better support user's needs. Public Library archival collections contain resources that support the genealogist's work.

The archivist, like the genealogist, must examine and interpret information to ensure the validity of the data. Genealogical societies serving a local town, city, or county will find local area libraries will have the same constituents (Litzer 1997, 40). However, public libraries that contain archival papers, but have no archivist and minimal staffing to maintain, build, and promote their collections, may not realize the commonalities they have between their institution and their local or regional genealogical society. The opportunities afforded to libraries and genealogical societies through such collaborations can bring about better access to collections, collection growth, increased patron usage, program building, facility sharing for workshops and meetings, and grant opportunities for preservation and care of collections. How do two separate agencies work together as a single unit, yet still retain their identity? What types of policies should each group have in place before embarking on such a collaboration? How does this collaboration affect library staff and what do they need to know? One such collaboration has begun between the Caribou Public Library (CPL) and the Aroostook County Genealogical Society (ACGS). This essay will share the ins and outs of a joint effort to combine holdings from both institutions to build a Genealogical Research Center.

A Brief History of the Aroostook County Genealogical Society

Genealogy is more than a table of names or a list of dates. Genealogy is the genetic history of a person or a family. It answers the questions, "Who are we?," "Where did we come from?" and "How did we get from here to there?" The genealogist's task is to investigate family origins, bloodlines, societal history, and human migration. It can tell us something about historical events through the lens of families living during a specific period in time. The genealogist's source of information is numerous—vital statistics, birth, marriage and death records, oral history, periodicals, baptismal papers and family bibles, correspondences, diaries, and military records.

The Aroostook County Genealogical Society (ACGS) began on August 12, 2003, with their first meeting held at the Caribou Public Library meeting space called the Caribou Room. That first year the ACGS elected officers, a board of trustees, a mission statement, and drafted its first informational brochure. They drafted and made plans for a monthly newsletter to keep everyone informed and hoped to bring in more members. In the meantime, the ACGS met in the Caribou Room at the library when it was available to them. In 2005, the ACGS became a chapter, named "The County" of Maine Genealogical Society. Although the Caribou Public Library had archives and space for research, it did not offer ACGS a permanent meeting space. Instead, the genealogical society was provided meeting space if a meeting room was available. ACGS would seek meeting space through the arrangement of field trips. These tours took members to various locations in Caribou such as the Family History Center Library located in the Caribou Branch of the Church of Jesus Christ of Latter-day Saints, the Vera T. Estey House, the Caribou Historical Center, Thomas Heritage House, and the University of Maine, Presque Isle Special Collections Room. The Caribou Lions building and the Chan Center at the Caribou Medical Center were available for a few years with occasional meetings in the Caribou Room. Late in 2014, the Caribou Library director invited ACGS to use the Archival area for meetings and to build a genealogical library within it. Print collections started to accumulate, through time, by the society and not secured in any repository. Instead, collections were spread out in various member's homes. Maintaining inventory of collections spread out was a challenge for ACGS. Before this time, a working relationship had been built with the library staff through members volunteering, so it was an easy decision for ACGS to make.

In 2006, the director of the Caribou Public Library loaned one file cabinet in which ACGS could store a few of their books in the archives. Later, a local business donated a lateral file cabinet for the society group, as they had outgrown the four-drawer cabinet loaned by the library. Although the library had a secure space for archives and special collections, the library did not have an archivist to organize, maintain or promote the collections. However, despite the challenges met by ACGS for a permanent meeting space and repository, between 2003 and 2014, the society was able to accomplish a great many things:

1. Aroostook County Cemetery Location map project using Global Positioning Software (GPS).
2. Cohosting Maine Old Cemetery Association with Caribou Historical Society in 2004.
3. Cleanup, repair, maintenance, and current caretaking of the Cochran Cemetery including photographing and documenting the gravestones.
4. Bringing in guest speakers, touring museums and history centers, offering workshops and classes on genealogy research.
5. Building liaisons with other groups such as the Nylander Museum in Caribou, Mark and Emily Turner Memorial Library in Presque Isle, LDS library in Caribou, Maine Genealogical Society, Maine Old Cemetery Association, Acadian Archives in Ft. Kent, Acadian Village in Van Buren and Libraries, Museums and Historical Societies in locations statewide.
6. Publishing *The Families of the Upper Saint John Valley in 1790* and *Aroostook County Towns that sent men to the Civil War*.
7. Assembling and indexing thousands of obituaries.
8. Providing information to people inside and outside of the Caribou area via the web site, through social media, emails, snail mail, and referrals.
9. Assisting Caribou Public Library in preparing the Hardison Collection; which is a donated repository of maps, deeds and related papers from generations of Hardison men who were surveyors. The goal was to make a public database of these holdings available.

Brief History of Caribou Public Library Archives

In January 2004, the library underwent some building projects, which included the reallocation of space opening up large meeting rooms in the lower level of the library. These were converted into archival space to house a large donation of the Aroostook Republican newspapers dated from 1887 to 2004 and continue to be updated and maintained to this day. The archives contained works of local writers and historians, photographs, local newspapers, school yearbooks, city reports, and postcards. The room was secured and only accessible when staff was available. Although the idea was to create a genealogical research center, there was no collaboration during this time between CPL and ACGS.

Between 2014 and 2016, a new director of the Caribou Public Library came onto the scene. She liked the Archive Room and welcomed the idea for ACGS to hold meetings there and join efforts to combine holdings and build a genealogical research center. Space was given to ACGS in the archives research area to house all their collections making CPL the official repository for the society.

The library provided storage shelving, bookcases, and storage space for ACGS to house their collection making the CPL Archives a repository for them. Plans to combine ACGS genealogical materials with the library's genealogical materials were discussed and then implemented. Because the library did not have a working archivist nor archival policies or standards for maintaining special collections, the collaboration had a bumpy start. The director, unfamiliar with archival standards, opened the archives room to the general public without supervision. Patrons used the space to eat, bring children to color or read, and used the space for various meetings. The director hoped that opening the space freely would give the patrons a sense of ownership. However, without advocating the archives, space was not considered special in any way by the general public. It was just another library space for patrons to congregate. Although the intention of the director was sincere, concerns for security was a major issue for ACGS. Again, a workable collaboration would have to wait a while longer.

In January 2017, a new director with a background in archives management took over the position of Head Librarian for the Caribou Public Library. In keeping with the previous manager's vision, the new director met with the President of ACGS, Brenda Bourgoine and past CPL librarian and now current Archivist for the Caribou Public Library, Wendy Lombard Bossie, to discuss policies and procedures that would benefit both institutions. New policies were set in place to help forge a stronger collaborative relationship that would benefit both institutions.

Working Policies for a Successful Collaboration

Since 2004, the library has maintained an archive to secure and protect historical collections, yet had no defined policies in place such as governing authority, purpose and mission, use and purpose of the archives and special collections, the role of ACGS within the library's archive, and appraisal guidelines to ensure its success. In 2014, collaboration was encouraged, but again, no archival policies were in place. These would need to be established first before collaboration could be implemented.

The Aroostook County Genealogical Society constituencies easily matched with Caribou Public Library thereby giving each an incentive to collaborate. ACGS and CPL are separate agencies with different mission statements. ACGS' primary mission focused on the members who were interested in increasing their knowledge in genealogy research and networking opportunities. The goals were to increase public awareness through programs and workshops and offer expertise in genealogical research:

> The Aroostook County Genealogical Society, a non-profit organization founded in 2003, is the society for everyone from the beginner to the most advanced family historian. The ACGS serves its members by, 1) providing genealogical skills development through education information, publications, research assistance, and networking opportunities; 2) promoting the highest standards of ethical research principles and scholarly practices; 3) establishing important links with other groups worldwide; 4) providing depth and breadth of knowledge and opportunities for our members; 5) creating programs to increase public awareness of opportunities to discover family history; and, promoting interest in the fascinating field of genealogy and family history [http://www.ac-gs.org/].

The mission of the Caribou Archives and Special Collections places primary focus on the collection, maintenance, and accessibility to archival resources. It is about stewardship of archival materials of historical, intrinsic, evidentiary and administrative value, and making these collections accessible to scholars, genealogists, students, historians, and visitors.

> … to identify, acquire, organize, preserve and make available materials pertaining to the history, culture, and people of the Caribou area and outline communities in Aroostook County and portions of the State of Maine that support our documents. These materials are available to genealogists, historians, scholars, students, and the general public. The library holds these materials in trust for future generations.

For the Caribou Public Library and the Aroostook County Genealogical Society, the decision to work collaboratively would require some written agreement, addressing ownership and access to materials. Each group must advocate for each other, which in turn offers strength and stability, increased access to users, visibility, and more opportunities for grants. The newly implemented archival policies that established the framework that would help define the relationship with ACGS were placed under its Research and References Services policies:

> The Caribou Public Library is the permanent repository of the Aroostook County Genealogical Society Research Center. Although a separate agency from the Caribou Public Library, ACGS and the Archival Collections at the library share their genealogy materials for easy access to users. As a specialized field, all inquiries for genealogical research will be provided by ACGS. The Archivist provides research services about Caribou history, its surrounding communities in Aroostook County, and the state of Maine as it relates to our collections.

Four types of collaboration were implemented: (1) exhibitions, (2) outreach/advocacy, (3) publications, and (4) grant writing. Of these four, outreach/advocacy services are the engines that drive our collaborative programs and overall partnership. It is beneficial to both groups when outreach/advocacy services are done collaboratively either in the forefront or in the background. Forefront advocacy is done when both groups are creating a program, event, or workshop together. For example, the Aroostook County Genealogical Society and the Caribou Public Library invited the public to an open house event. It was decided by both groups to have an open house as a way to introduce the community to both organizations and their collections. CPL and ACGS co-hosted the event with representatives from both groups attending. The open-house was an opportunity not only to promote both organizations but to exhibit an ongoing project ACGS has been working on since 2001—seeking information on the provenance of a "Mystery Quilt" found at the bottom of an old tool box in Wisconsin. The quilt is owned by the Caribou Historical Society. How it got to Wisconsin from Caribou is truly a mystery. Its approximate date was established as late 19th century although that may change.

Brenda Bourgoine, ACGS President began researching the names on the quilt to try and identify who made it, why it was made, when it was made, and perhaps how it traveled to Wisconsin from Caribou. The research was set aside for some years, until Wendy Lombard Bossie, Library Archivist, and member of the Caribou Historical Center and Museum, picked up the research. The open house was an opportunity to share the quilt and its mystery to the community. The turnout was a success for both groups. Many visitors of the open-house were not aware that the library had archival collections. The positive feedback from the community about the collaboration was another plus!

Behind-the-scenes advocacy relates to promoting each other's programs. For example, when the Caribou Public Library has an event, either archives- or library-related, ACGS shares the press with their members on their social media. This is done equally by the library. To do this successfully, both groups keep abreast of each other's activities. Since the library archivist is the liaison between ACGS President and the CPL Director, she is the connector between the two. This is what I mean by collaborations taking a "leap of faith." This "leap of faith" requires both groups having a vested interest in each other in order to succeed.

Any ongoing outreach of various forms, including but not limited to tours, presentations, workshop, sponsorships of meetings, seminars, and conferences related to ACGS and/or the Library Archives and Special Collections Mission will further the use and development of materials to serve the local and regional community.

Our publications policy is not to be confused with ACGS published works. Instead, it is an extension of Outreach/Advocacy. This is quite new for the library. Although ACGS has a brochure introducing themselves to the community, the Caribou Public Library has never had a brochure or booklet designed to market the archives. The Archives and Special Collections is in the process of designing brochures and descriptive guides (finding aids) to publicize its existence and information about its collaborative partnership with ACGS.

The Caribou Public Library archives and the ACGS will seek out and write grants collaboratively. Since we are both working together to strengthen each other's collections and provide research support to users, developing well-planned collaborative programs together may open up opportunities for grant writing. "A deeply collaborative program plan demonstrates dedication to making a difference by leveraging available expertise and resources" (Floersch 2015, para. 1). Such collaborations would help to generate funds to support and sustain both groups such as educational and staff training, programming, workshops, assessment grants, educational programming, facility and environmental control upgrades, new housing materials, and digital project grants.

Collection Ownership and Access to Content

One aspect of this collaboration is the sharing of genealogical print resources. Genealogical societies are less likely to contain family papers or business records—something common in archives. What can be found in ACGS possessions are indices of obituaries, publications by the Maine Genealogical Society, genealogy periodicals, and books on specific family histories. The library archives have additional print resources useful to ACGS including maps and gazetteers, which are valuable to genealogists in need to identify the names of localities within the geographic area (Duff and Johnson 2003, 94). For the family historian, key factors in research are ease of use and accessibility (Richards 2006, 78).

Both groups agreed it would be advantageous to combine these particular collections into one location for easier access. Library Archives genealogical research materials were shelved with ACGS genealogical materials. To differentiate what books belonged to which group, those belonging to the library are identified by their call number, whereas ACGS materials are identified by their name or specific recording keeping code. This decision has been beneficial in supporting ACGS while still maintaining ownership of each other's genealogical print collections.

Most important, ownership of print resources means good stewardship. The Caribou Public Library has an insurance policy for its materials and facilities. It is important that the society also has an insurance policy to protect its print collections from loss or damages. The policy must be for replacement value, and not depreciation value.

Research Support and Services: ACGS vs. CPL

We start to see differences within each group when you examine how research support and services are administered. The Caribou Public Library is a city department with non-profit 501(c)3 status through the Caribou Public Library Foundation. With numerous monetary trusts and support by the city budget through taxpayers, research service provided to our users at the Caribou Public Library is free other than making copies of documents using a standard photocopier or digital print. However, the Aroostook County Genealogical Society, also a non-profit 501(c)3 organization, relies on membership dues, donations, and research-based fees to a non-member of ACGS.

The archivist's knowledge specialty is local Caribou and Aroostook County history, not genealogy. Therefore, we are unable to serve users by attempting to do this highly specialized research. On the other hand, when genealogists and family historians come seeking photographs, city plans of neighborhoods, newspapers, school, church, or business records, or other resources that are part of CPL's archives, ACGS refers them to us.

The success of this type of resource/research collaboration only works because both parties communicate openly and often with each other. It also helps that the library archivist is the liaison between ACGS and CPL.

ACGS Provides Manpower for Library Archive Projects

One of the best assets of our collaboration with ACGS is their workforce support for Library archive projects. It is advantageous that ACGS know the scope of our collections. To do so requires interaction between the library archivist and the President of ACGS, who is also the archivist for their organization.

Approximately ten years ago, the Caribou Public Library received a collection of city plan blueprints dating from the late 1800s to mid–1900s from the University of Maine in Presque Isle. The plans are extremely useful to ACGS research, but difficult to use because they had not been processed since they were accessioned years ago. This year, a project partnership was established between ACGS and CPL to survey, organize, rehouse, and create finding aids for the city plans.

Conclusion

The genealogists seek practical information consisting of specific facts and dates using census records, vital stats, and obituaries, whereas the family historians are seeking needs of a more profound nature—a way to connect to their past and seek identity (Yakel 2004, 4). The archivist seeks information through primary sources such as diaries, journals, and correspondence. The similarities between the library archivist and the genealogist are to investigate the veracity of information found to determine its validity. However, at the same, we both understand the sensitivities of the family historian's need to connect with one's past.

What motivates the Caribou Public Library to collaborate with the Aroostook County Genealogical Society? For CPL, our motivation is visibility, stability, advocacy, and support. For ACGS, its motivation is space, stability, advocacy, and resources to help their users, which are our users. Wendy Bourgoine, President of ACGS is an active participant in the library archives. Brenda Bossie, the current archivist for the library, is an active member of ACGS. Their dedication is proof that such collaborations can make sense in organizations that have similar goals, missions, and stakeholders.

Lastly, our cooperation with each other is unique only to us and what works for us may not work for other libraries or genealogy societies. Collaboration is determined by the needs of the library and the local or regional genealogical society and what end results each one seeks.

ADDITIONAL RESOURCES FOR LIBRARIANS AND GENEALOGISTS

Best Genealogy Databases. http://www.familytreemagazine.com/article/50-best-databases.
Guidelines to Developing a Core of Genealogy Collections. http://www.ala.org/rusa/resources/guidelines/guidelinesdeveloping.
Ideas for Expanding Your Library Genealogy Programs. https://www.ebsco.com/promo/ideas-for-library-genealogy-programs.
Librarians Serving Genealogist Listserv. http://mailman.acomp.usf.edu/mailman/listinfo/genealib.
Random Acts of Genealogy Kindness. http://mailman.acomp.usf.edu/mailman/listinfo/genealib.

WORKS CITED

Barnwell, Ashley. 2013. "The Genealogy Craze: Authoring an Authentic Identity Through Family History Research." *Life Writing* 10(3): 261–275.
Duff, Wendy, and Catherine Johnson. 2003. "Where Is the List with All the Names? Information Seeking Behavior of Genealogists." *The American Archivist* 66(1): 79–95.
Floersch, Barbara. 2016. "How to Collaboratively Strengthen Grant Proposals." *LinkedIn* [Post] (16 June 2016). Accessed April 20. https://www.linkedin.com/pulse/how-strengthen-collaborative-grant-proposals-barbara-floersch.
Richards, Jennifer. 2006. "An Investigation into the Information Needs of Family History Researchers." MA Librarianship Thesis, University of Sheffield.
Yakel, Elizabeth. 2004. "Seeking Information, Seeking Connections, Seeking Meaning: Genealogists and Family Historians." *Information Research: An International Electronic Journal* 10(1): n1.

Part III: Case Studies

Making the Case for Genealogy Reference Instruction

Lisa A. Oberg

"Genealogy is hot!" said Tim Sullivan, CEO of Ancestry in 2012 (Farnham 2012). Since then interest has only become hotter. So much so that genealogy and its research have evolved into a TV genre (Smolenyak 2017). But shows such as *Finding Your Roots*, *Who Do You Think You Are?* and *Genealogy Roadshow* make genealogy research seem deceptively simple. The reality is it takes over "1,000 hours of research to put together 42 minutes of television" according to Jennifer Utley, senior manager of research at Ancestry.com. (Hendrickson 2015). Access to online records can turn anyone into an armchair genealogist with a simple *Google* search. Researchers may turn to librarians when their searches are unproductive or inconclusive. This essay describes a course developed specifically to train future librarians to effectively serve genealogists. Even librarians who think they will never work with genealogists may find themselves in need of this specialized training: how to locate an obituary—or write one—for a local business person or faculty member; assist a legal firm with locating heirs; help a patron determine a birth or death date for a historical figure; or determine the original owner of a home or business, all of which involve genealogy research techniques.

Genealogy Libraries Services is a graduate-level course open to Master of Library Science (MLIS) students enrolled in the Information School at the University of Washington. This course is designed to prepare students to provide library and archival service to genealogists. Students acquire a practical knowledge of genealogy library users and resources and explore related topics including reference, cataloging, collection development, digitization, outreach, and professional development.

Students who successfully complete the nine-week online course receive three credits. It is offered during the summer quarter when students typically have more room in their schedule to pursue electives. The course is divided into eight modules each of which focuses on a different aspect of genealogy research or reference service. The final week is left free for students to complete their final project, a Genealogy Portfolio. A pass/fail grade is based on class participation (50 percent) and completion of the Genealogy Portfolio (50 percent). Each module has specific learning objectives and is structured to include readings, a pre-recorded online lecture, and discussion questions. There is no required text for this course. The course was designed, in part, using the *Guidelines for a Unit or Course of Instruction in Genealogical Research at Schools of Library and Information Science* from the Reference and User Services Association (RUSA), a division of the American Library Association (RUSA).

The scope of the class is 18th-, 19th- and 20th-century American research of individuals with primarily European ancestry. This is based on the concentration of records available through the largest genealogy sites such as Ancestry.com and FamilySearch. For course assignments, students are encouraged to research their own family history or a historical figure of interest. A sample portfolio using Laura Ingalls Wilder's family history was created for students to use as an example. Because there is so much individual searching associated with the course, it lends itself to online instruction. The experience is greatly enriched for all when students actively participate in the discussion sharing their successes, failures, and discoveries related to their unique heritage.

The final project, a Genealogy Portfolio, is a compilation of original records and examples students collect in relation to the topics presented in each module. Students are encouraged to turn in elements of the portfolio incrementally throughout the quarter. However, the only assignment required before the final day of the quarter is a preliminary pedigree chart students turn in the first week of class. For this submission, students are asked to take 5–10 minutes to fill out a pedigree chart from memory. They are instructed not to worry if they do not know much information about their ancestors—or a historical figure they have chosen—off hand. They will submit a second pedigree chart with their Genealogy Portfolio which will highlight progress made throughout the quarter. For students unfamiliar with pedigree charts, tips and examples are provided to help them get started.

The Genealogy Portfolio also consists of a variety of record types typically used by genealogists, as well as examples of online library resources aimed at genealogists. The Portfolio elements include:

1. Table of Contents with full citations to records submitted
2. Original pedigree chart (due Week 1)
3. Updated pedigree chart (due at end of the quarter)
4. Federal Census Records from 3 different enumerations
5. W record from a state or special census (Mortality, Agriculture, Veterans)
6. Vital record: examples of a birth, marriage and death record
7. Archival records: 2 examples such a passenger manifest or military draft card
8. Published sources: 2 examples such as a county history or city directory
9. Citation to a social history topic related to their research, e.g., Civil War draft riots
10. Record or information from an index or database found through a genealogical or historical society, state library or archive not indexed by Google
11. Citation to a book or microfilm from a specialized genealogy library such as the Family History Library or Allen County Public Library
12. Citation/link to a genealogy education program or conference
13. Citation/link to a genealogy webinar, online video, or tutorial
14. Citation/link to a library research guide or pathfinder
15. Reflection paper describing what they learned over the course of the quar-

ter, how their perceptions of genealogists changed and whether the course contributed to their abilities to be an effective librarian [1200–1500 words]

The following outline lays out how the portfolio elements are associated with each of the eight modules, and strategies the students utilize, from researching their own family history to considering how they would assist others with research in a professional setting.

Module 1: Introduction to Genealogy and the Genealogical Research Process

Objectives

- Learn basic definitions of genealogy and gain knowledge of the history of genealogy in the United States.
- Understand how to record genealogical information.
- Identify steps for getting started with genealogical research, including developing research questions for locating missing information.

The first module orients students to the course and introduces them to the concepts associated with genealogical research. Readings for this module include an introduction to the standard forms genealogists use for recordkeeping, such as family group sheets and pedigree charts; an overview of the history of interest in genealogy in America from the Colonial period through today; and an explanation of the *Genealogy Research Process* (Tucker 2008). Students are also introduced to best practices for citing records. In the online discussion, students introduce themselves, share their reasons for taking the class, state what they hope to get out of the course, and describe their background, if any, in genealogy. Students are tasked with watching an episode *Who Do You Think You Are?* or some other genealogy TV show and share their impressions with the group, including their thoughts on how these types of shows inspire, yet sometimes mislead, genealogists and whether they provide enough information so that the research presented can be reproduced.

Module 2: Census Research

Objectives

- Understand what federal, state, and other special census records are available.
- Learn about how census records can provide a framework for genealogy research.
- Understand techniques and strategies for finding information in census records.

Module 2 focuses on the importance of census research for genealogists. The lecture and readings help students gain an understanding of census records, and ways to develop strategies for searching since information can often be difficult to locate. The lecture also covers where to find census records and describes the wide variety of census schedules available including state, slave, manufacturing, mortality, and agriculture. Availability of international census records is also discussed. As part of the course materials, students are given five optional skill-building worksheets which include a variety of searching challenges. The first optional worksheet accompanies the census module. In the discussion for this week, students share their experiences locating census records either from their own research or from the worksheet, as well as reflect on the impact of census records for genealogists. Students are also encouraged to submit items 4 and 5 from the list of required portfolio elements.

Week 3: Module 3

Objectives

- Understand what birth, marriage, and death records are available.
- Learn techniques and strategies for finding vital records.
- Gain knowledge of the information one can expect to find in vital records and the limitations and restrictions associated with these records.

The second optional worksheet focuses on searching for vital records. In the discussion, students again share their searching successes and challenges. Each of the major types of vital records; birth, marriage and death records, are defined and the information they may contain explained. An overview of other types of records which may contain important dates, funeral records, for example, is also presented. The Federal Government has a 72-year privacy restriction on records it collects, and each state has its own laws regarding access to public records. A second topic asks students to discuss the intersection of privacy protections and restrictions/challenges to access to records for genealogy purposes. This module is associated with portfolio element 6.

Week 4: Module 4

Objectives

- Understand the variety of archival records available to genealogists.
- Learn techniques and strategies for finding archival records.
- Gain knowledge of the information one can expect to find in archival records and the limitations and restrictions associated with these records.

Module 4 provides an overview of a variety of other records which are critical to genealogy research including church, court, land, military, immigration/naturalization, organization and institutional records. The importance of using maps to understand how boundaries have changed is also presented. A popular discussion ensues from the assigned reading "Why Your Family Name Was Not Changed at Ellis Island" (Sutton 2013). An overview of the National Archives and its wealth of resources is provided. To understand the breadth of the records at the Archives students read an article from *Prologue*, the Archives quarterly magazine, and report about the record group featured. Students are also tasked with reading entries from Trish Hackett Nicola's *Chinese Exclusion Act Case Files* blog to gain awareness into the wealth of information available in archival records and understand the effect public policy can have on individuals. An optional worksheet on archival research is also provided and students are encouraged to submit portfolio element 7.

Module 5: Weaving History into Genealogy

Objectives

- Understand the importance of weaving social history into genealogical research.
- Learn key resources and strategies for incorporating social history into genealogical research.
- Learn about and develop strategies for finding and analyzing newspapers, city directories, county histories, and other published sources.

Up to this point in the course, many students have had some exposure to the record types discussed. In this module, students are introduced to the concept of social history and resources that can provide texture to a family history especially when specific details are not readily available. *Merriam-Webster* defines social history as history that concentrates upon the social, economic, and cultural institutions of a people (Merriam-Webster). In addition, students explore newspapers, city directories, county histories and other published resources which help put their ancestors into historical context. Students are asked to find a piece of "social news" from a newspaper, generally using *Chronicling America* and post it to the discussion board. For example, "Left-Handed; Asks Divorce," a brief article which appeared in the *Seattle Star* on January 7, 1911, tells of a woman seeking divorce from her husband for his mental cruelty and ridicule. Hilarity often ensues from their discoveries.

Students are also introduced to deep web searching—an embedded search on a web page which many state libraries and archives employ but not indexed by web engines—and asked to share their strategies for locating key resources for an unfamiliar state or community for a patron. Optional worksheet 4 provides searches for published sources. Worksheet 5, the final optional worksheet, helps students develop critical reading skills when reading a biographical sketch from a county history or an obituary and use timelines as a way to identify discrepancies. Portfolio elements 8, 9 and 10 are associated with this module.

Module 6: Genealogy Reference Services

Objectives

- Understand the interests, characteristics, and motives of family historians.
- Develop strategies for assisting researchers with their questions.
- Learn about the types of specialized reference sources available and how to keep current.

The first half of the course deals with preparing students to do their own research in order to give them as much time as possible to work towards completing their Genealogy Portfolio. With Module 6 the curriculum turns towards providing reference service to patrons researching their family history. Readings discuss the genealogy reference interview, as well as the demographics of genealogists and some of the challenges associated with assisting them. Students are given an overview of major genealogy databases including Ancestry.com, FamilySearch and MyHeritage and Fold3. Other important internet resources available such as WorldCat, Internet Archive, HathiTrust, JSTOR, Google Books, and state library and archive sites are also introduced.

Important reference sources, such as handwriting guides, language, medical and law dictionaries, and guides to specific heritage groups are presented. Copyright, as it relates to genealogy, and interlibrary loan are also highlighted.

One discussion topic students respond to is an unexpected—and undesirable—discovery about an ancestor, such as a slave-holder, criminal or bigamist. The topic is introduced by a recent *Wall Street Journal* article "When a Genealogy Hobby Digs Up Unwanted Secrets" (Shellenbarger, 2013). Students are also asked to visit three public library sites: one servicing communities with a population over 500,000, one under 100,000, and one small/rural library and determine:

- If they offer genealogy programming?
- What services, if any, do they offer genealogists?
- If they provide service to non-residents?
- If they have any published policies regarding genealogy?

Students then compare and contrast their findings with that of a library known for having vast genealogy collections, such as Allen County Public Library in Fort Wayne, Indiana, and others. Portfolio element 11 asks students to identify a book or microfilm of interest in a genealogy-focused library they might not be able to access elsewhere.

Module 7: Preservation and Digitization

Objectives

- Learn about the relationship between archives and genealogy.
- Understand the need and strategies for preservation.
- Learn about how digitization can enhance access and support preservation.

Module 7 is a brief introduction to principles of archival organization and helps students develop criteria for assessing unique materials as candidates for both digitization and preservation. As the public interest in genealogy increases so does the desire for new, undiscovered resources. Identifying photograph collections, scrapbooks, card files and other material within a collection can be an opportunity to raise awareness for your library. Understanding the preservation needs of a collection ensures that it is well-cared for, is available for generations to use in the future, and identifies material for preservation grants and other funding opportunities. There are many crowdsourcing activities now that can help leverage unique materials and make them accessible via the internet, as well. The highly successful *FamilySearch* "Worldwide Indexing Event" in 2016 is a great model for libraries, large and small, to consider creating citizen archivists to aid with collections (FamilySearch 2016).

Module 8: Collections, Programming, Outreach and Professional Development

Objectives

- Understand various aspects of genealogy and local history collection development.
- Identify unique characteristics of cataloging genealogy and local history items.
- Increase awareness of the opportunities for public programming.
- Gain knowledge of professional development opportunities.

The final module explores a variety of common library activities through a genealogy lens. Students review *Guidelines for Establishing Local History Collections* and *Guidelines for Developing a Core Genealogy Collection* published by RUSA as part of their assigned reading (RUSA). Professional development opportunities for genealogy/local history librarians are discussed and the three remaining portfolio elements require students to identify examples of programming, outreach and education opportunities. The final discussion topic for the course asks students to imagine that they are asked to give a presentation on a topic related to genealogy. Their response includes a brief description of their topic and why they chose it; major categories of information to be covered; one online resource relevant to their topic they would feature/discuss in-depth in their presentation, and three additional resources (books, websites, etc.) they would recommend to help others understand the subject better. By this point in the quarter, students have gained the knowledge and confidence to move from being a student to becoming a teacher. The discussion for the quarter ends on a high note as students share their new-found expertise.

Feedback from students who completed the course has been very positive. A common refrain is that the research was harder than they expected. Students with non–European heritage were amazed by how much they were able to find. Even students who entered the course skeptical about genealogy experienced the thrill of unexpected family discoveries and gained new respect for the research process. Another unexpected realization many students commented on is that the research skills they learned in the course will have professional utility for them beyond assisting genealogists.

Although students do not gain a mastery of genealogy in eight short weeks, they do complete the course with a greater understanding of the complexity of family history research and an appreciation for documented, well-cited work. A popular refrain among family historians is that a genealogy without documentation is "mythology." Taking that analogy one step further, DNA test results without a well-researched family tree is just a topic for cocktail party conversation. The tantalizing commercials for DNA testing services, which imply a simple cheek swab is all it takes to uncover your ethnic heritage, only tell part of the story. To truly make sense of DNA results and leverage them, genealogy research is also essential. As more and more consumers get DNA tests, the need for librarians with genealogy expertise will increase. Offering an elective course in Genealogy Library Services prepares future librarians to assist patrons and approach new job opportunities better informed of the needs of family historians. Interest in genealogy will not be fading anytime soon as DNA tests become less expensive and increasingly more content is accessible online. Harnessing the passion of genealogists in ways that benefit the user and the library turns potentially challenging patrons into advocates and allows libraries to leverage collections unique to their library. The first step in making this happen is educating future librarians to embrace the opportunity to work with genealogists.

Works Cited

FamilySearch. "Worldwide Indexing Event 2016," FamilySearch Blog. Last modified June 22, 2016. Accessed July 26, 2017. https://familysearch.org/blog/en/worldwide-indexing-event-2016.

Farnham, Alan. "Who's Your Daddy? Genealogy Becomes $1.6B Hobby," ABC News. Last modified October 12, 2012. Accessed July 26, 2017. http://abcnews.go.com/Business/genealogy-hot-hobby-worth-16b-mormons/story?id=17544242.

Hendrickson, Paula. "The How of Who," Television Academy. Last modified February 26, 2015. Accessed July 26, 2017. http://www.emmys.com/news/mix/how-who.

Merriam-Webster. "Social History." Accessed July 26, 2017. https://www.merriam-webster.com/dictionary/social%20history.

Reference and User Services Association (RUSA). "Genealogy Guidelines and Standards." Accessed July 26, 2017. http://www.ala.org/rusa/sections/history/histcomm/genealogy/genealogy.

Shellenbarger, Sue. "When a Genealogy Hobby Digs Up Unwanted Secrets," *Wall Street Journal*. Last modified January 15, 2013. Accessed July 26, 2017. https://www.wsj.com/articles/SB10001424127887324734904578241822679163276.

Smolenyak, Megan. "Genealogy Is Officially a TV Genre." *Huffington Post*. Last modified April 5, 2017. Accessed July 26, 2017. http://www.huffingtonpost.com/megan-smolenyak-smolenyak/genealogy-is-officially-a_b_9609742.html.

Sutton, Philip. "Why Your Family Name Was Not Changed at Ellis Island (and One That Was)," New York Public Library. Last modified July 2, 2013. Accessed July 26, 2017. https://www.nypl.org/blog/2013/07/02/name-changes-ellis-island.

Tucker, Mark. "Genealogy Research Process Map," ThinkGenealogy. Last modified July 10, 2008. Accessed July 26, 2017. http://www.thinkgenealogy.com/map.

Introducing Genealogy to the Academic Library in the 21st Century

THOMAS MCFARLAND *and* JOAN M. BARNES

Introduction

This case study examines the development of a new program to foster genealogical research in an academic library that did not encourage or promote genealogical research. In early 2014, the University of Nebraska–Lincoln Libraries set a strategic initiative of increased outreach. As one way to reach the goal, the staff development officer and the community engagement librarian proposed a genealogical program with three objectives:

- to reach out to campus faculty, staff, and students
- to involve library faculty and staff
- to bring community users into the academic library

The staff development officer and the community engagement librarian became the program's coordinators. They developed the program by initiating Genealogy Over Lunch and Genealogy & Family History Day as focal points to bring people to the library for interesting discussions to help the library's staff understand how family historians can use their expertise, and to introduce more researchers to the library's underused large collections. Planning, resources, publicity, and assessment were crucial to the success of the program.

Background

For decades, like many other larger academic libraries, the University of Nebraska–Lincoln Libraries did not encourage genealogical research. This had not always been the case. The dean of the library in 1925–1937 was Gilbert H. Doane, the author of the 1937 genealogical classic, *Searching for Your Ancestors: The Why and How of Genealogy*. In the 1950s, however, the library transferred materials that librarians considered primarily genealogical to the Nebraska State Historical Society, which is just two blocks from the main campus library. Reference staff actively urged genealogical researchers to use the Historical Society's collections.

The re-introduction of genealogy into the library started more than fifty years later, in March 2012. The coordinator of Learn at Love, the library's public workshop series, asked the staff development officer to present a session on how patrons could use the library's collection to do genealogical research. The staff development officer used the library's online, print, map, and special collections to show how it was possible to research an unknown revolutionary soldier. Using Heritage Quest, he showed the soldier in the 1790 and 1800 censuses. The library's book collection and HathiTrust had many sources that helped to build out the story. These included lists of militia members, battle histories, effects of the war in the area, and even town histories that included genealogical information on the family. Fold3 provided payrolls, muster records, and personal dispositions. There were also sources to help find materials that were not in the library's collection, such as ArchiveGrid and WorldCat. These resources made it possible to get copies of articles and pages of books. Historical maps gave context and understanding to the movements of the soldier during the war. Bringing all of these documents together resulted in a substantive history. The Learn at Love coordinator actively advertised on campus and was able to get promotion for the event in the city newspaper. It brought in more attendees than the large room could accommodate. Librarians were surprised to learn how much information could be found. The success of the presentation resulted in adding genealogy in later sessions, and the staff development officer presented these programs for the library once or twice per year as part of that library-initiated series. Over the next two years, the attendance at all of the Learn at Love sessions dwindled, and the library discontinued the series.

With the termination of the Learn at Love series, campus colleagues approached the staff development officer to find a way to do something to assist faculty, staff, and students to learn more about doing genealogical research. In response to a new library strategic initiative to increase outreach, in January 2014, the staff development officer approached the dean of libraries with a proposal to have genealogically focused programs. The dean was enthusiastic, and they brought the community engagement librarian in as a co-coordinator with the staff development officer. The community engagement librarian was an adept genealogist and had the essential expertise to promote the program.

Genealogy Over Lunch

The coordinators met to brainstorm to get the program started and decided to emphasize family history over genealogy. The elimination of the strictly genealogical collection was not viewed as an obstacle by the coordinators because of the earlier success of showing how the use of academic materials led to the creation of a family history. They invited key faculty and staff in the library and a representative from the chancellor's office to give input on how to proceed. The group liked the idea of short presentations followed by an open question and answer period. The coordinators decided to start with outreach to the campus community. After discussing the pros and cons of various venues, the coordinators chose to hold the discussions in a library conference room with media and occasionally in one of the library's instruction rooms. The group determined a monthly hour session over lunch would most likely best meet the schedules for faculty, staff, and students and chose the third Thursday of the month from 11:30 until 12:30. Thus, they launched Genealogy Over Lunch with the first session, "Favorite and Unusual Sources." The community engagement librarian promoted the session, and it brought in thirty campus faculty and staff. This format began a successful series of sessions.

The coordinators led the programs and discussions. The attendance for Genealogy Over Lunch discussions fluctuated and ranged between five to twenty-five people depending on the session topic and work schedules. Over the next two years, they learned more about what attendees wanted and made incremental improvements to the program. At each session, they asked participants what they would like for presentations. The coordinators suggested themes to the attendees for about half of the sessions and the rest were suggested by the attendees.

Library faculty and staff were recruited to share their expertise in brief presentations covering various areas, including preservation of family documents, searching newspapers, and knowledge of collections specific to the university library.

Genealogy Over Lunch covered the following topics.

- DNA
- Cyndi's List
- MyHeritage
- Holiday traditions
- Google Scholar
- FamilySearch.org
- Question and Answer
- Crowdsourcing a problem
- Ancestry.com
- Success stories
- Draper Collection
- Court records
- FamilySearch and WorldCat for local records
- Open Mic discussion
- Finding death records/information
- Land records
- "Inspiration" software
- Building a family member timeline
- Beyond Ancestry.com
- Organizing your research
- GedMatch
- Online publishing
- Brick wall breakthroughs
- Proof and Evidence
- Crossing the Pond
- Archival preservation
- "Legacy" software
- Fold3
- U.S. Serial Set
- Favorite and Unusual Sources

Presentations that covered genealogically themed databases, such as FamilySearch.org, Ancestry.com and MyHeritage had the best attendance. Traditional library instruction topics, such as Google Scholar and how to organize research, had good attendance. Sessions that concerned a specific problem, such as crowdsourcing a problem or those that lacked a theme, like the general question and answer sessions, were not as well attended. It surprised the coordinators that the attendance at the DNA sessions was low. Nevertheless, there was a high level of interest by those that did attend. Recently more of the attendees have said that they took a DNA test, so it may become more popular. Faculty from the University's School of Biological Sciences have expressed an interest in working with the group on DNA for future presentations. This contact showed how the program connected to multiple disciplines and made genealogy in the library better known on campus.

The engagement and participation of attendees has been another indicator of success. During each session, discussion and questions flowed comfortably between coordinators and attendees. The coordinators encouraged attendees to present and several did so. This model gave the group more buy-in, was more inclusive, and took advantage of a larger knowledge base. Presentations by attendees were especially valuable for demonstrations of software, such as Legacy, RootsMagic, and Inspiration.

Publicity Plan for Genealogy Over Lunch

The publicity plan targeted a specific audience and marketed the programs in the channels where the audience members would discover them. The first step of the plan required listing each segment of the market audience and deciding on the best way to reach each segment with the program information. The breakdown of the audience for Genealogy Over Lunch included current faculty and staff, emeriti faculty, library personnel, and students.

After each type of marketable audience was determined, a plan was implemented to reach each group with the program publicity. For faculty and staff on campus, the community engagement librarian submitted the announcement of the upcoming Genealogy Over Lunch program to a campus-wide digital newsletter, entitled "Nebraska Today," distributed by the Office of University Communications several mornings each week during the academic year. This campus-wide digital newsletter was the primary means to reach faculty and staff across campus. The names and email addresses of every person that attended a Genealogy Over Lunch session was captured for future notifications of upcoming discussions or future events.

In addition to the digital newsletter, the program coordinators targeted emeriti faculty by sending an announcement to the designated chair with a request to share the announcement widely with their members. Past attendees, plus library faculty and staff, were sent an email notice by one of the program coordinators.

Students were targeted through a digital newsletter of announcements that the Student Affairs office manages, entitled "Next@Nebraska," which is emailed to students once a week. In addition, the Genealogy Over Lunch program was featured in the student-run campus newspaper twice. The second time a student reporter covered the program, she conducted an in-depth interview of both program coordinators. The result was a well-written article about the Genealogy Over Lunch program making it more visible to students (Rembert 2017).

Genealogy & Family History Day

After the success of doing the Genealogy Over Lunch series, the coordinators decided a day of free programs would be a good way to attract community members. They considered it important that the community users would feel welcome and view the library and its staff positively. Since the local community college and genealogical society offered classes for beginning genealogists, the coordinators decided their audience would be users with a basic understanding of doing genealogical research. It was important to highlight the family history aspect, as this was a library strength. They launched Genealogy & Family History Day in 2015.

A daylong event meant dealing with more logistics: themes, presenters, venue, extended marketing, registration system, welcome, and refreshments. As one of the goals was to bring community members into the library, the coordinators chose a large classroom auditorium in the building. It had the advantages of ample seating capacity and a full classroom presentation setup. It was a high priority to have a good speaker system and oversize display monitor.

The publicity focus for Genealogy & Family History Day was to take the core publicity efforts the community engagement librarian did for the on-campus audiences and to expand them to an off-campus audience in and around Lincoln, Nebraska. The additional marketing tools included a webpage, media release, and a visual/poster that could be printed, emailed or posted on social media.

The media release contained the elements of a standard event announcement, which included the date, time, place, link to register, and a brief description of the content of the day's program. The purpose of the media release was to drive people to the website for more information. The Office of University Communications distributed the media release to newspapers, radio, and TV media throughout the state.

To directly reach groups of people interested in a day of genealogy workshops, the community engagement librarian created a database of genealogical societies, historical societies, and public libraries. A student employee assisted in searching online and gathered email addresses and links to Facebook pages. The media release and a digital poster were distributed to all email addresses on the list. Part of the social media strategy was to post the visual or message to each organization's Facebook page with the poster.

The library's graphic designer created visuals for both Genealogy Over Lunch and posters for Genealogy & Family History Day. Figure 1 is the tree that accompanied the Genealogy Over Lunch announcements.

The poster for Genealogy & Family

Figure 1. Design for Genealogy Over Lunch: https://unl.box.com/s/6o7j22tt8e6wlmnx91n9oglru4ciqjxy

History Day (Figure 2) incorporated that tree and visually illustrated the theme of the second annual Genealogy & Family History Day. Visuals conveyed the theme of the program and grabbed the attention of the potential audience.

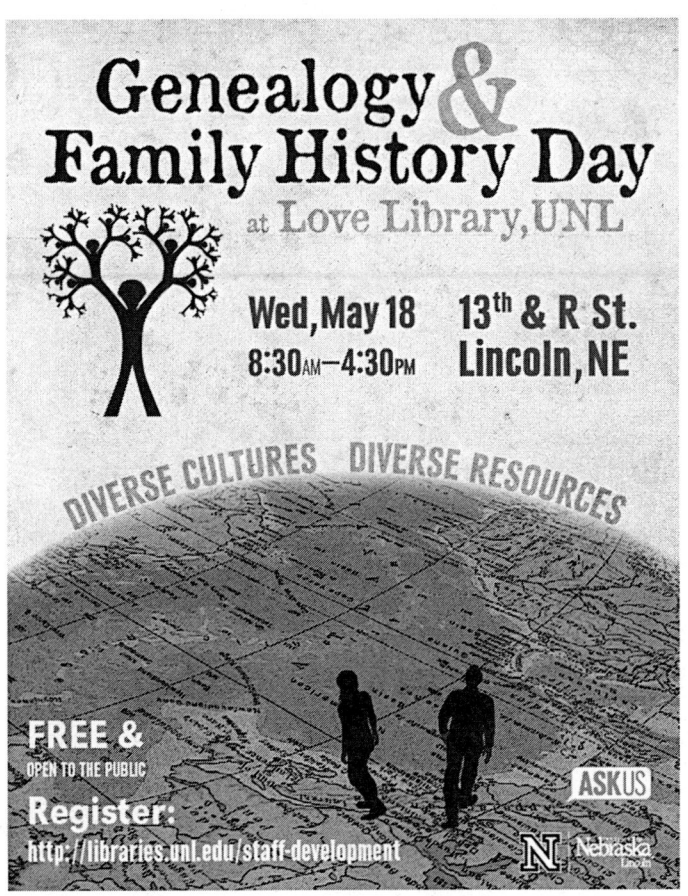

Figure 2. Poster for Genealogy & Family Day: https://unl.box.com/s/1u48vjotuhjlzq8jjst8vd1c9bhyb1wq

It was necessary to know the number of people attending in order to provide appropriate refreshments, distribute handouts electronically, and communicate final details. The coordinators used LibCal, a product of SpringShare, for registrations. This had several advantages. The coordinators could email directly from LibCal with reminders, directions, and updates. Setting up an event in LibCal created a URL that could be published in the promotional materials and that would take attendees directly to the registration page which interfaced with the library's staff development web page. The library web designers further developed the page to include details of the day's programs, speaker information, registration information, event location and directions, parking options, and recommendations for nearby restaurants that serve a quick lunch.

A part of the logistics surrounding the Genealogy & Family History Day included providing a welcome start to the day. This was especially important, as the library had not encouraged genealogical research for many years. Both coordinators and a student employee comprised the logistics team for the day. A successful event depends heavily on attention to detail. The student created the nametags and provided them for any walk-in registrations by transferring the names from the LibCal spreadsheet to a label-making program. The student was assigned to greet attendees at the welcome table, confirmed everyone was on the attendance list, and distributed the handouts. The community engagement librarian provided a script and went over possible questions that might arise at the registration table while the student greeted attendees. Specific talking points on the script were to show where the restrooms and vending areas were located. The library provided coffee, water, and an afternoon snack of popcorn for the attendees. The cost for each Genealogy & Family History Day was modest, as it covered coffee, popcorn, nametags, and one professional presenter.

For the first year, the coordinators chose to have presentations that highlighted databases and library collections. This was also a way to enthuse and educate librarians and staff as to how their expertise could help these researchers. The coordinators invited the reference coordinator, history librarian, architecture librarian, and university archivist to do presentations, along with the staff development officer. This covered a broad range of subjects by library experts. They included:

- Using the library website
- Newspapers
- Google Scholar
- Google Books
- HathiTrust
- Fold3
- Civil War Index
- Sanborn Maps
- University Archives
- ArchivGrid
- WorldCat
- Heritage Quest
- Draper Manuscript Collection

For the second year, the coordinators thought it would improve the event to have a theme. They chose "Diverse Cultures, Diverse Resources," which fit into the library's diversity focus. The theme worked well in promotional materials and in developing lectures. The presentations focused on Native American, African American, German, and Colonial American genealogy and showed a variety of resources held in the library and online.

Resources

When the new genealogy outreach program began, the library's only strictly genealogical online database was Heritage Quest. The library later exchanged that database for MyHeritage. These databases were important to the program, as they provided the United States censuses and other basic resources for assisting genealogists. MyHeritage also had the advantage of being more international in scope.

The program coordinators emphasized how the wider library collection could augment family history research outside of the strictly genealogical databases. They encouraged librarians to present sessions to show researchers how they could use the United States Serial Set, history, political science, map, and patent collections, as well as archives and special collections, in family history. It was also an opportunity to highlight underused large collections, such as the Draper Manuscript Collection, which included manuscripts and papers relating to the American West from the 1740s to the 1830s, and primary papers from the American Fur Company.

The genealogy program promoted the library digital initiatives of the Center for Digital Research in the Humanities (CDRH), a joint venture of the University Libraries and the College of Arts & Sciences. The CDRH digitized Nebraska newspapers as part of the National Digital Newspaper Program and its public website, Chronicling America.

They also digitized the Nebraska Homestead records. That collection became part of Fold3, a database that specializes in military records but includes non-military records. These opportunities highlighted to the campus and community users how the library contributes to the creation and dissemination of valuable record sets and how they could use these in their family history research.

Assessment of Impact

Attendance, engagement, and feedback were tracked to measure the success of both Genealogy Over Lunch and the Genealogy & Family History Day. Most importantly, both programs brought diverse members of the University community into the library. In the third year of Genealogy Over Lunch, new staff and faculty, from diverse offices and units across campus, are still discovering the discussion group. New attendees heard about this program through the campus e-newsletter announcement or by word-of-mouth.

Students were one group the program was unsuccessful in attracting to Genealogy Over Lunch. One student attended the very first session but never returned. The program has been featured in the student newspaper twice with no positive effect.

An objective of the program was to involve library faculty and staff in instruction and to make them aware of the needs of genealogists. This objective was essential to the success of the program. The genealogy sessions presented by the staff development officer as part of the Learn at Love series gave reference providers an in-house resource. The presentations also helped library staff understand that genealogists most often were not just interested in dates of birth, marriage, and death, but that they wanted to flesh out the family history. Starting with programs for campus researchers helped to overcome the negative stereotype some librarians had for genealogists. It also reinforced that their expertise could meet the needs of these researchers and was an exciting way to reach a new user base. Library staff also attended sessions to learn more about other resources.

One of the objectives of initiating Genealogy & Family History Day was to bring new community members into the main campus library. To gauge the success of that initiative, the coordinators used two main indicators: email addresses of registrants and the results of an evaluation questionnaire.

The online registration form for Genealogy & Family History Day captured registrants' names and email addresses. In 2015, twenty-eight of the emails addresses were from the domain used by the University of Nebraska–Lincoln (unl.edu); thirty-two email addresses were from non-university domains (.com, .net, .org, and .gov). In 2016, even more community members attended with twenty-three email addresses from the University's domain and forty-six email addresses from non-university domains. The numbers of community members increased in attendance from the first to the second annual day. The program coordinators knew, anecdotally, that a few attendees had returned to work on their family history or to use a resource in the library. Unfortunately, data such as reference or circulation statistics did not exist to support that supposition.

The coordinators used an evaluation questionnaire that yielded valuable qualitative feedback from registrants of the Genealogy & Family History Day. In 2015, the questionnaire contained seven questions and was returned by thirty-three of the sixty registrants. In 2016, an eighth question was added to the original evaluation questionnaire and thirty-four of sixty-nine questionnaires were returned to the coordinators. Below is a list of the questions:

1. Where did you learn about the conference? (added in 2016)
2. Please describe how the sessions met, or did not meet, your expectations.
3. What will benefit you most?
4. How will you apply what you have learned?
5. It would have been better to spend more time on…
6. It would have been better to spend less time on…
7. What would you like included in the next workshop?
8. General Comments

The results to question number one helped the coordinators determine whether the publicity for Genealogy & Family History Day was effective. Word-of-mouth and local genealogical societies were the top two answers to the first question on the evaluation. Sending the publicity announcement to genealogical societies across the state supported the attendance numbers and proved to be worth the time and effort.

In terms of rating the content of the Genealogy & Family History Day, attendees were overwhelming positive in 2015 and 2016. In 2015, there were only a few negative comments about one session. This highlighted for the coordinators the need to fully communicate to potential presenters about the type of audience that attends the workshops and that speakers need to be well-versed in their topic. All other questions on the evaluation form gave the coordinators feedback on content and guided future workshop topics.

Conclusion

The library developed a new genealogical program with the goals of reaching out to campus faculty, staff, and students, involving library faculty and staff, and bringing community users into the library. The assessment showed that the program met these goals, except for the ability to attract the student population. Reaching the student body is still a challenge. Factors that contributed to the program's success were the coordinators' good understanding of public service, genealogical expertise, and enthusiasm. It also was essential that there was a publicity system in place and that the coordinators had expertise in organizing events and marketing. It was important that the program proved itself able to support the library's strategic initiative. This meant that good record keeping and assessment were vital. Opportunities for library staff and attendees to have input resulted in their enthusiasm and good advice. The format of a shorter presentation followed by a question and answer session at Genealogy Over Lunch is recommended.

For the future, the program coordinators will test better ways to draw students into the program. They will also develop an online guide for reference providers and researchers on using the library for family history. They will continue to look at new topics and expanding the program.

WORKS CITED

Doane, Gilbert Harry. 1937. *Searching for Your Ancestors: The Why and How of Genealogy.* New York: Whittlesey House, McGraw-Hill Book Company, Inc.
Rembert, Elizabeth. "UNL's Genealogy Over Lunch Allows Family History to Be Discovered." *Daily Nebraskan.* February 7, 2017. http://www.dailynebraskan.com/news/unl-s-genealogy-over-lunch-allows-family-history-to-be/article_9735cbd4-ece0-11e6-b08a-97adedb77646.html.

PART IV: RESEARCH

Finding Military and Court Records
Strategies for Research
ROSEMARY L. MESZAROS *and* KATHERINE PENNAVARIA

Introduction

Military and court records are both subsets of government records, but are not usually accessed through the same channels. Most U.S. military records are held at the federal level, but court records can be found in state, county, and local offices and archives.

Even far back in the past, whenever an individual interacted with the government (including through military service), a paper record was prompted by that interaction. In fact, the little we know about the lives of people from the distant past usually comes from official records rather than private papers such as letters and diaries. Neither Johannes Gutenberg nor William Shakespeare kept a diary that has survived, so how do we know that Gutenberg went bankrupt and that Shakespeare's wife was eight years his senior? Both facts appear in court records.

Military records for other countries are difficult to obtain, but in the U.S. they are available and worth pursuing. These records are great sources for evidence of military service, of course, but also for residence history and physical descriptions, among other things. And court records, despite being somewhat challenging to obtain, can reveal a world of personal details for individuals whose lives are represented there. Many court records contain information that was deliberately not passed down to the younger generation: divorces, lawsuits over property claims and damages, crimes committed, restraining orders obtained—the list is long and sometimes reveals painful situations that were intentionally buried.

Librarians working with patrons doing family history research can offer those researchers the following information and strategies about military and court records.

Military Record Types

For the genealogist, all military records have inherent interest because they place someone within a known historical context that can be studied. Here are the most common types of military records available—see below for details on how to help someone access them.

Draft Registrations

The National Archives and Records Administration (NARA) has microfilmed millions of draft registration cards from the two World Wars, but only a percentage of cards from each conflict is available. Also, some cards were destroyed before they could be microfilmed, so failure to find a man's draft registration does not indicate failure on his part to register. The information on these cards is important because this is one of the few available official documents wherein the individual himself attested to the information. The forms asked for numerous personal details, including full name, birth date and place, current address, marital status, and current employer. Usually they included a general physical description as well. And each registrant signed his name or made an X.

Enlistment Records

There were, of course, many men who enlisted rather than registering for the draft and waiting for possible call-up. Females are represented in enlistment records, which is great news for the researcher because they do not appear in the draft registrations.

Muster Rolls

Where there are soldiers, sailors, marines, and airmen (the term, with peculiar military logic, applies to females as well), there will be lists. Muster rolls are lists of people—a human inventory—that have been produced throughout the long history of American military activities, during both war and peacetime. With luck, a researcher can trace a person's movements almost year by year as he or she appears first on one muster roll and then another. Many muster rolls are available online, but they represent only what has survived fire and other depredations of time.

Personnel Records

The federal government divides the personnel records it holds into *archival* and *non-archival*, with split responsibilities for storage and access control. Military personnel records belong first to the Department of Defense (or its predecessors), which created them; 62 years after a service member has separated from the military through discharge, death, or retirement, the records are considered archival and made available to the public through the National Archives and Records Administration (www.archives.gov). Records for individuals who separated from military service less than 62 years ago (i.e., non-archival records) are maintained in the National Personnel Records Center (NPRC) in St. Louis and are subject to access restrictions. Unfortunately, a 1973 fire at the St. Louis facility destroyed about 16 to 18 million personnel files that had no duplicates or microfilm backup—see below for details on how to get auxiliary records through the NPRC.

Pension Records

Military personnel are eligible to apply for pensions; if someone dies during or after military service, the surviving spouse or minor orphans are eligible to receive the pension money. Pensions have been part of federal spending since colonial days, when the new government promised financial support, sometimes in the form of land grants, to veterans of the Revolutionary War.

Patrons researching people who might have served in the Revolutionary War, the War of 1812, the "Indian" War, the Mexican War, the Civil War, or the Spanish-American War will want to investigate pension and bounty land warrant record sets. Pension applications (available from NARA) contain information such as branch and dates of service, date and place of birth, names of heirs, and locations of service during conflicts. Sometimes (especially if there was an appeal) the files contain supplementary material, such as affidavits, marriage and death certificates, discharge papers, and other testimonials offered by the claimant in support of his or her application. Land grants and bounties for the Revolutionary War can also be found in the American State Papers, part of the U.S. Serial Set—records of the earliest Congress and executive agencies from 1789 to 1838. An index to the U.S. Serial Set is available in microform and also digitally from Readex (a division of NewsBank which publishes collections of primary source materials) and via the Library of Congress page called "A Century of Lawmaking from Library of Congress" (memory.loc.gov/ammem/amlaw/lawhome.html). Between the two, Readex has the more flexible search interface. Sadly, fire has destroyed many federal pension and land grant records, including the earliest Revolutionary War applications, but most of the later ones still exist.

Compiled Service Records

This record set sprang out of a War Department initiative in the mid–1890s to reconstruct Union army and navy personnel information lost through fire, primarily to verify military service for veterans seeking pensions. The goal was to create a single card, called a compiled service record (CSR), to hold all the militarily relevant information about an individual. After the Union soldier card project was finished, War Department clerks began working on CSRs for Confederate soldiers and for participants in other conflicts, including the Revolutionary War, Spanish-American War, and War of 1812. The cards, which are held at the National Archives and at various state archives, range from 1798 to 1902; they usually provide, in addition to name, rank, and unit, the soldier's home state, enlistment date, and length of service. Also possible: age, physical description, wounds sustained, date of discharge, or death. The federal clerks creating the CSRs were doing essentially what genealogists do—they researched an individual's history by gathering information from primary records and created a data sheet summarizing what they found.

Remind patrons that CSRs were not created at the time of service, like enlistment records and muster rolls, but represent a data summary. Thus, they are derivative sources, extracts of information taken from original sources such as pay and casualty lists, regiment and hospital records, correspondence, and so on. They should be used as stepping stones to original resources. Compiled records are useful if the originals are difficult to access, but researchers should never forget that the copying/information transfer process inevitably introduces errors.

Militia Records

Militias were citizen groups providing military-type service, in contrast to the official national military—many records relating to these groups survive at the state and local levels.

Finding Military Records

A variety of military records can be obtained from the National Archives and Records Administration (www.archives.gov) and its subsidiary, the National Personnel Records Center in St. Louis (www.archives.gov/st-louis), and also through the subscription sites Ancestry (www.ancestry.com) and Fold3 (www.fold3.com). Quite often, city and county libraries hold locally relevant military records. Some of these collections have even been published in Google Books.

The 1973 fire that destroyed between 16 and 18 million military personnel files at the National Personnel Records Center (NPRC) in St. Louis was without a doubt a terrible blow for researchers. Eighty percent of the Army discharge records from November 1, 1912, to January 1, 1960, and 75 percent of the Air Force discharge records from September 25, 1947, to January 1, 1964, were lost. These documents were un-indexed originals with no microfilm or other copies extant. In the years following the fire, the NPRC collected other records (medical, dental, employment) and used them to reconstruct basic service information—some of those auxiliary records, such as the final pay voucher, can be ordered. Researchers should send requests to NPRC even if the individual records that they seek were likely among those affected. The response letter will explain options for ordering auxiliary records. They can request records from NPRC by filling out the form, *Request Pertaining to Military Records* (Standard Form 180), available online through the NPRC site.

Some of the federal census population schedules give military details: 1840 (Revolutionary War pensioners), 1890 (Civil War vets, for the 6,000 or so names that were not destroyed by fire), 1910 (survivors of the Union and Confederate army or navy), and 1930 (general veteran status). Also, family papers and letters might contain discharge papers, medals, citation certificates, etc.

The NARA site's dedicated area called "Access to Archival Databases" (www.archives.gov/aad) is a good place to steer patrons—it provides record information (though not images) for about 475 data sets, including many of military relevance. NARA also holds pension applications and records of pension payments to veterans, their widows, and other heirs for service between 1775 and 1916. Ancestry and Fold3 both offer subscribers many military record sets (both images and indexes). Fold3 is focused on records pertaining to specific conflicts from the American Revolution through recent wars in the Middle East, while Ancestry has two quite useful large indexes: "World War II Army Enlistment Records, 1938–1946" and "U.S. Army Register of Enlistments, 1798–1914." These index records usually contain, among other things, place of residence, place and date of enlistment, year and state of birth, and education status. The pre–World War I list is especially helpful in establishing the birthplace of people who came to the U.S. between the late 18th and early 19th centuries. Both sites offer downloadable images of compiled service records (CSRs).

One of the best free resources available for people researching Civil War participants is a database maintained by the National Parks Service. Called the Civil War Soldiers and Sailors Database (www.nps.gov/civilwar/soldiers-and-sailors-database.htm), this free index has extracted records of six million Confederate and Union military personnel—much of the information came from the compiled service records, but because this database includes information from other sources, it should be searched in addition to the CSR indexes. The system has unique information as well: regimental histories, which can give the researcher a picture of a soldier's movements; detailed descriptions of significant battles; lists of prisoners; and burial records. Another free resource worth checking out is Online Military Indexes and Records (www.militaryindexes.com), which offers federal and state resources organized by conflict (Revolutionary through Vietnam Wars).

Finally, if someone is researching relatively recent military personnel, suggest that they consider subscribing to the military's newspaper, *Stars and Stripes*. For current issues, they can find subscriber info at www.stripes.com; for the newspaper's archives, they can subscribe at starsandstripes.newspaperarchive.com. The latter site offers an inexpensive, one-day pass option.

Of course, there are many information resources relevant for military research other than the ones named here: casualty lists, lists of medal recipients, discharge papers, medical/hospital records, desertion and court martial records, and regimental histories among them. Some are federal; some are state controlled; and others might be with private organizations. The availability of military records, especially online access to them, is ever-evolving.

Court Records

Records of court transactions, which include much more than criminal cases, are not centralized or usually online, so some old-fashioned legwork is called for. The first step for the researcher is to understand the different types of court records.

Family Court

Covers events such as adoption, divorce (legally called "dissolution of marriage"), child custody/guardianship, and probate. These court records are rarely available online (Ancestry and FamilySearch do have a number of probate records) but can usually be obtained from the jurisdiction involved (adoption records excepted). In general, the records most likely reside where a case was initially filed, a hearing held, or a judgment rendered. Sometimes, however, county records are consolidated and archived at the state library, although the jurisdictional court may still have an index to those records.

Civil Court

Covers such things as lawsuits, property disputes, minor claims, etc. Sometimes older divorces and other family court matters are included in civil court indexes. These cases feature one party against another; for example, *Smith vs. Jones*—in which Smith (plaintiff) is suing Jones (defendant). With regard to divorce suits, before no-fault divorce, one party had to sue the other party, and thus each party's personal testimony became part of the court's record. These statements always reveal something about the parties involved—bitterness, resentment, and even allegations of violent and criminal behavior. A judge had to decide whether the case for divorce was legitimate, and who got what.

Criminal Court

Unlike civil cases, criminal court cases feature some level of government against an individual; for example, *U.S. vs. Smith* or *The State of Illinois vs. Jones*—in which the government body is the plaintiff and the individual (or corporation) is the defendant.

With only a few exceptions and with some privacy restrictions, court records are *public*; that means they are available to be ordered, sometimes under the federal Freedom of Information Act (FOIA). Getting to them usually isn't easy, but they are invaluable for providing details about a person's life that might otherwise not be known. Genealogy researchers sometimes discover through court records that a person was ordered to spend time in an institution such as a mental hospital or jail. Jail records are usually controlled by a government entity, but records from private institutions such as hospitals are difficult to obtain, as they are often discarded after a specified period or simply not made available. However, if an individual was committed (sent involuntarily) to an institution for criminal or mental issues, that commitment resulted from a court order, which means that a court record once existed, probably still exists, and might be available. The essential point is that court records are public and subject to laws governing their availability, whereas private records are not.

Researchers should pursue the strategy of "follow the money." A family's whereabouts and well-being can best be established and assessed by searching out employment, tax, property, and inheritance records, all of which are the province of local courts. Often, these proceedings were required to be mentioned in the classified section of the local newspaper.

Finding Court Records

As noted earlier, every time a city, county, or federal court has interacted with a citizen, a record was created—the Internet age has not changed that pattern. Today, some localities make court records available online, with open access; traffic violations and other minor criminal offenses pertaining to living people, for example, are often not considered private. Each state has a Bureau or Department of Vital Records, and each state also has an official state library or archive—those entities hold court records, as do local county archives and government offices.

Some county- and city-level court records in the U.S. have been photographed by the Family History Library in Salt Lake City and put on microfilm; many of them have already been digitized and made available at FamilySearch (www.familysearch.org). To find what's available in a particular jurisdiction, suggest that patrons do a "place" search in the catalog at FamilySearch (www.familysearch.org/catalog/search)—the catalog will indicate which records for that place are available in digital form, which are still on microfilm only, and which are available only in print at the Family History Library. If they don't find the court records available in any of these forms, they must travel to where the records are held or hire a local researcher to obtain them. Ancestry has a "hire a researcher" section, and there are several sites that can help researchers find someone to obtain on-site records for a particular area; e.g., Genlighten (www.genlighten.com).

Remind patrons that the people they are researching are more likely to appear in local court records than in federal or state. Unfortunately, legal actions at a local level (municipal, county, or state) are not usually recorded outside of that local jurisdiction, so will probably require an on-site visit. These cases do not appear in the widely available printed law books known as *reporters*, which contain the history of legal decisions in the nation, nor are they part of the biggest databases for legal research (see below for details).

But when a case is sent to a higher court, whether through appeal, retrial, or some other reason, it is likely to appear in one of the regional reporters, which are available both online and in print. The regional reporter system is managed by a private company called WestLaw, which divides the nation into seven sections: Atlantic, Northeastern, Southeastern, Southwestern, Southern, Western, and Pacific. These divisions were invented by WestLaw and do not correspond to the usual geographical divisions. For example, the six New England states (Maine, New Hampshire, Vermont, Massachusetts, Rhode Island and Connecticut) are broken up—all of them except Massachusetts fall under the Atlantic region, but Massachusetts is grouped with New York, Indiana, Illinois, Ohio, and Indiana into the Northeastern region. WestLaw reporters also cover the five permanently inhabited U.S. Territories (Guam, the Northern Mariana Islands, Puerto Rico, American Samoa, and the U.S. Virgin Islands) as well as some Native American Tribal jurisdictions.

To help someone determine what court records are online, consult the three biggest subscription databases: WestLaw, Nexis Uni (formerly LexisNexis), and HeinOnline. They all allow you to look up a case by the parties' names, by legal citation (e.g., 547 S.W.2d 435), or by topic. The search protocols are getting simpler to use with each update, but subject searching is not for the faint of heart. It requires the researcher to think like an attorney and use the terms that the law mandates. However, if the researcher is searching by names only, then the task will be easier. Remember: only cases that have moved up to a higher court will be in these national databases. The first appearance of a case is in local records that must be retrieved from the original jurisdiction.

Some differences among the national databases: HeinOnline covers nearly 10,000 Canadian cases from 1905 to the present, and more than 100,000 cases from the United Kingdom between the years 1220 to 1867. WestLaw and Nexis Uni include cases from Canadian courts and from several countries in Europe, including the European Union. The amount of information that can be retrieved from these legal databases differs from case to case, and sometimes from database to database. Usually a case record will contain only the court's final decision or opinion, and not the witness testimonies or trial transcripts. Oftentimes none of the other pleadings (complaint, answers, briefs, etc.) will be available online, but are still obtainable from the local court archive. Some landmark or precedent-setting cases do include those additional documents. All three national databases have full-text law journal articles from the first issues to the present, but these are not usually relevant for the family history researcher.

Personal subscriptions to these law databases are not available, but many libraries do subscribe, so suggest that patrons consider the "Friend of the Library" option of a nearby library if they don't already have an affiliation. And they should not forget to investigate two free legal databases—Justia (www.justia.com) and FindLaw (www.findlaw.com).

A Note on Interpreting Legal Citations

Legal citations look something like this: *Schreiber v. Beer's Widow and Heirs, 91 So. 149, 150 La. 676*. The parties to this suit are Schreiber (plaintiff) and Beer's Widow and Heirs (defendants). The numbers and letters that follow (*91 So. 149*) mean the case appears in Volume 91 of the *Southern Reporter*, starting on page 149.

All legal citations read the same: parties to the suit, then the volume number of the pertinent reporter to find the decision or other pleadings in the case, and then the page number where the case begins. Depending on the citation manual used, the year may be inserted in parenthesis in the citation. Sometimes the researcher will see a parallel citation; i.e., more than one reporter listed, as in the example just given.

In addition to the state cases, the United States District Court, the United States Court of Appeals, and the U.S. Supreme Court cases are printed in other volumes known as the *Federal Reporter* series. The researcher can determine which court heard the case by looking at where it was reported. The federal court reporters are: *Federal Supplement* (abbreviated *F.Supp.*), which covers cases in the U.S. District Courts, the lowest level of federal courts; the U.S. Court of Appeals (abbreviated *F.*); the Supreme Court's opinions and/or other documents in the case may take three different forms because there are three different publishers. Two of the publishers are private companies; the third, the U.S. Government Publishing Office (GPO), is the most authoritative. That abbreviation is *U.S.*; *LEd* stands for Lawyers Edition of Supreme Court cases, and *S.Ct.* means the Supreme Court case has been reported by WestLaw. The two private companies add headnotes and other aids. In the online versions, there are also links to law articles and the history of the case. U.S. Supreme Court citations look like this: *Santosky v. Kramer, 455 U.S. 745; 102 S. Ct. 1388; 71 L. Ed. 2d 599*. In this citation, the parties are named first; then the three parallel citations, which together refer to the three reporters which carry the opinion of the U.S. Supreme Court. Other pleadings and headnotes might be found in the *Supreme Court Reporter*, the *Lawyers Edition Reporter*, and the three online databases.

Legal citations can look confusing, so if you and your patrons encounter them, just call the nearest government documents or law librarian and ask for an interpretation.

Conclusion

As documents produced by, and almost always held by, a government entity, both military and court can be a challenge to track down. Genealogy researchers should make use of all the free resources offered by the federal government, but remember to spend time researching at the local courthouse or city government archive where records were created. The process isn't always user-friendly or cheap—many city and county governments have wised up to the opportunity they have to monetize their record sets, and they will charge, sometimes exorbitantly, for providing copies. Usually courthouse and government archive records are accessed via indexes on site, which are on microfilm or microfiche. Each researcher must balance the inconvenience and cost of pursuing government records against the value they have for a particular research project. In most cases, they are inaccessible any other way and so the cost must be paid. Although legal research may appear to be daunting, with some help from a librarian, usually in the government documents and/or law section of an academic or large public library, genealogy researchers will be able to explore this area of inquiry and get fascinating documents in return for their trouble.

Contemporary Chinese Genealogy
Value and Status in Academic Research and Library Collection

Hong Cheng

Contemporary Chinese genealogy is a cultural outcome of social development. Based on a tradition for over a thousand of years, the contemporary Chinese genealogy presents potential valuable resources to the academic research in many disciplines, and gets favorable attention from major university libraries in the United States. In this essay, I will review the historical context of Chinese genealogy, analyze its role and value in academic research, and promote the library's involvement in the growing process of this special resource. I wish that, through all the parties' efforts, the contemporary Chinese genealogy would play greater role in promoting and preserving history, culture and civilization.

Chinese Genealogy: From Traditional to Contemporary

Alfred M. Silberfeld gives a definition that "Genealogy is the recording of the descent of the person or family from an ancestor or ancestors from which a family tree can be created" (Silberfeld 2008, 1). This definition might be applicable to the Chinese genealogy, but the East and the West have different approaches in establishing family genealogy. Silberfeld says, "Genealogical research is different from most subjects you have studied in the past. Each of you must follow your own road through all the twists and turns of your particular journey." Starting from yourself and tracing your ancestors might be quite common in genealogical research in the West. However, such practice cannot apply to the Chinese genealogy. In the Chinese case, the starting point is not you; instead, it is the genealogy. If you can find your father, grandfather or great grandfather's name in the latest version of your family genealogy, you are connected to the Chinese genealogy.

As Gu Yan stated, "Chinese genealogies are histories that record a patriarchal clan's pedigree and events" (Gu 2008, 47). The origin of the Chinese genealogy can be traced back to a couple of thousands years ago, and it developed along with rapid social changes, which can be clearly divided into two stages, the traditional and the contemporary.

The traditional Chinese genealogy was a historical literature recording the patrilineal family lineage and major characters. Although some scholars thought that Chinese genealogy appeared as early as in the primitive clan society about three thousand years ago, the reliable evidence showed that the earliest genealogy emerged no later than West Zhou period (1046–771 BC). In 1976, archaeologists discovered a bronze in Shaanxi Province, carved with a genealogy of the Zhou royal family along with the Wei family for six generations (Wang 2010, 52–53). For hundreds of years since then, the Chinese genealogy was limited to royal and noble families. From later Han Dynasty (25–220) down to the South/North Dynasties (420–589), certain highly ranked officials with big family names often ruled the country. In response to such social structure, these big family names compiled their own genealogy for tracing the family roots and identifying inter-marriage relations (Zhou and Yan 2008, 18–19).

A transition occurred when the political structure changed during the Tang period (618–907), when the imperial examination system was induced to the political structure. Under the new system, big family name was not the only channel to the high positions; as a result, the compiling of family genealogy became more a private family affair, not a political issue. During the Song period (960–1279), especially later in the Ming (1368–1644) and Qing (1644–1911) Dynasties, the compiling of Chinese genealogy became popular among the ordinary people. Under the influence of Confucianism, which worships ancestors, most ethnic Chinese families had own family genealogies (Zhou and Yan 2008, 96–97). Even some minorities, such as Manchu minority, started genealogy during the time (Cai 2005, 430–431). This transition of Chinese genealogy marked the path of the historical literature developed from royal/noble documents to private ordinary family records.

Another transition came with the modernization of the Chinese society in the later 19th century, and peaked in the 1940s. As the West influence came to China after the First Anglo-Chinese War in 1840, social changes started from the coastal area and gradually reached the inner land. Three elements of the social transition affected the genealogy.

- *Decentralization.* During that period, China changed from a highly centralized empire to decentralized and unbalanced local separatist regimes. The central regime got weaker under the domestic and international crises. Each area in China experienced different levels of industrialization and modernization, which undermined stability of the patrilineal structure on which traditional genealogy was based.
- *Religion.* The Chinese genealogy was built on the belief of Confucianism, which was the ruling ideology in China for over thousands of years. With the Western influence, Christianity reached China's grassroots society, challenging and shaking the base of traditional Chinese genealogy. "Religions of the world each have their own sets of requirements of section and belief that adherents are expected to follow" (Otterstrom 2008, 138). The religious conflicts affected the Chinese genealogy so severely in some regions that some genealogies discontinued after Christianity spread, which directly detonated the rebelling at the turn of the 19th and 20th centuries.
- *Migration and urbanization.* In Chinese history, migration was commonly caused by wars, famines and rebellions, and normally organized by the clans or

groups of clans from the same region; as a result, genealogy could be carried over after migrating to a new region. However, the migration during the 100 years from the 1840s the 1940s became more of the individual, or small family, activities, which led to discontinuation of genealogical links. Especially, the rise of modern city reconstructed the society, and patrilineal link no longer existed in the urban area.

In general, the transitions of Chinese traditional genealogy did bring some substantial changes in content coverage, but its basic feature as a record of the patrilineal family lineage remained unchanged. The communists took over the mainland in the late 1940s, which officially ended the period of the traditional Chinese genealogy. In many researches as late as the beginning of the 21st century, scholars often regarded the latest Chinese genealogy that was compiled in the early Republican period before 1949 (Xu 2002, 30–31).

The contemporary Chinese genealogy started at the end of the 20th century, and its course continues even nowadays. The Communist revolution stopped all the new genealogy in mainland China from 1949 on. In the next 50 years, almost no genealogy was compiled, especially during the Cultural Revolution from 1966 to 1976 when most old genealogies were burned or destroyed. However, at the beginning of the 21st century, a new tide of genealogy compilation appeared, and it was much more spread than any time in Chinese history. The tide of the contemporary Chinese genealogy has many new characteristics.

Primarily, it was a result of modernization and urbanization, and it benefited greatly from the economic development. After 30 years of economic reform, people have more savings in the bank accounts, and their needs are extended from material to spiritual. Newly emerged entrepreneurs and local officials want their names and successes to be recognized in history, so many genealogies and local gazetteers are compiled under the spiritual and financial support of such new social "elites." Since such social "elites" are based in the cities or at least in the county towns, the contemporary genealogy is rooted in the urban areas, instead of the rural areas.

Also, it reflected the revival and revisionism of Confucianism in the grassroots society. Genealogy in China is certainly linked to Confucianist ideology of ancestor worship. After decades of Communist propaganda, people want the revival of the traditional belief; however, the contemporary genealogy is no longer based on traditional paternal society, which left little influence especially in the urban area. Compiling genealogy comes mainly from the interest in tracing back the history, not in rebuilding the paternal society. The contemporary values are dominating the process. For example, the traditional Chinese genealogy recorded only the male members of the clan, but the contemporary genealogy definitely records women, as well as overseas clan members. The 1937 version of Confucius Family Genealogy had four volumes, but the 2009 version of the genealogy reached 80 volumes. This phenomenon does not mean that the population of the Confucius family increased 20 times; rather that women and overseas members were also included in the genealogy.

In comparison to the compilers of the traditional Chinese genealogy, who were generally elders of the clans, the writers and the editors of the contemporary genealogy are often retired intellectuals and office workers. The social connections and work experiences these people had make the contemporary genealogy more close to the real world. The writing style contains many new techniques, such as statistics and interviews.

The contemporary Chinese genealogy is certainly a continuation of the traditional genealogy, but it is no longer a simple record of the patrilineal family lineage; in many cases, it becomes a comprehensive description of the enlarged family history, presenting various of aspects of the grassroots society.

Utilizing Chinese Genealogy: From Academic Research to Library Collection

Mary K. Mannix mentioned that "The published, or compiled, family history, is the ideal genealogy end product. Even those family histories that are poorly cited can provide exceptional clues and help guide research" (Mannix 2015, 5). Although in her book Mannix failed to provide meaningful guide to reference in Chinese genealogy, she did point out the value of genealogy to academic research. To understand the academic value of the contemporary Chinese genealogy, we need to analyze its special features, especially the differences with the Western genealogy and other Chinese grassroots resources.

- Uninterrupted continuation and coverage. An absolute majority of the contemporary Chinese genealogies are the continuations of the traditional genealogy, and its family history can be traced back for a thousand years or even longer. While Chinese nobles had family names (surnames) at the early time of the Chinese civilization, ordinary Chinese people got family names (surnames) during the Warring States period (475 BC–221 BC), relatively early in comparing to most cultures in the world. So almost every Chinese genealogy starts with the earliest ancestor with the family names, and traces from the top down generation by generation. Although some records about ancestors are not reliable, the records after migrating to a new area are often proved reliable. Such uninterrupted continuation and coverage is valuable to the academic studies of history, anthropology, sociology, demography, literature, art history and even medical history.
- Private compilation and independent publication. Following the practice of the traditional Chinese genealogy, the contemporary genealogy remains privately compiled and independently printed, with no inspection of the Chinese government. This feature makes its value for academic studies even higher than many official publications. Less or no censorship provides more true and vivid picture of the grassroots society to scholars in social sciences and humanities.
- Geopolitical links and social network. In Raffaele Mauriello's study on the genealogy of the Middle East, he said that "The role of genealogy in shaping political, religious and social realities appears to have been overlooked particularly, or even ignored, in the case of the contemporary history of the Middle East" (Mauriello 2014, 131). This is very similar to the Chinese situation. Both traditional and contemporary Chinese genealogy are locally based, but their geopolitical links with the same family names (surnames) in other regions present the regional even cross-regional power, culturally and politically. The family names in different regions could form social networks, offering help to the members with the same family names, such as scholarships to college

students or employment to newcomers, even promotions in business companies and government offices.
- Variety. The compiling styles of the contemporary Chinese genealogies are extremely different. It can be as simple as a chart of bloodlines only, or as comprehensive as a mini encyclopedia that covers categories from natural environment, political structure, and economic activities to cultural life. Especially, the contemporary genealogy includes many new fields and modern conceptions that the traditional genealogy did not have. Even in format, digital genealogy, either as compact discs or online databases, never existed historically.

Because of such characteristics of the genealogy, scholars in many disciplines of the Chinese studies paid more and more attention to this kind of new resources, especially in the fields of social and historical studies, folk and cultural studies, population and migration studies, and even natural science and biological and medical studies.

As a logical result, major academic libraries started to collect such rare and popular primary resources of Chinese genealogies, and some of them made even greater efforts for the contemporary Chinese genealogy. In some institutions, such as Harvard Yenching Library, Columbia Starr East Asian Library and the UCLA East Asian Library, as well as the Genealogical Society of Utah, a member of Mormon Church, the contemporary Chinese genealogy has become a specialized collection.

At the same time, we have to understand that the challenges to the library collection and services are tremendous, due to various reasons.

The biggest challenge is availability, the hardship in collecting contemporary Chinese genealogy. Since almost all the contemporary genealogies are self- and independently printed, with no publication and distribution channel, it is very difficult to acquire such materials. Even though some materials have printed ISBNs, the publishers are not responsible for their distribution. So far, no one really knows how many contemporary Chinese genealogies were published, and what percentage has been collected in the Library. Most academic or public libraries in China do not collect such materials, they are considered to be illegal publications without permissions.

Another major challenge to the libraries is the difficulty in processing contemporary Chinese genealogy. Such materials commonly lack a stable format and publishing standards, with a variety of formats from handwriting scripts to self-running online databases.

The challenge in library public service is no less than in collection development and technical services. Because of the lack of bibliographic tools and limited access points, it is always hard to locate the resource. We can assume that the Chinese genealogy is the largest genealogical resource in the world, due to China's population, culture and history. However, it is difficult to help scholars and users to find the materials they look for, and it is almost impossible get through interlibrary loan. It requires a huge amount of specialized knowledge for a librarian to help patrons with Chinese genealogy research.

In general, the special value and characteristics of the Chinese genealogy make the subject attractive to many researchers, and encourage major academic libraries, and even some public and special libraries, to pursue it. It is indeed a major challenge, but also a great opportunity.

Getting Involved in Chinese Genealogy: Modernization and Standardization

As mentioned in the earlier section, the contemporary Chinese genealogy started at the end of the last century, and is currently still in the high tide. It is a challenge to libraries, since the resource is so new and many issues need to be solved; on the other hand, it is also a rare opportunity for libraries' involvement, helping to shape the development.

In 2010 and 2013, I was invited as a researcher and library professional to attend the international conference of Chinese genealogy co-sponsored by the Association of the Chinese Genealogy. During the conference, I pointed some basic issues to the compilers and publishers of the contemporary Chinese genealogy (Cheng 2012, 61–64). At the same time, I also had the opportunity to listen to them to understand the direction in which the contemporary Chinese genealogy was heading. In general, there are four aspects commonly discussed.

- ***Standardization.*** Standardization is very important to modern publishing, and is a key element to the library service. Standardization can promote the accuracy and understandability of the resource, and make the resource more readable and accessible to academic researcher and to the public. Some standard measures might be difficult to reach. For example, ISBN and ISSN are not available to the self-publishers in China, which might be not understandable to the publishers in other parts of the world. Some Chinese genealogy compilers might purchase ISBN from the state publishing house, but it is too expensive to most genealogy compilers. If such standard measures are not a realistic solution for the contemporary genealogy, some other more essential standards can be adapted immediately.
    - *Personal Name Authority* is necessary in compiling the contemporary Chinese genealogy. In today's China, most Chinese individuals have only one family name and one given name for life and women do not change names after marriage. However, historically every ordinary Chinese could have several given names, including "*ming*" as the name at birth time, "*zi*" as the name when starting school, and "*hao*" as other names in later years. A person could have "*bi ming*" (pennames) or "*yi ming*" (artist names) and use different names in different periods or under different situation. On the other hand, family names could be changed because of marriage, adoption or other reasons. If a genealogy was unable to link all the names of the same person together, it would cause big confusion. I suggest compilers connect the names in their own genealogy with China's nationwide name authority or even the international name authority.
    - *Geographic Name Authority* is another major concern in Chinese genealogy. Even in the contemporary Chinese genealogy, the time span could be hundreds or thousands of years. During the time, geographic names have had many changes. The same as the personal names, establishing a geographic name authority is a key issue in the compiling process.
    - *Standardized Terminology* is no less important. Such terminology includes

various aspects. For example, China adapted to the Western calendar in 1912. If a historical document was dated in the 10th day of the 10th month before 1912, people cannot simply record it as on October 10. The names of the government offices were also changed from time to time, even in the recent years. If every genealogy uses its own terminology, we can imagine what could happen to the academic research.

- *Statistics* is a new feature of the contemporary Chinese genealogy. Historically, statistics were a weak part of the Chinese literature. A reliable statistical report can provide better description than words. In comparison with the traditional Chinese genealogy, the contemporary genealogy commonly includes statistical data in forms or charts, but concerns over accuracy still exist. For example, some genealogies included the data of college attendance, which is a progress; however, there was a lack of details of the percentage of college students in the age group and a historical comparison of college attendance. It is so important to include reliable statistical data in the genealogy, and we are looking forward to more and better statistics to come.
- *Bibliographic Reference and Citation* is a key element in academic writings. Basically the genealogy can be both the primary and secondly research resource. In either case, bibliographic reference and citation are important. Researchers and readers need to know the origins of the resources cited in the literature. Some genealogies did better job in listing the reference and citation, but there are many rooms for improvement for most compilers.
- *Digitalization and Networks* are issues primarily raised by the genealogy compilers and the Association of the Chinese Genealogy, rather than by the library professionals. The idea of using computers for genealogical research came out as early as in the 1960s, as Edward W. Wagner mentioned that "in particular I shall call attention to major problems I have encountered in the computer input and output of Chinese character data" (Wagner 1969, 260). When personal computers just got popular years ago, people were already aware of its meaning to genealogy. "Computerized databases generally offer many more access points than do conventional indexes and abstracts. This, of course, greatly increases searching options and effectiveness" (Cosgriff 1986, 39). In recent years, a new concept of constant updating was raised by some genealogy-compiling committees, which meant updating genealogical data online on a daily basis. They wished major domestic libraries in China, such as the National Library of China or Shanghai Library, or international libraries, could help hosting such online databases. I am very pleased to know that such creative collaborations are seriously under consideration, and might be put in action in the near future.

I believe the library involvement is a remarkable idea in developing contemporary Chinese genealogy. It offers necessary professional and technical support to the compiling activities, and benefits the library with access to the newest research resources.

The Chinese genealogy is an old resource that existed for centuries and has been used by the Western scholarship for decades. However, the contemporary Chinese genealogy is a relatively new resource which emerged in the last twenty years and is still growing and expanding. I hope that, through reviewing the development path of the Chinese genealogy, analyzing its value and characteristics, and recognizing the engagement of library profession, we are able to actively become an organic part of the growing process of this special research resource. In many cases, the library collects and processes resources passively; but, in the case of the contemporary Chinese genealogy, we can play a much more active role in promoting, supporting and reshaping the resource. It is indeed a huge challenge, but also an unprecedented opportunity.

Works Cited

Cai Yawen. 2005. "Cong ji bu Man zu jia pu yan jiu zhong tan pu shu de jia zhi" (On the Value of Genealogy Through the Research of Several Manchu Genealogies), in *Hetu'ala yu Man zu xing shi jia pu yan jiu* (Hetu Ala and the Studies of Man Family Genealogy), edited by Fu Bo, 430–436. Shenyang: Liaoning min zu chu ban she.

Cheng Hong. 2012. "The Value and Status of the Contemporary Genealogy in Academic Research and Collection," in *Proceedings of the Second International Conference on Chinese Genealogy*, 61–64. California: DaZhongHua Family Tree Development Association.

Cosgriff, John C., Jr. 1986. "The Use of Online Searching in Genealogy," in *Genealogy & Computers*, edited by Charles Clement, 38–59. Chicago: American Library Association.

Gu Yan. 2008. "A Chinese Cultural Project: The Compilation of the General Catalogue of Chinese Genealogy," in *International Genealogy and Local History*, edited by Ruth Hedegaard and Elizabeth Anne Melrose, 47–51. The Hague, Netherlands: International Federation of Library Associations.

Mannix, Mary K. 2015. "Introduction: Genealogy Source," in *Guide to Reference in Genealogy and Biography*, edited by Mary K. Mannix, et al., 3–5. Chicago: American Library Association.

Mauriello, Raffaele. 2014. "Genealogical Prestige and Marriage Strategy Among the Ahl al-Bayt: The Case of the al-Sadr Family in Recent Times," in *Genealogy and Knowledge in Muslim Societies*, edited by Sarah Bowen Savant and Helena de Felipe, 131–148. Edinburgh: Edinburgh University Press.

Otterstrom, Samuel M. 2008. "Genealogy as Religious Ritual: The Doctrine and Practice of Family History in the Church of Jesus Christ of Latter-Day Saints," in *Geography and Genealogy: Locating Personal Pasts*, edited by Dallen J. Timothy and Jeanne Kay Guelke, 137–151. Burlington, VT: Ashgate.

Silberfeld, Alfred M. 2008. "Ancestry," in *Genealogy Workbook: Sources for Research of your Ancestry*, edited and compiled by Sylvia Furshman Nusinov, 1. Delray Beach, FL: Jewish Genealogical Society.

Wagner, Edward W. 1969. "A Computer Approach to Genealogical Research in East Asian," in *Studies in Asian Genealogy*, edited by Spencer J. Palmer, 260–269. Provo, UT: Brigham Young University Press.

Wang Heming. 2010. *Zhongguo jia pu tong lun* (General Theory of Chinese Genealogy). Shanghai: Shanghai gu ji chu ban she.

Xu Jianhua. 2002. *Zhongguo de jia pu* (Chinese Genealogy). Tianjin: Bai hua wen yi chu ban she.

Zhou Fangling and Yan Mingguang. 2008. *Zhongguo zong pu* (Chinese Genealogy). Beijing: Zhongguo she hui chu ban she.

Supporting Genealogists in Oral History Research
The Role of the Library

Noah Lenstra

Oral history is increasingly important in the work of family historians. Ancestry.com, the world's largest genealogy and family history company, states "we feel that gathering the memories of the living is just as important as discovering the lives of our ancestors" (Ancestry.com 2017, n.p.). This essay provides practical advice for librarians seeking to provide genealogists with the support they need as they record, preserve, and disseminate oral history interviews. The first part of this essay discusses some of the reasons that genealogists do oral history interviewing. This section includes suggestions for resources librarians may wish to include in public programs. The second part of this essay consists of an outline for a tried and tested program targeted at genealogists (of all levels and backgrounds) interested in getting started with oral history interviewing.

The advice in this essay comes from two sources: (1) For three consecutive years, the author led workshops on "Oral History Interviews for Genealogists" at the Urbana Free Library, Illinois, through its Champaign County Historical Archives; and (2) The author analyzed over 50 manuals on how-to-do genealogy, focusing on advice provided to genealogists seeking to record interviews with family members. Based on these two sources, this essay discusses how librarians can, through public programs, provide genealogists with the resources and advice they need to succeed in being competent oral historians of their families.

Why Genealogists Do Oral History

Understanding how to help genealogists do oral history requires first understanding why genealogists do oral history interviewing. Thus, this essay first analyzes how manuals on how-to-do genealogy discuss oral history interviewing. In fall 2012, all genealogy manuals in four libraries in Champaign County, Illinois, were systematically coded and categorized for references to oral history, oral traditions and interviewing. Libraries consulted included the University of Illinois's Main Library, Undergraduate Library, and Center for Children's Books, as well as the Champaign Public Library. Although not all genealogical manuals ever published were analyzed, this convenience sample, built across multiple libraries with different collecting foci, enables understanding of the diverse roles of oral history within genealogical research.

This investigation found that different genealogists see oral history differently. This fact is important to understand because supporting genealogists interested in oral history requires understanding how those genealogists wish to use oral history within the context of their broader projects and interests. This section discusses these different perspectives on oral history, and suggests resources librarians may wish to include in programs related to these perspectives.

Perspectives on oral history within genealogy include:

1. disregarding oral sources in genealogical research
2. family stories inspiring genealogical research
3. separate from genealogy, but equally important
4. containing clues or kernels of truth
5. adding "flesh" to the bare-bones of the genealogical chart
6. intrinsically rewarding

Ignoring Oral Sources in Genealogical Research

Traditionally, genealogists have seen oral history as irrelevant, at best. Leaving no space for oral traditions within genealogy, Donald Lines Jacobus, one of the pioneers of contemporary genealogical research, writes that oral "tradition is a chronic deceiver, and those who put faith in it are self-deceivers" (Jacobus 1930, 3). However, over time this opinion has become a minority one among genealogists. A professional genealogist stated in a more recent manual that: "I don't know of a single researcher who has not conducted a personal interview to obtain information about his or her ancestors" (Cerny and Eakle 1985, 67). Nonetheless, librarians need to be aware that some genealogists may not see oral history as relevant to genealogical research. If you do programs on oral history interviewing for genealogists, be prepared to answer questions from genealogists who hold this view of oral history. In past programs, the author has found that one good way to grapple with this type of challenge is to let other genealogists explain why oral history interviewing is valuable to them. That way, rather than directly contradict someone with no interest in oral history, or who thinks oral history has no place in genealogy, you allow other genealogists to explain why they see oral history as important to their genealogical work.

Family Stories Inspiring Genealogical Research

Many genealogists say that interest in genealogical research emerged from hearing family stories. One manual states that "Setting out to discover the truth behind such stories is precisely the impulse that sparks many people's interest in genealogy" (Beard 1977, 1). Those who cherish family oral traditions and stories wish to thoroughly document and verify these beloved stories. In this model, oral history interviewing can be used to inspire interest in genealogy. For example, some libraries have genealogy programs targeted at young people in which youth interview their relatives in order to be inspired to do genealogical research (e.g., http://www.ala.org/programming/2014jaffarianaward/perrymeridian). This type of program could be done collaboratively with schools or with youth organizations (such as Scouts).

Separate from Genealogy, but Equally Important

Some manuals urge genealogists to document family stories, even if these stories play no substantive role within the genealogical research itself. This perspective sees oral history as a corollary to genealogical research. One manual urges the genealogist not to "ridicule the family traditions, even when you suspect they are false. Respect the feeling of those who believe them" (Rose & Ingalls 2012, 13). Even if peripheral to genealogical research proper, these oral stories deserve to be documented. Some genealogists struggle to reconcile their desire to record family stories with the suspicion that the stories may not contain much factual veracity. This ambivalence is powerfully vocalized by Arthur Kurzweil, the author of the first Jewish genealogy manual in America:

> The stories become an important part of the family history—not as fact, but as legend.... Even if stories are "false" ... I still think it's important that the story has survived and has come down to me.... Don't perpetuate a fraud, but don't rob your family history of its richness by being "scientific." A tale which is not "true" in fact, can be quite "true" in its message [Kurzweil 1980, 76].

Some genealogists may worry that their family stories may not be true, and thus may be reticent to include them in their research. Programming in libraries could talk about the value of recording family stories, even if those stories turn out to not be based in fact. A resource useful to such programs is the 2003 film *Big Fish*, based on the 1998 novel of the same name, in which a son learns to cherish his dying father's tall tales after denigrating those stories earlier in life.

Containing Clues or Kernels of Truth

When genealogists more directly incorporate oral history interviewing into the genealogical research process itself, they often see oral sources as clues requiring decipherment. Genealogists are advised to listen intently since "you'll be surprised how often a seemingly insignificant detail can become a major clue three or four months later" (Blockson and Fry 1977, 18). This process of discovering facts from oral sources requires the genealogist to amass a large number of oral histories. Some authors recommend collecting multiple versions of family legends to better determine the legends' factual truth, which presumably would repeat across all telling of family legends. Henry Louis Gates, Jr., notes that when doing interviews "you'll throw out a lot ... some wheat will emerge from amid a lot of chaff" (Gates 2007, 13). A good resource to use in public programs based on this type of research is Alex Haley's *Roots*, which revolves around Haley deciphering oral stories passed down in his family across generations through exhaustive genealogical research. Other good resources are the television programs *Who Do You Think You Are?*, *Genealogy Roadshow*, and *Finding Your Roots*, all of which tend to feature individuals discussing family stories in the context of genealogical evidence.

Adding "Flesh" to the Bare Bones of the Genealogical Chart

Many manuals frame oral history as adding texture and nuance to genealogical research. Genealogists encourage collecting "colorful anecdotes" since "funny, embarrassing, tragic, strange, and unimaginable stories add the necessary flavor and personality to a satisfying genealogy project" (Jamison 1999, 32). With the increasing availability of home media tools, multi-media oral history recordings add texture to genealogical publications. A manual for Native-American genealogy states that doing audio-visual oral histories during genealogical research "can turn your family history project into a vibrant, living document" (Kavasch 1996, 88). Authors refer to oral history recordings as family heirlooms to be passed down along with photo albums and scrapbooks. One manual notes that "From relatives you can learn the anecdotes and personalities in a way seldom possible from public records" (Cosgriff and Cosgriff 1986, 8). Based on this perspective, librarians may be asked to help genealogists not only in searching for records and information. They may also be called upon to assist in helping genealogists preserve and make use of their oral history recordings. A good resource to help librarians thinking of developing programs in this area is the Library of Congress's website *Personal Archiving: Preserving Your Digital Memories*, which has ample resources for genealogists (and others) interested in preserving and utilizing oral history recordings made with digital media.

Intrinsically Rewarding

Finally, a recent and emerging perspective found among some genealogists is that oral history interviewing is an intrinsically rewarding process. Even if the interview leads to no new information, is still worth doing. This perspective appears most frequently in manuals written by and for African American genealogists. One author states that oral history is "the Most Important Thing You Can Do" (Burroughs 2001, 73) as a genealogist. Another author tells readers that through genealogical research they participate in a cultural movement to recover lost memories: "You're reviving one of the oldest traditions of black culture ... oral history" (Blockson and Fry 1977, 13). Another genealogist writes that genealogy "can contribute a new positive history" for African Americans: "Perhaps we sometimes believe the worst about ourselves because we stopped sharing ... stories" (Jamison 1999, 15) within families.

Although most clearly and forcefully articulated in manuals written by and for African Americans, this perspective appears throughout many genealogy manuals. Kurzweil writes: "Remember: The books, archives, and libraries will wait. The people will not" (Kurzweil 1980, 71). Another authors states that "For a genealogist, the time spent re-establishing contact with older relatives by interviewing them ... can be the most fascinating and emotionally gratifying phase of research" (Beard 1977, 22). Genealogists frequently experience remorse because many relatives have passed away before they could be interviewed: "Almost every ancestor-hunter will say to you, 'If only I had talked to my great-aunt and listened to her stories when she was alive. Now she is dead, and all her knowledge of the family went with her'" (Baxter 1987, 3). In organizing programs on oral history interviewing for genealogy, you may attract individuals who may not be interested in conventional genealogical research, but who are interested in participating in oral history interviews as an intrinsically rewarding process. An excellent resource to use in programs focused around this perspective is the StoryCorps.me website, which frames oral history interviewing within families as an intrinsically rewarding process.

Programs on Oral History Interviews for Genealogists

Based on reading these manuals, as well as the author's own experiences doing oral history and family history research, he organized a program on "Oral History Interviews for Genealogists," which was presented for three consecutive years at the Urbana Free Library, Illinois, through their Champaign County Historical Archives. After each program, participants completed a survey, which enabled the program to be fine-tuned. The following outline contains suggested topics to be included in such a program. This outline can be used as a starting-point to organizing interactive programs in libraries for participants to learn about oral history interviewing, and to develop the skills needed to successfully record, preserve, and disseminate those interviews.

During the programs, individuals attended who were found to fit into each of the six approaches to oral history sketched in the preceding section. Some attendees had no interest in conventional genealogy, but wanted to interview their relatives because they saw interviewing as an intrinsically valuable process. Others had been doing conventional genealogical research for decades, and now wanted to learn how to do oral history interviewing so that they could add family stories to their genealogical data. Others were excited about using oral history as a way to collect stories and quotes that could be included in genealogical publications distributed among family members. Still others were seasoned genealogists suspicious of oral history, but wanting to learn more about it nonetheless. This program outline is deliberately designed to cater to different types of individuals, with different interests in using oral history interviewing as part of genealogical research.

Outline for "Oral History Interviews for Genealogists" Program

Time: 1–2 hours
Equipment needed: None (but having handouts and equipment to demo are a plus).
Suggested partners: Local genealogy societies, community colleges, adult education centers, Osher Lifelong Learning groups.
Structure: This outline consists of core content, and suggested discussion topics to be used as time allows, in order to make the program interactive and engaging.
Outline:
    1. Introductions: Ask participants to introduce themselves and briefly address these questions "Have you tried doing any oral interviews for your family history? How did they go?"
        a. Introducing oral history interviews for genealogists. Interview types include:

b. Gather basic facts for beginning genealogical research.
   c. Oral memories contain "clues" that need close listening to decipher.
   d. Adds texture to Family History–Publications and Multi-Media Presentations.
   e. Create family heirlooms and/or public records to share with others.
   f. Inspire interest in family history among others.
   g. Interviewing for itself can be intrinsically rewarding.
2. Whom to interview:
   a. Family members—including siblings and cousins (not just older generations).
   b. People who knew family members—neighbors, co-workers, friends.
   c. Don't forget about yourself!! Have someone interview you. A resource to get started: http://www.lifebio.com/.
   d. If time permits, engage participants in a discussion of whom they most want to interview, and why.
3. What equipment to use (try to have equipment to demo during this part of program). Test (and re-test) your equipment. Don't use equipment you aren't thoroughly familiar with!
   a. Analog audio-tape recorder
   b. Digital audio recorder
   c. Laptop with microphone (internal or external)
   d. Smartphone
   e. Digital video camera with tripod
   f. Skype also as option—MP3 Skype Recorder
   g. If time allows, engage participants in a discussion about what equipment they may have available to use for oral history interviewing.
4. How and where (logistics of the interview)
   a. Art of the possible. Don't miss opportunities because conditions are not ideal, but do strive for quiet environments with minimal distractions.
   b. If you can, record someone talking in the room you will use prior to the interview. Do this to make sure you know what you will be recording when the interview starts.
   c. How to get people to sit down with you? Some people may refuse. That is OK. They may change their mind later. Be persistent and tactful but not pushy.
   d. If time allows, engage participants in a discussion about experiences they may have had trying to set up oral history interviewing in the past. What will they do differently in the future?
5. What to ask (prompts)
   a. Prompts include questions, objects, and visuals. Some people can only remember when prompted with objects (e.g., heirlooms) or visuals (e.g., pictures of places).
   b. Goal here is to record interviewee's life experiences in as much detail as possible.
   c. Ask open-ended questions to elicit storytelling. Ask, "Could you tell me about" (open-ended) instead of "Do you remember" (yes/no). More examples http://storycorps.org/great-questions/.

d. If time allows, ask participants to interview their neighbor with one question, using the "Could you tell me about" prompt. Discuss as a group how this exercise went.
6. What do I do after the interview?
   a. Import the audio, video, or text file into your computer, and back it up in multiple locations.
   b. Audacity—best free program for simple-to-advanced digital audio editing.
   c. Transcribe, if time permits.
   d. Think about depositing interview recording at library or archives—they may be able to make the interview more accessible for you and for others—resource to show participants: http://www.oralhistoryonline.org/.
   e. If you are thinking of depositing the interview, be sure to get interviewee to sign a waiver. For one you can use visit The American Folklife Center, Library of Congress. *Folklife and Fieldwork: An Introduction to Cultural Documentation.* 2016 (4th ed.). http://www.loc.gov/folklife/fieldwork/, page 40.
   f. Other resources: https://storycorps.me/, http://digitalpreservation.gov/personalarchiving/.
   g. Time permitting, download on the computer you will be using for the program the Audacity software. Have loaded in the software an oral history recording file. Show participants how they can use Audacity to make quiet sections louder, and to do other manipulations on the recording to make it more usable. Introduction to Audacity: http://write.flossmanuals.net/audacity-workbook/introduction-to-audacity/.
7. Conclusions: Wrap up by going around the room and having participants say what they think they will do with the information they have learned.

Conclusion

Genealogists increasingly see oral history interviewing as an important part of what constitutes a successful genealogical research project. Based on a review of how-to-do genealogy manuals, this essay first discussed some of the ways genealogists use oral sources. The essay then outlined a successful model of how to do a program focused on oral history interviewing for genealogists. By supporting the interests of genealogists in oral history interviewing, librarians can demonstrate their value in new ways. Libraries not only provide people with access to information, they also offer educational opportunities through public programs. This type of program has been found to be engaging and tends to attract a large audience, especially if done in collaboration with local genealogical societies or adult education entities.

WORKS CITED

Ancestry.com. 2017. "Personal Family History Interviews." Accessed March 1. http://www.progenealogists.com/interview.htm.
Baxter, Angus. 1987. *In Search of Your German Roots*. Baltimore: Genealogical Publishing Co.
Beard, Timothy Field. 1977. *How to Trace Your Family Roots*. New York City: McGraw-Hill.

Blockson, Charles L., and Ron Fry. 1977. *Black Genealogy*. New York: Prentice-Hall.
Burroughs, Tony. 2001. *Black Roots: A Beginner's Guide to Tracing the African-American Family Tree*. Los Angeles: Fireside Press.
Cerny, Johni, and Arlene H. Eakle. 1985. *Ancestry's Guide to Research: Case Studies in American Genealogy*. Ogden, UT: Myfamily.com.
Cosgriff, John, and Carolyn Cosgriff. 1986. *Climb It Right: A Hi-Tech Genealogy Primer*. Christiansburg, VA: Progenesys Press.
Gates, Henry Louis, Jr. 2007. *Finding Oprah's Roots: Finding Your Own*. New York: Crown Publishers.
Jacobus, Donald Lines. 1930. *Genealogy as Pastime and Profession*. New Haven, CT: Tuttle, Morehouse & Taylor.
Jamison, Sandra Lee. 1999. *Finding Your People: An African-American Guide to Discovering Your Roots*. New York: Perigee.
Kavasch, E. Barrie. *A Student's Guide to Native American Genealogy*. Phoenix: Oryx Press.
Kurzweil, Arthur. 1980. *From Generation to Generation: How to Trace Your Jewish Genealogy and Personal History*. New York: William Morrow.
Rose, Christine, and Kay Germain Ingalls. 2012. *The Complete Idiot's Guide to Genealogy*. New York: Penguin.

Preparing for Genealogical Reference Work

Beth Stahr

Librarians in every type of institution encounter genealogists. According to a 2012 Pew Internet & American Life Project survey, "25% of Americans ages 16 and older used their library to access historical documents or archives or genealogical records (Pew Research Center 2012)." In some larger library systems, a specific "room," department or branch functions as a local history or genealogy service point. However, at small library systems, staff may serve genealogical patrons in addition to other normal responsibilities.

Long before I was a librarian, I was a professional genealogist, and I frequently traveled to small towns and large cities to conduct research on my own ancestors and those of my clients. While I generally had very specific questions, I sometimes found that the answers received from staff at research repositories, including libraries, were not very specific. What was the educational preparation and continuing education of the many librarians and archivists helping genealogists?

For one month in the fall 2014, I distributed a thirteen-question online survey to three listservs [Librarians Serving Genealogists (genealib), the American Library Association (ALA) Reference and User Services (RUSA) list (rusa-l), and ALA RUSA History Section list (history-l)], and a LinkedIn Group for Historians, Librarians and Archivists. Survey results were first reported in a paper, "Who Can Help Find Grandma: Educational Preparation of Genealogical Librarians and Staff," delivered at the Popular Culture Association/American Culture Association Annual Conference in New Orleans in April 2015 (Stahr 2015). Although this was not a scientific survey, and was not tested for reliability and validity, it provided fascinating information about genealogical reference services at American research repositories. This essay presents the survey findings and suggests additional avenues of genealogical education and genealogical librarian education for librarians who work with genealogists.

Genealogical Educational Preparation for Librarians

One hundred eighty-nine persons responded to the survey, and 69 percent of those who answered the survey worked in a public library. Over 92 percent of the respondents researched their own families. Almost 76 percent of the respondents had a master's degree in library science, and 37 percent had at least one additional graduate degree. Only 5 percent reported a certification/accreditation by one of the most likely bodies [The Board for Certification of Genealogists (SM), the International Commission for the Accreditation of Genealogists, or Academy of Certified Archivists (ACA)]. Almost 68 percent of the respondents reported no formal genealogical education. For the survey, I provided the following examples of formal genealogical education, along with the opportunity to write in other answers or to answer, "None":

- an undergraduate degree in genealogy (e.g., Brigham Young University's BA in Family History)
- attendance at genealogical institutes, e.g., Institute of Genealogy and Historical Research (IGHR) formerly at Samford University and now hosted by the Georgia Genealogical Society and housed at the University of Georgia; the Salt Lake Institute of Genealogy (SLIG); or the Genealogical Research Institute of Pittsburgh (GRIP)
- attendance at the Genealogical Institute on Federal Records (Gen-Fed), formerly known as the National Institute of Genealogical Research (NIGR) held at the National Archives in Washington, D.C.
- enrollment in the National Genealogical Society (NGS) Home Study Course
- enrollment in the National Institute for Genealogical Studies (NIGS) through Continuing Education at the University of St. Michael's College in the University of Toronto
- enrollment in the Boston University Certificate in Genealogical Research

Genealogical Librarian Education Preparation

When asked about formal genealogical librarian education, 44 percent of the survey respondents reported they had none. I provided the following examples, as well as the opportunity to write in answers:

- graduate course(s) in library school in genealogical librarianship or genealogical reference
- participation in the Library Juice Academy online course, *Introduction to Genealogical Librarianship*
- participation in the ALA RUSA online course, *Genealogy 101*
- attendance at a RUSA History Section pre-conferences
- attendance at a Librarian's Day pre-conference held before the National Genealogical Society (NGS) Family History Conference or the Federation of Genealogical Societies (FGS) National Conference
- enrollment in a genealogical institute that includes a genealogical librarian focus [e.g., IGHR, SLIG, or Gen-Fed]

Most respondents (73 percent) indicated that local or state genealogical society conferences were their method of maintaining their genealogical librarian education skills. A few attended pre-conferences at the FGS and NGS annual conferences, vendor demonstrations or trainings, and ALA RUSA pre-conferences. Other techniques included online discussion groups, blogs, journal articles and applying their personal experience and research to their work. Many augmented their professional knowledge with the Genealib e-mail listserv.

Five Trends Emerged

Based on the survey responses, five trends emerged:

1. Genealogical experience was valued as much as educational preparation. Thirty-eight of the respondents mentioned that their strength as a genealogical librarian came from their personal research experience or the length of time in their library job, and another thirty-six wrote about their familiarity with their geographic locality or its local history records.

2. Many librarians want specialized educational preparation to work with genealogists. Only eight of the respondents indicated they did not need further education, and nine did not know what they needed. Six respondents said they needed anything or everything, while most listed very specific training or content needs. These ranged from learning about specific ethnic group record types, to software training, to learning new websites, to outreach and programming training. Some respondents listed specific examples of education about social history, the law, records beyond their own collection, or documentation formats in genealogy. Others wished for technical service and collection development training or training to improve their people skills to work with genealogy patrons. The mere variety of answers indicated the huge need, and confirmed that the combination of a strong educational background in both genealogy and genealogical librarianship was rare among respondents.

3. Online classes or webinars were most preferred for specialized formal education, with many indicating that this was the best fit for busy schedules and limited travel budgets.

4. Educational opportunities for genealogical librarians were fragmented and ill-defined. Some respondents were unaware of the examples I included in the survey, and wrote they had to learn about genealogy and genealogy reference service on the job.

5. Genealogical librarians and staff love what they do. Many wrote about how long they had been conducting research or working as a genealogical librarian, and how proud they were of their local collections. Twenty-four respondents wrote about tenacity, persistence, their passion, or the challenge of the search.

Formal Genealogy Reference Service Education

The RUSA History Section Genealogy Committee developed "Guidelines for a Unit or Course of Instruction in Genealogical Research at Schools of Library and Information Science" in 1995. The Committee revised the Guidelines in 2004, and the RUSA Board of Directors approved them in 2007. (Genealogy Committee of the History Section of the Reference and User Services Association. American Library Association 2017). In the past ten years, much about genealogical resources and genealogical research has changed, and educational preparation for librarians who help genealogical patrons has changed as well. To determine how many of the ALA-accredited master's degree-granting library schools offer a course in genealogical reference, I conducted a second, shorter survey in spring 2017. I sent an online survey to representatives from each graduate program with these questions:

- Does your MLS/MLIS program offer a course in genealogy reference service or family history reference service?
- If yes, is the course an elective or core course?
- How frequently is it offered?
- What textbook(s) are currently selected for this course?

Only 29 of the 60 programs replied to the four-question survey. Eight of the twenty-nine responding programs offer such a course. Another four graduate library schools that did not respond to the survey are known to offer some type of genealogy or local history course. This means that 20 percent of the programs definitely offer a course to prepare librarians to work with the highly specialized genealogical library user. The courses employ a variety of textbooks, all listed at the end of this essay. All of the courses are elective courses. Since many library students decide on their graduate coursework before they know the type of position or library where they will be working, many of the librarians who actually work with genealogical patrons have never taken such a course in graduate school.

Continuing Education for Genealogy Reference Service

Many librarians who work with genealogy patrons reported in the initial survey that they had to identify and fund their own continuing education. Vendors who supply licensed products used by genealogists (e.g., ProQuest's Ancestry® Library Edition, EBSCO's MyHeritage Library Edition, etc.) often provide free training through webinars or online videos. However, librarians also need a working knowledge of the free electronic resources like FamilySearch.org or FindAGrave.com. As new products and websites appear, the librarians must maintain their skills and identify training sources. Training for the use of these genealogical reference tools is often a "Help" page or blog on the website. They must also know what educational resources are available for patrons, and how to find and evaluate quality genealogy programming for the library.

In the original survey, librarians cited lack of time as an impediment to staff development. ALA's website provides a representative list of pathfinders, print resources and websites for librarians (American Library Association 2013). State Library organizations and consortia can provide affordable educational opportunities. One such professional network of librarians who serve genealogists is the Georgia Library Association Genealogy and Local History Interest Group, which was formed in 2016 (Stanley 2016).

When travel distances and costs to conferences are prohibitive, library trade journals and publications can be a cost-effective alternative. Verma (2016) shared useful examples of library reference service and programming in her *Library Journal* article. Another example is the quarterly publication, *Kentucky Libraries*. Since the fall 2010 issue, Katherine Pennavaria has edited a column in *Kentucky Libraries*, "Genealogy Gems." Pennavaria seeks expertise within her state to write the columns on both state genealogical topics and topics with a broader reach. (Pennavaria 2010). Examples of columns on local resources include "Old News—The *Louisville Leader's* Genealogical Gems," and "Two Microfilm Resources for Kentucky Genealogists." Examples of columns that would be helpful to genealogical librarians elsewhere are "Beginning African American Research" and "Understanding and Using the United States Census." This informative column gave Pennavaria the opportunity to write a book, *Genealogy: A Practical Guide for Librarians* (Pennavaria 2015). It is one of several books currently used as a textbook in library reference courses at master's degree programs. It would be a valuable tool for any librarian who needs to help genealogists.

Another recent textbook is *Fostering Family History Services,* written by library science professors Clark and Miller (2016). They coined endearing terms to categorize genealogy patrons based on common observations: The Newbie, The Gusher, The Confused, The Optimist, The Disorganized Patron, The Wounded, The Monopolizer, and The Shooter. Chapter 6 of their book provides guidance for successful reference encounters with each type of genealogical patron. (Clark and Miller 2016, 115–147). While most textbooks used in library schools for general reference service courses adequately address the art of the reference interview, they do not provide sufficient tools to meet the needs of the genealogical patron. One size does not fit all for these focused researchers. The Pennavaria and Clark and Miller books can meet many of the needs mentioned by genealogical librarians in the survey.

Librarians can peruse trade publications for helpful, timely articles addressing a rapidly advancing field. Francis presented two separate helpful articles: "The Genealogy Reference Interview" (2004a) and "The Genealogy Search Process" (2004b). She included a flowchart of questions to guide librarians through the genealogy reference interview in one article, and she created a Genealogy Search Process Model (GSP) in the other article. More recently, Zastrow (2015) provided a four-step "Family Recipe" for research, "The Big Five Databases" used in genealogy, and a list of other important tools for genealogical reference work. Librarians will find all these resources beneficial as they work with genealogists.

The RUSA History Section Genealogy Committee ("RUSA HS Genealogy Committee Facebook Page") launched a Facebook page in February 2017. The initial posts offered tips on genealogical and historical resources, programming, collaborations, organizations and societies, public records and so much more. This is a free, easy tool for librarians who work with genealogists, and an excellent way to stay current with available resources.

DNA and Genealogy

Perhaps the most daunting challenge for librarians is the addition of genetic genealogy as evidence in family history research. Librarians will need to understand the basics of genetic genealogy as their library users will surely expect information. According to the International Society of Genetic Genealogy, "Genetic genealogy involves the use of genealogical DNA testing together with documentary evidence to infer the relationship between individuals" (ISOGG wiki 2017). Genetic genealogist Blaine Bettinger wrote that while DNA never proves a genealogical relationship, "the modern genealogist who ignores DNA does so at their peril; beware a genealogist that intentionally ignores *any* potential source of evidence" (2016). In 2015, a group of genealogists and scientists drafted the first Genetic Genealogy Standards. They continue to develop additional standards regarding specific types of genetic genealogy tests (The Genetic Genealogy Standards Committee 2016). Judy G. Russell, The Legal Genealogist, wrote that DNA evidence is a "high quality source" of genealogical information (Russell 2014):

> It is not a replacement for traditional paper-trail genealogy but can be combined with it to build a solid proof argument. It is one more tool to consider in each case where it is appropriate, may be helpful, and is reasonably available. Where DNA testing is not appropriate or not helpful or not reasonably available, it is no different from any other evidence [Russell 2014].

Bush and Woodbury (2014) provided a description of how DNA evidence fits into the Genealogical Proof Standard (Board for Certification of Genealogists 2017), a five-part "best practices" approach to establishing kinship and genealogy. In January 2017 AncestryDNA, the largest commercial genetic genealogy testing company, announced that its DNA database surpassed three million people (Ancestry Team, 2017). With all this attention to DNA testing, librarians will continue to field questions from increasing numbers of genealogical researchers who want to know how genetic evidence and traditional genealogical evidence are used together to establish family histories. As the Genetic Genealogy Standards evolve, librarians will direct library users to the appropriate guidebooks, online resources, and educational opportunities. Many libraries will want to plan programming with qualified outside speakers on this advanced topic.

The Local Touch

While most genealogists use web services to find information about their ancestors, some will want to learn about the places where their ancestors lived. Local libraries, archives and museums are the source for local records and the place to study local history. In addition to the regular library users, out-of-town visitors may use local libraries in the areas where their ancestors lived. Indeed, librarians need to be able to provide that special local touch to these customers, too. Local libraries can also serve as a home base for genealogical and historical societies. Others have documented the importance of the partnership between libraries and community groups. Recent examples show how public libraries and community partners use genealogy as a marketing tool (Rzepczynski 2013). Given the ubiquitous nature of family history research in our culture, support for the collections and the staff who serve genealogists in libraries can be a significant marketing tool and community service. Genealogical education and genealogical librarian education for genealogy reference librarians are essential to satisfy the needs of these library users. They also represent a value-added service that library administrators seek.

Genealogical Education Resources

Boston University Center for Professional Education. "Programs in Genealogical Research," accessed March 17, 2017, https://genealogyonline.bu.edu/.
Brigham Young University. "Family History Program," accessed March 17, 2017, https://history.byu.edu/Pages/Programs/FamilyHistory/.
Genealogical Institute on Federal Records (Gen-Fed), accessed March 17, 2017, http://www.gen-fed.org/.
Genealogical Research Institute of Pittsburgh (GRIP), accessed March 17, 2017, http://www.gripitt.org/.
Institute of Genealogy and Historical Research (IGHR), accessed March 17, 2017, http://ighr.gagensociety.org/.

National Genealogical Society (NGS), "Educational Courses: American Genealogical Studies," accessed March 17, 2017, http://www.ngsgenealogy.org/cs/educational_courses/american_genealogical_studies.

National Institute for Genealogical Studies (NIGS), "Courses," accessed March 17, 2017, http://www.genealogicalstudies.com/eng/courses.asp.

Utah Genealogical Society. "The Salt Lake Institute of Genealogy (SLIG)," accessed March 17, 2017, http://ugagenealogy.com/aem.php?eid=16.

Genealogical Librarianship Education Resources

American Library Association (ALA) Reference and User Services Association (RUSA), "History: Genealogy Preconference Planning," accessed March 17, 2017, http://www.ala.org/rusa/contact/rosters/history/rus-hisgenpre.

American Library Association (ALA) Reference and User Services Association (RUSA), "Online Learning with RUSA," accessed March 17, 2017, http://www.ala.org/rusa/onlinece.

Federation of Genealogical Societies (FGS), "Conferences," accessed March 17, 2017, http://www.fgs.org/cpage.php?pt=43.

Librarians Serving Genealogists list serve. Accessed March 17, 2015. http://mailman.acomp.usf.edu/mailman/listinfo/genealib.

Library Juice Academy, "Introduction to Genealogical Librarianship," accessed March 17, 2017, http://libraryjuiceacademy.com/056-genealogical.php.

National Genealogical Society (NGS), "Annual Conference," accessed March 17, 2017, http://conference.ngsgenealogy.org/.

National Institute for Genealogical Studies (NIGS), "Librarianship Certificate Courses," accessed March 17, 2017, http://www.genealogicalstudies.com/eng/courses.asp?certificateID=22.

"RUSA HS Genealogy Committee Facebook Page." Facebook.com. Last modified March 23, 2017. https://www.facebook.com/rusahsgenealogy.

Textbooks, Supplemental Textbooks and Resources Reported Used at ALA-Accredited Master's Program Courses

Clark, Rhonda L., and Nicole Wedemeyer Miller. 2016. *Fostering Family History Services: A Guide for Librarians, Archivists, and Volunteers*. Westport: Libraries Unlimited.

Croom, Emily Anne. 2001. *Unpuzzling Your Past: The Best-Selling Basic Guide to Genealogy*, 4th ed. Betterway Books.

Curran, Joan F., Crane, Madilyn Coen, and John H. Wray, John H. 2008. *Numbering Your Genealogy: Basic Systems, Complex Families, and International Kin*, rev. ed. Arlington, VA: National Genealogical Society.

Cyndi's List. Accessed March 17, 2017, http://www.cyndislist.com/us/.

Gates, Henry L. 2006. *African American Lives*. Alexandria, VA: PBS Video.

Gates Jr., Henry L. 2009. *In Search of Our Roots: How 19 Extraordinary African Americans Reclaimed Their Past*. New York: Crown.

Meyerink, Kory L., ed. 1998. *Printed Sources: A Guide to Published Genealogical Records*. Salt Lake City: Ancestry Publishing.

Mills, Elizabeth Shown. 2015. *Evidence Explained: Citing History Sources from Artifacts to Cyberspace*, 3rd ed. Baltimore: Genealogical Publishing Company.

Moore, Dahrl Elizabeth. 1998. *Librarian's Genealogy Notebook A Guide to Resources*. Chicago: American Library Association.

Morgan, George C. 2015. *How to Do Everything: Genealogy*, 4th ed. New York: McGraw-Hill Education.

Pennavaria, Katherine. 2015. *Genealogy: A Practical Guide for Librarians*. Lanham, MD: Rowman & Littlefield.

Simpson, Jack. 2008. *Basics of Genealogy Reference: A Librarian's Guide*. Westport: Libraries Unlimited.

Swan, James. 2014. *The Librarian's Guide to Genealogical Services and Research*. New York: Neal-Schuman.

Szucs, Loretto Dennis and Sandra Hargreaves Luebking. 2006. *The Source: A Guidebook of American Genealogy*, 3rd ed. Salt Lake City, Ancestry Publishing.

Works Cited

Academy of Certified Archivists, accessed March 17, 2017, http://www.certifiedarchivists.org/.

American Library Association. 2013. "Professional Resources: A to Z Index of Topics>Genealogy," last modified December 10, 2013, http://www.ala.org/tools/atoz/genealogy.

American Library Association. "Reference and User Services Association List," accessed March 17, 2017. http://lists.ala.org/sympa/info/rusa-l.

American Library Association, "RUSA History Section Discussion List," accessed March 17, 2017. http://lists.ala.org/sympa/info/history-l.
Ancestry Team. 2017. "AncestryDNA Surpasses 3 Million Customers in DNA Database," *Ancestry Blog* (blog), 10 January 10, 2017, https://blogs.ancestry.com/ancestry/2017/01/10/ancestrydna-surpasses-3-million-customers-in-dna-database/.
Bettinger, Blaine. 2016. "The DNA Era of Genealogy." *The Genetic Genealogist* (blog), http://thegeneticgenealogist.com/2016/12/17/the-dna-era-of-genealogy/.
Board for Certification of Genealogists(SM). 2017. "The Genealogical Proof Standard." Accessed March 17, 2017. http://www.bcgcertification.org/resources/standard.html
Bush, Angie and Paul Woodbury. 2014. "DNA and the GPS." ICAPGen Conference 2014 Syllabus, Brigham Young University, Provo, UT, November 1, 2014. http://icapgen.org/wp-content/uploads/2014/10/Bush.Woodbury.GPSandDNA.Final_.pdf.
Francis, Laurie S. 2004a. "The Genealogy Reference Interview." *PNLA Quarterly* 68.3: 13–15.
Francis, Laurie S. 2004b. "The Genealogy Search Process." *PNLA Quarterly* 68.3: 12, 22.
Genealogy Committee of the History Section of the Reference and User Services Association. American Library Association. (2017) "Guidelines for a Unit or Course of Instruction in Genealogical Research at Schools of Library and Information Science," approved January 2007, http://www.ala.org/rusa/resources/guidelines/guidelinesunit.
The Genetic Genealogy Standards Committee. 2016. *Genetic Genealogy Standards,* January 10, 2016, http://www.geneticgenealogystandards.com/.
Historians, Librarians and Archivists Linked in Group. Accessed March 17, 2017. https://www.linkedin.com/groups?gid=1322227.
International Commission for the Accreditation of Genealogists. Accessed March 17, 2017. http://www.icapgen.org/.
International Society of Genetic Genealogy (ISOGG) wiki. "Genetic Genealogy," updated March 2017, https://isogg.org/wiki/Genetic_genealogy.
Pennavaria, Katherine. 2010. "Genealogy Gems." *Kentucky Libraries* 74(4): 5.
Pew Research Center. 2012. "Pew Internet & American Life Project Survey: Librarians, Patrons and E-Books," released June 22, 2012, http://libraries.pewinternet.org/2012/06/22/part-4-how-people-used-the-library-in-the-past-year/.
Russell, Judy G. 2014. "DNA and the Reasonably Exhaustive Search," *OnBoard* 20 (January 2014): 1–2, 7. http://bcgcertification.org/skillbuilders/skbld141pf.html.
Rzepczynski, Mary. 2013. "Tourist Attractions." *Public Libraries* 52(4): 8–10.
Stahr, Beth. 2015. "Who Can Help Find Grandma: Educational Preparation of Genealogical Librarians and Staff." Paper presented at the Annual Conference of the Popular Culture Association/American Culture Association, New Orleans, LA, 2015.
Stanley, Angela. 2016. "Georgia Library Association—Genealogy and Local History Interest Group." *Georgia Library Quarterly* 53(2). http://digitalcommons.kennesaw.edu/glq/vol53/iss2/.
Verma, Henrietta. 2016. "Rooted in Research: Genealogy." *Library Journal* 141(8)26–31.
Zastrow, Jan. 2015. "Genealogy: A Cheat Sheet for the Unsuspecting Librarian." *Computers in Libraries* 35 (5):16–20.

PART V: INSTRUCTION

Education Techniques for Genealogy Instruction

Carmen Nigro

Library staff engage with genealogy researchers at a variety of levels, from curious passers-by to professional genealogists preparing for publication. Instruction can happen informally as part of a standard reference interaction, or formally as researchers elect to attend classes taught by library staff. Using techniques of the field of education, particularly social science education, librarians can maximize the effect of genealogy instruction for their users to help them navigate this complex research. No matter what the researcher's level of skill, a librarian's familiarity with the following concepts can aid them in providing better instruction for these users.

Teaching to Standards

Most educational disciplines have a set of standards that instructors work to attain. These standards are often designated by state boards of education or another body of authority in a relevant discipline. For the topic of genealogy, the Board for Certification of Genealogists (BCG) created standards in the field that apply to documenting, researching, writing, and education. The BCG released the *BCG Genealogical Standards Manual* in 2000 and published an update in 2014 as *Genealogy Standards* (Board for Certification of Genealogists 2014).

Genealogy instructors should familiarize themselves with standards in the field and conscientiously work to teach to these levels of quality. The standards the BCG set forth for genealogy instruction pertain to planned outcomes, content titles, enhancements, presentation style, ownership, course design, and student evaluation (Board for Certification of Genealogists, *Genealogy Standards* 2014, 41–42).

In addition to standards for educators, genealogy instructors should be familiar with the Genealogy Proof Standard (Board for Certification of Genealogists, "The Genealogical Proof Standard"), which is the minimum standard of work genealogists should complete in order for their work to be considered credible. The Genealogy Proof Standard was also established by the BCG and encompasses the following elements: reasonably exhaustive research; complete, accurate citations to the source or sources of each information item; tests—through processes of analysis and correlation—of all sources, information items, and evidence; resolution of conflicts among evidence items; and a soundly reasoned, coherently written conclusion. Because the Genealogy Proof Standard establishes a basis for credibility, genealogy instructors should communicate to their students and patrons what that standard is and that its adherence is expected amongst professional genealogy researchers.

Having standards in the field in mind when creating classes and programming will enable instructors to shape worthwhile, meaningful genealogical programs. Standards also encourage educators to be reflective and critical when creating instructional content.

Scaffolding

In education, the concept of scaffolding is providing the support that a student needs to solve a problem, complete a task, or learn a new concept (Bilash, "Scaffolding"). Scaffolding is often illustrated by the proverb "if you give a man a fish, he eats for a day; if you teach a man to fish, he eats for a lifetime." At its core, scaffolding is empowering students or researchers to complete the research on their own by allowing them the opportunities to learn processes and skills needed.

Librarians as instructors can provide scaffolding in their classes and reference interactions in a variety of ways. Demonstrations of techniques such as how to properly use an index, how to perform wildcard searches in a database, how to locate a digitized book or dataset, or how to search a library catalog by subject heading can empower the user to do these things independently in the future. When providing scaffolding in your instruction, aim for clear instructions, provide examples, demonstrate visually when possible, and point researchers to the best known sources for their tasks (Bilash, "Scaffolding").

It is important that the librarian as an instructor not only perform tasks in front of the researchers but also either verbally walk them through the processes or have the researchers do the tasks with the librarian as a guide to the process. Researchers should be made aware of methodology texts—handbooks and how-to guides—and websites that librarians consult in answering reference questions and designing classes. Librarians and instructors should also remain approachable for the researcher to revisit the process if support is still needed. Researchers will gain confidence in their abilities as they experiment with the techniques and especially after they have successes in solving their own research problems. Mastery of these skills allows for researchers to move on to higher levels of research and knowledge creation.

Collaborative Learning

Many library users who are interested in their family histories became interested through the discovery of some of their family stories, whether factual or lore. However, it is the story element which drives them to share their discoveries, and as they add to them with an accumulation of evidence, to work out where and whether the new evidence fits into these stories.

Collaborative learning is a concept that emphasizes peer-to-peer learning and facilitates the learners by organizing them into groups in which they discuss projects, concepts, and techniques (Cornell University Center for Teaching Excellence, "Collaborative Learning: Group Work"). Collaborative learning is most successful when learners have already been introduced to basic concepts and then use discussions with peers to further their understanding and explore more techniques.

Collaborative learning opportunities for group-based problem solving encourages other researchers to share successful research experiences as well as help analyze and decode a problem at hand. Beneficial impacts of collaborative learning include higher-level thinking, oral communication, self-management, and leadership skills. Collaborative learning also leads to an increase in student retention, self-esteem, and responsibility; and exposure to and an increase in understanding of diverse perspectives (Cornell University Center for Teaching Excellence, "Collaborative Learning: Group Work"). These outcomes are also desirable in instruction for genealogy users who do not fit the same profile as typical university or high school students, as many of them are older, sometimes retired, and are often amateur researchers instead of being directed by a professor or teacher.

Setting up collaborative learning opportunities in the library for genealogy users may not be as easy as letting users know that they can reserve available meeting rooms. A facilitator should be on hand and be familiar with the types of problems that genealogy researchers often need to solve. This can be an experienced librarian, a representative from a genealogical society, or a professional genealogist.

At the New York Public Library, through a grant which encouraged experiments in library service which was funded through the Charles Revson Foundation, a professional genealogist was hired to facilitate a meet-up group and encourage the collaborative learning process. Called "The Innovation Project," (Charles H. Revson Foundation, "Education") the Revson Foundation grant provided funding and support library staff to proposed creative programs.

The genealogist led the meet-up group for six sessions to provide the collaborative learning space where library users could consult not only her professional expertise but also each other. The sessions were well attended, and the attendees indeed spent more time talking and collaborating than consulting items in the research collections. This may have been precisely because the collaborative experience is not always offered at libraries, particularly research libraries where the normal environment is oriented toward individual research.

Collaborative learning is a skill-building and socially supportive opportunity for genealogists and family history researchers. Libraries can encourage this learning style by offering space and staff for these types of learning sessions.

Problem Based Learning

In education, "problem based learning" is presenting students with an open-ended, real world applicable problem and letting them work, often in groups, toward devising a solution to the problem at hand (Cornell University Center for Teaching Excellence, "Problem-Based Learning"). In genealogy, users come to the library with their problem already in mind, though they may need substantial help formulating and expressing what their questions are so they can focus their research on finding the answer to the problem.

The genealogy instructor should guide researchers to formulating a problem-based query and then structuring their research experience around that query.

The first time a genealogy researcher approaches a reference desk, he or she may pose the research question in vague terms that will more express the researcher's interest in the field than it will truly help direct research in a meaningful way. Common queries include, "I want to research my family name," or "Do you have anything about my great-grandfather?" An adept librarian will help these users focus the intent of their research visit in order to achieve a goal, or at least create a reasonable plan of approach to the research question at hand.

As part of the Genealogical Proof Standard, a fundamental concept is to create a focused research question that concerns a documented person and seeks specific information about that person (Jones, *Mastering genealogical proof*). Questions should not be too broad or too narrow. Questions that are too broad allow for several correct answers and are difficult to assess for accuracy. "Who was Eleanor Medly? could have many unrelated answers.... Better questions would be Who were Eleanor Medly's parents? Where did she live? What was her religion?" Questions that are too narrow may be unanswerable with the records available at a certain place or time, such as determining exact date of birth (Jones 2013, 7). A good research question gives the researcher a specific problem to solve so finding sources can be focused to the exact problem at hand.

Researchers have better success in their research when it is focused on a specific problem because they, with support of research staff, can develop a research plan. They can look for specific record sets, consult specific methodology books, look into the history of specific localities, or know when to search for alternative records. Helping researchers turn vague questions into specific problems to solve creates a problem-based learning inquiry for which research plans can be created.

Primary Sources Versus Original Sources

Humanities educators are familiar with "primary" and "secondary" source materials. Primary sources provide "direct or firsthand evidence about an event" while secondary sources "describe, discuss, interpret, comment upon, analyze, evaluate, summarize, and process primary sources" (Ithaca College Library, "Primary and Secondary Sources"). Currently, history instructors prioritize the analysis of primary sources as par for their courses.

In the field of genealogy, practitioners focus instead on "original" and "derivative" sources and "authored works." Genealogy researchers also analyze content by placing it into categories of "primary information," "secondary information," and "unknown origin." Evidence is the interpretation of this information and is categorized as "direct evidence," "indirect evidence," and "negative evidence" (Mills 2015, 24–25). Genealogy researchers investigate the source itself: is it in its first oral or recorded form? Or is it created by copying an original and manipulating the content? An authored work is the hybrid of the two, created by authors who have evaluated many sources and created a piece of writing. Once the source is analyzed, the information must be categorized: are the details provided by someone with firsthand knowledge of the event? Or secondhand information? Or can the informant not be identified? And finally, does this information give a direct answer to the research question at hand? Can it be combined with other evidence to answer a research question? Or is the absence of information a provider of negative evidence? (Mills 2015, 24–25).

The application of Genealogical Proof Standard and *Evidence Explained* requires researchers to analyze sources and the information contained within, and to further analyze the evidence they attain from that information in a critical manner. Those who are interested in genealogy as a hobby may balk at this level of higher-order thinking, but instructors should encourage researchers to be thorough and captious. Genealogists that thoroughly develop their research skills and think analytically about their research will be more sure of their conclusions and may be more satisfied with their long-term investment in genealogy.

Evidence-Based Writing

Supporting claims with evidence, sometimes also called evidence-based writing, is the process of evaluating evidence to support or disprove a claim. Often it is taken for granted that genealogy researchers base their conclusions on evidence, but that assumption can be false. Like any history research, the genealogy inquiry can be based on rumors, exaggerated stories, assumptions, innuendo, gossip, hearsay or other inventions. Family trees often list relationships with no evidence cited to underpin those assertions. Genealogy instructors should emphasize that evidence is needed to support claims and move researchers toward a systematic research process.

In education, writing teachers strategize how to get students to include evidence in their writing in persuasive essays, research papers, and document-based writing exercises. A key part of using evidence to prove and disprove claims is critique and evaluation of the evidence itself. The National Council of Teachers of English recommend steps for the process of teaching students to incorporate evidence in their writing to include first finding and interpreting evidence, followed by evaluating the quality of the sources and data and analyzing the data (National Council of Teachers of English 2012).

This process parallels that which is laid out in *Evidence Explained: Citing History Sources from Artifacts to Cyberspace*, the widely accepted genealogy citation style guide by Elizabeth Shown Mills (Mills 2015). Mills' citation guide is based on *The Chicago Manual of Style* but with additions intended to help users evaluate the reliability of sources. Mills' guide drives researchers to appraise their sources and seek out original sources if they are using derivative sources. She writes, "at each step of that process, we appraise the credibility of *each* detail in *each* document. We apply every conceivable test for authenticity, contemporaneousness, and credibility of informants" [original emphasis included] (Mills 2015, 16). Mills' approach is integrated into the Genealogical Proof Standard, and professional organizations and journals require the same in-depth evaluation and inclusion of evidence in writing. Mills defines proof as "a conclusion based upon the sum of the evidence that supports a valid assertion or deduction…. Proof must be backed by thorough research and documentation, by reliable information that is correctly interpreted and carefully correlated, and by a well-reasoned and written analysis of the problem and the evidence" (Mills 2015, 17).

Genealogy instructors should be familiar with both the concept of evidence-based writing as the desired outcome of genealogical research and with Mills' *Evidence Explained* as a standard style guide in the field of genealogy. Genealogy classes should articulate the importance of supporting claims with evidence and well as the critical evaluation of sources of information.

Bloom's Taxonomy

A framework for educators routinely called Bloom's Taxonomy was originally published in 1956 as *Taxonomy of Educational Objectives* (Bloom). This framework has been applied by generations of educators and instructors in their teaching. The original framework consisted of six major categories: Knowledge, Comprehension, Application, Analysis, Synthesis, and Evaluation (Vanderbilt University Center for Teaching). The underlying concept of this framework was that the goal of educators was to move student learning from the lowest tier, knowledge, to the highest tier, evaluation, with each tier representing a level of attainment and progress. In 2001, a revised look at Bloom's Taxonomy was published—*A Taxonomy for Teaching, Learning, and Assessment*—with the scheme of classification as Remember, Understand, Apply, Analyze, Evaluate, Create (Anderson and Krathwohl 2001).

An awareness of Bloom's Taxonomy enables instructors to create classes and programming with educational outcomes in mind. By setting learning goals, educators create more effective instructional materials and exchanges that align with their specific goals. For genealogy instructors, one could look at the intended objective. For example, a class called *Getting Started in Genealogy* would cover the first levels of learning objectives (Remember, Understand) with the intent of moving those learners into applying their new information. Mid-level classes would focus greatly on application of principles and move learners toward analyzation of evidence. A more advanced class in genealogy, such as *Writing Your Family History*, would be designed to have learners analyze and evaluate their own research and ultimately create something new out of it.

With its structures from the field of education, Bloom's Taxonomy can fit into the field of library and information science, where the conceptual terms "data," "information," and "knowledge" are used. These terms are often thought to be sequential in a manner similar to the sequenced tiers of Bloom's Taxonomy, though that concept is certainly a matter of some debate (Zins 2007). Common views are that information is created out of data and that knowledge is created from information. This view is compatible with Bloom's Taxonomy's movement of a learner up a ladder of increasing knowledge, from remembering to understanding to applying, analyzing, evaluating, and finally creating.

Information Literacy

Librarians are, of course, concerned with information literacy as it is a concept promulgated by the American Library Association. Information literacy is a person's ability "to recognize when information is needed and have the ability to locate, evaluate, and use effectively the needed information" (Association of College and Research Libraries 1989). Widely discussed since the 1989 publication of *Presidential Committee on Information Literacy: Final Report*, the Association of College and Research Libraries has also set standards in their publication *Information Literacy Competency Standards for Higher Education* in 2000 (Association of College & Research Libraries 2000).

Genealogy instructors have ample opportunity to address information literacy with researchers. Users need to understand what information was created, where that information is housed or digitized, how it can be searched, how to evaluate it—especially information that produces conflicts—and how to analyze it. Not unlike academic fields in higher education, genealogy researchers must grasp a patchwork of available information and attempt to create statements of proof from what they find. The records that genealogy researchers use vary greatly from place to place and in different time periods. Information literacy can help them navigate more effectively through this variety of records and understand what creates roadblocks for their research and where information is held that may reopen a research pathway.

Instructors can focus classes and researcher consultations on elements of information literacy—especially helping them determine what records are needed and where they are located. In particular, showing researchers how to determine this in itself is important—what genealogy handbooks and methodology works are most useful, and what websites are up-to-date and appropriate for the problem at hand. Instructors should avoid simply telling known information without demonstrating how they came to know that information.

Librarians who are pedagogically trained or conscientious of the relationships between teaching and learning can be better advocates of information literacy. Because information literacy is a focus of college and university libraries, many of which employ instructor librarians who are pedagogically trained, it sometimes falls out of the mindset of librarians who do not expressly work with students. If genealogy instructors revisit core concepts of information literacy and the standards set forth in the ACRL's *Information Literacy Competency Standards for Higher Education*, they may be more effective in their instruction.

Graphic Organizers: Family Group Charts and Trees

Educators often use graphic organizers to support students in organizing content, appealing to visual learners, and communicating complex ideas in simple formats. While traditional graphic organizers in the field of educations tend toward Venn diagrams, mind maps, and double-entry journals, the field of genealogy uses graphic organizers such as family trees, family group charts, genograms, pedigree charts, fan charts, and timelines.

The West Virginia Department of Education lists types of graphic organizers on its website and also defines them: "Graphic organizers are visual models that can assist students in organizing information and communicating clearly and effectively. Students can use graphic organizers to structure their writing, brainstorm ideas, assist in decision making, clarify story structure, help with problem solving, and plan research" (West Virginia Department of Education). This translates well to genealogy education, where researchers need to group generations, separate specific branches, or perhaps sort out marriages and divorces in their family histories.

Graphic organizers assist in scaffolding content. They also contribute to understanding links between content, such as relationships and timelines. Reformatting data into graphic organizers can help users transition facts into information and knowledge.

Using Maps to Support Family History Research

In the classroom, the use of maps has been effectively demonstrated to improve student behavior, class participation, attendance, confidence, and student achievement in comprehension and application of social studies materials (Yousaf, Aziz, and Hassad 2012). Likewise, in family history research, maps greatly enhance the learning experience and add value to the research performed.

Genealogists should be intimately familiar with the geographic locations of their ancestors in order to understand where to search for records. "Genealogy is a geographically driven subject.... Records are made and kept by locations. That makes geography as important if not more important than history to the genealogist" (Kashuba 2005, 1–2). Maps will aid the genealogist in finding specific locations and understanding their relationships to other locations, understanding the natural terrain of an area, helping visualize migration routes, and providing insight to historic places. Maps users will be able to see a layout of a neighborhood; identify natural boundaries like rivers or mountains; find local religious institutions, cemeteries, or schools; understand the boundaries of a township and determine neighboring municipalities; see landowners plotted; and possibly find geographic features named with the surnames they are researching.

Instructors should strive not only to introduce genealogy patrons to maps but to inform them of their usefulness and the potential insights gained from using them. Understanding an area geographically will aid them in their genealogical research, and maps are key to that understanding.

Conclusion

An awareness of pedagogy, even without formal study of the subject, leads to better instructional techniques in libraries. Genealogy instructors have a variety of methods to enhance their teaching and informal instruction at the reference desk. Social science education techniques are particularly adaptable to the genealogy field. Genealogy instruction should include teaching to standards, scaffolding, collaborative learning, problem-based learning, use of primary/original sources, application of Bloom's Taxonomy, information literacy, using graphic organizers and maps.

Works Cited

Anderson, Lorin W., and David R Krathwohl. 2001. *A Taxonomy for Learning, Teaching, and Assessing: A Revision of Bloom's Taxonomy of Educational Objectives*. New York: Longman, 2001.

Association of College and Research Libraries. 1989. "Presidential Committee on Information Literacy: Final Report." American Library Association: Chicago, 1989. Accessed 31 March 2017, http://www.ala.org/acrl/publications/whitepapers/presidential.

Association of College and Research Libraries. 2000. *Information Literacy Competency Standards for Higher Education*. Association of College & Research Libraries: Chicago. Accessed 10 April 2017, http://www.ala.org/acrl/sites/ala.org.acrl/files/content/standards/standards.pdf.

Bilash, Olenka. "Scaffolding" University of Alberta, Department of Secondary Education, accessed 10 April 2017, http://sites.educ.ualberta.ca/staff/olenka.bilash/Best%20of%20Bilash/scaffolding.html.

Bloom, Benjamin S. 1956. *Taxonomy of Educational Objectives*. New York: Longmans, Green.

Board for Certification of Genealogists. 2000. *The BCG Genealogical Manual*. Orem, UT: Ancestry Publishing.

Board for Certification of Genealogists. 2014. *Genealogy Standards*. Washington, D.C.: Ancestry.com.

Charles H. Revson Foundation. "Education," accessed 10 April 2017, http://revsonfoundation.org/projects/new-york-public-librarys-innovation-project/.

Cornell University Center for Teaching Excellence. "Collaborative Learning: Group Work," accessed 10 April 2017, https://www.cte.cornell.edu/teaching-ideas/engaging-students/collaborative-learning.html.

Cornell University Center for Teaching Excellence. "Problem-Based Learning," accessed 10 April 2017, https://www.cte.cornell.edu/teaching-ideas/engaging-students/problem-based-learning.html.

"The Genealogical Proof Standard." Board for Certification of Genealogists, accessed 10 April 2017, http://www.bcgcertification.org/resources/standard.html.

Ithaca College Library. "Primary and Secondary Sources," accessed 3 April 2017, https://library.ithaca.edu/sp/subjects/primary.

Jones, Thomas W. 2013. *Mastering Genealogical Proof*. Arlington, VA: National Genealogical Society.

Kashuba, Melinda. 2005. *Walking with Your Ancestors: A Genealogist's Guide to Using Maps and Geography*. Cincinnati, OH: Family Tree Books.

Mills, Elizabeth Shown. 2015. *Evidence Explained: Citing History Sources from Artifacts to Cyberspace*. 3rd edition. Baltimore: Genealogical Publishing Company.

National Council of Teachers of English, Office of Policy Research. 2012. "Using Evidence in Writing: A policy Research Brief," accessed 3 April 2017, http://www.ncte.org/library/NCTEFiles/Resources/Journals/CC/0222-nov2012/CC0222Policy.pdf.

Vanderbilt University Center for Teaching. "Bloom's Taxonomy," accessed 10 April 2017, https://cft.vanderbilt.edu/guides-sub-pages/blooms-taxonomy/.

West Virginia Department of Education. "Graphic Organizers," accessed 10 April 2017, https://wvde.state.wv.us/strategybank/GraphicOrganizers.html.

Yousaf, Shakeela, Shamsa Aziz, and Hamid Hassad. 2012. "Effectiveness of Maps & Globes in Social Studies Teaching." *International Journal of Social Sciences & Education* 3, accessed 7 April 2017, http://www.ijsse.com/sites/default/files/issues/2012/Volume%203%20issue%201/Papers/Paper-20.pdf.

Zins, Chaim. "Conceptual Approaches for Defining Data, Information, and Knowledge." 2007. *Journal of the American Society for Information Science and Technology*, 22 January. Accessed 29 March 2017, http://www.success.co.il/is/zins_definitions_dik.pdf.

Instructing Patrons on Using Free Online Genealogical Resources

Andrew Hart

The Basics

Powerful subscription search engines and databases like Ancestry and Fold3 make genealogical research easier, and provide opportunities for linking information and finding new leads. However, this comes at a cost to researchers who are charged a fee. Many non-subscription sites provide free, quality information resources. Genealogical research should not cost an arm and a leg. Knowledge of free, online genealogical resources is a boon for librarians instructing patrons, especially patrons who are just beginning family research. As a side note, subscription services charge a fee for a reason: they synthesize a ton of information and allow users to search multiple places at one time. They are a great tool, and if patrons wish to use them, librarians should be able to explain what each provider offers and the kind of information that can be obtained.

A great place to start online genealogical research is Google. While Google should not be the only search engine one uses for research online, it can provide information that is useful in other engines. It can also retrieve information located on the web that would not be found anywhere else. For example, I tried everything to find information about my great-grandmother. I used well-known search engines, including Family Search (covered later). Frustrated, I typed her name and death location into a Google search. I was shocked to find my grandmother's obituary and picture in a newspaper someone had digitized. I discovered the reason why my previous searches were not working: the date of birth was wrong.

Google offers a multitude of advanced search options that many might not know exist. Advanced search options improve the quality and accuracy of search results. As of 2017, to access Google's advanced search options, users will first have to complete a normal Google search. After the search results populate, a settings option will appear under the right side of the search bar. Clicking on this will open a dropdown menu. Clicking on advanced search gives users multiple search fields to narrow down search results for the information that they want to find. Users can search using a group of words, an exact word or phrase (useful for people's names), some of the words provided, any of the words provided, and numbers. Librarians will notice immediately that this is common Boolean searching made easy for non-information specialists. Search results can also be further narrowed by selecting a language, region, file type, and domain type. Google provides instructions on the side of the search menu in case users forget what search option/limiter does what.

If users find Google's advanced search page cumbersome, they have the option to complete a normal search, using specific symbols and syntax that offers the same results. For example, if a user is searching for Robert Emmanuel in Ohio, and wants Google to understand that Robert Emmanuel should be searched as a combination of both words, and not just Robert and Emmanuel separately, quotation marks should be placed around the search phrase. So, a search might look something like this: "Robert Emmanuel" Ohio (leave out "in"). A search using the information above without quotation marks produces 10.2 million hits. A more controlled search with quotation marks produces only 3,370 hits. An online researcher's goal should be to get the most accurate results possible. Using advanced search features on Google and other search engines will help in this endeavor.

Search engines like Google, Bing, and Yahoo do a great job at retrieving information located on funeral home and legacy/memorial websites. There are two caveats that accompany an information search of this type: funeral home announcements and legacy pages are typically for recently departed individuals, and this information is sometimes only briefly available (especially on funeral home website announcements/obituaries). For researchers wanting information about a recently departed individual, this is a particularly useful option. In addition to funeral home websites and online legacy pages, obituaries are sometimes available through a newspaper's website. Depending on the newspaper, this information may only span back a few months.

To perform a search for online death and funeral announcements using a general search engine, users will need to provide as much data as possible in the search query. If available, the following information should be included: full name of the deceased, year and month of death, and state and city of death. A search might look like the following: "Robert Emmanuel" death January 2017, Philadelphia, Pennsylvania. If the death was recent enough, the funeral home that was used may still have information on their website regarding arrangements and the obituary.

It is important to verify search engine and database results. This can be done by instructing users to compare known information against data obtained through a search. There are thousands of people with the same name as a patron's ancestor. If results are not verified, a researcher might copy information that is not correct, potentially sabotaging an entire family line. For example, if you know that Robert Emmanuel died in 1962, and a record is found that states he died in 1978, then you know you do not have the correct Robert Emmanuel. Patrons should try to verify at least three pieces of information to make sure data matches their own. This can include the person's full name, including middle, the date of birth, city of residence, date and place of death, mother and father's names, children's names, and occupation.

The following is a list of free, online genealogical research databases and websites. Each resource is described, including tips on how to get the most information out of the resource. The sites were chosen for their quality and prominence in the genealogical research community.

Family Search

Family Search offers a treasure-trove of resources for online researchers. The site is operated by The Church of Jesus Christ of Latter-day Saints (Quillen 2015, 87), and has billions of online genealogical records. What makes Family Search a valuable resource is the searchability of digitized records. This is afforded by indexing. Seasoned genealogists and information professionals volunteer for Family Search and index digitized genealogical documents. There would be no Family Search, or any online genealogical database, without dedicated indexers. A cool feature of the site is the ability to view the digitized document along with the indexed information. This allows researchers to double-check the record and to gather related information pertaining to other individuals. This is most helpful when researching the U.S. Federal Census.

To begin research, visit FamilySearch.org/search. The left side of the page is titled *Search Historical Records*, and the right is titled *Research by Location*. Researchers who are just beginning should use the *Search Historical Records* option. *Research by Location* is for advanced users who are comfortable with finding information located in Family Search's thousands of digitized and indexed collections. For the *Research by Location* option, users are presented with a map of the world, and below that, a search bar to search by collection title. Hovering over the map allows one to select a certain region. Once clicked, an option menu appears for the region. Clicking on the United States will present clickable options for all fifty states, including the District of Columbia. Hovering over a state reveals information related to that state's online records. This includes the amount of collections in Family Search, years of coverage, amount of indexed records, and images associated with those records. As of 2017, there are a total of 1,050 collections, 2,622,199,218 indexed records, and 704,701,518 images for the United States of America. The period of coverage is from 1500 to 2015 (FamilySearch.org/search).

Searching for genealogical records using Family Search is quite straightforward. Using the *Search Historical Records* side of the page, users should be instructed to put in as much information as possible. There is a checkbox at the end of each search field. Clicking on the box tells Family Search that you want an exact match. Leaving the box unchecked will return records with variant spellings of the information provided. It is recommended that the boxes be left unchecked. During the Federal Census, names were sometimes misspelled by enumerators (those who conducted the survey). If you know there are variants for the way a family name is spelled, "Emanuel" instead of "Emmanuel," then consider keeping the boxes unchecked. The first thing Family Search asks for is a first and last name (or multiple first and last names, which helps to find records that contain maiden names). If only the first or last name is known, just put that.

The next set of search options centers on life events. These are extremely helpful in pinpointing records for an ancestor. There are fields for birthplace and year, marriage place and year, residence place and year, death place and year, and any place and year. Be as specific as possible. If you know that an ancestor was born in Chattanooga, Tennessee, then include Chattanooga in the search and not just Tennessee. Extra special attention needs to be paid when listing years. Sometimes genealogical records contain wrong year information. A birth in 1894 might be recorded as 1895, or a marriage that took place in 1921 might be recorded as 1919. It is recommended to instruct users to subtract two years and add two years (even three) for the year search fields. For example, if you believe a date of birth to be 1870, you would put 1868 and 1872 for the beginning and ending year fields.

After life events, information related to relationships is collected. This includes spouse's first and last names, father's first and last names, mother's first and last names, and other person's first and last names. It is recommended to keep the exact match box unchecked, but again, researchers have this option at their disposal. The last set of search options includes limiting records by type (birth, marriage, death, census, etc.), batch number, and film number. It is recommended that users do not use any of these options unless they know exactly where the information is located.

Once the search fields have been filled, click "search." Family Search will comb multiple collections including the United States Social Security Death Index and U.S. and state-specific censuses. When viewing results, it is best to take it slow. Results with the most relevant information are generally at the top of the results list. Results are displayed in rows with four columns: name, events, relationships, and view. In the Name column, the person's name will be displayed along with the collection that the information came out of. In the Events and Relationships columns, information that matches what was searched appears, including birth, death, spouse, and parent information. The View column contains a button to view the record.

There are three ways to view the record: clicking the view button, clicking the hyperlinked name in the Name column, or clicking anywhere in the record listing. Choosing the first two view options opens a new page where the record is displayed. Clicking anywhere in the record listing opens a drop-down view of the record on the results page. The same information is displayed using any of the options. If a digitized document is available, there will be a choice to view it on the right-hand side of the record. If the search did not obtain results, users can refine their search by modifying search fields on the left-hand side of the results page.

Find a Grave

A unique and sometimes surprising resource is Find a Grave. The site concentrates on cemetery information, including photos of the deceased's headstone. The information located in the Find a Grave database is provided by volunteers and amateur cemetery catalogers (FindaGrave.com). Data about the cemetery including cemetery location, entrance photo, size, date of establishment, number of interments, and a listing of famous interments is provided. Records for individuals in the cemetery offer the following information: names, date of birth, date of death, obituary (if available), grave marker (if available), and hyperlinks to family members located in the same or different cemeteries. Find a Grave's linking feature is one of the most powerful features of the site. Sometimes genealogies are available for an entire family, ancestors linked to one another's graves.

Creator information is provided at the bottom of each record, including the creator's Find a Grave username and the date the record was added. The username is hyperlinked to the creator's contact page. Patrons who wish to contact a record's creator should be instructed to do so in a respectful manner, identifying themselves and the reason for contact. Patrons may find that the person they contact is a lost relative that is working on the same genealogical research that they are! Besides providing the information listed above, Find a Grave allows users to leave notes and virtual flowers on records.

To begin a search, go to FindaGrave.com. The left-hand side of the page presents information on finding famous graves, and the right-hand side has resources for finding regular graves. Librarians may want to familiarize themselves with the famous grave search feature: you never know when it will help answer a reference question. Patrons should be instructed to either click on the *Search 159 million grave records*, or the *Search for a cemetery* hyperlinks on the right-hand side of the page. Clicking on the first option allows researchers to provide information about their ancestor and to obtain a grave record; the second allows users to provide information about a specific cemetery and to get a cemetery record.

Clicking on *Search 159 million grave records* opens a search form. Fields for name, birth and death dates, and cemetery location are provided. A memorial number field is also available if a patron knows a record's Find a Grave memorial number. The *date* and *order by* filters should be left alone. Unlike Family Search, dates should be as specific as possible. The information in Find a Grave is taken from death records and headstone data; documents which usually provide accurate information. If it is unknown what state or province an individual is buried in, only specify the country. The same goes for dates of death or birth: list what you know. If this is the case, instruct patrons to verify information already known about the ancestor against the record.

Liberty Ellis Foundation

Patrons conducting research on ancestors who immigrated to the U.S., will find Liberty Ellis Foundation invaluable. The site is the online record database for The Statute of Liberty—Ellis Island Foundation, Inc. The late nineteenth and early twentieth centuries saw millions of immigrants enter the United States through Ellis Island and the Port of New York. In return, millions of records were created. Liberty Ellis Foundation makes indexed and digitized ship manifest records from 1892 to 1957 available for genealogical researchers (LibertyEllisFoundation.com). Several bits of information can be obtained from these records including passenger's year of birth, age at arrival, month/day/year of arrival, marital status, gender, and ethnicity. Please note, records do not just include those for passengers, but also for crewmembers, as well.

The site offers a few ways to search, and users should be guided depending on skill level. To begin, visit LibertyEllisFoundation.com/passenger. The most basic search can be conducted by typing in a first name, or the initial of the first name, accompanied by the last name of a ship passenger. Last name is mandatory and a search cannot be completed without one. There are six options to narrow the most basic search: contains, exact matches, close matches, sounds like, alternate spellings, last name as first. Just like Family Search, choosing an exact match is not a good idea (at least not initially). Workers recording ship manifests may have written a variant or even a completely different name than what was presented by a passenger. Users can choose as many limiters as they wish. If patrons are not having any luck finding a passenger, instruct them to try different narrowing functions.

To use more advanced search settings, click the *wizard* or *one page form* option below the basic name search bar. Either option presents the same search fields. The only difference is that the *wizard* opens on the same page and the *one page form* opens in a new page. Clicking on the *one page form* presents an orderly series of search-narrowing options. Patrons are presented with the same fields as the basic search, including options for gender, marital status, year of birth, current age, age at arrival, year of arrival, ship name, port of departure, and ethnicity. Patrons should be instructed to include any limiting information that they know.

Results are presented in a similar fashion like Family Search. Rows present information as directed by the following columns: name, arrived, last place of residence/birth place, ship name, and action. Hovering over the "i" symbol next to the passenger name provides information including marital status, port of departure, passenger ID, and date of arrival. Patrons should be instructed that in order to see more detailed information, they must create a free user account with Liberty Ellis Foundation. An email address is required and used to verify the account creation. After an account is made, patrons can access the passenger record, ship image, and ship manifest under the Action column.

Clicking on the ship manifest option allows users to view the actual digitized manifest on which their ancestor was recorded. Please note, Liberty Ellis Foundation offers the manifest for sale, and that will be the first thing listed on the page. Instruct researchers to scroll down until the digitized and viewable manifest comes into sight. For the best viewing experience, instruct patrons to click the blue Full Image button above the right-hand corner of the manifest image. Below the digitized manifest is the indexed information for the manifest, including the line on which passenger information is found.

Cyndi's List

Cyndi's List is an awesome resource that should be introduced to every patron who is conducting research. The site is a hub where researchers can find over 300,000 indexed and categorized links to online genealogical resources (Cyndislist.com). To peruse this wonderful collection of links, visit Cyndislist.com. The site is quite simple to navigate. At the top of the home screen, instruct patrons to click on the *Categories* or *What's New* hyperlinks. Clicking on the latter will list links recently added to Cyndi's List offerings. Clicking on the former will display a page of various genealogical categories and the last time the category was updated with new links. Before clicking on a category, instruct patrons to become familiar with the list so they are aware of the different options at their disposal. Jotting down pertinent and interesting categories is a good idea.

Once a patron has some idea of what is available, they can begin clicking on hyperlinks and opening webpages. Patrons should be instructed to bookmark sites they find useful for easy access later. Taking notes on each website and saving the notes in a text/Word file should be suggested. This way, when patrons come back to the bookmarked site, they know why they bookmarked it and what they hope to accomplish by using it. Categories include *Law & Genealogy, Humor & Prose, Taxes, Evidence Analysis & Evaluation*, and most curiously, *Myths, Hoaxes & Scams*. When clicked, the category's page is displayed with a *category index* on the left and a *related categories* column on the right.

Patrons should inspect the *category index* for a subtopic that matches what they are looking for. For example, clicking on the category *Africa* will provide a *category index* that lists *census, general resources*, and *maps & geography*. Clicking on a chosen subtopic will produce a page with links to online resources pertaining to that subtopic. For example, clicking on the *Birth, Marriage, Death* subtopic of *Africa* produces links to *Family Search-Zimbabwe, Death Notices, 1904–1976*, and *Depouillement Seychelles Page Principale*, among others.

Family Echo

After a patron conducts research, they are going to want to record the information they have found. A neat way to store and visualize genealogical data is through a digital family tree. Many sites provide such opportunities, including Ancestry, but a lot of them fall short in visualization and options. Family Echo is not one of these sites. It offers a robust array of tools for researchers to use, store, and share the information that they have discovered. To sign up for a free account, visit FamilyEcho.com. Users are greeted with a home screen introducing the site. The left-hand side of the page contains data fields that, once filled, create a jumping point for a researcher's family tree. The tree starts with the researcher and branches out as new members are added. The site is extremely interactive. Once more people are added to the tree, users can move the tree around by clicking and dragging it in whatever direction they like.

Patrons should be instructed to fill out data profiles as much as possible. Each data profile contains a *personal, contact,* and *biographical* tab where information can be provided about an individual. This data includes first and last names, date of birth and death, address, phone number, birthplace, interests, and biographical notes. Once a patron completes their own data profile, they can begin to add members to their family tree. Instruct patrons to click on one of the three add options: *parents, partners,* and *brothers and sisters*. Once clicked, a branch will be added to the patron's profile bubble. On a side note, an individual's bubble is color-coded for gender: pink is for women, blue is for men, and white is for other. If the individual is dead, clicking on the checkbox next to *this person is living* will provide a death date field and wash out the individual's bubble. It will also add additional data fields in the *biographical tab* for *death place* and *burial place/date*. A picture can be uploaded to an individual's data profile by clicking on the *add photo* button under the individual's name.

Another useful feature of Family Echo is the ability to share a family tree and to export data. To share a family tree with someone, click on the *share* button located in the upper right-hand corner of the screen. You can send an email with a link directly to someone in the family tree (if their data profile has an email), or you can copy the link provided by Family Echo. Be aware! Those who have access to this private link can potentially change records in the family tree, which could be disastrous. To export data, researchers should click on the *download/export this family...* button located in the bottom left-hand corner of every data profile. Researchers are presented with several options for exporting family tree data, including GEDCOM.

Conclusion

While helpful, free, online genealogical resources only go so far. Primary source materials that have not been digitized, and genealogical research books/manuals are other tools that should supplement internet research. While instructing on the resources in this essay, librarians should recommend these other materials, offering to show patrons how to use/access them. Additional free, online genealogical resources will appear in the future, and it will be up to librarians to instruct on their proper use.

Works Cited

Cyndi's List. "Welcome to Cyndi's List." Accessed March 25, 2017. Cyndislist.com.
Family Search. "Research by Location." Accessed March 18, 2017. https://familysearch.org/search.
Find a Grave. "Who Is Behind Find a Grave?" Accessed March 19, 2017. https://Find *a Grave*/cgi-bin/fg.cgi?page=whois.
Liberty Ellis Foundation. "About Passenger Search." Accessed March 19, 2017. http://Liberty *Ellis Foundation*/about-passenger-search.
Quillen, Daniel W. 2015. *Mastering Online Genealogy*. Centennial, CO: Cold Spring Press.

Special Collections Librarians Assisting Patrons in Finding and Preserving Family History

NANCY RICHEY

For many archives and special collections libraries, "family history researchers often make up the largest group [of users] comprising forty-five to ninety per cent of all archival researchers" (Tucker 2014). Many will be 50 years old or older (Henry 2015) and they will be coming to special collections near you because of the renewed interest in genealogy fostered by such programs as *Who Do You Think You Are?* and *Finding My Roots*. They are seeking information that requires extensive use of libraries and archives and this includes visiting the physical collections that are not yet online and may never be. According to *Family Trees: A History of Genealogy in America* by François Weil,

> Genealogy has filled many needs-social, economic, moral, political, racial, religious, and familial, depending on time, place, and the individuals concerned. Family trees in other words, have always contributed to the fabric of America. This suggests now more than ever, they will continue to offer insight into American culture.

Genealogists are often characterized metaphorically as having a fever and infected by a strange bug. So much so, "that the fever of the chase leads them on [because] the detective instinct is stimulated, the collector's passion for completeness roused" (Wagner 1960). So be prepared to deal with enthusiastic, "infected" researchers who are at different skill levels. Younger genealogists, who grew up in the advent of the web will be more web-oriented and require less assistance after an introductory tour. Other genealogists may be divided into three broad categories: (1) the filiation genealogist, (2) the genealogist researcher, and (3) the master genealogist. A filiation genealogist conducts research in primary and secondary sources to produce a pedigree chart. The genealogist researcher takes this first level of genealogical participation further, not only finding family information, but also solving complex genealogical problems and often collecting information found in a family history. The master genealogist possesses the skills of the previous two categories, completes complex information searching, and has high-level analytical skills. The master genealogist's work leads to such outputs as publications, conferences, training, and major research projects for private and public organizations" (Fulton 2016).

I would add a fourth category: the novice genealogist or family historian who simply walks in the door. They will consider the use of special collections as difficult and forbidding. All will know that professionals have sought to collect and preserve genealogical materials but may ask what exactly "special collections" are. You may even wish to share with them a more literal and descriptive term coming into use, "unique and distinctive collections" (Cullingford 2014). But, regardless of experience, I believe all types of researchers need a comprehensive definition and introduction to the concept of special collections and/or primary resource material. Each of the researchers is looking for information to place themselves and their family history in society's grander narrative.

What's so special about special collections? These distinctive aspects may include:

- Format: irregular materials that need special handling, such as film, photographs, slides, audio/video recordings, maps, ephemera
- Rarity: holdings that are old, scarce or unique
- Comprehensiveness: materials accumulated that jointly create an significant resource
- Housed and attached to institutions both large and small

All genealogical questions have their basis in the following questions:

- WHO are you searching for?
- WHAT do you want to find?
- WHERE was your family member located?
- WHEN did they live and die?
- WHY are you seeking this information?

As Special Collections librarians and archivists, we are uniquely qualified to open the doors to the materials because of our knowledge of a record's creation and its evidential value. We seek its preservation and best use and ensure this through trusted custodianship noting provenance, and the preservation of context. They quickly discover that the collections comprise materials unduplicated elsewhere and include items treasured because of their rarity. This also means that the items have an integrity and "speak for themselves" without added interpretation. All of which are vital to a family historian as they seek to prove or legitimize their conclusions.

Additionally, Special Collections librarians and family historians share many basic skills and views about recordkeeping, documentation and perpetuation. They, just as we are, are taught to develop a "thorough understanding of the nature of records … and to know how to "analyz[e] the credibility of data from individual records" (Devine 2001). Our bibliographical and well-honed research skills, as well as our familiarity with the holdings, are of great value to the genealogist. As the *Librarians Genealogy Handbook* states,

> Genealogy is the study of the descent from one ancestor in a direct line to another by verifying birth, marriage, and death dates. Family history-historians broaden our understanding of who our ancestors were; how and where they lived, worked, and traveled; and how you can relate to them with a better understanding of who you are. In other words, family history puts flesh on the skeleton of dates and facts that genealogy uncovers.

Any researcher coming to a special collections library or archive is ready to go beyond unreliable online searching and even valued databases such as Ancestry.com, to a deeper pool of resources. Certainly, not all special collections libraries will have all these materials but many historical collections will have some of them. Much of the material will be geographically centered to the location and will have come in through donations. The following list offers anyone an idea of the breadth and comprehensiveness of the types of resources available in many special collections libraries. It may also serve as an aide-mémoire prompting places to search:

- Account books (merchants' interactions with customers in the area; records of financial obligations which shed light on ancestors living in the area)
- Bibles (family/parish/church with valued vital statistic records; sometimes the only listing of births, deaths, marriages, may also list dates of church sacraments)
- Biographies/individual family histories (many self-published or from vanity presses)
- Cemetery Records (sexton, plates, flower gifts, monument/tombstones purchases)
- Census Records/Schedules (transcribed, microfilmed or digitized, 1790 to 2010)
- Church Records and minutes (with deaths-births-excommunications-removals, ordinations, disciplinary proceedings, minister's records, christenings, annulments)
- City and Telephone Directories
- Citizenship Papers
- Club Records and Minutes
- Court Records, "a piece of paper for every interaction with the government" (wills, probate and appraisals, settlements, inventories, marriage licenses and bonds, property maps, mortgages, plat books, surveyor's records, tax lists, powers of attorney, guardianship and adoption, poor house payments and residents, naturalization papers)
- Ephemera (think ephemeral, paper items designed to be useful or important for only a short time, invitations, pamphlets, tickets, flyers, advertisements, political leaflets)
- Family Group Sheets
- Farm and plantation records (many on microfilm as part of larger collections such as "Records of Ante-Bellum Southern Plantations from the Revolution through the Civil War")
- Historical Manuscripts (family and personal papers, journals and diaries, professional papers, correspondence, business papers and ledgers, architectural drawings, legal documents, maps, photographs, oral histories)
- Immigration "Jumping the Pond" and Naturalization records (passenger manifests, ship's logs, passports, change of name papers)
- Indexes to Historical and Genealogical Periodicals (electronic and print)
- Individual Family Files
- Institutional Records (mission and historical societies, seminary, orphanages, Masonic lodges)
- Land Records/Real Estate Records (land grants, deeds, land ownership, and land transfers)
- Lineage Society Records (Daughters of the American Revolution (DAR), National Society Daughters of the American Colonists (NSDAC), Sons of Confederate Veterans (SCV)

- Local History Resources
- Manumission Records (manumission is the legal document freeing a slave)
- Maps (cemetery, plat, farm, fire and land)
- Military and conscription records (service files, bounty awards, muster rolls, discharge papers, draft cards, local regimental histories)
- Memorial Cards and Funerary (contains the deceased's name and information, may contain a lock of the deceased's hair or a button from a uniform.
- Mortuary Records (burial registers, funeral home books, other types of funeral cards)
- Newspaper Notices/clippings (birth and marriage notices, obituaries, accidents, crimes)
- Newspapers and Periodicals (microfilmed and original; maybe the only extant copy)
- Plaques or awards
- Poll tax records (AKA 'head tax' or 'capitation,' head of the household (whether male of female) and other men over age 16 were taxable in a household)
- Poorhouse, workhouse, almshouse, and asylum records
- School and college yearbooks, records, diplomas, report cards
- School and Church certificates
- Scrapbooks
- Slave Registers
- Sharecropper Agreements
- Specialized "one-of-a-kind" serials such as *Confederate Veteran* containing reminiscences of Confederate soldiers.
- State Records (land taxes and personal property taxes, land office records including military certificates, land patents and grants, state pension, non-military public service claims, muster and payrolls, applications for pensions from Confederate veterans)
- University Archives (photographs, school records, papers, letters requesting financial assistance, student and faculty correspondence, personnel files)
- Vital "of or relating to life" Records (birth certificates, adoption records, death certificates, marriage and divorce records)
- Union Catalogs (National Union Catalog of Manuscript Collections, NUCMC, "describing archival and manuscript collections held by eligible repositories located throughout the United States and its territories")
- United States Serial Set (land claims, law suits, divorces, requests for financial relief, lists of pensioners, artificial limbs furnished to soldiers, includes women, African Americans, Native Americans, students, soldiers, sailors, pensioners, landowners and inventors)
- Voter records (possibly naturalization information, signature, occupation, marital status, if owned land)
- World War 1 and 2 discharge papers (originals/microfilmed, may have restrictions)
- WorldCat access [this catalog of catalogs has records for unpublished and ephemeral materials held in special collections and archives around the world]

Genealogical researchers are just like any other patron who approaches a reference assistance desk. Some may require ten minutes of your time; others two hours. Be prepared for some of these types of queries. The patron may approach with only one question. "Can you help me find my grandfather?" "Sure, I will be happy to assist you. What is your grandfather's name?" "I don't know." Or "I want a copy of a death notice for my Great-Grandmother Mary Smith who died in Kentucky in 1916." "What was the month date of her death?" "I don't know." Another question: "I know you have the local newspapers on microfilm from the 50s and 60s. My father played football then. I want all the newspaper articles about him that were in the paper."

Also there may be multiple questions about timelines, immigration-emigration, missing persons, name changes, illegitimate births, adoptions, social and local area history, evolution of counties and the best ways to organize and cite the materials. Regardless, they want a welcoming attitude not one as noted in "A Gentle Reminder to Special-Collections Curators." The author described "a cold or condescending reception from curators [librarians]" when he went to collections seeking to use the holdings (Gilman 2010). We must also remember, "research is research, whether it is science or family history-it should always be done according to established best practices" (Pennavaria 2015).

Be Ready! How Can Special Librarians Be Prepared?

- Have clear policies in place about how much research assistance you can offer in person, by mail or e-mail and clearly state charges if you have them.
- Be a knowledgeable librarian that can connect them with the information they need. All reference staff should be able to answer a core set of reference questions about genealogy and the resources located at your institution. But the researcher may ask for the librarian/staff member most familiar with the genealogical collections.
- Look for ways to develop and adapt policies to minimally process "hidden" collections.
- Create as much as possible finely, detailed finding aids and catalog records and digitize in order to create surrogate copies.
- If possible, make more materials browseable to facilitate easier use of the collections.
- Present a welcoming attitude and assist each patron to the limits of time and expertise.
- Find low cost or no-cost training and professional development for all staff members who assists patrons.
- Purchase how-to genealogy books to educate staff on how to aid patrons such as *Genealogy: A Practical Guide for Librarians* by a practicing librarian, Kath Pennavaria.
- Promote an attitudinal change from "get it, catalog it, and preserve it" and modify by adding [protect] and promote it.
- Don't get left behind; use social networking technology resources.
- Cultivate local genealogists as excellent potential volunteers and donors.
- Ask for copies of relevant family materials to assist other patrons such as family bible records.

The Family Group Sheet includes the names of the husband, wife, and children of a family with birth, marriage, and death information, additional spouses (if any) of the parents, and children's spouses. The Ancestor Chart/Pedigree Chart shows family relationships in a conventional tree structure with names, as well as space to record critical information about his or her life, such as birth date and location, death date and location, and marriage date and location.

Caveats or How You Can Prepare Visiting Researchers?

- Make it clear that access to special collections involves more stringent security measures; sign-in registration with valid identification; they may be asked to lock up belongings, and bring in only a pencil, notebook, laptop.
- Special Collections libraries usually have limited weekday hours and no weekend or major holiday access.
- Formulate and prominently post polices about cell phone use as cameras and for calls, electronic scanners devices and their use.
- Library may require copied items to be stamped with institutional name, watermarked or require a special credit line such as: "Courtesy of the Department of Special Collections—WKU."
- Educate users that methods of describing and housing the collections and the techniques for accessing them will be different from those of general library collections.
- Let them know that not everything has a finding aid online, there may be collections that still use paper based "analog" finding aids and catalogs.
- Instruct users that we do not hold copyright to all we possess; they are ultimately responsible for compliance with laws governing copyright and so we cannot copy entire works. However, they may inquire about special circumstances for copyright, and they should be told that some material may be restricted at the request of the donor.
- Educate users to look at all materials objectively; that creators may filter facts through their own world view.
- Be careful with long tutorials or excessive dos and don'ts.
- Request that researchers narrow down their focus to decide exactly what they would like to accomplish on their visit.
- Provide a list of current, respected local genealogical researchers available for hire.
- Make researchers aware that all special collections material must be handled carefully which may involve the use of gloves and special devices such as book cradles.

As genealogists research their families' lineage and history, they collect documents, papers, family bibles, photographic images, and other artifacts that tell and document the ancestors' stories. They seek advice, along with the general public from special collections professionals, on how-to preserve these inherited and collected family history treasures. Questions will be asked about photographs and paper-based items such as newspaper clippings, letters, scrapbooks and family bibles. The special collections library can make available simple reference sheets that offer basic conservation and preservation best practices. We can also show the patrons many reputable websites with this information.

Questions about photograph care and identification are among the most received. To assist the patron, it is helpful to know what kind of photographic process was used. The most common photographic processes are the following. They will be the types of photographs that patrons most likely bring into the library. The care and preservation will be according to the process used. Note: all dates are circa.

Daguerreotype (1839–1855)

- highly reflective, "the mirror with a memory," silver-coated copper plates and are often found in ornate cases, rare and one-of-a-kind
- *Ambrotype* (1854–1870)
- non-reflective photographs, collodion on glass negatives viewed against a dark background

Tintypes (1854–1900)

- durable, inexpensive images produced on sheets of iron coated with dark enamel. Very popular during the Civil War which helps to date them

Glass Plate Negatives (1850–1865)

- collodion wet and the gelatin dry emulsions coated on a glass plates, very fragile

Paper Prints

Salted Paper (1830–1855)

- earliest photographic prints on paper.

Albumen Prints (1850–1895)

- most common type of photograph from the 19th century; finely detailed; sample sizes of mounts:
  - Carte-de-visite—4¼ × 2½
  - Cabinet—4½ × 6½
  - Promenade—4 × 7
  - Boudoir—5¼ × 8½

Cyanotype (1885–1910)

- Blue tinted on uncoated paper, very stable, used also for blueprints

Gelatin Silver Print/Platinum (1880–1930)

- dominant black-and-white photographic process of the 20th century.

Film-Based Photographic Materials and Negatives (1890s)

- Kodachrome: the first commercially successful color film for the novice; other film-based photographic materials: cellulose nitrate, cellulose acetates and polyester. If the patron asks about film negatives, make them aware of how dangerous cellulose nitrate film can be as opposed to "safety" acetate film.

After determining a type and age for a photograph, storage and preservation issues can be addressed. For housing the images, let the patron know to choose appropriate enclosures for storage such as envelopes or "Hollinger" boxes, PVC-free sleeves, plastic bags and acid-free paper, mats and backboards. Tell them to beware of broad terms, "Acid-free" does not mean "lignin-free" and "photo-safe" does not mean PVC-free. Share with them reputable dealers who offer products that have truly met ANSI/NISO standards. These types of materials limit both damaging light and dust and reduce chemical deterioration. Let them know "tape is evil." If possible, they need to remove any paper clips, rubber bands, pressure sensitive tapes (Scotch), labels, rubber cements and glues from the original image. Make it clear lamination is never used as it violates the cardinal rule of preservation: "do nothing that is irreversible." There are paper enclosures that are sold as buffered which contain an alkaline material that can neutralize acids as they form. These types of buffered enclosures last longer than non-buffered and will offer more protection to photographs that may have been previously mounted or stored with poor quality mats or boards.

Optimally, the types of acceptable plastics that you choose for the storage of photographs should be uncoated polyester (often sold as Mylar®), polypropylene, and polyethylene. Do not use polyvinylchloride (PVC) plastics. If something smells like a new shower curtain, avoid it. These are never recommended as they are chemically unstable and can cause further damage to a vulnerable image. Many individuals still have the self-adhesive or "magnetic" albums in their procession and they are extremely detrimental to photographs. If possible, remove the images from these types of albums and re-house. All materials that come in contact with images should pass the (PAT) Photographic Activity Test (high quality vendors will note this), and this designation should be on all purchased materials. The PAT was developed by the American National Standards Institute. Further information can be found at http://www.ansi.org/ and http://www.archives.gov/preservation/.

After choosing correct enclosure for the images, label and identify them. Correctly identifying the subject(s) of photographs enhances their enjoyment, importance and use. Descendants are less likely to discard well-labeled family photographs. Labeling with a soft graphite pencil is recommended because it is considered harmless to the photograph and fade resistant. Other archival quality marking pens, or blue photo pencils can be used on other types of contemporary color prints which may resin-coated and difficult to mark with a pencil.

Examples of paper-based family treasures that special collections staff receive questions about are family bibles, prints, certificates, letters, diaries, and scrapbooks. For the patrons with particularly fragile paper albums and scrapbooks, keep these intact and advise them that they should be stored horizontally in a high quality acid free box or wrapped with quality paper. Every item, regardless of type, will benefit from following basic preservation guidelines which are really the same for all materials. Keep all precious family items in cool, dry, dark environments and at as stable a temperature as possible. You cannot control the chemical and physical composition of the materials but you can avoid the enemies of all: light, heat, and humidity.

To preserve family materials, watch for:

- Light exposure
- Temperature (ideal temperature range 68–72[deg] F)
- Relative humidity (ideal conditions 30–50%)
- Dirt and dust
- Pests
- Chemicals

Questions will also arise about digital items and scanning. Digital photography began to be common in the 1990s and is now the standard. If the images are not printed out, they can be housed on discs, flash drives or the cloud. However, caution the patron that technology ages out and so to maintain the images, migration to the latest technology (at least every 5 years) must always be followed. Warn patrons to keep multiple digital copies in numerous places.

By assisting a researcher in finding, accessing and preserving materials and other resources, we "flesh out" the ancestor and the why and how of the past. For the special collections librarian, preserving the heritage of the community, in this way, can be one of our most important roles. When one looks at good successful special collections departments, connections have been made and relationships formed with people at the local level.

Preservation issues will constantly be transforming as the materials preserved change. Collecting, maintaining, and providing access to historical records entails significant expense with staffing, space and funding issues. State of the art conditions will be beyond the limits of most library budgets but a minimal level of best practices can be accomplished by an informed librarian or archivist. These "best practices" can be easily shared with all researches to enable them to create a lasting legacy. Special Collections librarians, by partnering with researchers in this way, collect and preserve those materials that will democratize interpretation for all. We also promote original scholarship as researchers "plow over new ground." Special Collections librarians recognize that all stories and collections are legitimate parts of an American past and know the importance of opening access to these collections and preserving them for the scholar and family researcher.

Works Cited

Cullingford, Alison. 2014. "Unique and Distinctive Collections: Opportunities for Research Libraries." *RLUK: Research Libraries UK*: 1–52. http://www.rluk.ac.uk/wp-content/uploads/2014/12/RLUK-UDC-Report.pdf.

Donn, Devine. 2001. "Defining Professionalism," in *Professional Genealogy: A Manual for Researchers, Writers, Editors, Lecturers, and Librarians, 10,* Elizabeth Shown Mills, ed. Baltimore: Genealogical Publishing Company.

Fulton, Crystal. 2016. "The Genealogist's Information World: Creating Information in the Pursuit of a Hobby." *Journal of Multidisciplinary Research* 8 (Spring): 85–100.

Gilmore, T. 2010. "A Gentle Reminder to Special Collections Curators." Chronicle of Higher Education. http://www.chronicle.com/article/A-Gentle-Reminder-to/65235/.
Hendry, M. 2015. "Narrating the Past, Enhancing the Present: The Effects of Genealogical Communication on Family Satisfaction." Unpublished thesis, Department of Communication Studies, Texas Christian University, Ft. Worth, Texas.
Tucker, Susan. 2014. "Archival and Genealogical Collections." *Collections: A Journal for Museum and Archives Professionals* 10 (Fall): 408.
Wagner, Richard. 1960. *English Genealogy*. Michigan: Clarendon Press.

EXAMPLES OF ARCHIVAL RESOURCE SUPPLIERS

Conservation Resources International www.conservationresources.com
Gaylord Brothers www.gaylord.com
Hollinger Corporation www.hollingercorp.com
Print File, Inc. www.printfile.com

Beyond Names and Dates on a Tree

How Librarians Can Help Explore Family Heritage and Preservation

Barry L. Stiefel

The pursuit of genealogy has traditionally been the development of a tree diagram decorated with the names and dates of ancestors and other relatives. Some may also write a historical narrative, and in rare instances, even self-publish it. But there is the potential to do so much more with genealogical research materials and skills. Just like each of our own experiences today, the lives of our past family members were immersed in culture and customs, as well as occurred in dynamic historic places and used extraordinary artifacts. In some instances the cultural traditions, things, and places of what our ancestors once experienced are gone, but for others they survive. Because genealogy hobbyists—and they are the majority of people with family history-related inquiries—are frequently not aware that more could be done regarding the safeguarding of their heritage information than the tree diagram, little more happens. Therefore, how can librarians, archivists, and others who work at institutions where historical information pertaining to genealogy is maintained, as well as hired genealogical consultants, help their guests and clients explore broader preservation-related opportunities? Becoming well informed and knowledgeable of opportunities is essential.

Within this essay I will provide guidance to those who wish to assist others who are open to doing more about their family beyond the tree diagram or historical report, especially ascertaining the state of preservation pertaining to cultural traditions, heirlooms, and places (e.g., buildings, neighborhoods, property). For instance, the information gathered through genealogical research can provide additional usefulness for a National Register of Historic Places nomination. My premise is, if one does not take a proactive interest in the preservation of one's heritage, then who will and when?

The Second Conversation

The first conversation between new hobbyists who are just beginning their genealogical exploration and those providing assistance (librarians, archivists, hired researchers, etc.), following greetings and informal pleasantries, usually addresses the basic questions of investigation (i.e., what do you want to know about your family members?) and where to find that information (canvasing the family scrapbooks, interviewing knowledgeable family members, using online databases and social media, tracking down vital records and other primary sources). As the process in response to the first conversation evolves—preferably before it is over, and loses momentum—is a time to have a second conversation pertaining to meaning of information found.

Based on what has been learned, encountered, discovered, and so forth, what does the hobbyist find meaningful and what might they like to do with this information? The creation of a tree diagram and some form of family history narrative are common interests, as well as their duplication and sharing with others, but is there anything more? These are worthwhile conversations within their comfort zone. For example, over the course of the self-discovery process did the hobbyist encounter any heirlooms, places, or cultural traditions that impacted them profoundly in one way or another? If so, what and where? The subject of heritage meaning does not have to be from some distant past either, many generations ago. Indeed, the major premise of historian David Lowenthal magnum opus, as well as title, is that *The Past Is a Foreign Country* (1985), implying that the further back one may go in time the more alien it might seem. Therefore, for most hobbyists, the meaningful aspects of their heritage may be from a more contemporary period—possibly even people or customs that they knew in their lifetime when they were much younger. Indeed, it may be difficult for many hobbyists to find a meaningful heritage association with an object or custom from a far distant past because of the differences in contemporary society from historical ones. For example, the author has not found much personal meaning in the heritage lifestyle of his ancestors from the late sixteenth century, even though he has been able to research his pedigree that far into the past. It is more recent centuries that interest him, starting from the late eighteenth century unto the mid twentieth century. Thus, it is also recommended that librarians, archivists, and professional genealogists reading this essay and with an intent on implementing its recommendations conduct this process on themselves first, if they have not already, so that they also have some applicable experience.

The subsequent sections of this essay are organized according to the following three themes: Preserving Moveable Objects; Preserving Aspects of the Immoveable Built Environment; and You Can't Touch It: The Complexities of Intangible Heritage Preservation. The first section on moveable objects pertains to tangible objects where it is relatively easy to move or take them with you, though they don't necessarily have to fit in your pocket (many families have heirloom automobiles, for instance). The immoveable built environment comprising of those things that cannot be easily moved, such as buildings, large structures, neighborhoods, and landscapes. While there is some overlap in the material conservation of moveable objects with immoveable things and landscapes (wood, metal, ceramics, and so forth are common in both instances) there are different logistical issues and opportunities that need to be considered as well. The last one addresses intangible traditions, which of course, is very different than tangible things or places. Lastly, I shall tie together preserving tangible things (moveable or immoveable) and places and intangible traditions, because often things/places involve some sort of cultural expressions or customs to facilitate meaning, as well as intangible traditions may rely upon things/places as they are observed.

Preserving Moveable Objects

The topic of preserving and maintaining moveable objects that are often described as heirlooms has been well covered in literature in recent decades. Publications include *Tales from the Attic: Practical Advice on Preserving Heirlooms and Collectibles* (Wilson 2002), *Saving Stuff: How to Care for and Preserve Your Collectibles, Heirlooms, and Other Prize Possessions* (Williams and Jaggar 2005), and *Conserving, Preserving, and Restoring Your Heritage* (Kim 2010). Each of these publications takes a different approach to the subject of preserving moveable objects, many of which are encountered during genealogical research and family history sharing. For example, in *Saving Stuff*, a couple of the chapters explore such topics as controlling and maintaining the environment (often inside your home) in order to prevent harm to objects, as well as deciding what things are worth saving and what is expendable so that one is not overly burdened by material possessions. Additional chapters explore the individual circumstances of things such as old photographs and films, toys, children's crafts, kitchenware, furniture, books, collectables (i.e., stamps, coins, etc.), fine art, textiles, musical instruments, and so forth (Williams and Jaggar 2005). This is in contrast to *Conserving, Preserving, and Restoring Your Heritage* where not only such things as books, textiles, and fine art are covered, but Kim takes a materials typological approach through paper, film, wood, bone, plastic, rubber, glass, ceramics, metal, and digital media because the maintenance or preservation treatment of moveable objects is largely based on what they are made of. In each of these instances the authors address heirlooms that are small enough in nature that can be moved by either an individual or a small group of people, such as in the instance of furniture or a large piece of fine art.

Larger objects that often can be relocated by some form of steering, driving, or towing, are sometimes found within families as well, and can have great sentimental value besides that determined by market value. These can include any number of things, but are frequently some form of watercraft (boats, ships, rafts, etc.), motor vehicles (automobiles, motorcycles, recreational vehicles, etc.), or even aircraft (planes, helicopters, etc.). Organizations such as the Historic Naval Ships Association, the Fédération Internationale des Véhicules Anciens (International Federation of Historic Vehicles), and the Vintage Aircraft Association have technical resources available that can be consulted on how to properly maintain and preserve these; as well as address such issues as continued use of them and insurance protection. Moreover, besides the material stewardship of historic watercraft, motor vehicles, and aircraft, these items are sometimes eligible for historic register designation, including the National Register of Historic Places and the relatively new National Historic Vehicle Register (for motor vehicles). The purpose of honoring a historic vehicle or craft is more than just family stewardship; it is also a public history outreach that "will help document historic vehicles as they exist now, preserving their information for future generations." Accordingly, "[i]t is by no means a directive as to how these vehicles should be used and maintained, but rather a chance to take inventory of the historically significant vehicles that are of our history or within our care" (Historic Vehicle Association 2013). If there is a historic heirloom vehicle or craft of some kind in your family that matters to you, consider the further research and heritage documentation in order to have it recognized for purposes of informational posterity.

Preserving Aspects of the Immoveable Built Environment

The National Trust for Historic Preservation has a promotional campaign program called "This Place Matters," which is about "encourage[ing] people to celebrate the places that are meaningful to them and to their communities" (National Trust for Historic Preservation 2017). Family history is often part of community history, and so exploring the two together is a natural outgrowth of a genealogical research project. The goal of the "This Place Matters" is to take photographs of places that matter to you and to share them, for example, through social media. Places that matter are those where old buildings (as well as other structures, or old vehicles or air/water craft) have intrinsic value. They can also serve as reminders and monuments to a place's culture, history, and social complexity. There are many technical resources for finding information on the physical maintenance, preservation, and restoration of historic buildings. Usually, it is best to consult a local historic district commission or board of architectural review near you, if one exists. Other sources include the National Park Service's Preservation Briefs (2017a), which include a variety of treatments from cleaning exterior masonry to repairing decorative ceilings and walls. The state of condition of a historic place can have a significant impact on long-term maintenance costs, market value, as well as consideration for historic registry designation. This type of preservation-related work is very place-based. It will have to be done within or near the locality of where a property is. Attempting to conduct a historic place investigation or nomination project becomes increasingly more difficult the further one is geographically separated.

The primary reasons for wanting to have a place officially designated as historic is because that place matters to the family historian and that the history of that place is also significant to the community, the state, or the country; and thus recognition is desired. Depending on the type of historic designation obtained it could lead to some protection of the place, as well as eligibility for some historic preservation-related financial programs, such as conservation easement tax credits, rehabilitation tax credits, repair loans, etc. Historic registry designation can take place at one or more of three levels—local, state, and national—depending on the locality. Contrary to popular misconception, the most restrictive regulations pertaining to historic property protections are frequently at the local level, in contrast to the state or federal level that are less stringent. Many municipal governments—both urban and rural—have some form of historic preservation or designation program, as well as state governments. The place where one lives as well as the initial history of a place that has been uncovered during the process of genealogical research will, of course, have a bearing on which historic registry one can consider. Also, many historic registry programs require owner consent at the time of designation—so if one is not the property owner, be sure to get permission in writing.

At the national level the most widely used historic registry program is the National Register of Historic Places. Many state- and local-level registry programs also emulate this one. If considering nominating a property to the National Register of Historic Places the first step in this process is to contact your respective State Historic Preservation Office (SHPO); or territory if located in American Samoa, Puerto Rico, U.S. Virgin Islands, Guam, etc.; or Tribal Historic Preservation Office (THPO) if located on a Federally recognized Native American Indian Reservation. In many instances SHPOs/THPOs have a preliminary questionnaire to assist in ascertaining if a property is eligible for the National Register of Historic Places, or a State Register instead, as well as for what historic reasons. The National Conference of State Historic Preservation Officers and the National Association of Tribal Historic Preservation Officers maintain up to date directories of SHPOs (http://ncshpo.org/directory/0) and THPOs (http://nathpo.org/wp/thpos/find-a-thpo/), and SHPOs and THPOs can also direct you to local government historic preservation opportunities.

There are four assessment criteria for property consideration to the National Register of Historic Places:

> **A.** That are associated with events that have made a significant contribution to the broad patterns of our history; or
> **B.** That are associated with the lives of significant persons in our past; or
> **C.** That embody the distinctive characteristics of a type, period, or method of construction, or that represent the work of a master, or that possess high artistic values, or that represent a significant and distinguishable entity whose components may lack individual distinction; or
> **D.** That have yielded or may be likely to yield, information important in history or prehistory [often through archaeological resources] [Sprinkle 2014, 214].

These four assessment criteria are also evaluated for level of integrity (how truthful or authentic is the condition of the place to its period of significance), which is described in great detail within *How to Apply the National Register Criteria for Evaluation*, a bulletin by the National Park Service (1995). As a rule of thumb, it is preferred that places that are being considered for the National Register are at least fifty years of age, though exceptions are made for truly extraordinary places. When a place that matters is more vernacular in design or use, consult the National Park Service Bulletin *Guidelines for Evaluating and Documenting Traditional Cultural Properties* (Park and King 1998). Much of the information found during the genealogical research investigation pertaining to a historic place may be applicable to a preliminary review. If the review is found to be favorable, then additional research may need to be conducted to the full nomination in order to fill in missing gaps on the place's history. Besides the regularly consulted vital records for genealogy, property records (such as chain of title or deeds), a combination of historical images, maps, and other documents may need to be investigated, depending on the property. The genealogists/family historians should see this additional research as an opportunity to further discover the broader context of their family's history. Those working on a property nomination for a local, state, or the National Register of Historic Places should be mindful that the process can often be lengthily due to the various governmental reviews that will take place, so communication with professional staff at the respective government agency and the property owner is encouraged in order to avoid logistical problems, as well as patience.

Another option besides nominating a property for a historical register is simply to conduct what is called a heritage documentation project, especially when unable to find sufficient historical significance. A heritage documentation project is a means of preserving in perpetuity the information and documents found from genealogical- and property-related research for future generations to easily access, so that it is not lost. The grandest type collection is the Historic American Buildings Survey/Historic American Engineering Record/Historic American Landscapes Survey, which is managed by the

National Park Service and the Library of Congress. With contributions from the American people, "[t]he collections document achievements in architecture, engineering, and landscape design in the United States and its territories through a comprehensive range of building types, engineering technologies [including vehicles], and landscapes" (Library of Congress 2017a). The National Park Service (2017b) administers the Standards and Guidelines for what is expected in a heritage documentation project, as well as the contribution process. Many state and local libraries and archives will also accept heritage documentation projects, and thus should also be consulted regarding their quality control expectations.

You Can't Touch It: The Complexities of Intangible Heritage Preservation

Family heritage is more than just things, places, and a family tree chart. It is also about the customs and traditions that help both individuals and family groups form a sense of identity and togetherness. According to UNESCO "[t]he importance of intangible cultural heritage is not the cultural manifestation itself but rather the wealth of knowledge and skills that is transmitted through it from one generation to the next" (2017). While relatively abstract, intangible heritage is also "[t]raditional, contemporary and living at the same time…, inclusive, representative, and community-based" (UNESCO 2017). In respect to the maintenance and continuation of intangible family heritage, the way to do so is through experiential education and communication with younger generations, so that they can continue the traditions. Conveying the relevance, meaning, and significance of intangible customs is also important. According to journalist Daffnee Cohen, "[t]radition remains one of the few practices that truly belongs to your family and close friends, and allows you to cherish the very valuable memories created with your loved ones over the years. While maintaining family tradition is important, it can be a challenging feat with the fast paced and technologically driven world we occupy today" (2015). Since each culture is uniquely different from the other, the manner on the best way to preserve and continue family traditions should be done through the respective culture one identifies with. Reaching out to organizations that specialize in this, or even informal groups, communities, or ethnic-religious congregations, may be the way to provide some assistance and guidance.

For where and when there are circumstances that inhibit the passing on of intangible family traditions to a younger generation, documentation may be considered to create a tangible record for others who may benefit. Both the Library of Congress and the Smithsonian provide opportunities for archiving documented intangible heritage traditions, but they should be consulted first regarding their expectations for quality control, documentation formats, and acceptable content. These include the American Folk Life Center and American Memory Project at the Library of Congress (2017b and 2017c) as well as the Cultural Programs of the Smithsonian's Cultural Centers (the Asian Pacific American Center, Latino Center, Center for Folklife and Cultural Heritage, and Smithsonian Folkways) (Smithsonian 2017). Depending on the state and municipality, state and local libraries, archives, and museums might also be involved in the archiving of documented intangible heritage traditions, and could be considered as well.

Tying It All Together

While a tree chart is informative in understanding familial and biological connections to one another, there is more to appreciating family history. Our ancestors, extended kith and kin, and friends of the past spent their lives using things, residing in and moving around places, as well as had customs and traditions that brought meaning to the relationships they had, the things they used, and where they sojourned. When a genealogist or family historian obtained an understanding of each facet of their heritage—the family tree chart, the preservation of heirlooms, the investigation of places that matter, and the cultural traditions of importance—then one has achieved a panoramic perspective of family heritage and the preservation needs. The process ought to be seen as the objective because as time evolves there is always updating that needs to be conducted. As Jay Robinson of the National Park Service has observed, "Cultural Heritage Preservation keeps cultural practices and identities alive in our memory as a part of what has shaped us as a people and nation. Tangible and intangible cultural heritage are often deeply intertwined and they cannot be fully separated" (2017). Thus, just because each facet has been addressed individually within this essay, the research exploration and preservation-related activities do not have to be done in this way.

When we participate in family traditions, the cultural and social aspect is intangible, but we often use material things while the custom is taking place. For example, we may enjoy a family celebration that uses heirloom recipes, with antique objects, and in a home, house of worship, or garden setting that has hosted such events over many years or generations. Transportation or pilgrimage to and from the event or place may also be part of the experience, and not simply a conduit between points "A" and "B." The objective of going beyond names and dates on a tree is to share both knowledge and meaning with others in one's family—however that might be defined—as well as to package what has been learned in such a way so that others in the future may benefit as well; whether it be family, a community, or some other unforeseen knowledge seeker. Moreover, when others understand why a particular tradition, thing, or place is meaningful and valuable, they are more inclined to respect its importance and continuance.

Works Cited

Cohen, Daffnee. 2015. "Why We Need to Maintain Family Tradition," *Huffington Post*. http://www.huffingtonpost.com/daffnee-cohen/why-we-need-to-maintain-family-tradition_b_6279268.html. Accessed 6 June 2017.

Historic Vehicle Association. 2013. The National Historic Vehicle Register. https://www.historicvehicle.org/national-historic-vehicle-register/. Accessed 5 June 2017.

Kim, Kennis. 2010. *Conserving, Preserving, and Restoring Your Heritage*. Toronto: Dundurn Press.

Library of Congress. 2017a. *Historic American Buildings Survey/Historic American Engineering Record/Historic American Landscapes Survey*. http://www.loc.gov/pictures/collection/hh/. Accessed 6 June 2017.

Library of Congress. 2017b. *The American Folklife Center*. http://www.loc.gov/folklife/index.html. Accessed 6 June 2017.

Library of Congress. 2017c. *American Memory*. http://memory.loc.gov/ammem/index.html. Accessed 6 June 2017.

Lowenthal, David. 1985. *The Past Is a Foreign Country*. Cambridge, UK: Cambridge University Press.

National Association of Tribal Historic Preservation Officers. 2017. *Find a THPO*. http://nathpo.org/wp/thpos/find-a-thpo/. Accessed 6 June 2017.

National Conference of State Historic Preservation Officers. 2017. *Directory*. http://ncshpo.org/directory/. Accessed 6 June 2017.

National Park Service. 1995. *How to Apply the National Register Criteria for Evaluation*. Washington, D.C.: U.S. Department of the Interior, National Park Service.

National Park Service. 2017a. *Preservation Briefs.* https://www.nps.gov/TPS/HOW-TO-PRESERVE/BRIEFS.HTM. Accessed 5 June 2017.

National Park Service. 2017b, *Standards and Guidelines.* https://www.nps.gov/HDP/standards/index.htm. Accessed 6 June 2017.

National Trust for Historic Preservation. 2017. *This Place Matters.* https://savingplaces.org/this-place-matters#.WTWi4I61tXh. Accessed 5 June 2017.

Parker, Patricia L., and Thomas F. King. 1998. *Guidelines for Evaluating and Documenting Traditional Cultural Properties.* Washington, D.C.: U.S. Department of the Interior, National Park Service.

Robinson, Jay. 2017. "Tangible and Intangible Cultural Heritage," National Park Service. https://www.nps.gov/articles/tangible-cultural-heritage.htm. Accessed 6 June 2017.

Smithsonian. 2017. *Cultural Centers.* https://www.si.edu/CulturalPrograms. Accessed 6 June 2017.

Sprinkle, John H, Jr. 2014. *Crafting Preservation Criteria: The National Register of Historic Places and American Historic Preservation.* New York: Routledge.

UNESCO. 2017. *What Is Intangible Cultural Heritage?.* https://ich.unesco.org/en/what-is-intangible-heritage-00003. Accessed 6 June 2017.

Williams, Don, and Louisa Jaggar. 2005. *Saving Stuff: How to Care for and Preserve Your Collectibles, Heirlooms, and Other Prize Possessions.* New York: Fireside.

Wilson, Colleen. 2002. *Tales from the Attic: Practical Advice on Preserving Heirlooms and Collectibles.* Victoria, BC: Royal British Columbia Museum.

Finding Death-Related Records
Strategies for Research

KATHERINE PENNAVARIA
and ROSEMARY L. MESZAROS

Introduction

Family history researchers love trouble. Not for themselves or for anyone living, of course, but they do benefit from the trouble experienced by people in the past. Because quite often, when something bad happens, a genealogically useful record is created. And the worse the trouble, the more interesting the record. Of course, records are created for positive reasons (marriages, baptisms) or neutral ones (census, property transfers). But records created because of trouble are often the most useful and fascinating ones available, and at the top of that "trouble" list is when someone dies.

Most of us feel a natural compassion and empathy for the losses suffered by people in the past. They suffered and grieved when someone close to them died, just as we do. But the cause of their grief gives researchers some valuable records to study. And the more dramatic the death, the more records there are. If an 86-year-old man dies of heart disease at his residence, the event will be noted most likely by a death certificate, an obituary, and a grave marker. But if a 23-year-old woman is found dead under mysterious circumstances in a field, that death also triggers newspaper accounts and inquest/autopsy reports.

Death-related records are all over the place—literally. The thousands of cemeteries in the United States are blanketed by memorial markers and stones, which serve not only as personal memorials at the time of burial but as genealogical records that can be studied hundreds of years later. Online, one can find death-related records by the millions on Ancestry and FamilySearch (the online presence of the Family History Library in Salt Lake City). Obituaries have for decades been published in newspapers that are now possible to access through subscription services such as Newspapers.com, NewspaperArchive, and GenealogyBank. And many more records connected to death are available offline—by special request in person, electronic order, or through the mail. Some of these records require time at a microfilm reader; others are in private family papers.

Librarians working with patrons doing family history research can offer those researchers the following information and strategies about death records.

Death Record Types

Death records are useful for many reasons, but especially because they are the most recent documents created in a person's life. Here are some of the most useful and accessible types:

Death Certificates

Official records of death are part of a larger category called "vital" records, which are, for the most part, created and maintained at the state or county level. The three vital records types (birth, marriage, death) are sometimes humorously designated by genealogists as "hatch, match, and dispatch" records. Death certificates created in the past few decades usually contain the full name of the deceased; the date, time, and location of death; the deceased's last address and occupation; and a physician's assessment of the cause of death. Usually they also indicate whether an autopsy was performed, and the burial/interment/cremation plans. Prior to the mid–20th century, less information was given. The earliest certificates in the United States contained the bare minimum of information (usually the deceased's name and age plus the date and place of death). In most states, death certificates filled out by a physician were not required by law until around the start of the 20th century. Researchers should be reminded that records of births, marriages, and deaths have long been kept by churches as well as civil institutions. Ancestry and FamilySearch both offer extensive collections of church records of these events.

They should also be reminded that a death certificate is excellent testimony to only *some* of the facts contained in it. Any details not immediately observable (time, place, and cause of death) must come from an informant, who is usually a family member. That person might or might not have accurate information about the date and place of birth for the deceased, so information other than that relating to the death itself should be viewed cautiously. In other words, a death certificate provides primary (firsthand) information for the date and place of death, but only secondary (secondhand) information for earlier events.

Obituaries

Who doesn't love (and deserve) a well-written obituary? These newspaper notices of community deaths have been around for centuries; the detailed entries we're all familiar with today were preceded by simple lists of people recently deceased. Remind patrons that the information in obituaries does not usually come from an official source, but from family members. Family grudges can lead to individuals being slighted in the list of survivors, and other information might be incorrect as well.

Funeral Notices

Like obituaries, these notices are the province of community newspapers, and often appear as a separate listing from the obituary. The information usually comes from funeral homes.

Memorial Notices

Families sometimes place memorial statements in the classified ads area of a newspaper for years after a loved one dies. If researchers can't find an obit, suggest that they check the paper for a possible memorial notice the following year on the date of death, or even five/ten years after.

Funeral Home Records

Usually not accessible, because funeral homes are private companies, but some record sets have been photographed and microfilmed by the Family History Library.

Inquest Proceedings

An inquest is a jury trial convened by a judge to establish the means by which a person died, if the cause cannot be determined by a physician or coroner. The jury's charge: to weigh evidence and interview witnesses, and then declare whether the individual's death was accidental, suicidal, or homicidal. Many counties make older inquest records available upon request; start with the specific location where the death occurred and find out whether the inquest files are kept locally or have been transferred to state archives. The best clue to whether or not an inquest was performed is usually the death certificate, in the "cause of death" section.

Coroner's Autopsy Reports

Usually done when a death is suspicious, but no inquest is held. Availability varies by municipality, and there is no standard form. The researcher who manages to get a copy of an autopsy report will probably need a medically trained person to interpret it.

Probate Proceedings

Probate is triggered when a person dies, so that any inheritable property can be passed on to the legal heirs. Many probate records have details about the person's death.

Funeral Bills and Receipts

Quite often preserved among family papers, along with other ephemera such as memorial service cards and programs.

Burial Deeds

When you buy a cemetery plot, you are literally buying a (tiny) piece of land, so the transaction is governed by real-estate laws. It's now your property, although the cemetery retains the right to determine how the space is used. Families investing in a multi-space plot almost always keep the deeds and certificates issued by the cemetery, because eventually someone else will need to go into the space. Often these deeds are with other important family papers.

Cemetery Records

Cemetery records are private—they belong to the corporate entity that owns the cemetery. As such, researchers have no "right" to see those records, but most cemetery offices have a procedure in place for helping people find graves. See below for suggestions about researching on cemetery grounds.

Gravestones

Some cemeteries contain gravestones so whimsical and artful that they have become tourist attractions. Most, however, just stick with the facts. Whatever the inscription and however well (or not) preserved, remind patrons that a grave marker should be treated with care (i.e., no rubbings or manipulation of them, which can cause damage).

Finding Death Records Online

Ancestry (www.ancestry.com)

This essential resource for family history researchers is the best place to start looking for death-related records. In addition to national-level and state/county-specific indexes, Ancestry also offers, for some locations, images of death certificates, church burial records, and several other record types. Best of all, the search interface is easy to use; searches can be limited to death-related records with just a few clicks. Most public libraries offer on-site access through their institutional subscription; patrons should be reminded, however, that a personal subscription offers them far more, including the ability to create a "tree" using proprietary software (other companies offer excellent tree builder software without the extensive database access; e.g., MyHeritage, Legacy Family Tree, and Root-Magic). Point curious patrons to library.si.edu/sites/default/files/tutorial/pdf/ancestry-library-edition-and-ancestry-com-comparison.pdf for a detailed comparison between the library edition and a personal subscription.

There is no national index for deaths apart from the well-known Social Security Death Index (SSDI), and that covers only people (a) who had a Social Security number, and (b) whose death was reported to the Social Security Administration. So people whose work career and/or death occurred before the mid–1930s will not be represented; in fact, most of the entries are for people who died in the past few decades. The SSDI contains around 90 million names, and includes around 400,000 railroad retirement records (after 1935, railroad employees had a separate Social Security–like retirement plan).

SSDI entries usually contain the deceased person's first name and surname, birth and death dates, Social Security number, the state where that SSN was issued, and last known residence. But—a few caveats to pass along:

(1) SSDI records are *extracts*, not original sources for any of the information. The database contains errors, as any database does, because it resulted from data entry. It is not a primary source for birth information or the spelling of names.

(2) The deceased's last residence does not equal "place where person died." Official death location is established by the death certificate.

The SSDI is available in Ancestry and also through FamilySearch, which is free to access.

A few years ago, Ancestry added a companion index to the SSDI, called the "U.S., Social Security Applications and Claims Index, 1936–2007." Entries often include parents' names and birth place, as well as other names used by the individual. Since it specifically covers claims, it often includes people whose deaths were not reported or not included in the SSDI. A search on death records should pull up both indexes. Like the SSDI, this database consists of extracted information, not original records.

FamilySearch (www.familysearch.org)

What's not to like about a free resource that offers millions of original records? For several decades, the Family History Library in Salt Lake City has been collecting genealogically relevant records and putting them on microfilm. Those microfilms are slowly but steadily being digitized (completion is scheduled for the end of 2020) and made available to anyone who signs up for a free account. In other words, the FHL is giving away access to records that Ancestry and other sites charge to see. All family history researchers need both Ancestry and FamilySearch. Their offerings overlap on many record sets (the federal census, the SSDI, national draft registration cards), but each has record sets the other does not.

Where FamilySearch leaves Ancestry in the dust is with non–U.S. records—they have lots more, and (once again) are giving them away whereas Ancestry charges extra for an "international" subscription. If you have genealogy patrons who have reached the immigrant generation for the families they are researching and they need to "jump the pond," then the Family History Library catalog is the best place to go. Tell them to forget about going to other countries to do research—they won't get access to original records or have even a fraction of the time needed to study them.

The Family History Library catalog, available at FamilySearch, offers the option to search by location; results will show what records are already available digitally, which are still on microfilm only or are held only in print form (and thus accessible only on site at the FHL in Salt Lake City). The Family History Library has records from just about every country in the world, though some locations are better represented than others. The difference in holdings reflects the difference in opportunity to photograph records. If the local authorities refused permission, then the FHL did not collect the records.

The key for the researcher pursuing non–U.S. familial history is identifying the specific town or city someone lived in prior to settling in the U.S.—that information might have been passed down orally within a family, it might be written in private papers, or it might be represented in preserved correspondence. That crucial detail can also be found on some official documents as well, such as the declaration of intent to become a citizen, a passport application, and a draft registration. Death certificates might contain that place name, if a knowledgeable family member was asked for it.

Bottom line: To research deaths and other lifetime events in a family's U.S. history, patrons should make use of these two powerhouse resources side-by-side, making sure to focus on state and county-specific indexes as well as national-level ones. Then, before they spend money on Ancestry's "international" option, encourage them to explore the Family History Library's vast holdings of international records.

Newspapers

Of primary interest to family history researchers are actual name mentions in a newspaper: obituaries, engagement and marriage announcements, birth announcements, news about military activity, hospital admissions and releases, police reports, car accidents, and so on. Real estate transactions and legal proceedings required to be published in newspapers give a glimpse into who sold what property to whom, who had not paid their taxes, and who was notified in the case of probate. In general, the smaller the place, the more newsworthy each person's actions were. Items reported in a small-town paper (visits abroad, anniversary parties) did not usually appear in big-city publications.

Something patrons might not know: newspaper items (including obituaries) are not public records and citizens have no special right to see them. Instead, newspaper archives are made available at the publisher's discretion. This elusive record type has become a big business online, and today's researchers have unprecedented access, usually through subscription sites. One major free source for older local newspapers is the Library of Congress's *Chronicling America: Historic American Newspapers* (chroniclingamerica.loc.gov), with about 7 million historic newspapers available.

It is always worth checking to see if a small town or city has digitized its papers and made them available online. Some localities are following the Library of Congress model and digitizing their newspapers going back to the beginning—in many cases, access is free with registration.

Several subscription sites—chiefly NewspaperArchive, GenealogyBank, and Newspapers.com—offer access to newspapers and are worth exploring, and Ancestry provides partial access to more than a thousand historic publications. One resource sometimes overlooked is the ProQuest Historical Newspapers database, accessible through library subscription. This resource offers the full text of many city papers; researchers with ancestors in New York, Washington, D.C., Chicago, and Los Angeles, among other places, will benefit from tracking down a subscriber library and arranging access through the Friends of the Library or guest program.

For genealogists, obituaries are often the most sought-after newspaper items. Recent obituary extracts are available at several sites, but original publication images (the gold standard) are harder to come by. For recent notices, Ancestry has its "United States Obituary Collection"; for a wider date range and more comprehensive geographical spread, individuals can access "America's Obituaries and Death Notices," a NewsBank product offered through library subscription. Also, GenealogyBank subscribers can search for older obits through the "Historical Obituaries" option. One major free source for recent obits (extracts only) is Legacy.com's ObitFinder, a trademarked searching tool that covers more than 1,000 newspapers in the United States and Canada. Searching is free, but access to some documents requires payment.

Find a Grave (www.findagrave.com)

Cemeteries contain genealogical records literally by the acre, and Find a Grave offers the best way to access them without an actual visit. Find a Grave contains around 160 million entries (called "memorials"), and thousands are added daily. Ancestry now owns the site, but it is still free and open to the public through direct access. Think of Find a

Grave as Wikipedia for death information—submitted and corrected by users themselves, but with links to primary information sources.

Here's how it works: All across the country—and increasingly across the globe as well—volunteers visit cemeteries and photograph or record tombstone information, then upload that data. Interment records are also added by genealogical societies or from the records of institutions such as the U.S. Veterans Affairs Department.

Information available nowhere else can be obtained here for no cost or registration (an account is necessary only to create records and post messages). Most memorials indicate, at minimum, the location of a burial, but usually contain dates as well, and many who submit data supply photographs of the burial site. Any memorial can potentially contain photographs of the individual, other uploaded documents, and transcriptions of other records. Each memorial is managed by its creator unless management is transferred to someone else.

Researchers can search across the entire database, within a state or county, or within a particular cemetery. The tombstone photographs are especially valuable, because they provide verifiable evidence of death and burial; if a memorial has no tombstone photo, the user can submit a request for one to be taken by a volunteer who lives near the cemetery. There are other free burial site databases available worth checking as well: BillionGraves and Interment.net are two.

Finding Death Records Offline

Library patrons will always need to be reminded that what's available online does not represent all the records necessary to carry out a family history research project. Far from it. In fact, the farther back one goes, the less likely it is that the records needed to prove location and kinship connections will be available in digital form. But online info can often help researchers understand what is not online. One unique site does just that: "Online Searchable Death Indexes and Records: A Genealogy Guide" (www.deathindexes.com). The site's offerings are not limited to death indexes—there are links to online obituary resources, burials, probate records, and death certificates (where available) as well. The site is clean and well organized, and supported by almost invisible ads from Ancestry. The links are mostly to online resources, but (and here is the important bit) some of them point to location-specific resources for ordering vital records that are not online.

Cemeteries

Most people today rarely visit cemeteries, but for many families, such visits were once a normal part of their routine, especially on holidays. Decades ago, people tended to make a day of it, bringing a picnic lunch along with their sunhats and floral arrangements.

Cemeteries have always attracted genealogists because the stones are lasting testimonials to those who have passed. People once made a hobby of gravestone rubbing—making an image on paper of something carved into stone, by rubbing charcoal, wax, or graphite over the paper while it is pressed against a stone—but the practice has become rare with the advent of digital photography, and because it potentially damages the stones.

Doing field research on cemetery grounds is practically inevitable for the genealogist who desires to be thorough, but it requires some preparation. Remind patrons considering cemetery research that cemeteries were not set up to facilitate research, and that cemetery records are usually private, not public—access is determined by the record-holders. Before those researchers go wandering among the headstones, they will want to establish the exact burial location for everyone on their list. The first stop inside the cemetery should be the office. Cemeteries grounds are usually organized by section, then by block (or row), and then by grave. Most of the time, the burial records held by the office are precise and match the labeling done out on the grounds. The older a cemetery is, however, the less likely it is that the blocks and graves will be labeled effectively. Finding crypts and mausoleum burials (as opposed to in-ground burials) is usually easier, though the plaques labeling each interment unit almost always contain far less information than a traditional grave marker.

Responses from cemetery office personnel vary widely, and researchers will sometimes encounter resistance to looking up long lists of names. Some administrators have made their records searchable at on-site stations, but others require interaction with a desk clerk. If the latter occurs, researchers should be advised to watch the clerk carefully. Maybe the clerk will sit down at a computer, but just maybe he or she will pull down some heavy, interesting-looking volumes called *platbooks*—the term comes from geographical mapping and is connected to the fact that burial plots are sold as real estate (an exact map of the boundaries for real estate plots is required by law). The gold standard for time spent at a cemetery office is a photo of the platbook page showing the burial location being inquired after. The researcher should always ask, "Can I please photograph that page?" If the clerk says no, they should go back later when someone else is staffing the desk and ask again. Even if permission is not given to photograph the platbook, the clerk should be asked to note the location on a map of the cemetery. A blank map of the cemetery grounds should also be obtained, so it can be scanned later. Then it can be used to create a customized map of all the burials for a particular family.

To help patrons prepare cemetery research, check to see if the place has a website or is part of a site that lists the area's burial grounds. If you find online information, note down the cemetery's hours, parking availability, the nearest entrance to the office building, and where the nearest restrooms are. Most cemeteries close well before dark. Researchers should make a printed list of names that they want to look up, and bring along some additional note-taking supplies. Remind them to wear sturdy shoes—cemeteries do not usually have walkways or smooth paths along the rows, and the ground can be treacherously uneven. Other essential cemetery research supplies: water, a hat, sunscreen and, of course, a camera. For researchers planning to visit cemeteries with older graves, tell them to bring along gardening gloves and something to trim away the grass that has most likely overgrown the stones (that happens especially with the ones that lie flat).

Cemetery searching can be frustrating and rewarding at the same time. One can spend hours searching for graves without success and then find another one right away. If the researcher persists, the hours of effort will be rewarded with data for particular individuals and also a sense of connection with long-gone family members, some of whom might have been previously unknown.

Conclusion

Death-related records are merely one type among many that are essential for family history research, and should always be used appropriately. If you are assisting genealogy patrons and the issue of death certificates comes up, remind them that they should not assume that these certificates contain accurate birth information, and that they should pay close attention to cause of death, and whether an autopsy was performed or an inquest held. All researchers should use online sources, but to do thorough research, they must not stop there—they should track down the ordering information for vital records not yet digitized, and get out among the tombstones if they can. And above all, library genealogy patrons should be encouraged to share the information they discover with other researchers by creating memorials in Find a Grave and linking documents to their posted family trees.

Genealogy Literacy

Helping Patrons Build Stable Trees Through Information Literacy Standards

Cheri J. Daniels

Today's genealogy patron can be hard to size up for reference assistance. The reference interview itself is usually too brief to get a complete understanding of their skill level, desired research outcomes, or even the question itself. These challenges appear due to the broad spectrum of genealogy research and inquiry that we lump together in the hopes of hitting an answer target. With the proliferation of new genealogists beginning their journey on the internet, we are forced into a quagmire of false expectations of instant gratification, flashy marketing coated with unrealistic promises, DNA testing, and a flood of fictitious family trees. The goal of this essay is to identify the various types of genealogy patrons you will encounter, followed by a Genealogy Literacy reference plan that combines the competency standards of Information Literacy with the Genealogical Proof Standard.

Background

This Genealogy Literacy reference plan of assistance and guidance was born when I first implemented this structure for my library staff, and later shared at our state library association conference in 2014. This concept was directly related to a shift in patron assistance. After eleven years on library staff with a University that served a student population of over thirty thousand, the atmosphere of critical thinking and source analysis had been firmly engrained in my reference strategy. Within that decade, Information Literacy standards provided the foundation of instruction and inquiry. All of our instructional interactions with the students were now based on this approach that helped them evaluate the legitimacy or bias of the information they were gathering, as well as how to produce an end product that demonstrated understanding with a well-sourced foundation. My shift in career took me to a state historical society that houses the largest genealogy collection in the state. With a book collection of over ninety thousand, and an archival holdings area of over two thousand square feet, the clear majority of our patrons are in the pursuit of ancestors. As the Head of Reference Services, it has been my duty, as well as challenge, to not only instruct these researchers regarding sound methodology, but to introduce an element of reason and analysis at every opportunity. By implementing a Genealogy Literacy reference plan, the patron reference experience has become more efficient, balanced and comprehensive.

Information Literacy

Despite our increasing information challenges of the 21st century, Information Literacy is not a new concept. The term was first coined in a 1974 report from the National Commission on Libraries and Information Science. According to this report, people known as "information literates" had mastered "techniques and skills for utilizing the wide range of information tools as well as primary sources in molding information solutions to their problems" (Zurkowski 1974, 6). The goal of this report was to urge the creation of a national program that would "achieve information literacy by 1984" (Zurkowski 1974, ERIC abstract). In 1989, the American Library Association's Presidential Committee on Information Literacy defined information literacy as a set of abilities that would allow the learner to "recognize when information is needed and have the ability to locate, evaluate, and use effectively the needed information" (1989). By the turn of the current century, this approach to research methodology was gaining huge momentum, specifically within the education parameters. The technology explosion and its following influx of information fueled the creation of a set of *Information Literacy Competency Standards for Higher Education* in 2000. This same explosion of technology and information both revolutionized and forever altered the approach to genealogical pursuits. With the fundamental goal of Information Literacy focused on creating "lifelong learners" dedicated to evaluating information they encounter, these standards are easily adapted to assist genealogy patrons (American Library Association 2000, 4):

> the ability to seek, find, and decipher information can be applied to countless life decisions, whether financial, medical, educational, or technical.... An informed and educated citizenry is essential to the functioning of our modern democratic society [United States President, 2009].

While the Competency Standards of 2000 were developed for Higher Education, they reiterate a need for developing "informed citizens and community members" (American Library Association 2000, 4). In simplified format, these standards are as follows:

- **Determine** the extent of information needed
- **Access** the needed information effectively and efficiently
- **Evaluate** information and its sources critically and incorporate selected information into one's knowledge base
- **Use** information effectively to accomplish a specific purpose
- **Understand** the economic, legal, and social issues surrounding the use of information, and access and use information ethically and legally

Genealogical Motivations

Above all of the common motivations, two dominant questions lie at the heart of the genealogical pursuit: "How do we know what we KNOW; and how do we KNOW what we know?" (Durie 2017, 4).

> Genealogy, in short, is first and foremost a way of thinking. Indeed, thinking genealogically is one of the distinctive characteristics of human cognition. As the very objects of our genealogical imagination, ancestors and relatives therefore deserve a prominent place among the foundational pillars of the human condition [Zerubavel 2012, 131].

Researching and discovering the unknown is a fundamental delight among all genealogists. Those who are in pursuit of their own lineage, as opposed to those who research for clients, are even more delighted by this discovery because it reveals something about them. When attempting to help genealogists, the main thing to remember is that they take this endeavor very seriously. They can become extremely passionate about their research, because it's inherently very personal.

On a more individual level, some of the motivations behind genealogical inquiry include:

- Who am I?—Sense of family: charting ancestors, or adoptees attempting to connect, DNA cousins and ethnicities
- Sense of place: Understanding their family's role in history or the community
- Leaving a legacy: Preserving their family's historical identity for future generations
- Building memorial: Honoring their ancestors, or recently passed loved ones—death in the family can be a watershed moment that sparks the genealogical journey
- Health concerns: Some embark due to a troubling family medical history (Case 2008)
- Connecting to celebrity: Finding famous people in the family tree—or being able to boast that their ancestry is illustrious, stretching back to royalty or historically respected characters—sometimes in the hopes of joining a lineage society
- Tradition: Carrying on research from a family member that has passed, or taking the tree farther back—with each generation, a new genealogist
- Curiosity: Sorting out that wild family story passed down over the years

How Did We Get Here?

With the development of internet resources, such as Ancestry.com, Family Search, Find a Grave, RootsWeb, etc., the amount of information shared online revolutionized the genealogy field. No longer was the pursuit of lineage reserved for the elite, but now open to all as "self-understanding superseded self-assertion (Weil 2013, 181). From the early days of internet genealogy, the information being shared was in the form of transcribed records and shared family trees, developed and maintained by volunteers. Despite a lack of original images, users were beginning to be swayed by a form of instant genealogy gratification. In 1999, the television series *Frasier* aired an episode called *A Tsar Is Born*. In this episode, Frasier and his brother Niles are attempting to connect a Russian clock that had belonged to the Romanov family back to their own family tree. In order to accomplish this connection, they decide to look into their family history, excitedly declaring: "Just a few hours on the internet, a trip to the library, we could sketch in the entire family tree!" (Hauck 1999). Even though online research was still in its childhood, the seed had taken root and from there, the impression of an instant family tree had solidified in our psyche.

With the development of digitization programs, images made their way to the forefront, making users aware of the need to see original documents. Sadly, as these image repositories have continued to grow, the statistically large number of images available has deceived many into believing that the majority of records are now online. Unfortunately, this is way off the mark, and what they see is only a fraction of the records available in libraries and archives around the world. Which means, when advising the patron, we have an uphill battle against the record romance of the internet and the expensive marketing that tells them that one subscription will provide the means to fill in their entire family tree.

Typecasting: Who Is Coming to Your Reference Desk?

Despite the common foundational concept of hunting down ancestors, "the reasons why genealogists explore family histories and their contexts are as varied as the individuals concerned" (Durie 2017, 3). When encountering genealogists in the library, it may be helpful to get a sense of their varied backgrounds to better serve their research needs.

Traditional Genealogists. These patrons are usually very focused in their research goals. They are visiting in the hopes of finding that piece of written/printed information that can help. Technology is not foreign to them, but is regarded as another tool; they prefer published lineages or transcribed records from official organizations. They could be advanced hobbyists, or professionals.

Ancestry.com Groupies. These patrons might actually skip your reference desk, opting instead for a computer terminal to take full advantage of your Ancestry.com Library Edition subscription. They have completely bought into the marketing message that tells them their family tree can be found here, and they needn't look anywhere else. This group is the hardest to engage because, while they are proficient with Ancestry, they aren't always willing to learn about other sites or discuss the need for analyzing the information found within the Ancestry gold mine. Print sources are not on their radar, and they will not be interested in your catalog. Sadly, the number of genealogy-focused TV shows out there that simplify the research process in order to produce a sensational reveal at the end have fostered the growth of this patron type.

Techno-Junkies. Very closely related to the Ancestry devotees above, their horizons are a tad broader in the fact that they can navigate many different sites in all of their complexity. They are firm believers that everything they need is online, and are adept at hunting out free sites with needed content. However, as much as they relish the online hunt, many in this group are not big fans of subscription databases. They believe all of the records online should be available for free due to their original creation as government records—failing to understand the cost associated with digitizing documents. They are comfortable recording their research in genealogy software, but citing their sources can be hit or miss.

Family Historians. These patrons navigate both print and digital sources well. Their motivation lies in understanding the historical world in which their ancestors lived. They are fairly well versed in citation standards, but still learning. The positive characteristic of this group is their willingness to take time with the historical context, and as a result, they usually discover valuable supplemental documents, often in your archival collections.

Social Media Addicts. These patrons use all tools at their disposal, leaning heavily on the social community for assistance. They love sharing what they discover, across many social media platforms, and monitor current trends. Conferences and the social nature of these events inspire and excite them. Usually, one driving force behind them is the trend toward family connections—sharing what they have with distant cousins via Social Media tools. DNA is widely embraced by this group, and some have become something of genetic genealogy evangelists. Standard research skills can vary widely with this group.

Educators. These patrons are at the top of the genealogical field. Usually professionals or certified genealogists that teach or write regularly on the subject. *Evidence Explained* by Elizabeth Shown Mills is their citation Bible, and the Genealogical Proof Standard is the only legitimate research method. While their research skills are highly advanced, their technology skills can be hit or miss. Do not assume that their credentials or apparent research organization means that they will know all about your catalog, or even the wonderful databases out there that can help with their research. However, they are very receptive to resource suggestions.

Lineage Society Members or Potential Members. Sadly, these patrons can be the most demanding with little to no understanding of the necessary research process. If you are lucky, the lineage society member contacting you for information is a genealogy-educated registrar or historian, attempting to help a potential member fulfill their requirements. If you are unlucky, the person contacting you will be the potential member who is trying to confirm their descent from a qualifying ancestor, on their own. I have actually had this patron group demand that we create some sort of document in our state capacity, verifying the birth or parentage of an ancestor, especially when an original document does not exist.

Clueless. These patrons have no concept of the term "genealogy." Perhaps they have seen an exciting episode of *Who Do You Think You Are?*, and want to delve into their own family history. Sometimes, the death of a loved one, advanced age, or physical illness can spark the desperate search to know more. Either way, they are looking for quick gratification. Original records confuse them, because they just want to know what it means. They often have no interest in the research process, nor in the recording process. If they can see a Find a Grave memorial, or an Ancestry family tree, they are usually very happy. Unless, of course, they are searching for that elusive grandmother who happened to be a long lost Indian Princess.

Genealogy Reference

With all of this complexity for one patron group, how do we meet their wide range of needs? Professional development for staff in the area of genealogy is a safe investment. By spending a little time and budget funds on current webinars, local genealogy presentations, and perhaps national or regional conferences, libraries can keep up to date with current trends in the field. This will also help with collection development for your print sources, as well as the difficult database choices made each year. Databases remain one of the most expensive consumers of collection development dollars, simply because they change and fluctuate with popularity.

Another challenge you will face is keeping your diverse genealogy patron base up to date on the changes you make. While some embrace the trends and new software, others will dig their heels in and object to the changes. You will not be able to satisfy all of the varied opinions that come with change, but this is where your genealogy literacy plan comes into play. By applying information literacy standards to genealogical pursuits, you can help them conduct more solid research, as well as provide a voice of reason that cuts through the marketing hype.

Tip: Prior to reading the below Information Literacy applications, be sure to supplement your collection with titles about the Genealogical Proof Standard (GPS). Similarly, this standard also contains five steps followed by professional genealogists. By incorporating the GPS into IL standards, you are naturally assisting genealogy patrons with field standards and language that will help guide them in a responsible methodology.

IL Standard—Define/Determine

Begin with the standard reference interview already in place. Train staff in the art of leading the patron to key words that help them formulate a single question. Streamline term usage by repeating to the patron what is needed based on correct terms to simplify the inquiry.

Tools of the Trade. Terms should be repeated often in reference interviews, training sessions, and information sheets or libguides. This is when professional development regarding genealogy processes and resources will help in narrowing down the needed information to formulate the question and identify the corresponding resource. Feature a new genealogy term each month for staff and patrons: post it, and tie it into programming so that everyone is on the same page.

Corresponding Genealogical Proof Standard: Conducting a "reasonably exhaustive search in reliable sources for all information that is or may be pertinent … to the situation in question." (Board for Certification of Genealogists 2000, 1)

IL Standards—Access

Reinforce staff's consistent effort to help patrons access and use the correct resource, which is related to teaching them to fish. Be quick to make them aware of your catalog and databases and how to use them. Point out reliable databases and print sources, which help guide them to reliable information.

A note on navigating access: Navigating changes can result in choppy seas. Changes in resources or development of tech features happen pretty frequently among genealogy databases. It is very helpful for staff and programming efforts to stay abreast of these changes.

Corresponding Genealogical Proof Standard. Backing up the research with complete and accurate citations to assist others in accessing the original source used.

IL Standards—Evaluate

By far, this is the most difficult challenge when serving genealogists. Even though you may have just pointed them to Ancestry.com as a reliable source, you have to keep this IL standard in mind. Do not forget that Ancestry is full of trees that have little to no citations, or are full of wrong information. You will be fighting the false impression that the trees contain reliable information. Constantly ask patrons about authorship of the resource they are using. What sources are attached to this tree? How did they reach their conclusion? What bias may be included? It is usually in this part of the assistance that you refer the patron to the Genealogical Proof Standard. It's a great way to let them know you understand their research needs, as well as demonstrating an understanding of the responsibility of reliable information for their research.

The GPS will also provide an authoritative source to help with the argument for citations and the difficulty of proof. Make sure your staff is fluent in the definition of primary versus secondary information or sources. This concept is vital to assisting patrons produce well-sourced genealogies. Note that I used both "information" and "sources." In genealogical study, the standard is to differentiate between primary and secondary information. The history and education fields prefer primary and secondary sources. Just be aware that a genealogist may try to correct you if you use the word "sources," but you are perfectly within your right to do so, explaining your preference for education or history standards.

Corresponding Genealogical Proof Standard. Analyzing and correlating the "collected information to assess its quality as evidence." (Board for Certification of Genealogists 2000, 1)

IL Standards—Use

Once they have determined that they have collected legitimate pieces of information, they must be organized into citations. Only with proper citations can the research be followed by subsequent generations. For the genealogist, *Evidence Explained* by Elizabeth Shown Mills, is the standard citation formatting guide. It is large and thorough, with its foundation in the *Chicago Manual of Style* (Mills, 2017). However, EE can be intimidating, and I often remind new researchers that it is not mandatory to use Mills' style guide. As long as they are consistent with their usage, they are encouraged to pick a comfortable style early on, and stick with it. Other possibilities include: Chicago, MLA, Turabian, etc.

Corresponding Genealogical Proof Standard. Conflicting pieces of evidence are analyzed and resolved. One way we do this is by citing correctly each piece, with the majority of documents leaning toward a certain truth.

IL Standards—Understand

After citing the sources, a narrative should emerge. Sometimes that narrative may not yield the expected result. Understanding may need to come in the form of additional research to learn more about the context of the information they have uncovered. We must also remind them that information collected and cited can still fall under copyright restrictions, and a responsibility lies in adhering to these laws. Putting the pieces together into a coherent argument or conclusion is a big goal of the entire GPS. Understanding goes hand in hand with the last corresponding Genealogical Proof Standard: writing a proof argument.

Corresponding Genealogical Proof Standard. Arriving at a well reasoned, "coherently written conclusion" (Board for Certification of Genealogists 2000, 2). One that supports the "answer" to the original question (Jones 2013, 3).

Performance Indicators and Outcomes

Within each IL competency standard, a set of performance indicators exists to monitor student literacy and progress. In order to simplify this process, the list below is an adaptation to help with monitoring your patrons' progress as well as your staff's implementation.

- Evaluate patrons' behaviors; make note of the questions they are asking on a regular basis; determine how your staff help streamline question formulation using correct terminology.
- Assess needs and progress. Are patrons finding what they need, or are they leaving very frustrated? Are researchers stuck in one area, or do they exhibit progress? Fluency in resource information systems remains a goal.
- Encourage review of current research. By re-evaluating their past research, patrons may uncover errors, or, with an additional set of eyes, an entirely different research path may appear. If staffing permits, this is a great way to help struggling patrons, it forces them to slow down and look more closely at the evidence.
- Continue to shape programming around the standards. By using the Genealogical Proof Standard as your skeletal Information Literacy framework, you are teaching patrons responsible methodology that will result in sound genealogies.
- Keep abreast of the changing landscape. What are genealogists talking about or what needs and issues are coming to light? Social media groups can help with this; use Twitter chats, free webinars, RootsTech conference sessions (free online), Facebook groups, local meetings.

Overarching Goal

In 2016, the Association of College and Research Libraries voted to reevaluate the approach to Information Literacy, thereby abandoning the competency standards. This move made the structure more inquiry-heavy to focus on students' understanding of where information comes from. Gone are the simple five steps. In their place is a multi-step framework involving IL pedagogy. With the rapid nature of reference service, minus any long-term classroom approach, the 2000–2016 standards are easy to implement, and correspond wonderfully with the five-step Genealogical Proof Standard. Our goal remains focused on creating lifelong learners through this Genealogy Literacy plan. It is wise to remember that genealogy patrons are unique in resources, methodology, and challenges, but they are not unique in the process necessary to help them reach their learning goals.

WORKS CITED

American Library Association Presidential Committee on Information Literacy. 1989. *Final Report.* Report. ERIC document reproduction service no. ED315074. Chicago: American Library Association.

The Association of College and Research Libraries. 2000. *The Information Literacy Competency Standards for Higher Education.* Chicago: American Library Association. http://www.ala.org/acrl/standards/informationliteracycompetency.

Board for Certification of Genealogists. 2000. *The BCG Genealogical Standards Manual.* Orem, UT: Ancestry Pub.

Case, Donald O. 2008. "Collection of Family Health Histories: The Link Between Genealogy and Public Health." *Journal of the American Society for Information Science and Technology* 59(14): 2312–319.

Durie, Bruce. 2017. "What Is Genealogy? Philosophy, Education, Motivations and Future Prospects." *Genealogy* 1(1): 4. http://www.mdpi.com/2313-5778/1/1/4/htm.

Frasier. By Charlie Hauck. Performed by Kelsey Grammer. Television Sitcom. Episode 77: *A Tsar Is Born.* United States: Paramount/NBC, 1999.

Jones, Thomas W. 2013. *Mastering Genealogical Proof.* Arlington, VA: National Genealogical Society.

Mills, Elizabeth Shown. 2017. *Evidence Explained: Citing History Sources from Artifacts to Cyberspace*, 3rd edition. Baltimore: Genealogical Publishing.

United States. National Commission on Libraries and Information Science. National Program for Library and Information Services. 1974. *The Information Service Environment Relationships and Priorities. Related Paper No. 5.* By Paul G. Zurkowski. NCLIS-NPLIS-5. Washington, D.C. ED100391.

United States. President of the United States. Government Publishing Office. 2009. *National Information Literacy Awareness Month, 2009.* By Barack Obama. Proclamation 8429. Washington, D.C.

Weil, François. 2013. *Family Trees: A History of Genealogy in America.* Cambridge, MA: Harvard University Press.

Zerubavel, Eviatar. 2012. *Ancestors and Relatives: Genealogy, Identity, and Community.* Oxford: Oxford University Press.

PART VI: FAMILY

Finding Family, Friends, Neighbors and Community in Patent Records

BARBARA J. HAMPTON

Genealogical researchers may be inspired by family lore about an inventive ancestor, perhaps a patent holder. They may be curious about a mysterious old tool found in the attic, barn or workshop. With about 10,000,000 patents granted by the United States, this challenge calls for the research skills of a librarian. Patents can help define biological and legal relationships in a family tree. Patents can also lead to a rich historical context and help complete a family history:

- Where did they live?
- Were they citizens of the United States or another country?
- What was life like for this person?
- How did the family spend its days?
- What inspired them?
- What challenged them?
- How were they connected to their community?
- Where did they work, and with whom?
- How were they connected to business, trade, and manufacturing?
- What impact did they have?

These users may have been frustrated by quick-and-dirty results in a Google search or confused by the sometimes-arcane terminology and tools of the U.S. Patent and Trademark Office ("USPTO") records. Your fluency with classification systems, Boolean searching, and field searching will help you guide and support genealogical patent research, using the best free, open-access databases and resources.

Panning for Patent Gold

What treasures await researchers beyond the name of the inventor and the title of the patent? The earliest patents were manuscript documents, copied from the inventor's application, and signed by the President of the United States, the Secretary of State, and the Attorney General. Quite often, all three names are familiar to us today. Regrettably, some archival documents have been vandalized by autograph thieves. Libraries and archives in possession of these documents should collaborate with archival and security experts to protect these irreplaceable documents.

Another valuable nugget is the identification of the inventor as an American citizen, a requirement of patent law from 1793 to 1836 (Dobyns, 48). Many include the inventor's residence (town and state or territory). But patents do not classify inventors, focusing instead on the invention. Patents do not describe the inventor as native-born or naturalized citizens, English-speaker or not. No mention is made of the inventor's educational achievements, employment, wealth, racial or ethnic heritage, marital status, or even gender. Sociologists, anthropologists, as well as genealogists and local historians must look to other sources for this information.

The names of witnesses and/or the patent attorney may be disclosed. The witnesses are likely to have been family, co-workers, neighbors, or employees. While some early American lawyers advertised expertise in patent law, many patents were prepared by local general practitioners. Researchers can construct a slice of a community with these names. Witnesses shown on two of Christopher M. Spencer's repeating rifle patents include R.S. Spencer, J.W. Coombs, J.S. Strong, M. Welles (Spencer 1860), E.A. Stansbury, E.R. Stansbury, Atty. Chas. F. Stansbury, Chauncey Smith, and H. Farnam Smith (Spencer 1865).

When a community is identified, archival maps can locate the inventor's neighbors and perhaps the shop where the invention was made and related businesses. Christopher Spencer, born in Manchester, later worked in machine shops there and in Windham and New York, lived in Boston, and built factories in Hartford and Windsor ("Invention and Technology"). The machine shops of the greater Hartford, CT, area became a synergistic "Place of Invention" for firearms, bicycles, sewing machines, automobiles, milling machines, and much more (Moella and Karvellas 2015).

The Civil War gives context and significance to Spencer's invention. In 1860, he patented a "magazine gun" or "repeating rifle" that could fire seven shots (1860). Its power on the battlefield is demonstrated by its use by several Union army units, including several at the Battle of Gettysburg (Hollbrook 2011). In 1865, an inventor in Virginia received a patent from the Confederate States of America for a method for making cartridges to be used with Spencer repeating rifles (Sibert).

Patents are said to "teach" about the invention, with descriptions, drawings, and references to prior inventions, often describing a problem not solved with the old way of doing things. The very large number of patents for washing machines (going back to the early 1800s) is some indication of what a challenge this chore was (Leggett 1874). Some inventions are designed to serve the particular needs of a community. Even when your ancestors weren't part of the patenting, an invention may reflect their lifestyle. The White Frost Icebox, a unique cylindrical design, efficiently kept foods chilled (without electricity) and accessible (using turntables). It is still treasured in the backcountry lumber camps of the Olympic Peninsula, where this artifact, patented in 1906, was found (Boeck).

Although models were originally required to accompany patent applications, the USPTO sold the models to private collectors about 100 years ago. Some have become part of museum collections, with a large number now held by the Hagley Museum and Library in Wilmington, DE. Many examples are shown in a book by collectors Alan and Ann Rothschild (2016). Encourage genealogical researchers to investigate patent documents and patent models held by archives and museums, particularly in the areas where ancestors lived and worked (Hampton 2016). Make them aware of the three different uses of the term "patent" in library and museum catalogues. In addition to inventive patents, the term can refer to lands conveyed to an individual by the sovereign. Also, some military and government officers are appointed with a document called a patent. Usually, a careful reading of the description will make clear when the patent concerns land or an appointment of an officer.

Jump Start Your Patent Research

The surest way to access patents is following research trails that have been cut by experts. Once you're acquainted with the patent terrain, you can carve your own patent trails. Start by gathering any facts you've found about the person(s) you're researching:

- Name (and variations)
- Dates of birth and death
- Citizenship
- Residence(s)
- College affiliations as student or faculty
- Trades, professions, businesses
- Employers or partners
- Descriptions or drawings of inventions in diaries, letters, newspaper or magazine articles, advertisements, etc.; look for notations of patent date, patent pending, patent applied for, or a patent number.
- Archival documents or artifacts concerning the person and/or invention
- References in local maps and histories to the person's trade, invention, business, etc.
- Relevant items in business accounts and estate inventories

Next, look for the person, location, or invention in an appropriate specialized database and bibliography. Keep an organized list of any additional persons, places, trades, and inventions that may connect with the subject of your research. Many states have created their own searchable database of patents granted to local individuals:

- Alabama—http://bpldb.bplonline.org/db/inventors
- Alabama—http://invention.si.edu/alabama-inventors-database-1821–1974
- Arkansas—http://arkansas.patents.com/
- Connecticut—http://museumofcthistory.org/2015/09/connecticut-patents-2/
- Delaware—http://genealogytrails.com/del/patents.html
    - References extracted from newspaper archives
- Florida—http://www.floridainvents.org/
- Hawaii—http://www.waybetterpatents.com/comingsoon/digests/patents/HI/HI_20150331_patents.html
- Idaho—http://db.lib.uidaho.edu/patents/
- Illinois—http://illinois.patents.com/
- Iowa—http://www.statelibraryofiowa.org/cgi-bin/patents/
- Kansas—http://www.waybetterpatents.com/comingsoon/digests/patents/KS/KS_20150310_patents.html

- Maryland—http://maryland.patents.com/
- Massachusetts—
  - Annual Index of Massachusetts Innovation Economy/Technology Patents—http://index.masstech.org/research/indicator9
- Montana—http://montana.patents.com/
- Nevada—http://guides.library.unr.edu/nvinventors
- New York—http://www.rootsweb.ancestry.com/~nyononda/patents/NYSPatenteesAssignees.html
- Ohio—http://staff.lib.muohio.edu/shocker/ohist/
  - Cincinnati–http://www.cincinnatilibrary.org/resources/invent/
  - Miami Valley—http://www.libraries.wright.edu/patents/
- South Carolina—http://biblio.clemson.edu/sci/
- Texas—https://texashistory.unt.edu/explore/collections/TXPT/browse/
- Wyoming—http://inventors.wyo.gov/

Some databases include additional unofficial categories, such as gender or race. Some include supplemental materials, such as photographs. Be aware that the dates of coverage vary, and the listings may contain errors. Some cities, counties, regions and colleges have also built custom patent databases. If your location isn't listed, check with the USPTO Patent and Trademark Resource Center in your area (see References list), state library, or historical society to see if one has been developed. If not, this could be a valuable project that genealogical researchers and librarians could support.

Additional specialized databases include:

Racial or Ethnic Heritage

- African American History—African American Inventors: http://inventors.about.com/od/blackinventors/a/Black_History_J.htm
- Black Inventors by State or Country of Residence, 1834–2008, Index (downloadable Excel Spreadsheet prepared for PTRCA): http://ptrca.org/files/handouts/stliblkin-10-09-2008-1C-with%20headings.xls

Women

- Women of Invention: Women Inventors and Patent Holders (Library of Congress bibliography)—http://www.loc.gov/rr/scitech/SciRefGuides/womeninventors.html
- Women inventors to whom patents have been granted by the United States government, 1790 to July 1, 1888; also included Appendix 1, July 1, 1888–Oct. 1, 1892; Appendix 2, Oct. 1, 1892–Mar. 1, 1895 / [compiled under the direction of the Commissioner of Patents]; digitized book, searchable text—https://catalog.hathitrust.org/Record/100594552

Technology and Tools

- American Artifacts (medical, surveying, and farm tools and instruments)—http://www.americanartifacts.com/smma/index.htm

- Directory of Tool and Machinery Patents—http://www.datamp.org/. Database includes both commercial and household tools and machines. DTMAP supports searches by manufacturing company, technology type, and partial name matches. Some entries include drawings or photographs of invention.)
- HistoricIP (includes search by inventor's names from 1790 forward)—http://historicip.com/

Wartime Patents

- "Some Civil War Era Patents: List of Confederate Patents." In Dobyns, App. A, 2016.
- "U.S. Alien Property Custodian Documents: Patent Applications Published During World War II." Database of bibliographic data for WWII patent applications that were seized from nationals of enemy and enemy-occupied countries during World War II by the Alien Property Custodian in 1942 to make enemy technology available to American industry. Subsequently, these were published by the USPTO, though little known. http://db.library.queensu.ca/apcdocuments/

The Library of Congress's Science, Technology, and Business Division has extensive bibliographies available online, including biographies of selected inventors and scientists from various backgrounds. Historical organizations may provide information about inventors and patents on their websites, such as the "Invention and Technology" project of Connecticut Humanities. These narrative sites generally feature "famous" inventors, with only a sampling of patentees. Depending on the persons and inventions sought, a well-researched site may help a genealogist. However, the searchable databases listed above are much more comprehensive.

Digging In with Keyword Searching

Genealogical researchers will be tantalized by actual patents found in the specialized databases. From there, help them organize and develop their personal search of the complete United States patent records:

- Name(s) and Variations. What names could be associated with this patent (Jeffrey J. Fielding)? Initials (J.J. Fielding)? Full name (Jeffrey James Fielding)? Nicknames (Jeff Fielding)?
- Towns or Cities. Primary town name (Southbury)? Village name (South Britain)? Historical name (Pomperaug)? Prior or subsequent residence (Woodbury)? Use local gazetteers to discover alternatives.
- Invention description. What are current and historical terms for the device: Bicycle? Velocipede? Running machine?
- Features, components of invention: Gears? Pneumatic rubber tires?
- Purpose of invention: Fold up compactly? Pull a passenger carriage?

Google has released a new (and very good) patent searching tool https://patents.google.com/. As of this writing, their early basic (https://google.com/patents) and advanced patent searching (https://www.google.com/advanced_patent_search) tools are still operational. Beside differences in the site layouts, the results and features of each differ. Your users may have a preference for one or another; good results can be obtained with any of these. On your own, try each with a simple keyword search (e.g., "bicycle") and compare. Google automatically includes plurals and compounded words (seat belt AND seatbelt) Use the (?) link to get the specifics of the search protocols. This can be found on the Result page for the newer version and on Prior Art Search page in the older version. Wildcard character options for left and right truncation, as well as mid-word wildcards, can be useful:

- ? (zero or one character)
- * or $ (zero or more characters)
- $x (zero to × characters)
- # (exactly one character). You can include more than one wildcard symbol per word.

Most likely, genealogical researchers will begin with searching their subject's name as inventor. Use the Advanced Search screen's Inventor field for this purpose and minimize bad hits occurring when part of the inventor's name appears elsewhere in the patent (in a reference source, as part of another name [Henry Fielding], or as a homonym ["fielding a baseball"]).

Google's default setting is to include patents and applications for patents from about sixteen nations. Check the "US" option in the drop-down "Patent Office" settings on the Advanced Search screen menu. Removing all but the U.S. patent office results will reduce the number of false positives for genealogical researchers. To see only granted patents, choose "Grant" under the "Filing Status" settings.

Google searches digitized versions of patents prior to 1976 (when the USPTO began full-text searchability). Using OCR, Google will do a keyword search of all patents on file from 1790 forward. However, since older patents use many different fonts and layouts, as well as some documents that are manuscript-only, many letters are misinterpreted. For example, in one case the town name Woodbury was rendered unsearchable as "\I\Ioodbury." Some numbers and letters are easily misread in OCR: B/8, O/zero, S/5, T/7, for example. Additional strategies to overcome these issues are presented below.

The inventors listed on a patent are limited to individuals who believe themselves to be the "true inventor" of the claimed invention. Thus, family lore of an inventor may relate to an employee or friend of the individuals who actually received the patent. That person may well have participated in the development and marketing of the invention without qualifying or being credited as the inventor. However, researching patent records will not provide anything beyond the names accepted by the USPTO.

Power Tools for Mining Patent Gold

As professional librarians know, field searching and classification are powerful strategies to locate relevant information. The USPTO does this with precision (in both methods and results) via the "PatFT" database (http://patft.uspto.gov/netahtml/PTO/search-bool.html). Before beginning a search here, read the limits (in red) on searches prior to 1976. The "Select Years" box on the bottom left side of the screen defaults to "1976 to present." Fields other than Issue Date, Patent Number, and Current U.S. Classification are the only officially searchable fields for patents prior to 1976. However, OCR files going back to 1920 may return additional results from 1920 to 1976 if the 1790 to present option is selected.

About forty search fields are available from a drop-down menu in the "Quick Search" two-term search tool. The most important ones of genealogical research are:

- Inventor Name
- Inventor City
- Inventor State
- Inventor Country
- Issue Date
- Current CPC Classification
- Current US Classification
- Patent Number

The absolutely critical detailed formatting rules for each of these fields are available on the USPTO's Tips for Field Searching page (http://patft.uspto.gov/netahtml/PTO/help/helpflds.htm). Failure to follow these protocols will result in failed searches; recheck your formatting. Also, consider the use of wildcard characters and truncation for name searches to allow for variations. When searching for a city/state location, these are separate searches. Thus searching for city: Portland and state: CT, results could include patents with inventors from Portland, OR and Storrs, CT. If the field search generates too many irrelevant results, try a keyword phrase search: "Portland, CT." To eliminate false positives when a location occurs elsewhere than the inventor's residence (e.g., attorney, assignee, etc.), the second search term can use the Inventor City field. Google Patents does not offer a field search for Inventor City or Inventor State, although keyword search can be used.

The field of invention is described with classifications, allowing searchers to discover related inventions even when different terminology is used. Likewise, the same word may apply to very different items (e.g., paddle—for boats; paddle—for games). Beginning in 2015, the USPTO is using a new classification system (CPC) developed in cooperation with the European Patent Office. Since that time new patents are no longer classified under the previous system (USPC), although those classifications are still attached to patents prior to 2015, as well as being reclassified with the CPC system. Using each system in a historical search will offer alternative perspectives on a field of invention. One easy way to harvest classification numbers for a type of invention is to see what numbers were assigned to a relevant patent which you've found. They are listed on the cover sheet at the beginning of each patent file and on the patent itself for newer patents. The USPTO offers an Index to the USPC at (https://www.uspto.gov/web/patents/classification/uspcindex/indextouspc.htm). The best look-up tool for the CPC system is offered through the European Patent Office's Espacenet site (https://worldwide.espacenet.com/classification?locale=en_EP). Classification searching can find relevant patents when you may not know the name of the inventor or other details.

Google Patents Advanced Search offers many of the same fields, with less stringent input rules. Google's sophisticated algorithms can vary and add terms to a search without you being aware of it. Google also includes non-patent publications (books, articles, websites) relating to a patent. While these are important for new inventors, they can clutter the genealogical researcher's results. Do not check the Google Patents box to "Include non-patent literature" during an initial search.

Researchers may have a reference to an official Patent Number. This is the surest route to an exact patent. However, formatting matters. Letter codes precede all patent numbers other than utility patents:

- D—design patents
- PP—plant patents
- X—patents prior to 1837 numbering system established

In the USPTO database, patent number searches must use seven characters, including the prefix letters and sufficient leading zeroes to comprise seven characters. Google Patents does not offer a Patent Number field search. Entering a patent number in the general keyword search is likely to produce confusing results, since numbers can occur in many places in a patent that are irrelevant to the assigned patent number.

Traps for the Unwary

An 1836 fire at the Patent Office destroyed all patent records to that date. Only about a quarter of these have been reconstructed, many only partially and are part of the X Patent files. The *List of Patents* (1872) and *Subject-matter Index* (Legett 1874), USPTO publications now digitized and searchable, provide names, residences, broad classifications, and brief titles. These may reveal names and towns missed by the OCR search. The *Journal of the Franklin Institute* regularly published information about patents filed in the nineteenth century. Sometimes patents were described in newspaper articles or advertisements. Occasionally, original patent documents are discovered by researchers in family papers or archives, which may be added to the reconstructed records in the database.

Google has created the only fully searchable OCR database of U.S. patents, including those prior to 1920. Its interface is comforting familiar and intuitive for users. However, Google's algorithm may lead you astray in its interpretation of your search, substituting the machine's approximations and choices for the user's. Several other sites offer "free patent search," generally part of a marketing program for intellectual property businesses. The free content on each is generally limited and contains erroneous or misleading information. Subscription databases available for walk-in use at libraries and the resources at PTRCs can provide quality resources. Ultimately, the more complex rules of the USPTO's field-searching tools should be part of patent research.

Understanding the Boundaries of United States Patents

The United States patent system began in 1790 under the U.S. Constitution (art. II, §8, cl. 8), with the goal "to promote the Progress of Science and useful Arts." "Anyone who invents or discovers any new and useful process, machine, article of manufacture, or composition of matter, or any new and useful improvement thereof," (35 U.S. Code §101 [2015]) may be granted a patent, with the right to exclude others from making, using, offering for sale, selling or importing the invention for a limited period of time (35 U.S. Code §154 [2015]).

Patents include more than gadgets and machines (utility patents). Ornamental designs (appearance) for items to be manufactured (such as a design for china, jewelry, or a cell phone case) can earn a design patent. Asexually reproduced plants can earn a plant patent ("Plant Patents"). Librarians at USPTO-sponsored Patent and Trademark Resource Centers (PTRCs) can provide additional information about these various systems ("Patent and Trademark Resource Centers [PTRCs]").

Two other important intellectual property systems are trademarks and copyright. Trademarks (and their close relations, servicemarks, and trade dress) can be registered with the USPTO as source identifiers of a product or service. They are *not the product*, are *not included* in patents, and often aren't developed until long after an inventor applies for a patent. Copyright is the exclusive rights granted to authors regarding their works, including writings, music, photographs, and several other forms of authorship. These topics are beyond the scope of this essay. Interested users should be referred to a PTRC Library for further assistance.

Connecting the Innovation Dots

Successful patent searching is iterative. As a search progresses, new names, new locations, and new invention information should be incorporated and re-searched. Geographic and cultural context for invention can be found in historical records and maps (Moella and Karvellas 2015). Many libraries now include digital archives of early maps and photographs that may allow users to see the family, co-workers, and location of the shop where the inventor worked. Adjacent resources such as power supplies, natural resources, transportation, and collaboration with others in an industry can be assessed. Even isolation and the lack of resources can define the problems an invention solved. With your help as an expert researcher, your community could also become known as a "Place of Invention."

WORKS CITED

(Note: For the convenience of the reader, anonymous publications of the U.S. Patent and Trademark Office are alphabetized and cited according to the title of the publication.)

Boeck, Charles H. 1906. Design for a Refrigerator. US Patent D38,237, filed April 18, 1906, and issued September 11, 1906.
"Connecticut Patents." Museum of Connecticut History. Connecticut State Library. http://museumofcthistory.org/2015/09/connecticut-patents-2/.
Dobyns, Kenneth W. 2016. *The Patent Office Pony: A History of the Early Patent Office*. Boston: Docent Press.
"General Information Concerning Patents." 2015. US Patent and Trademark Office. https://www.uspto.gov/patents-getting-started/general-information-concerning-patents.
Hampton, Barbara J. 2016. "Building the Patent Knowledgebase with Life-Size Patent Models." *Journal of the Patent and Trademark Resource Center Association*, 26. http://ptrca.org/system/files/Building%20the%20Patent%20Knowledgebase.pdf.
Hampton, Barbara J. 2015. "White Frost Icebox." Photograph taken at Lake Quinault [WA] Museum.
Hollbrook, Tom. 2011. "Weapons at Gettysburg—The Spencer Repeating Rifle." *From the Fields of Gettysburg: The Blog of Gettysburg Military Historical Park*. Posted 1 Sept. 2011. https://npsgnmp.wordpress.com/2011/09/01/weapons-at-gettysburg-the-spencer-repeating-rifle/.
"How to Conduct a Preliminary U.S. Patent Search: A Step by Step Strategy—Web Based Tutorial." (38 minutes) US Patent and Trademark Office. https://www.uspto.gov/video/cbt/ptrcsearching/.
"Invention and Technology." 2017. *ConnecticutHistory.org*. Middletown, CT: Connecticut Humanities. https://connecticuthistory.org/topics-page/invention-and-technology/.
Journal of the Franklin Institute. Digitized copies available at Internet Archive. https://archive.org/search.php?query=journal%20of%20the%20franklin%20institute.

Leggett, Mortimer Dormer (Commissioner of Patents), comp. 1874. *Subject-Matter Index of Patents for Inventions Issued by the United States Patent Office from 1790 to 1873, Inclusive*. Washington, D.C.: Government Printing Office. https://hdl.handle.net/2027/miun.agl4739.0001.001.

A List of Patents Granted by the United States from April 10, 1790, to December 31, 1836. 1872. United States. Patent Office. Washington: [Am. photo-lithographic Co., NY]. https://hdl.handle.net/2027/mdp.39015030257284.

Moella, Arthur P., and Anna Karvellas. 2015. *Places of Invention: A Companion to the Exhibition at the Smithsonian's National Museum of American History*. Washington, D.C.: Smithsonian Inst. Scholarly Pr.

"Patent and Trademark Resource Centers (PTRCs)." U.S. Patent and Trademark Office. https://www.uspto.gov/learning-and-resources/support-centers/patent-and-trademark-resource-centers-ptrcs.

"Plant Variety Protection." US Dept. of Agriculture, Agricultural Marketing Service. https://www.ams.usda.gov/services/plant-variety-protection.

Rothschild, Alan, and Ann Rothschild. 2016. *Inventing a Better Mousetrap: 200 Years of American History in the Amazing World of Patent Models*. San Francisco: Maker Media.

"7-Step U.S. Patent Search Strategy Guide." U.S. Patent and Trademark Office. https://www.uspto.gov/sites/default/files/documents/7_Step_US_Patent_Search_Strategy_Guide_2015_rev.pdf.

Sibert, Joseph L. 1865. "Patent Drawing, and Specifications for a Machine for Forging Spencer Rifle Cartridge Cases." Issued by the Confederate States of America. Evans-Sibert family papers, 1800–1928. Library of Virginia.

Spencer, C[hristopher] M[inor]. 1860. "Improvement in Self-Loading Fire-Arms." U.S. Patent 27,393, issued 6 March 1860.

Spencer, Christoper M. 1865. "Improvement in Self-Loading Fire-Arms." U.S. Patent 45,952, filed 27 April 1864, and issued 17 Jan. 1865.

Stanley, Autumn. 1993. *Mothers and Daughters of Invention: Notes for a Revised History of Technology*. New Brunswick: Rutgers Univ. Press.

35 U.S. Code §101 (2015).

35 U.S. Code §154 (2015).

U.S. Constitution, art. II, §8, cl. 8.

Putting Family History on the Map

Creating Visual Representations of Family Migration, Settlement and Encounters

Leslie A. Wagner

Introduction

Library patrons who find themselves in the library tracking down clues to their family history often began with simple curiosity about their own personal history. They've heard the family stories and they've begun documenting the facts to prove, or disprove, what they've heard over the years. They've gathered clues and they're beginning to see a bigger picture. They've poured through the family photo albums and scrapbooks and quizzed their elders to identify family members no longer living, thus passing simple, yet valuable, information from one generation to another.

After years of compiling research, family genealogists become the interconnecting links amidst the five or six generations they have known during their lifetime. They want ways to continue the interest of younger family members in preserving the fruits of their research, the tenuous thread they have built between past and future generations. One way we can assist them in their quest is to point them in a new and exciting direction that provides a visual perception of place and time by creating digital family maps. Digital family maps allow family genealogists to reveal where on Earth their family branches have trod and settled in to take root, sharing the sense of place and belonging in the grand scheme of things.

With new ways, we can share information through the very technology to which we are constantly exposed. Thanks to modern technology, librarians can help genealogists and family historians expand their research and analytical skills beyond just adding another leaf to their family tree. Traditional genealogy software programs are adding mapping features in their newer, updated editions to allow their users to depict where their ancestors lived, where they worked, and where they played, because family historians want to see where the leaves fall and what patterns they create across a landscape of time and place.

Librarians can assist the genealogy and family history patrons showing them ways to organize their information and create digital family maps to depict just how near, or how scattered, their ancestors ensconced themselves across the landscape through the centuries. Such maps will enable researchers to trace the paths of their ancestors across the continents and provide them with virtual evidence of whether their lives intersected or ran in parallel.

There have been numerous conference workshops and training classes, usually presented by savvy Geographic Information Systems librarians, explaining the use of software packages for data visualization while pulling information from government databases to depict statistical information on a digital map. While helpful for librarians who assist their patrons in manipulating statistics, the sessions involved far more complex processes to acquire and ingest types of data that most genealogists do not need. When it comes to digital maps, there is no handy database containing the data required to address their special needs. The effort of genealogists who want to create a map representing an aspect of family history essentially boils down to creating a set of data so unique and specific to their family line that it is shared only with their full siblings.

Online genealogy resource giants like FamilySearch, Ancestry, and their many competitors have convenient ways of searching their databases, building a family tree online, and storing digital documents and images online. However, it takes the researcher considerable effort to comb through those materials to gather the appropriate information needed to create a digital family map. Once gathered, it must be arranged and organized into a usable format that translates easily into a digital map. Librarians have the opportunity to guide their researchers through the simple steps introduced in this essay that allow family genealogists create digital family maps to depict, for example, the geographic presence of one individual family member, three distinct generations, or an entire family branch. Digital family maps can tie to a particular theme like cemeteries, schools, or religious affiliations. Digital family maps provide engaging ways to show just how amazing their ancestral journey has been.

In reviewing available online resources for creating maps, we came up with a number of resources to create our maps, however, some were either too complicated or didn't provide the results we expected. We will actually walk you through the two resources with which we had the most success. So hang on to your hat. We're going to show you how to create digital family maps!

First Things First, Let's Start with a Simple Project

Perhaps your researcher has yet to track down where their ancestors resided between census years. Or maybe they've only found information on where a few of them lived. Have they ever checked a map to locate their hometown? And just how much information (that's data) is needed to create a family map, and do they have enough to get started? Let's start out using broader locations first, and work our way down to more exacting locations—street addresses—later:

1. country
2. state, territory, or province
3. county, parish or enumeration district

4. city, town, suburb, or village
5. neighborhood, subdivision, or community
6. address number, block and lot number, or survey tract number (remember, this level of detail can come later)

Did a particular ancestor live in a town so tiny that it wasn't even on the map? Then stop at the broader level of county/parish/enumeration district. This also works well for earlier ancestors, as street addresses were likely non-existent in smaller communities; farmland was prevalent and location details were recorded at a community level in earlier census records.

Start Small, Simple and Easy

If you or your patron hasn't already dealt with locating a business or restaurant on an online map, you may want to start with any number of free online map programs that will allow pinning (placing a marker on) multiple locations. But before we create an online map, we need our location information.

Addresses—specific or general—can be found in city directories and on census sheets. City directories often cover a number of years that will reveal whether our ancestor resided in the same place or moved around in the same community or neighborhood. Old directories are such popular resources that libraries and genealogy websites are continually expanding their collections, and digitized directories are increasingly available.

While census records provide a location for an ancestor every ten years or so, there are census maps that can show us the boundaries of the enumeration district displayed at the top of most census sheets. In recently available census records, for those taken within a city, the far left column usually notes a street name and subsequent columns will have an address number for the residential structure. Addresses also appear on birth certificates, death certificates, and draft registrations. These bits of information provide us enough data to pin a general location using an online mapping program. And when we say data, we mean the information that gives us the who, the where, and the when we need to create our family map.

Whether for our own needs or for a patron, we can also begin with a set of existing addresses that we already have on hand, such as those of living relatives or those recently deceased. Each address, along with city and state, is typed into the search box of the online mapping program to automatically place a pin on the given location. Using a program that allows us to pin and save multiple addresses, albeit one by one, lets us quickly create a digital family map. It is important to be able to save the visual representation of our information so as not to have to repeat the process again. We used Google Maps to plot and save our first family map.

From your own personal computer, you can use Google Maps to pinpoint a location and save that location. Google Maps will know it's you when you return to the website because your computer has created a cookie (unless your computer is set to prevent "cookies") for the website and your computer stores this information for you. If you start broadly by adding in just the cities, along with states, that your ancestors lived in, you will quickly create your first digital family map. If you want to see where your ancestors lived in proximity to each other within the same community, then you need to type in the street address, followed by the city and state. When the pin appears in the expected location, you can save the pin to "Your Places" by clicking "save" and can also select "label" to add their name or whatever information you want to display for that pin.

Google Maps also works well and is fun to use for small family groups when you have street addresses for each household. Once entered, if you have pinned locations for several family members in a larger city, when viewing the entire state or a broad view of the city, only a single pin may be visible. However, when you zoom in (using the + or— feature at the lower right-hand corner of the map) on the city, the streets appear, along with the individual pins.

However, typing and pinning each address one-by-one is a time-consuming process if you have more than a handful of addresses for input. How do we deal with larger batches of information? Once again we look to our computer.

Any mainstream spreadsheet software program will allow you to input and organize each ancestor's data and to save it, add more data later, and save it again. By organizing your data in a single spreadsheet, you will be able to load an entire batch of data at once as you create your map with most online mapping software programs. A spreadsheet is a simple way to create a list of repetitive types of data in a table format of rows and columns. The whole table becomes a set of data. If you have basic skills in using, for example, Microsoft Excel, you will be able to create a spreadsheet for your data.

Whatever means you use to organize your data, use it consistently in all of your spreadsheets. For our examples, we included the full name of an ancestor (or a married couple) in the first column because it displays nicely when you click on or hover the cursor over a pinned location. Here are the essential categories we used for our column headers to represent the information necessary to create a digital family map from a spreadsheet:

- Full name (add birth year-death year to differentiate same-named individuals)
- Street Address
- City
- County (unnecessary if all addresses in same city or town)
- State
- Dates at address

If an ancestor lived in several locations, reenter their name with each additional address on a new line in the spreadsheet.

While it is possible to create multiple spreadsheets in a single "workbook" file (that's multiple spreadsheets, or pages, saved as a "workbook" under one filename), most online mapping programs allow only one set of data at a time. A file with two spreadsheets saved under one filename will not transfer the data correctly. Save each spreadsheet that you have created as a separate file with its own unique filename. If you have a sizeable amount of location data for your ancestors, spreadsheets provide an easy way to store and use large batches of information.

Gathering Geographic Coordinates

We're also going to add two more columns to our spreadsheets to enable our mapping programs to create accurate representations of our locations with geographic coordinates. Geographic coordinates are the numerical representations of a single point on the globe and are traditionally measured in degrees, minutes, and seconds. These coordinates are based on the latitudinal lines (horizontal lines which wrap around the globe), and the longitudinal lines (vertical lines which stretch across the globe between the North and South Poles). The accepted standard for geographic coordinates used in online mapping programs is based on the Greenwich Meridian near Greenwich, England, where longitude equals zero degrees. All longitudinal lines from that point to the west or east are counted upward from zero. The latitudinal value at the equator is also zero degrees and all points north or south count upward and end at 90 degrees at each pole. The direction for the counted measurement is reflected by the addition of N, S, E, and W. When these numbers are converted to decimal representations of a location, numbers to the west and south become negative numbers and will be preceded by a minus sign. Decimal formatted values are used in the examples shown in this essay. The important thing to remember about geographic coordinates is to type or copy them onto your spreadsheet accurately. Lop off a starting digit and you may find your ancestor floating somewhere in the Pacific Ocean or chilling at the North Pole.

It will take a little more time to acquire your geographic coordinates for each address. Some mapping software programs will take just the addresses and pinpoint the locations on your map, but for older addresses that no longer exist, the pins will not be accurate. Adding latitude and longitude to pin your locations on the map will increase the accuracy of your pins and is required for some online mapping programs. The coordinates must be used when you don't have an address.

The tables shown in this essay mimic the data setups in the spreadsheets which we used to create our sample digital family maps. Here are suggested ways to organize your spreadsheet data:

- By location
- By family group
- For an individual over a lifetime
- Individual or family locations for a particular time frame

Examples

Our first example represents a family group of adult siblings who moved their respective families to El Paso, Texas, to run a family business. The information sources used for the addresses were taken from the 1930 United States Census and online Hudspeth's city directories for El Paso from 1930 to 1932. Today, however, most of these locations lie beneath major interstate highways. To pin down the exact location under these circumstances, several methods can be used:

- Fire insurance maps for the particular city
- Street directories, found separately or as part of many city directories, showing cross streets and block numbers
- City maps dating from the same approximate time period

Because all the addresses are in the same city, we have eliminated the column for county.

To ensure the accuracy of your map coordinates, set the number format for latitude and longitude fields in your spreadsheet to 6 decimal places.

198   Part VI: Family

Full Name	Street Address	City	Dates at address	Latitude	Longitude
Leslie Cookie Company (Robert Leslie, owner)	909 Bowie	El Paso	1930–1931	31.782743	-106.441183
Hilman & Johnie Leslie	3029 Oro	El Paso	1930–1931	31.778310	-106.458424
Claud Leslie	909 Bowie	El Paso	1930	31.782743	-106.441183
Robert & Bethel Leslie	909 Bowie	El Paso	1930–1931	31.782743	-106.441183
Hilman & Johnny Leslie	2712 N. Piedras	El Paso	1931	31.801051	-106.461075
Alma Leslie (widow of G.C.)	4200 Montana (rear)	El Paso	1931	31.783627	-106.441573
Leslie Cookie Co. (Britt Mfg. Co., proprietors)	907 Bowie	El Paso	1932	31.782739	-106.441183

Our second example covers highlights of one individual's lifetime, including a military career with overseas assignments. For those locations without detailed addresses, a single pin on the country is shown, using coordinates at the approximate center point of that country. Geographic coordinates for individual countries can be found on Wikipedia. At the top of a Wikipedia page for a country, the map coordinates appear above the main map on the Wikipedia page, or just below the map. Clicking on the displayed coordinates will open another window with the coordinates in decimal form, ready to copy and paste into your spreadsheet.

Full Name	Street Address	City (County)	State or Country	Dates at Address	Latitude	Longitude
S.G. Jones	121 Clinton Street	Abilene (Taylor)	Texas	1927–1944	32.450962	-99.744491
S.G. Jones	Texas A&M University	College Station (Brazos)	Texas	1944–1947	30.610369	-96.344056
S.G. Jones	None	None	Japan	1948–1949	35.000000	136.000000
S.G. Jones	None	Granite City (Madison)	Illinois	1949–1951	38.717778	-90.129444
S.G. Jones	None	Gondreville (Loiret)	France	1951–1954	48.063200	2.654900
S.G. Jones	None	Fort Hood (Bell)	Texas	1954–1955	32.000000	-97.780000
S.G. Jones	None	None	South Korea	1955–1957	36.000000	128.000000
S.G. Jones	None	Fort Campbell (None)	Kentucky	1957–1960	36.650000	-87.467000
S.G. Jones	6 Heinrich-strasse	Frankfurt am Main (Hesse)	West Germany	1960–1962	31.130000	-97.780000
S.G. Jones	None	Rhein Main (None) Air Base	West Germany	1962–1964	50.030194	8.588047
S.G. Jones	480 Holiday Hill Drive	Florissant (Saint Louis)	Missouri	1964–1966	38.787367	-90.303354
S.G. Jones	None	Long Binh (None)	South Vietnam	1966–1967	10.940518	106.900892
S.G. Jones	2835 Derhake Drive	Florissant (Saint Louis)	Missouri	1967–1971	38.790755	-90.288348
S.G. Jones	1901 Carter Creek Parkway	Bryan (Brazos)	Texas	1971–1995	30.656192	-96.357327

Finally, we have a spreadsheet containing addresses of various ancestors during the same year, 1926 (thus no column is used for dates at address). Since these names and addresses were taken from city directories, young children are not listed. However, it is interesting that once the information is put together, we can see that several individuals resided with other family members. Frances Wade is grandmother to Lada Cox. Claude Leslie is father to Hilman and Lucille.

Full name	Street Address	City	County	State or Country	Latitude	Longitude
Frances E. Wade	3521 Hamilton Avenue	Dallas	Dallas	Texas	32.771377	-96.755327
Lillie A. Fitzgerald	401 Olive Street	Cleburne	Johnson	Texas	32.352504	-97.378253
Lada F. Cox	3521 Hamilton Avenue	Dallas	Dallas	Texas	32.771377	-96.755327
Morris J. Roberts	1518 Hughes Circle	Dallas	Dallas	Texas	32.765824	-96.784523
Hilman Leslie	208 W. Davis	Dallas	Dallas	Texas	32.749489	-96.825457
Claude C. Leslie	208 W. Davis	Dallas	Dallas	Texas	32.749489	-96.825457
Lucille Leslie	208 W. Davis	Dallas	Dallas	Texas	32.749489	-96.825457
William B. Jones	None	Anson	Jones	Texas	32.755731	-99.896376
S. Guy Jones	125 Parramore Street	Abilene	Taylor	Texas	32.456933	-99.737449
H. Edgar Jones	141 Sayles Blvd.	Abilene	Taylor	Texas	32.448387	-99.747067
Fred L. Leslie	437 Pembroke	Dallas	Dallas	Texas	32.738075	-96.818873
Robert Leslie	605 Melba	Dallas	Dallas	Texas	32.747523	-96.832457
Cream Cookie Company	113 East Colorado	Dallas	Dallas	Texas	32.759035	-96.822936

It's time to create an online digital map from our spreadsheet.

There are numerous online mapping software programs available for purchase which will allow you to try out the product for free, using limited features, for a limited time, to create your very first digital family map. One product, ZeeMaps, will let you create up to five maps before requiring a subscription to use the product. Before you start plugging in your data to create a map, you will want to make sure your information is complete, thorough, and accurate. In testing out several of the programs, we found ZeeMaps one of the easiest to use. Thus, the examples in this essay were created using ZeeMaps. Methods for other online mapping software programs should work essentially the same way, with only minor differences:

1. Open ZeeMaps on your computer.
2. Select "map my spreadsheet" and a window opens.
3. Select "choose file" and a list of files you have saved on your computer opens up.
4. Select the spreadsheet file you want to import into ZeeMaps and select choose. Your selected file name will appear next to the "browse file" box.
5. Leave the default selection as "marker pin" and select "submit."
6. A box will open to confirm your selections; you must select a country from the box in the upper right hand of the window; you can also select a different color for your pins. When finished with your selections, select "submit."
7. A pop-up box will appear telling you your map is scheduled to upload and you can expect an email with a link to your completed map shortly.

Once you know how to create a map displaying the data you or your patron provide, you can use it for a number of purposes:

- Planning family history trips to visit some of the locations.
- Planning cemetery visits in a particular area.
- Visualizing the community where your ancestors worked and lived.
- Following a single life journey.
- Tracking immigration routes of your ancestors.

Problem Solving for Researchers

They've done their research. They've gathered and organized their data. They've looked on Google Maps until they're cross-eyed but they can't locate the tiny hamlet where their ancestor was born or the address or even the street where their great grandparents live. What now? How can we help our researchers next? We might consider whether the town was annexed by its larger neighbor. Was the town renamed? What about the spelling? Did the county boundaries change? If you're looking in the early 19th or the 18th century, state, territorial, or county boundaries may have changed. Did the town simply fizzle out and become a ghost town? Refer to older maps to find that little hamlet. As for street addresses, the numbering system may have changed (this was the case in Dallas in 1911), or perhaps the street name was changed. Or, as is the case for several addresses shown in our examples, they are now beneath the ribbons of pavement of major interstate highways, plowed under for shopping malls, or destroyed by storm, flood, or fire. You can still get a feel for the neighborhood by viewing remaining nearby neighborhood streets using street view in Google Maps and similar online applications. Some additional resources to help you find those hard-to-find places:

- Gazetteers
- Almanacs
- Historical street maps
- Original survey maps

Online and Downloadable Mapping Software

- ZeeMaps
- Scribble Maps
- Google Maps
- StepMap
- Click2Map
- ESRI ArcGIS
- Tableau Public
- Maptive
- MapQuest MyMaps
- SimplyAnalytics
- Mapline
- eSpatial
- QGIS

Online mapping utilities are as various as any online applications and are certainly subject to updates and changes. Technology changes, problems are corrected, competition comes out with a new or improved product, and poorer products disappear from the market. The essentials presented here should get you good results and your success, or lack of success, will help you decide if you want to pursue a commercial product for expanded digital family map projects.

PART VII: OUTREACH

Genealogy Behind Bars
Professional Development Through Prisoner Requests, a Case Study

KATHRINE C. AYDELOTT

As an academic librarian at the University of New Hampshire (UNH), I work primarily with my university community, but I also support the people of New Hampshire and the public with their research agendas. So when a letter addressed to the Reference Department was delivered to me, I opened it as I would any similar request sent to our email account. However, "snail mail" is incredibly rare. The request was from a prisoner.

Prisoners are forbidden to use the Internet, so requests come in hard copy, and although he was writing from Arizona, the request was for help with New Hampshire genealogy. Genealogy isn't my primary professional responsibility but I am interested in moving my 20 years of experience in a more professional direction. This requires practice and opportunities to use new and diverse sources of information. I read the letter eagerly.

The prisoner's name was Carl Hughes, and the envelope contained two sheets of paper (name and text used with permission, edited for length). On the first, Carl told a compelling story stemming from the Civil War:

> I am searching for anyone that may have information on the descendants of Albert E. Emery, the son of Barzilla & Hannah (Emery) Emery, born Dec. 29, 1828, in Bartlett, New Hampshire. He married Caroline O. Harriman, daughter of Henry & Sarah Harriman, Sept. 19, 1850. Caroline and Albert had one child: Barzilla Emery, born July 4, 1859, in Bartlett, NH.
>
> Albert enlisted with Company B on Sept. 15, 1862, entered into the 16th Infantry Regiment of NH, Union Army, Oct. 18, 1862, and mustered out on Aug. 20, 1863. Then he met Martha Jane Littlefield. They married in 1863/64 and had one child: Susan/Susie Emery, who was born in 1864/65 in Bartlett, NH. After Albert's death on Sept. 7, 1866, in Bartlett, Martha married Phineas Sherman, March 6, 1868, in Whitefield, NH. They had three children: Eliza, born in 1870; Joseph, born in 1872; and Josie Sherman, born in 1875.
>
> For unknown reasons, in 1880, Albert's daughter Susan Emery was adopted out to Olive Hurd in Jackson, NH. Then, on March 20, 1883, Susan received word that her mother had married Joel Perkins, son of William Perkins of Jackson, NH.
>
> On Jan. 24, 1886, in Bartlett, NH, Susan/Susie Emery gave birth to a boy, Charles Albert Emery. Then in 1887, Susan and Charles were placed in a poorhouse in Ossipee, NH. After four years, Susan gave birth to her second son, Fred Emery, on May 7, 1891, in the Ossipee poorhouse. Five years later, Susan and Fred left the poorhouse, leaving her son Charles behind with a promise to come back for

him within a few months. Soon after, Susan married George E. Johnson of Conway, NH, April 4, 1896, in Kearsarge, NH, but Susan would not be able to keep her promise to Charles: she died on Sept. 21, 1897 giving birth to her daughter Susan Johnson.

In 1900, Charles was taken from the poorhouse, along with Henry Davis, who was two years old, by Weare T. Davis, who lived in Effingham, NH. Charles lived on the farm under the name Albert C. Emery until Mr. Davis's death in 1904/5.

For whomever reads this please contact me if you are a descendant of anyone on this page. For that would make you kin to me, and I would love to hear from you. I never knew my grandfather's people because he died when my mother was nine years old.

This was a plea for family connections, and clearly indicated that some research had already been done.

Next, Carl outlined three requests:

1. Confirm Albert's date of death as Sept. 7, 1866.
2. Obtain the adoption record of Susan Emery to Olive Hurd.
3. Obtain school or marriage records for Susan Johnson, the daughter of Susan (Emery) Johnson, to prove that she lived to adulthood.

He concluded:

Thank you for any help you may have on these subjects.
P.S. I don't have much money, but I can pay for copies and postage. Thank you [Hughes 2016].

Carl further included more family history on the second page, with names and dates of the key players listed above. Charles Albert Emery later moved to Alabama and started a family, which included Carl's mother.

This was not the standard "My great-grandfather was in the Civil War" narrative we often hear from patrons. The story provided names, dates, and context, and Carl knew what he needed to prove the facts.

In my mind, Carl's letter could not have fallen into better hands. I have extended my own family research to trace as many affiliated lines as possible back to the immigrant ancestors. My database contains more than 170,000 individuals spanning more than four centuries, most of whom lived in the Colonial period of New England, particularly Massachusetts, New Hampshire, and Maine. It wasn't long before I had traced Carl's line back, according to his listing, and connected his family to the extensive Emery research I had done myself.

I then worked to confirm the facts of Carl's story using several key online tools:

1. My personal Ancestry.com subscription (although I could have used UNH's Ancestry Library Edition subscription, if necessary);
2. FamilySearch.org;
3. RootsWeb's WorldConnect database search; and
4. FindAGrave.com

Ancestry and FamilySearch both provide access to primary-source documents, including census images and vital records, and all four tools contain secondary sources, including user-submitted information and trees. Recognizing that this isn't professional genealogical work, I generally have luck using these sources in conjunction, along with careful source evaluation.

All of Carl's individuals were born when the U.S. Census should list their names, ages, and, after 1860, relationships. But this was still before most states mandated keeping vital records: New England towns at this time mostly kept simple ledgers to record births, deaths, and marriages, and it was not uncommon for these records to be incomplete, lost, or destroyed. Bartlett, a tiny town in the White Mountains, was not unusual in being a challenging place for genealogical research, particularly from across the state, where I was located.

But a few days later, I sent a letter back to Carl indicating the work I had completed:

Dear Carl,

I have examined your request for genealogical information:

1) I am unable to find an online record confirming Albert Emery's death. I did find a letter that mentions this Emery family, posted by the Bartlett Historical Society (BHS), which I will include ("Emery Genealogy"). They don't have a record of Albert's death either, and they further indicate that records for Bartlett, NH, during this period are very scarce. Since the BHS researcher has actively looked for this information in other places, my best interpretation is that local documentation may no longer exist.

2) I confirm that on the 1880 US Census for Jackson, NH, Susie Emery is living with Olive Hurd and is listed as "adoptive daughter" (FamilySearch); however, a legally adopted daughter would simply be listed as "daughter." Further, Susie does not appear in Olive's will ("New Hampshire, Wills"), as her natural children do. So I suspect that the census taker wrote down whatever was said, which was somewhat overstated. Children were "adopted out" when family circumstances made it difficult to support everyone in the household, but this is a different term than simply "adopted." With Martha J. (Littlefield) Emery remarried, and with other young children in the house, the oldest daughter may have sought employment and/or housing elsewhere.

3) According to the U.S. Census, Susan, Susie's daughter, is age 4 and living with her father, George E. Johnson, in Conway, NH, in 1900 (Ancestry). Notably, the 1900 census lists month and year of birth, and Susan's is listed as May 1896, which is a year before Susie's death on 21 Sept. 1897. This could easily be dismissed as an error, either by George or by the census taker, but you would think that George would know the date of his daughter's birth, especially if it coincided with the death of his wife.

I have been unable to trace Susan further in the census. It's possible she went by another name—perhaps a middle name not associated with her mother—but other documentation, such as a marriage record should still list parents' names; I haven't been able to locate such information, but again, few sets of records are absolutely complete. My suspicion, though, as is perhaps yours, is that she died.

School records from this date are rare as copies weren't typically made, but the Conway Historical Society might have more information on George E. Johnson or on the schools in Conway. The historical society might also have more information as to whether Susan died young.

But back to George and Susie. I found a user-submitted record on Ancestry.com for a Minnie B Johnson (reedcarroll1). Minnie's birthdate is listed as 21 Sept 1897, the same day as Susie's death. The owner of the record lists Minnie's parents as George E. and Susie (Emery) Johnson of Conway. Further, Minnie B Johnson, aged 12, is on the 1910 US Census for Conway, NH, living with the family of John Towle and his wife Abbie (Ancestry). On the census, Minnie is listed as "niece," which would make Abbie George's sister. There's a record for Abbie's tombstone on FindAGrave.com (Geary 2012), which lists her maiden name as Johnson and her birthplace as Denmark, Maine, the same place George lists as his birthplace on his marriage record to Susie ("New Hampshire, Marriage"). The 1870 US Census for Conway, NH, does list both Abbie (aged 10) and George (aged 2) in the household of Ivory H and Maria Johnson (Ancestry). This is decent evidence that Minnie is another child of George and Susie, and the child born at the time of Susie's death [Aydelott, Jan. 11, 2016].

I further traced out Minnie Johnson through the census and other sources to her death in 1959 in Bangor, Maine (Dale & Patti 2009).

This hadn't been challenging research, and although the discovery that Susie (Emery) Johnson had two children with husband George was groundbreaking, I didn't feel that this work was anything more than routine. The investigation took a few hours on a Saturday morning, a time I try to dedicate to my own genealogical research, and I printed and mailed the response from work the following week.

Carl wrote back with his thanks, and thus began a series of letters that has continued to the present. Sometimes Carl writes with requests to examine a book for a family reference, or to share information he has received from his apparently extensive letter writing, such as burial locations and photographs of Minnie's tombstone in Bangor.

But sometimes the requests lead to opportunities to use new sources and extend my experience. For example, Carl asked me to examine David Wagner's book *The Poorhouse: America's Forgotten Institution* for the pages citing Susie's time in the Ossipee almshouse. I was pleased to find that UNH had the book in our collection, and I wrote back the following week:

> Wagner's info does indicate that in 1899 Charles Emery, as a long-term resident, was at the almshouse in Ossipee with his mother and brother (2005, Table 4.1).
> Wagner seems to round his dates, for example he says:
> "Charles Emery, the boy in the almshouse since he was one year old, appears with his mother, Susan, who stayed in the almshouse from 1888 to 1897 and gave birth to Fred in the almshouse in 1892" (2005, 70).
> Your letter of March 6 mentions that Susie didn't name Fred for a few days after his birth, and you have his birthdate specifically as 7 May 1891. Fred's birth is recognized as having been in 1891—maybe the 1892 rounded date comes from the Carroll County Annual Report for 1891, published in 1892.
> Fred is not with Susan's husband George in 1900, nor is he with his brother Charles Albert at the farm in Effingham, per the census (Ancestry). He is also not in the broader region as I've looked rather creatively across the census and haven't found him. There are Fred Emerys, but each one traces back to identifiable parents.
> I suspect that Fred died. Maybe not immediately, but perhaps before 1896 when Susan married George. Do you know for sure that Fred ever left the almshouse? [Aydelott, April 2, 2016].

I followed up Wagner's work with a search of Ossipee Town Reports that our library held in our Special Collections Department. There I was able to trace Charles A Emery's stay in the poorhouse from 1888 to 1900, Susie Emery's stay from 1887 to 1896 and notably the three children that Martha J. Littlefield (Emery) Sherman Perkins had with her second husband Phineas Sherman, who were also supported throughout the 1880s and 1890s (*Carroll County Annual Reports* 1877–1893). I wrote to Carl:

> Ultimately the mystery around Fred's whereabouts continues. He disappears, at age 4, sometime between 1 Jan 1896, when the records were reported, and when the next records were collected for the year ending 1 Jan 1897. If he does leave with Susan, and he survives, I would have expected to find him on the 1900 census with George Johnson and (daughter) Susan in Conway.
> Speaking of the Johnsons, here's an update on Minnie: she is living with George's sister's family in 1910, and I think she's living with them in 1900, too: there's a daughter transcribed as "Mary J" (but could be "Mary B," "Mary" being probably just an error) who is about same age that Minnie would be ("1900 U.S. Census"). Still no Fred [Aydelott, April 15, 2016].

Although I was tempted to jump in the car and drive more than an hour to Ossipee to look for poorhouse burial records and other information, I decided that such a trek was outside of the scope of my work with Carl. Professional boundaries should be kept. But in every exchange, I provided Carl with more addresses for people or institutions to whom he could write for more information.

Early in our correspondence, Carl asked whether I would be willing to request Martha J. Perkins's application for Albert Emery's Civil War pension record from the

National Archives and Records Administration (NARA). I never had reason to request a file before. The $30 cost was modest, but I refused to take money from Carl for documents or postage; I requested the file and chalked up the cost to professional development. It was exciting when the NARA record arrived as a scanned file in my email, and more so that indeed it was a treasure trove:

First, the file confirms Albert Emery's Civil War service as a private in Co. B, 16th Regt. of the NH Infantry. In Feb. 1863 and "similar report in" April 1863, Albert Emery was absent from duty for being "sick at Marine Hospital, N[ew] O[rleans], LA. Medical records show that he had typhoid; later, from May to July 1863, he suffered from "chronic diarrhea" but was returned to duty. He was mustered out 20 Aug. 1863.

Second, the "Declaration of a Widow for Original Pension" reiterates Albert Emery's service record, and confirms again his reported death date of 4 Sep 1866 from "chronic diarrhea due to service."

Third, for Martha's part, she reports that she married Albert Emery in Bartlett, NH, on 15 October 1864. This is information we didn't have before. She also reports that Albert Emery had been married before, which we knew; however, Martha states that "[h]is wife died while he was in service," which we know isn't true because I have traced his first wife through two other marriages. Note that I have not located Albert and Caroline's divorce record.

Fourth, Martha falsely reports that her next marriage is to Joel Perkins, whom she married in Bartlett, NH, on 20 May 1883. She completely overlooks Phineas Elkins Sherman, another veteran, whom she married on 6 March 1868 in Whitefield, NH ("New Hampshire, Marriage and Divorce Records"). Her third marriage would have made her ineligible for Albert's pension, and her marriage after the war to Phineas made her ineligible for his.

Fifth, under the category: "That the soldier [Albert] left the following named children under 16 years of age at the date of his death," Martha lists Susan, who was born on 7 December 1865 in Bartlett. We haven't had Susan's birthdate before. I will use Martha's reported date as she is the mother and should know the date her daughter was born, although in other cases she's an unreliable witness.

Martha then reports that Susan "Died about ten years ago, she left no children." This is notable. Susan died in 1897, which indeed is "about ten years ago," but it's interesting that Martha doesn't (or can't) indicate the specific date, or even the more accurate "12 years ago." We know from records that Susan wasn't with her mother after the 1870 census, and it may be that Martha knew only general details about Susie's life in the years since. This, then, doesn't provide any evidence for either the death or survival of Susie's son Fred Emery or daughter Susan Johnson.

Next in the file comes a series of testimonies on Martha's behalf.

A record is submitted noting that the town clerk of Bartlett reported that "Albert Emery and Miss Martha Jane Littlefield, both of Bartlett," were married 15 October 1864. This is affirmed by the town clerk serving in Bartlett in 1909, and further witnessed by the Justice of the Peace. We didn't have this information before.

Note that Martha's third husband, Joel Perkins, died 6 June 1908 in the Carroll County Almshouse, Ossipee, NH ("New Hampshire, Death and Burial Records"). At this point, Martha, now in her mid-sixties, is again eligible for Albert's pension, as she wouldn't be if she were still married. But she also would have been deemed ineligible for the pension if she had contracted more than one marriage since the death of the soldier, or if she divorced. This seems to be why she neglects to mention her marriage to Phineas. Note: I haven't found Martha's and Phineas's divorce record. Phineas dies in Lisbon, NH, in 1902 ("New Hampshire, Death and Burial Records"). In the 1900 U.S. census for Lisbon he is living as a boarder and identifies himself as a widower (Ancestry). Martha, to the best of my knowledge, dies in 1921 in South Paris, Maine ("Maine, Death Records"). Given that there is no certificate number, it appears Martha's claim for pension was not approved, if not outright rejected.

This was an exciting exercise and was certainly worth the $30 for the amount of information contained, for the practice I gained working with such files, and for exploring the complexities of Civil War widows and the pension system.

Carl has continued to write and share information, and I continue to flesh out (genealogical pun) his extended family as my time permits. There is still no sign of Fred Emery outside of the almshouse. Carl's recent requests have asked me to examine more family genealogies for references to the Bartlett families, and I'm currently tracking down Free Will Baptist records.

The experience that I have gained broadly, and the opportunity I have had to work with new sources, both electronic and print, and to track down other sources using UNH's own library collection and Interlibrary Loan has allowed me to build expertise. I encourage librarians to take on these public requests as professional development opportunities when possible, even if pursued on one's own time.

Points to consider when working with the public at large, including prisoners:

1. Keep it private. It's none of my business why Carl is in prison, and I have not used my research skills to investigate. He knows nothing more about me, and I know nothing more about him.

2. Keep it professional. My correspondence relates specifically to the research questions Carl asks and anything else genealogical I find during my investigations.

3. Follow policy. Genealogy is part of my portfolio but not a significant part, which is why this is work I generally take home (also: my genealogy database is on my home computer).

4. Set expectations. If you can only do a little, or if genealogy isn't the main work of the library, say so.

5. Provide timely answers. Don't leave requests unanswered. If you're too busy to respond, either pass the request on to someone else or send a brief note saying support is unavailable at this time.

6. Set and keep boundaries. Consider whether you are willing to travel to investigate further. Consider how much, if anything, you would be willing to pay for documents or to mail photocopies (and/or ask whether the library will reimburse you). If a policy is required, write one.

7. Know your collections. Your library's local history collections, special collections and archives, and genealogy collections might hold the answers you seek.

8. Take the opportunity to investigate: this is professional development, good service, and good practice, particularly if you use sources or venues you haven't used before.

I don't know how long my communication with Carl will continue, but I look forward to his letters. I never know where the next request will send me looking. Carl and I are 8th cousins.

WORKS CITED

Aydelott, Kathrine. 2016. Kathrine Aydelott to Carl Hughes, Jan. 11. Letter.
Aydelott, Kathrine. 2016. Kathrine Aydelott to Carl Hughes, April 2. Letter.
Carroll County (N.H.). 1877–1893. *Annual Report of the Commissioners for the County of Carroll.* Dover, NH: The Commissioners.
Dale & Patti. 2009. "Minnie Anthony (1897–1959)." FindAGrave.com. https://www.findagrave.com/cgi-bin/fg.cgi?page=gr&GRid=38139835&ref=acom. Accessed 1 April 2017.
Deposition of Claimant, 4 Dec. 1909, Martha J. Perkins, widow's pension application no. W.O. 931,691; service of Albert Emery (Pvt., Co. B, 16th Reg., NH Inf., Civil War), Civil War and Later Pension Files; Department of Veterans Affairs, Record Group 15; National Archives, Washington, D.C.
"1880 United States Federal Census." Database. *FamilySearch.* 2016. Susan Emery in household of Olive Hard, Jackson, Carroll, New Hampshire. http://www.familysearch.org.
"1870 United States Federal Census." Database. Ancestry.com. 2009. Abby M. and George E. Johnson in household of [Ivory] H Johnson, Conway, Carroll, New Hampshire. http://www.ancestry.com.
"Emery Genealogy." Bartlett (NH) Historical Society. http://www.bartletthistory.org/directors/EmeryGenealogy.pdf. Accessed 1 April 2017.
Geary, Lynne. 2012. "Abbie Maria Johnson Towle (1861–1921)." FindAGrave.com. https://www.findagrave.com/cgi-bin/fg.cgi?page=gr&GRid=100264760. Accessed 1 April 2017.
Hughes, Carl. 2016. Carl Hughes to Reference Librarian, University of New Hampshire Library, Jan. 3. Letter.
"Maine, Death Records, 1617–1922." Database. Ancestry.com. 2010. Martha J. Perkins, South Paris, Oxford, Maine. http://www.ancestry.com.
"New Hampshire, Death and Burial Records Index, 1654–1949." Database. Ancestry.com. 2011. Joel Perkins, Ossipee, Carroll, New Hampshire. http://www.ancestry.com.
"New Hampshire, Death and Burial Records Index, 1654–1949." Database. Ancestry.com. 2011. Phineas Sherman, Lisbon, Grafton, New Hampshire. http://www.ancestry.com.
"New Hampshire, Marriage and Divorce Records, 1659–1947." Database. Ancestry.com. 2013. Martha J Littlefield and Phineas Sherman, Whitefield, Coös, New Hampshire. http://www.ancestry.com.
"New Hampshire, Marriage Records Index, 1637–1947." Database. Ancestry.com. 2011. Susie Emery and George E. Johnson, Conway, Carroll, New Hampshire. http://www.ancestry.com.
"New Hampshire, Wills and Probate Records, 1643–1982." Database. Ancestry.com. 2015. Olive Hurd, Northwood, Rockingham, New Hampshire. http://www.ancestry.com.
"1900 United States Federal Census." Database. Ancestry.com. 2004. George Johnson, Conway, Carroll, New Hampshire. http://www.ancestry.com.
"1900 United States Federal Census." Database. Ancestry.com. 2004. Phineas Sherman, Lisbon, Grafton, New Hampshire. http://www.ancestry.com.
"1900 United States Federal Census." Database. Ancestry.com. 2004. Charles A. Emery, in household of Weare T. Davis, Effingham, Carroll, New Hampshire. http://www.ancestry.com.
"1910 United States Federal Census." Database. Ancestry.com. 2006. Minnie B. Johnson in household of John P. Towle, Conway, Carroll, New Hampshire. http://www.ancestry.com.
reedcarroll1. Ancestry.com Family Tree. "Minnie B. Johnson." CPPC(1). https://www.ancestry.com/familytree/person/tree/83591967/person/44488819722/facts. Accessed 1 April 2017.
Roberts, Richard P. 2003. *Vital Records of Effingham and Freedom, New Hampshire, 1888–2001.* Bowie, MD: Heritage Books.
"U.S., Social Security Death Index, 1935–2014." Database. Ancestry.com. 2011. Fred Emery. http://www.ancestry.com.
Wagner, David. 2005. *The Poorhouse: America's Forgotten Institution.* Lanham, MD: Rowman & Littlefield.

Community Outreach
Making Your Collection Known and Used
Larry Naukam

It's important to not only have a good collection, but to have people know that you exist and value what you do. Here are some ideas and methods for making your collection more known and being considered more valuable to your users and your community. What you are hoping to achieve is the a-ha! moment when patrons find just what they are looking for, and their work of getting to the library and searching for the answers is rewarded. If you make your collection more accessible, it will get more use. It does take time and energy. The payoff is worth it because your library will be used more, valued more, and considered a must-have in the community. And unless you are a lone practitioner, make sure that the staff are in agreement and work as a team.

Create Indexes for Special Groups and Advertise Them

Make and market soldier indexes, newspaper indexes, hard to find ready reference indexes, subject specialty indexes, death dates from city and suburban directories, high school yearbooks, local authors, records of early pioneers, cemetery records, census extracts, cross-indexes to heraldry and genealogy books, and whatever other specialty indexes that you can think of to create. Make them available and searchable electronically on a computer in the library or even on the Web. Adopt 21st century searching techniques, such as federated searching (allowing users to cross-search multiple indexes at one time, like the big commercial sites or FamilySearch do). Merge these indexes into a searchable database, with the data on the original cards now contained in a text field, and with the sources of the information on the original cards also noted in the entry. Your staff can use the same databases on the computer in front of them for daily reference and referral.

Offer Classes on Using Your Collection

There are many users who could benefit from tips you could provide on what's available at your location and how to search and use it. Find representatives of a commercial historical publishing or genealogical database company. They do training to advertise their databases but the information on their content and how to search is very useful. Try to schedule something at least monthly, and weekly if you have the staff.

Team Up with Local Colleges

Identify and collaborate with local educational institutions. Make your library a valuable resource for students working on assignments for courses at these schools. Ask if there are courses that could use your materials. Seek out the instructors, meet with them, give them a tour of the collection, and explain how the great collection you have would complement the task which they may want their classes to accomplish. If it involves local history and genealogy, become their go-to place, local and free, where these students could do their work. After the papers are done, try to host the results, or link to them. Students learn something about how to use a library with a specialized collection. Plus, all of this increases collection usage, user traffic, and question counts.

Have an intro class for them early in the semester where they come in for a couple of hours, which includes an interactive talk, hands-on examination of sources, and some successful—and some sad—stories. Find out what history assignments local colleges and high schools are requiring, and provide support material. Develop guide lists that have the ten or so most likely sources for this material and their locations, along with a short description of the source.

Do Public Speaking

Offer to speak at conventions attended by people who may be interested in your collection. Look for opportunities to talk to local genealogy, history, or even seniors' (or children's!) groups, and also at district or regional library resource council classes, quarterly and annual meetings; regional archives annual gatherings; state history conferences at colleges, and even a few state or national genealogical conventions such as the Federation of Genealogical Societies. Subjects of these talks can be primarily about local sources for historical and genealogical research, or Internet genealogy, or a specialized interest—computerized genealogy and hardware, and ethnic research.

Mention digital projects, such as scanning directories, newspaper indexes, and having an index of the births, marriages, and deaths from the local papers. Make sure that you do a good job, talk to a lot of attendees, and make sure that you have professional-looking business cards. Do not write on spare scraps of paper—have real cards. Make sure to talk to conference coordinators and organizers, and offer your services and talents for next year. Get on email lists and mention that you are available. Maintain contact with sales reps from the major genealogical databases, which have contact with all sorts of conference and meeting organizers. They know the names and numbers and can give you contact information. Have a backlog of experience and contacts to draw upon.

Contact local historical and genealogical societies, library school professors, regional library associations, state library special interest groups, and even the county office for the aging to meet with town seniors' groups. Have decent speaking and presentation skills. There are numerous books and organizations that can help you brush up on your presentation skills. Two that can be mentioned are Jeff Slutsky's *The Toastmasters International Guide to Successful Speaking* (Chicago, IL: Dearborn Financial Pub. 1997) and a simple web page (http://www.liscareer.com/osborn_presentation.htm), *The Librarian's Guide to Developing Presentation Skills* by Jennifer Osborn. Get onto a list of speakers for local historical, genealogical, library, and even seniors and school groups.

Examples of Libraries That Do This and More

This is an illustrative list, not an exhaustive one:

- *Fort Wayne, IN—Allen County Public Library.* This site (http://www.acpl.lib.in.us/genealogy/index.html) shows a breadth and depth of a collection that is nationally renowned for its comprehensiveness and service orientation.
- *Godfrey Memorial Library—Middletown, CT* (http://www.godfrey.org/index.html). This library is a leader in research in the fields of American genealogy and biography.
- *Rowan Public Library—Salisbury, NC.* This library is mentioned for a great study showing the substantial financial trickledown benefit to their area from having a destination library.
- *Halton Hills—Burlington/Hamilton, Ontario, Canada area.* On their page at (http://www.halinet.on.ca/localhistory/forms.htm) users can cross-search a large number of names for their research purposes.
- *Indian River County Main Library—Vero Beach, FL.* Their page (http://www.irclibrary.org/genealogy/) has a large listing of diverse collection holdings. Clicking on the holdings links gives a more detailed list of what the library's specific holdings are.

Develop Library Displays

Nothing will bring your collection to life more than an attractive, well-done display. Decide whether you want to be catchy or erudite. Use copies of items that you want to show off. If you are a public library with display cases that are not in your line of sight, you have a risk of theft of the originals. Only show copies that can stand the exposure to light, have duplicates or triplicates, and in fact if possible and appropriate make actual modern copies of items and display those. It is advisable to have a small card describing the view, the item, the date of creation, etc. It gives casual viewers a time and place frame to think about. Pictures capture the eye and stir memories and questions. They capture attention better than print. An autographed letter (a copy!) shows the mind's eye "picture" of the famous person's signature.

What are good subjects for displays? Items that speak to the local experience and that can be supplemented with reference materials available in the collections. Be prepared to handle the increase in queries that happens when are doing a display on a subject. Specific places or items are the province of the library where you work and the area in which you live; here are some ideas that have proven useful as beginning points: waterways; recreation and sports; transportation; clothing; people who stir local pride; roadways and highways; weather; buildings; industries.

Here are several suggestions for making a display. This list is based on years of experience; it incorporates experience with not-great display areas, iffy practical security, and adverse environmental conditions. It also addresses the ways to keep these displays inexpensive:

- Use copies so that originals do not get worn, faded or stolen.
- Keep displays in tightly locked cabinets, or on stand-up poster boards on tables, or cases where people can see them.
- Think about height off the ground. Those who are reasonably tall can stoop a bit—shorter folks appreciate items at their eye level.
- Consider having one-sheet takeaways describing the display.
- Use items that are appropriate for a display. Pictures, postcards, and pamphlets usually are good, while print usually isn't captivating.
- Do subjects on which you have supplemental information, and for which you are willing to provide follow-up reference.
- Avoid heraldry. It's usually considered part of genealogy but it takes a lot of time to answer questions about it, and 99.9 percent of the viewers will not want to do the necessary research.
- Consider the times. There is more interest in woman suffrage. If anything, it's a good opportunity to teach young women about how life was just 100 years ago in great grandma's time.

You want to draw attention to locally notable places and people and happenings and give people information about them. You want to increase use of underutilized materials, and highlight events and issues of local importance. Modern pictures can also be manipulated to look better! What you are doing is not scholarship, nor telling lies. It's trying to give a little information to pique curiosity and get more traffic to you. Here are a few references to other sources for displays:

- The University of Lethbridge, in Canada, has a nice web site with information on presenting displays (http://www.uleth.ca/lib/displays/display-policy.asp#goals).
- A good book is Wendy Barteluk's *Library Displays on a Shoestring: 3-Dimensional Techniques for Promoting Library Services*, Rowman & Littlefield Publishers, Inc., 1993.

Get Free Interns to Help with Your Outreach Efforts

Younger people in school or college have a good feel for what will be interesting to them. Library school students or history majors are a good pool to draw from.

Use the Internet: Have a Facebook Page, a Twitter Account and So On

Publishing costs and updates there are cheap.

Get Involved with Local Genealogical Groups

Be a member of the local societies; if you have an interest, serve on the Board of Directors. There is the natural cross-pollination of seeing what an important customer base wants from attending the meetings and talking to people. Many librarians are not known in the community, therefore the people who have an interest in a subject do not know to whom to go. Use this to market your materials in a personal, pleasing, and interactive manner. An invitation to a tour and a handshake makes more of an impression than yet another cute bookmark.

Groups can also supply volunteer docents. Make sure that the library staff welcomes them and aren't so insecure that they consider the volunteers to be intruders, doing their work. What's the practical payoff? Much greater awareness of the library, its collections, and possible users; actual contributions of cash and materials to the library; volunteer hours providing helpful assistance; and good community relations.

Take business cards to meetings. Talk to other speakers at various gatherings, as they can be great professional-related contacts. Set up meetings for later, so you and the speaker can see what common ground you might have. If they are local to you, see what they can suggest as new directions for collection, displays, etc. If they are from out of the area, then they give an outsider's clear view of what you seem to be doing because they look at it with experienced fresh eyes. The history and library worlds are not that big, and making contacts helps get you known and keep you known.

Provide Information for Movies and Books

Use television as well. Local producers are always looking for research materials to spruce up their video productions. If you have these materials, especially photographs, colorful books, postcards, maps or broadsides, then you are a good resource for their work. See if there are local reporters looking for items of interest and make connections with them. Meet and make contact with local radio and TV people or filmmakers and other media producers, and encourage them to use your resources for their stories. See if there are local filmmakers who do short documentaries for public television or as filler for commercial stations. You can work with them in providing source materials, photographs, old newspapers, and microfilmed accounts of the subjects being researched, maps and other sources. Make a point of giving them a long tour of your collection. If they do a good job, it can show—for free—hundreds of times on local outlets, and you likely can get copies (in whatever the latest format happens to be) for free from the filmmakers. This raises community awareness of your site, but also can serve as a great presentation for prospective donors. Allow local media groups to tape your talks at various community presentations.

Utilize the professional skills of these folks. Be ready to have materials for your local media TV stations. When you get a call from a national producer, be ready to provide the kinds of items that they are looking for. Make it a point to cooperate and expedite requests for materials that such entities request. Respond affirmatively and quickly. Deadlines are just that, and agonizing over getting a duplicate copy of something made for three months is quite unproductive. Follow your policies but use common sense. Being overly rule-oriented and methodical is a real hindrance. You have the goods and you have their attention. So go for it and supply what they can use, and ask for a copy of the production and a listing in the credits. Have your materials in a format that can easily be supplied—read, digitally—to producers who can get you up there on the screen.

It is a wise idea to build your collections to help reporters out when they need specific information. If you can amplify what is in their own paper's morgue, you are going to be well thought of indeed. The kind of information that a reporter might be interested in can either be historical or current. Build relationships so that they will come to you. When they approach, find items for them reliably, easily, and quickly. Make sure that the information is good—not a half-baked guess, but something that they can use for their story by the deadline. If you reliably help them do their job, you will be valued as a source.

Write Articles for Local Publications— Become a Go-To Source

Oftentimes there is room in a local paper or publication for a "from the library corner"–type article. Submit these to the paper on a regular or agreed upon basis; in a smaller town this may be easier than in a larger city. You can write for a weekly or monthly online publication—they are always looking for new talent to use, and if you can write but don't feel comfortable speaking in public, here is a way for you to express yourself and get your collection known. There are also online state encyclopedias (the American Association for State and Local History had an interest group on this called IDEA); consider putting entries into the FamilySearch research wiki.

Find and Book Speakers on Related Topics

Your staff does not have to do all the work. Many times there are very interesting and qualified people who are happy to do their act or talk for you. Examples would be local experts on a subject, or re-enactors for a locally or nationally famous person with connections to your area.

Build Special Collections, e.g., Civil War, Veterans and Women's Suffrage

For example, the sesquicentennial of the Civil War was just over. Collect Civil War regimental histories, the Official Records, the state muster rolls, the Adjutant Generals' reports, and other related materials—such as soldiers' letters home—and create a separate shelving area for it. Index the newspapers of the time into notations of local soldiers; make a list of persons who bought someone else to serve for them, with bounties. Create a mini research area for that particular interest and it may be regularly and decently used.

Do as Many Tours as You Can Handle

When you give a talk to an outside group, for example, offer to give a tour of the building if you work in a larger society or library. In a smaller setting it would be intimate, and you can show specific items that would interest them. Ditto for graduate students at local colleges, or social studies teachers, or politicians or new library board members.

Participate in Local, Area, Regional, State and National Digital Partnerships

If you decide to digitize some photos, get together with other collections that are amenable to the idea. Banding together looks good to grant awarders. Decide who will host the actual unified collection (which can easily run into the terabytes if you have photographs and maps). Write letters of support for one another. Those who decide that they would lose control of their images by being partners get no net exposure at all because their pictures are not mounted. You don't collect copy fees and use fees on a collection that is unknown and inert.

There are often library or history groups who have an interest is using technology to further the discovery and use of their collections—and perhaps impress some donors who will support this. Get involved with local, area, regional, state and national organizations that will host your work and provide a referral back to your institution. One that comes to mind immediately is the Digital Public Library of America. It has gone from zero to over 15 million items referred to in that collection.

Develop Relationships with Vendors and Commercial Publishers

Meet and talk with people working as sales reps or content acquisition staff for various commercial entities. If you have something they want, figure out what that is. If you can get people to visit and offer to partner in the production of your collection, you might get lower cost, or discounted or free access to a product in exchange for some PR work or being a test or demonstration site for a concept or product. If you can get good help producing a valuable product for users where everyone benefits, then it behooves you to talk. Some of the biggest content providers will do digitizing and indexing for you. Show a vendor or publisher the creative ways that you have of marketing your collection—and ask for a piece of the action. Ancestry.com has done this for all 50 state archives. Partners can digitize your manuscripts and old volumes, index what you have in your locally created databases, and convert them to a more useable web or network version so that you can sell copies of what is indexed. Make sure that you have written contracts that are clear and enforceable. A handshake agreement or "we'll finalize this later" can and will—trust me on this—come back to bite you later.

If you are concerned with staffing, buying equipment, production schedules, and quality, you can work together with a commercial entity. Keep your eyes open. They won't bother with you unless they can make a profit from what you have. Be sure to have some good negotiators on your side—and if you don't feel comfortable doing this, bring in a tough negotiator to work for you. The national and international vendors and database suppliers deal with locals everywhere. Get your best deal.

Sell Your Library

Selling your library means that you find the time and energy to get out from the desk and make people aware of what you have. Think of whatever you can create that didn't exist before: items such as impulse buys, like a 1900 map of your small—or large—town that people can purchase at the circulation desk for a dollar or two. Pictures of canal boats, aerial views, parks, and natural formations that are noteworthy are some ideas. If you have them, put a credit line "find out more at the [name of your organization]." While this is not a new idea to some (there are many very well-known historical and genealogical collections across the country), it is a new initiative for others.

Measure Results Quantifiably

Set up a counter to see how many hits your web pages get. Get readings of web usage from your commercial partners. Keep track of how many images or copies of obituaries you sell. See how many takeaways are taken away. Count your reference questions, phone calls, emails, letters and visits. Putting up a display, giving a talk, having a class—all these activities can be quantified and measured against a baseline of when you didn't do the outreach.

Staffing and Practical Considerations

Of course, there needs to be a physical place and money. Make a commitment and follow through. If a collection exists and is known about, and the staff there doesn't know much about it or give it much more than cursory care, it wastes their time and that of the users coming to see it. What you have to do is ensure that what you have is useful, accessible, and adequately described.

If you are a single practitioner—a historian working 15 or 20 hours a week maximum for a nominal salary, or are a library director with a college degree but not a library school degree, and you are the only full time staffer in the building then you are in a vastly different situation than if you are in a public library in a larger city. What you do in your own library depends on your real life situation. Starting small taking one or a few of these ideas and working with it for a while, and then going on to another, will give you a feel for which of these ideas works for you.

Make sure that you do something and do it right!

Crowdsourcing Genealogy with Tea and Sympathy

Outreach Approaches That Instruct and Engage

CHERI J. DANIELS

The Kentucky Historical Society is a state organization that serves a diverse community, across 120 counties. Besides housing three museums and a learning department, the library holds a significant archival collection alongside the largest genealogy collection in the state. Despite a steady stream of visiting researchers, programming and outreach remain continual challenges. In order to better engage with our genealogy community and to connect our collections to families in the far corners of the state, two outreach programs were developed that remain strong components in our strategic plan of being relevant to the communities we serve: *Genealogy Tea and Sympathy* and *Piecing Together History*.

Genealogy Tea and Sympathy

Beginning in 2013, this program was born out of a desire to better engage with our genealogy patrons through dialog. For many years, lecture style instruction has remained the standard programming format. With recycled topics and limited feedback from attendees, planning fresh and relevant programming was increasingly elusive. Additionally, despite a growing need for one on one research assistance, ever shrinking budgets and staff numbers prohibited personal consultation appointments. The *Genealogy Tea and Sympathy* program implements a format that allows for engaging, yet educational, dialog and consultation, with fewer staff commitments. Additionally, tea is very popular, providing a natural appeal to many visitors. What could be better than genealogy conversation over a cup of tea? This simple concept continues to be one of our most popular and consistently attended programs.

How to Get Started

The concept is very simple: Placing pots of tea and treats in a room with genealogists for a couple of hours, while they discuss research challenges. One thing we have done to keep this program fresh is limit its occurrence to every 5th Saturday of the month. On average, this means the events will occur about four times per year.

Ingredients

- Room large enough to hold 15–20 attendees.
- Tea: preferably several hot varieties, with flavored iced teas in the summer months.
- Treats: as simple or elaborate as you choose.
- Staff to serve as moderators: with 15–20 attendees, a couple of staff in attendance will suffice.
- Whiteboard or large paper for notes (optional): can be used to diagram a problematic family tree, but most sessions remain strictly conversational. Think about taking notes for programming topic ideas.

Cost

For the first few years, the event was free. The cost of tea is so minimal that it's of little significance. The cost of treats is where cost can arise, so budget accordingly. Recently, our organization implemented a campus admission fee, with the tea event now being included in the cost of general admission, or free with membership.

Pre-Event Planning

Prior to each event, promotional tools include: e-mail blast, social media posts, and local events calendars. Attendees are required to pre-register for accurate seating and treats count. An appropriately sized meeting room is reserved based on the number of incoming registrations.

Event Proceedings

After setting up the room with tea and treats at one end, attendees are instructed to help themselves. They are also reminded that this is not a formal tea party, allowing for multiple refill trips at their leisure, even while discussion is in progress. For the 15–20 attendee range, I make a few pots of tea in various varieties, but also include a couple of pots of hot water next to a bowl of various teabags. While the pots might empty in due course, you can keep pots of water heating to replenish and keep the tea flowing.

As soon as everyone has settled back at the table with their tea, the discussion begins with individual introductions. Attendees are instructed to include their names, where they are from, and a few of the surnames they have been researching. As soon as the introduction rounds have been made, the floor is opened up for anyone to introduce individual research challenges. This is also a moment that you can tailor to organizational goals or seasonal themes. When bringing in the new year, you may want to discuss upcoming research goals, or challenges encountered in the previous year. Regardless of topic or discussion direction, both novice and expert are encouraged to attend to provide a knowledgeable mix to the group. This event illustrates the power of the crowd when harnessed to brainstorm through research challenges. Despite the advertisement to help attendees break through their brick walls, the number of experts and rookies in attendance is fairly even. Both groups enjoy the lively discussion and learn from each other's experiences.

Event Challenges

Our regular attendance level at the Tea event runs around 15 to 20. This size of crowd works very well together, but be aware of your room acoustics prior to reservation. This range also allows for plenty of time to go around the room for introductions plus challenge discussions. With fewer attendees, it creates a nice intimate feel where conversation flows freely and informally, creating a space that makes everyone comfortable speaking in front of the others. At two hours, it never feels rushed, and keeping limits on the conversation direction is fairly easy. When the group grows past twenty, nearing thirty, the group can get out of hand quickly. While they may quietly listen to the introductions, the discussion of challenges provides moments of interpersonal deviation. When one person brings up a challenge that others have had, they chime in, and if they are sitting near one another, they naturally begin to break off into smaller conversations to work on the mutual challenge. Once this happens, others diverge in the same manner, and you can quickly have a room full of small groups talking about various challenges, minus the crowdsourcing benefit of learning from the solution. The first time this happened, I wasn't too concerned, simply because they all seemed to be having a marvelous time, and they were actually discussing genealogy challenges. The second time this happened, I attempted to reign the crowd back in so everyone could benefit from the conversations happening in the room.

Solution: Limit the number of attendees with a registration cap, or have extra staff on hand to break up the group into smaller groups, in different rooms, although this is not ideal.

Topics

Be prepared to cover any topic imaginable. Since the topics are driven by the attendees and based on real research, the conversation is genuine and not contrived. This dynamic maintains a fresh feel to each event, thereby fostering attendance. However, there have been a couple of occurrences when the conversation lagged slightly. To avoid these moments, come to the event equipped with a few questions or topics that you could introduce if the crowd is a little shy. The benefit to a live crowdsourcing event such as this is the topic diversity. Attendees will bring up such subjects as technology, records access/usage, DNA, preservation issues, repositories, and brick walls. Some conversations have intersected with current issues that challenge previous views of lineage and race, resulting in conversations that were enlightening, challenging, but also healing in nature. For example, one conversation drifted to membership in a Confederate lineage society. An African American attendee was curious as to the reasoning behind such a membership. The result was a group-wide discussion about the implications of having Confederate ancestors, enslaved ancestors, and the thin line between honoring your ancestors but not their efforts to retain the system of slavery.

Takeaways

Issues discussed help with future programming topics. Several of our regular experts are affiliated with lineage societies which helps foster organizational collaboration and relationships. Even when conversations create conflicting opinions, the group is respectful and everyone comes away having learned a great deal. For very little preparation and cost, this event provides us with the maximum benefit of assisting our patrons on an individual level, that meets their complex research needs.

Piecing Together History

Taking a slightly different direction in community crowdsourcing, the *Piecing Together History* series has significantly helped in the areas of archival and genealogical outreach. Each year, many collections are donated to our archival holdings. In most cases, the collection is delivered by an individual, who may or may not be directly connected to the contents. Since processing research is limited, a clear need for community input was identified. The format versatility of this program has yielded great success in not only connecting families and individuals back to their community collections, but also providing information necessary for future research and access.

In essence, an archival collection is chosen to be reintroduced to its family or community of origin. Once the selection has been made, the method of introduction is determined, followed by context preparation, venue arrangements, and marketing for the event. A typical *Piecing Together History* can be achieved by following these basic components.

Collection Selection

Any type of collection can be selected for an event, whether it is photographic, manuscript, or oral history. The key to successful selection is based on the collection profile. Is it large enough to require input from many family or community members? Will the contents resonate with the community you are attempting to engage? This part is important; many people will attend if the goal is to identify unknown people, places, or locations. With manuscripts, the appeal is trickier, but as long as the collection contains a popular subject, and individual connections can be made, people will attend. Also, think about potential community relationships you may want to foster: genealogical or historical societies, libraries, political or educational groups.

Identifying Your Audience

Once you have the collection selected, take a moment to think about the audience you are trying to attract. Clearly define this portion in order to move forward with timing, location, and event format. Think about this audience in its full spectrum, including their age, accessibility, technology challenges, and location. What if the audience you need is scattered and not easily corralled into one event location? This is where off-site participation should enter the planning phase.

Identifying Your Goals

You have the collection, and you have your audience selection, but what information do they have that will enhance your understanding of the collection? Not only will they be able to identify individuals, locations, or events, but can they fill in more of the story, or provide family links for this collection? You must identify your goals for the event to drive your information-gathering plan.

Location/Timing for Event

If the community you are attempting to engage with is located elsewhere, you should entertain the idea of partnerships for the event. You will need to choose an event location, and the best way to do this is to partner with other local organizations whose mission may be similar to your own, and which would benefit from a local event geared toward historical/genealogical crowdsourcing. Societies, museums, libraries, government entities, religious groups, schools, or even local colleges could be instrumental in making the event a success. After all, if you are an outside organization coming into a community, suspicion may hamper local participation. Gaining the trust of community participants can be easily accomplished if a local partnership exists.

Participation Format

While the above sections suggest in-person events, online-only crowdsourcing events are also an option. For most of our PTH events held in the past, a two-pronged approach was implemented; both in-person and online. Chosen format will affect your processing duties prior to the event. For either option, processing includes digitizing the collection—the entire collection or just the portions needed for the event. Once the images are digitized, complete with available metadata, a slideshow can be developed to create a portable version of the images. The idea here is to load onto tablets for easy zooming with the option to run in the background via large screen projection serving as group conversation triggers. Once the slideshow is ready, several hard copies can be printed and placed in binders for distribution around the room. The physical copies are there for hands-on information gathering. Attendees are invited to write all over the copies, adding their knowledge to the individual photos.

For online participation, the processing needs to be taken up a notch to make the images available and ready for crowdsourcing. The most important element of hosting an online event is making sure that the digital hosting platform used contains multiple engagement opportunities for crowdsourcing in the way of comments, contact submissions, social media sharing, etc.

Knowledge Sharing

While processing is always a time-consuming part of the preparation, it is worth your while to put extra effort into your metadata development. When entering a community, or inviting participants, the relationship starts out on a better foot if your staff has a significant understanding of the collection in relation to the community. Taking the time to research the community of impact shows that you are invested in this collection and the relationship. In fact, due to the diversity of the participants, we shifted away from the term "crowdsourcing" and instead opted for "Knowledge Sharing." While "crowdsourcing" can be a buzz word, not always known by your audience, "Knowledge Sharing" is self-explanatory, and conveys a message that you are there to participate in a knowledge exchange, or partnership. The more sharing and informed conversations you can have with the participants, the more engaging the event.

Marketing and Attendee Takeaways

Marketing is an important element of success with an event so dependent on community involvement. It is worthwhile to develop evergreen marketing tools in order to recycle the format when planning for subsequent community events. Some marketing elements include: series title, logo, and pamphlet/print advertisement templates. One helpful feature that places history or genealogy into the hands of the attendees is a half-sheet or pamphlet that includes collection information: timeline, biographies, family tree, etc.

During the Event

The room set-up should include several tables dispersed throughout to promote flow, with reduced crowding. Every table should contain the binders of images, along with post-it notes, pencils, and magnifying glasses. Sign-up sheets at the entrance are a must in order to allow for follow-up communication. The slide show should also be running to catch attention. As attendees inspect the binders, staff should walk the room with tablets and offer to zoom in on image details that may be hard to see in the photocopies. Become something of an eavesdropper. Listen for opportunities to capture the information being discussed, or to point out the pencils and binders. Most of the conversations will be informal, so feel free to ask questions that come to mind. Record what you can with your tablet, or within the binders. You will find that collecting the information is challenging. Many like to talk and reminisce, but few like to document this information. As for taking note of who provided information, little half slips of paper with areas for notes should be made available. Again, as people get excited about their memories, conversations can happen very rapidly, but instructing staff to be vigilant about noting the contributors is crucial to supplementing your metadata after the event. While the new information can be added with a note about the past community event, it is much more valuable if you can identify who contributed the information.

Previous Events

Over the past five years we have hosted about eight events, sometimes hosting one collection at multiple locations. Since each event was different, here is a brief synopsis of each.

Ogden

The Ogden Photograph Collection was hosted in more than one location and incorporated different information-collecting techniques. The first attempt was on-site at KHS, inviting community historical society members to assist in building the metadata for the photographs. Unfortunately, the participants were brought in at the digitization stage to create more of a streamlined process. By working in tandem, we assumed things would happen together, with little follow-up processing necessary. The problem with this approach is that since we only have a limited number of scanners, it meant a severe reduction in the number of supportable participants. We attempted this same format a second time, with the addition of local high school students to assist with the information collection, in the hopes of building relationships and dialog among different age groups within this community. But again, the same timing and scanning limitations reduced the amount of information gathered. For the third Ogden event, we took the images offsite, back to their community, in partnership with their local museum. We followed the standard format, which involved pre-scanned images, binders, tablets, etc. The results were much broader in scale, resulting in many more participants and a wealth of information gathered.

T.T. Wendell Collection

This collection of African American photographs from the early part of the 20th century provided an amazing connection to a large African American community in our state. This event was also held more than once to attract the maximum number of attendees, but the on-site version did not include binders. Instead, we actually brought out a large selection of the original photos, placing them under mylar, and affixing numerical labels. As participants examined the photos, they were encouraged to write down their information by using the half sheets, and placing the corresponding number at the top of the page. We also made several enlargements with a photocopier and had these in drawers below the images. If someone wanted to share this photo with a person not in attendance, they were encouraged to take a copy back with them to gather information. While we made sure to have the images up online for outside participation, taking the paper copies to nursing homes was a wonderful option, and resulted in a few being returned, complete with identification notes. One of the highlights of this event: the current owner of Dr. Wendell's house brought a photo album found in the attic that contained many duplicate images from the family, complete with contemporary labels! For the off-site event, we partnered with a Church congregation located near Dr. Wendell's original neighborhood. The result was an entirely different group of attendees whose roots were from this neighborhood, and who possessed a more intimate knowledge of the community and family.

Watson and Robinson Family Letters

With a collection of letters written by enslaved individuals during the 1840s and 50s, the format and connection to the community would be precarious. No contemporaries of the authors were alive to help us identify the writers or recipients, but since we had the names and locations, we were hoping that families and community attendees could help with context. Isabella Watson, the author of most of the letters had been removed to the far south with her owners' relocation. Being separated from friends and family, she was eager to send word on a regular basis about her condition, and to inquire about loved ones back on Kentucky plantations. She named many enslaved individuals in her letters, as well as several who were free or from the owner class, creating an amazing genealogical network. We partnered with the local public library, and brought the letters on site, complemented with binder copies to share around the room. Pre-processing was intensified, because the letters needed to be transcribed completely, with the help of academic historians. Once transcription was completed, we created a large index of all of the names and locations we could find within the letters. This helped immensely when trying to connect family members. This event was also hosted in partnership with the state African American genealogical society, which co-hosted a panel discussion regarding the community, slavery, and connecting families. While few family connections were directly made, the event was well attended, and some people even arrived with their family trees or scrapbooks in hand to contribute information. In order to permanently connect this collection back, we left behind a full copy of the letters, transcriptions, and index with the local library.

Other Events

We continue to host these events on a regular basis, choosing different collections to feature for each event, such as: local city collections, bourbon industry photographs, regional collections, etc. Each event is always a little different due to the collection composite or the community it touches.

A Word About Trust

Communities can be close-knit, wary of outsiders, and suspicious of government entities, such as ours. There are also the racial, ethnic, and cultural hesitations that may exist among some groups. In a couple of instances, information shared was controversial, or uttered in confidence, forcing us to make difficult decisions regarding entrusted information. In one instance, a photographer was being discussed by a few locals. The conversation lowered to a whisper, as it was remembered that locals knew enough about the photographer to make sure young girls did not go see him alone due to his penchant for photographing them in a state of undress, without their permission or knowledge. But a woman's voice got louder as she said "that's off the record, by the way!" The moment happened so fast that we didn't quite know how to respond. In the end, much of what they reported was hearsay, and not from a direct witness. We decided to record the conversation in our notes for the collection, but in context as second hand, and chose not to include this in the metadata for the individual photo.

In another instance, a group of African American women were speculating on the identity of a group of women in a photo. The photo was taken at a party, and once again, the whispering started as they decided not to identify one of the girls in the group as she was the only one who could freely attend any party of her choice because she was "passing." The group knew I was standing there, and one of the older ladies came up to me and put her arm around my waist. She leaned in and said, "Do you know what they are talking about, honey?" I shook my head as I continued to listen, and she leaned in to whisper, "She was passing as white." In that moment I was given a glimpse into this privileged circle, yet I was very relieved when the women refused reveal the identity of the woman in question. This removed the burden of whether or not to lift this woman's lifelong veil of secrecy. The conversation taught me more about this circle of women and their protectiveness, than any article or book could have done. These moments of confidence or hearsay will happen. However you choose to handle these situations, it is best to be prepared prior to the event.

Conflicts of Memory

In some cases, one person may identify a person or place with complete certainty, only to have that information contradicted by another participant across the room. Our policy in these instances is to record both identifications and include them in the metadata. This allows for both perspectives to be included, and with comments below, later participants could provide supplemental information that may confirm one or the other.

Metadata

After the event, you now have loads of new information to supplement your metadata. Be sure to schedule staff time right away to process these additions. You want to avoid the inevitability of fading memory. During the event, your staff will gather notes, and make notes, sometimes in the form of illegible scribbles. You need to interpret what was written while you have a fresh memory. Standard processing involves changing the metadata description, including the contributed details, the name of the informant, and the details of the event.

Takeaways

These events have created invaluable relationships in communities we could not easily reach in a state with 120 counties. This format is also versatile enough to allow us to connect various collections back to families and communities long after the event itself. We have noticed a ripple effect that has resulted in donations (both monetary and physical collections), local digitization initiatives, post-event oral history interviews, and introduction to the educational community. After six years of consistent success, the *Piecing Together History* series shows no signs of slowing down.

Part VIII: Management

Accessing and Creating Local Digital Services for Genealogy

Rhonda L. Clark

Increasingly, today's patron expects digital access for genealogy resources—access to local, unique resources; access to virtual reference; and access to support family archiving and genealogical research. The desire of the public to utilize digital access can be seen in the enormous popularity of both free and subscription genealogy databases. Where does the genealogy librarian fit into this evolution? What skills and knowledge are vital in providing relevant, reliable services to our patrons? To answer the needs for curation of local digital materials, the MSLS program at Clarion University provides a concentration in local and archival studies, with a unique focus among library and information programs on genealogical and family resources. This degree path requires not only a course in genealogy reference, but also Digital Libraries, Metadata for Local Special Collections, and other courses to support the varied demands that are put upon those curating local collections in a variety of cultural heritage settings. In the few years since this concentration began, we have seen students place successfully into a wide variety of internships, whose learning objectives increasingly demonstrate site emphasis on digital access. Our students, faculty, and program alumni are actively engaged in technology projects with libraries, historical/genealogy societies, and archives.

In reflecting upon the courses and skills that our students are finding useful in both internships and job placement, some key concepts emerge that may be valuable for both new genealogical librarians and for those who would like to update their skills in critical areas. Three areas of innovation and evolution stand out:

1. a new expanded notion of what is necessary for an effective genealogy/local studies web presence
2. an evolution in collaboration for digitizing local resources
3. the need to understand the use of metadata and related concepts in connecting local collections to patrons

The New Web Presence: Social, Expanded and Collaborative

In this era of web access to genealogy information, it is clear that libraries need to maintain a presence for their local collection. Well-established web design literature recommends that websites provide accurate, accessible information with graphical features and top-level access to information (Morris 2016). In addition, at the very least, the web page for genealogy and local collections should provide:

- access to key information about your physical site
- access to the library catalog
- information on subscription databases
- links to digitized information
- supporting information on how to use resources for genealogical and family history research

So, in other words, the casual visitor to a local site should be able to identify what services and resources are available. But many of our visitors are virtual-only. They Google the name of their relatives' hometowns in hopes that the libraries will provide something more. How can librarians with a bare-bones web presence take the site to the next level?

Take Advantage of Easily Established Social Media Tools

It may not take a major effort to jump-start a successful web interaction with the public. Social media tools can provide patrons personal access to stories, photos, information, a question forum, and some personality. Patrons want to interact by submitting comments and questions; they enjoy immediate feedback. So a social media interface like Facebook, a blog, Pinterest, and Instagram can provide the tools libraries need to connect their patrons with genealogy services and resources. While many of our students have used social media tools, they are less familiar with the potential of such sites for genealogy librarianship. In addition, the day to day demands of genealogy librarianship may not allow for time to be spent on a social media account, yet we teach our students the desirability of using at least one tool on a local special collection website.

So, what are the immediate advantages of social media tools? They are:

- easy to launch
- provide intersection with the fabric of patrons' day to day lives
- quickly incorporate video and still images
- allow for patron messaging, comments, and interaction
- provide frequent, timely information to spark interest in the collections and programs at the library.

The power of these tools should not be underestimated. Recently, for example, the Titusville, PA, Historical Society launched a Facebook presence with a daily posting consisting of images and links related to local history and genealogy. By far, the most popular of those links, a photograph of a historic downtown Titusville drug store that recently closed, reached over 4,800 people in a few days (Titusville Historical Society 2017). The posting also generated lots of comments with information on the drugstore and its impact on the lives of citizens. This historical society has a membership of around 40; it sees 10–15 persons a month at meetings; it hosts up to 50 people at its most successful events in town. And, yet, through the power of a Facebook posting, this small society reached thousands of individuals with their image and words. By maintaining a site that posts quality information on a regular basis, the Society is able to provide far more support and service to local history and genealogy patrons than they could otherwise.

Of course, there are many potential downsides to social media, including:

- the need to provide consistent, daily or almost daily postings
- the possibility of destructive, negative feedback on the site
- a significant demand on library staff time from patrons who are virtual and do not utilize the physical site nor pay taxes locally to support it

Fortunately, there exist multiple resources that can streamline the launching of successful social media. In the case of the Titusville Historical Society, the technology committee spent time working through a Non-Profit Social Media Handbook (2012) and developed a social media policy that was posted on the site. The team of three persons successfully maintains the site and plans for rotation of new members to avoid burnout for the original developers. With regard to the issue of resources, a PayPal button or other method to encourage donations can go a long way towards mitigating potential costs or perceived importance of these sites in the daily workflow of a genealogy librarian. Additionally, reimagining the methods for counting circulation statistics to include online usage of digitized resources should be discussed in the library community.

Expand the Web Presence

We also teach our students to evaluate the web presence of local special collection sites. As noted by Clark and Miller, all items in a local special collection should be catalogued, indexed, or otherwise represented in some form that is accessible via the web interface, even if the access is to a surrogate or description of the materials in the collection (2016). In other words, make sure that someone accessing the website for a genealogy or local collection can see a list of all the information/databases/catalogs that make up the collection. Increasingly, patrons expect to see full-text genealogy sources available through cultural heritage institution websites. Websites should be expanded to include:

- digitized local resource materials
- links to other genealogy sites for the area
- catalog links to fully digitized resources for the area (why re-invent the wheel?) Good places to check for digitized publications, such as county histories and maps include:
    - The Library of Congress
    - Internet Archive
    - State and local repositories

Additionally, thought should be given to easy methods for providing virtual reference. Many libraries have done this for decades by telephone, but, increasingly, email and even chat reference have become available on local collection pages. Like social media tools, virtual reference options should be employed only after planning to ensure that responses are swift, high quality, and consistent in depth and approach. Like on-site genealogy reference services, virtual options should be well described, with a defined response time for inquires, specified geographic and/or content limitations, and any applicable fees posted visibly near the portal for launching a virtual request.

It may be that the laundry list of desired content on expanded local collection pages may be overwhelming or nearly impossible for small public libraries and genealogy societies. This is where use of a collaborative approach can advantageous.

Build a Collaborative Web Presence

Genealogy services differ from many other patrons' needs at a local library because the types of information requests made by the genealogy patrons may be fulfilled at a wide variety of cultural heritage sites within the same town, county, or region. In fact, it is difficult to predict where the bulk of genealogical materials reside in any given town. The locations, accessibility, and services for genealogy materials may differ significantly in each locale, even for towns in the same county. With this in mind, often collaboration between genealogical societies and libraries or between historical societies and other groups in town can provide for programming and references services that would be difficult to pull off with just one institution. For example, it is common to see historical or genealogical society volunteers providing genealogy reference in libraries either in addition to the normal reference there or as the only specialized genealogical reference support available.

With the advent of an expected digital presence for institutions, the notion of a collaborative web presence for all those institutions in a town with genealogy or local studies materials holds much merit. Such a page may reside on the web page of one of the interested partners in town or on an independent site. In Titusville, PA, Clarion students and faculty have helped facilitate the development of a local digital portal on Omeka.net. The portal was developed with the cooperation of four institutions in town that have genealogy/local history materials (the local public library, the local high school alumni society, a state-affiliated history museum and the local historical society). The site currently provides contact information and basic questions on the goals of the digital visitor so they can be directed to the right institution, using the right methods and at the best times to get their request fulfilled (Titusville PA Heritage Connection 2017). Eventually the site will house digitized materials, particularly from collections in town that have other priorities for their own digital sites, such as businesses, churches, and family resources.

The process of developing this site provided a learning opportunity for the graduate students involved and for the faculty member liaison to the project. We learned that to develop such a project we should:

- Have at least one real-time meeting where all potential partners can discuss what their individual goals and information might be for the site.
- Keep in in mind the digital possibilities for volunteerism and external support. For example, our graduate intern provided organization and information flow,

though she physically was located several states away. We choose the cloud-based version of Omeka (Omeka.net) for the site, so our snowbirds and other interested parties who did not live in the area could still participate in information update and even digital reference down the road.
- We realized the importance of creating a list of goals for the site, both now and in the future, as well as the importance of revisiting these goals at regular intervals for evaluation and tweaking.
- We realized that a shared digital portal requires shared branding or clear textual affirmation of the role for each participating entity.

If the notion of a social media presence, local digital portal, or other enhanced web presence for local collections sounds daunting, remember that you may ask the public for task-specific volunteers, some of whom might offer to help build the site, provide regular content, monitor email, schedule annual portal planning meetings, etc. Just set in place a good training session and establish clear, written guidelines for each task. But what about expanded digitized collections? How does one go about adding these to a site or portal without great expertise in the area of digitization? The answer lies in collaboration.

The New Digitized Collection: Collaboration and Support

Libraries, certainly major public sites and academic libraries, have been in the business of digitizing unique resources for many years now. Even small public libraries all over the country have been able to get into the act by digitizing small collections of postcards, photographs, or historic newspapers. Generally, these projects require funding and some expertise for project management or even digitizing on site. LSTA funding and other local initiatives have given many sites the opportunity to post their unique content online, which has provided ample help to genealogists all over the country. Discovery of such collections, however, remains challenging. Though many libraries upload a catalog record for their digital collection to WorldCat, including a link back to the site and collection, the average patron does not know to check that resource.

Happily, a number of developments in recent years are allowing for greater participation of small societies in large-scale digitization sites:

- Many non-profit and library digital collaborations provide opportunities for sharing the challenges of digitization and platform hosting, for example, statewide sites such as Arizona Memory, Maine Memory and AccessPA Digital Collections provide an access tool for digital content, as well as instruction in digitization and metadata.
- FamilySearch.org will work with cultural heritage sites to digitize their genealogy materials.
- Internet Archive.org will host digitized material on its site.
- Digital Public Library of America (dp.la) is providing education and outreach to allow existing digital collections into a single access portal. DPLA is creating service hubs, with webinars to assist with creation of a DPLA-compliant collection.

What do you have to do to be a part of these efforts? First, look to see if you have materials that meet the standard requirements:

- Published material that no longer has copyright attached or you have secured it from the owner. For a chart on determining copyright coverage, see the Peter Hirtle's chart on Copyright Term and the Public Domain in the United States (2017). Additionally, you can get help with determining copyright or help with taking steps to protect the library if copyright ownership is not clear through educational seminars, paid consultants, or sometimes through district and state library consultants.
- Material is highly relevant for family historians, such as vital documents, photographs with identified persons, historic newspapers, obituary files, cemetery records, family genealogies.
- Material has not been digitized already. If you locate published materials about your region that have been digitized, just add a catalog entry for these items and link to them. County histories, for example, are commonly found on Internetarchive.org, with downloadable cataloging records. See individual items for specific limitations and uses.

Genealogy librarianship can be greatly enhanced by participating in new digital projects, even starting with a small collection. There are many ways to connect genealogy programming to digital collections. In addition, the use of digitized items is expandable to a global population. The effectiveness of your digital collection outreach often lies in the cataloging information, or metadata, attached to your digital files.

The New Metadata Landscape: Connecting Us All

We feel it is critical to teach our students about cultural heritage resources-specific concepts related to cataloging our digitized items. Below are several terms that new genealogy librarians or seasoned librarians hoping to improve their digital collections should be aware of:

Metadata. The term most often used for cataloging of digital items or objects is "metadata." A wide variety of metadata schemas exist. Very commonly we see Dublin Core being utilized to describe digital collections. This set of fifteen main descriptors for digital objects can be learned fairly quickly. When a site sets out to digitize, there are often suggested rules for applying metadata standards to a collection, as seen in publications available to contributors to the Arizona Memory Project (Arizona State Library 2016). Specific interpretations of each category of metadata are provided, as well as syntax rules. Controlled vocabulary can be utilized, as well as keywords and descriptions of the objects. It is important to understand that participation in specific digital projects will require adherence to their specific applications of a metadata schema. While that concept may seem difficult to someone who has not yet worked on a digital project, in fact, metadata schemas for digital objects are much more accessible than standard cataloging rules. Certainly a trained cataloger would have a good grasp of controlled vocabularies that could be input into certain fields in a metadata schema, but teams of individuals at a site can generally be trained to apply basic metadata required for submission to a digital host.

So, in short, it is good to understand that metadata is generally not a barrier to a digitizing project, rather, creation of the metadata rules are often already accomplished and the focus of the local team can be on training to input information from both the conceptual and logistical perspectives. Within most metadata schemas are fields that will provide ample opportunity for the local genealogy/history librarian to input valuable descriptions, names, dates, and keywords to enhance discovery of genealogical information.

Tagging. Tagging may seem like old news, a fad that never quite caught on for describing books in library catalogs. Tagging, however, can provide invaluable information for local digitized objects in a genealogy collection. Objects with tagging or comment fields enabled allow the patron or user of the digital library to provide information about the items. These terms generally are not originating from any controlled vocabulary. They are not a part of the fields that are catalogued by the site staff. Instead, they provide an opportunity for the patron to add personal information that could not otherwise be found, much like the user-added information on many genealogy websites. Of course, like user-generated family trees, the information is not vetted nor validated in any way by the site. Others must take responsibility to check the information before using it in research. But the potential for genealogical research gains far outweigh the potential for errors over large numbers of records. How else would we know that "Aunt Edna lived in this house," or "That man in the photo is my grandpa, James Everett Smith." Tagging for genealogical purposes is most valuable when contact information is provided by those who supplied information, but having some clues and searchable names in the tagging fields can aid tremendously in discovery and use of a local digitized collection. In addition, tagging allows for multilingual access to family photos and other digitized materials.

Linked Data. On the horizon is the goal of linking key metadata from MARC records and other cataloging methods to allow for automatic use of the metadata in other cataloging systems. This notion of "harvesting" key search information hinges on successful mapping of metadata fields in different systems. While the nuts and bolts of this system is beyond this introductory essay, it is good to keep your eyes open for training and information about linked data, particularly if you are a cataloger.

In sum, at Clarion, we try to impart to our local and archival MSLS students the need for continual education to stay current in the field of digital access for local collections. We emphasize interaction with other professionals at conferences, applied projects, and an open mind for the expansion of digital access and services for genealogy resources. For more information and educational opportunities on emerging trends in genealogy digital services, try some of the following resources and links:

- DPLA webinars and materials from past webinars (note especially Tamika Maddox Strong and Amy Johnson Crow, "Using DPLA for Genealogy and Family History": https://dp.la/info/get-involved/workshops/
- Advanced DC and linked data webinars: http://dublincore.org/resources/training/
- Introductory webinars on a wide variety of library topics: http://www.webjunction.org/find-training.html
- Library of Congress Personal Digital Archiving Day Kit: http://www.digitalpreservation.gov/personalarchiving/padKit/index.html

Works Cited

Arizona State Library. Last modified 2016. "Arizona Memory Project Metadata." http://azmemory.azlibrary.gov/ui/custom/default/collection/default/resources/custompages/amp_docs/AMP-MetadataGuidelines.pdf.

Clark, Rhonda L., and Nicole Wedemeyer Miller. 2016. *Fostering Family History Services: A Guide for Librarians, Archivists, and Volunteers*. Santa Barbara, CA: Libraries Unlimited.

Hirtle, Peter B. Last modified January 9, 2018. "Copyright Term and the Public Domain in the United States." http://copyright.cornell.edu/resources/publicdomain.cfm.

Idealware. April 2012. *Nonprofit Social Media Workbook*. http://www.idealware.org/reports/nonprofit-social-media-policy-workbook/.

Morris, Terry Ann. Last modified October 31, 2016. "Web Design Best Practices Checklist." http://terrymorris.net/bestpractices/.

Titusville PA Heritage Connection. 2017. http://titusvillepaheritageconnection.omeka.net.

Titusville (Pa) Historical Society Facebook Page. Entry of May 31, 2017. https://www.facebook.com/titusvillehistoricalsociety/.

Genealogy for Academics
Utilizing Genealogy Resources for More Than Family History

NANCY A. BUNKER
and JENNY L. PRESNELL

Genealogy has become more than just a pastime. Aside from personal family history, genealogical sources have been used to tell the stories of famous or significant individuals. With the popularity of such programs as *Finding Your Roots* and *Who Do You Think You Are*, genealogy is more mainstream than ever. In the case of *Finding Your Roots*, Henry Louis Gates uses famous individual's family to narrate American history. However, genealogists and professional historians seldom collaborate. This essay will explore their hesitancy to reach across disciplinary boundaries, look at the history of genealogy, and present a sample course currently offered in an academic department. Understanding the historical development of American genealogy from the mid–18th century to the present helps to understand genealogy's role in academia. Academic courses, such as the one described, face challenges, including students' weak understanding of American history, their inability to create a cultural context for individuals, and the lack of available resources for certain ethnic and racial groups.

Historians and Genealogists Can Be Friends

Historians and genealogists have always had a tenuous and contentious relationship. "To historians, genealogists are obsessive collectors of meaningless minutiae, enthusiastic, but woefully untrained…. To genealogists, historians are utterly out-of-touch academics, offering one jargon-dripping tome after another…" (O'Hare 2002). Professional genealogist Elizabeth Shown Mills has spent her career trying to rectify this divide by advocating and creating research methodology standards and courses for genealogists, believing professional genealogical education raises the standards for genealogists will ultimately, gain respect from historians (Elizabeth Shown Mills). She defines three kinds of genealogists (Mills 2003, 272–3):

- "Family Tree Climbers." Collectors of past family members with little interest in documentation.

- "Traditional Genealogists." Data compilers that produce meticulously searched and documented lineages with names and dates of significant family events, but without historical context.
- "Generational Historians." Researchers of all types combining the work of Traditional Genealogists while contextualizing individuals and family data within a historical time period. (See also Howe and Strauss [2000] for the development of the term "generational history.")

This last category mentioned, "Generational Historians," is the meeting place for both genealogists and historians. This will create a richer understanding of the cultural heritage of the United States, both for individuals and for the nation as a whole.

History and Purposes of Genealogy

The history of the practice and uses of genealogy has evolved from proving legitimacy of rulers and ties in medieval Europe, to a history of the everyday man; from a practice by the elite to an avocation of everyday individuals. François Weil in *Family Trees: A History of Genealogy in America* defines four phases of genealogical practices and uses of family data (Weil 2013, 5–7). Understanding how and why genealogical data was collected and used informs the teaching of genealogy practices.

- *To mid/late-18th century.* Weil calls this "status related genealogy" (Weil 2013, 16). Families connected to each other to affirm ties to kin both in Europe and in the new republic. It was important to come from "good," moral extended families, even if family members had never met. Newly formed societies like the Massachusetts Historical and Genealogical Society began to document and publish registers of early settlers (Weil 2013, 43, 50–62).
- *Antebellum: 1760s to 1860s.* Merchants and other middle class families practiced genealogy to establish a sense of self and of the family in moral, egalitarian, and civic terms. By using published genealogies of "blue blood" families, these middle-class folks could tie into the new American version of aristocracy. Claiming to be part of "Puritan Stock" or "Southern Gentry," individuals labeled their families as responsible for the success of the new nation, contributing to the sectionalism of the Civil War (Weil 2013, 6, 45, 85–94).
- *Post–Civil War to Mid-20th Century.* Post–Civil War United States through the mid–20th century would see vast and drastic changes due to industrialization, urbanization, migration, and immigration. Genealogy proved to be a way to include (to be a member of) and exclude (to be differentiated from) desirable or less desirable groups. Racism and nativism gave rise to eugenics as well as societies based on ancestry (Sons of the American Revolution, for example). With the professionalization of historians and the founding of the American Historical Association in 1884, this era begins the divide between historians and genealogists. The market for pedigrees in part leads to the professionalism of genealogists (Weil 2013, 112–114, 130, 173).
- *Mid-20th Century to Present.* The end World War II began a long and gradual rise in interest in ethnic history especially in light of the civil rights movement. People became interested in their own cultures and looked for a sense of their

history, no longer looking to establish a pedigree for a kind of moral authority. Historians began to study the new "social history," a history the daily life of the common person. In 1894, the Church of Jesus Christ of the Latter-day Saints decided that tracing ancestry was integral to their mission and beliefs. By the 1960s, the church had begun massive microfilming projects and regional libraries. Perhaps the biggest impetus for family history, of all races was the television series *Roots* (1977) demonstrating historical context interweaved with a family's history (Weil 2013, 173, 183–187,194–196). In the early 21st century, interest became so strong that several television series were developed around genealogical research on families of famous people. *Who Do You Think You Are* (2010–), an adaptation of a British television program (2004) by the same name, looks at specific events in celebrities' pasts in historical context. Henry Louis Gates, Jr., renowned Harvard University historian hosts *African American Lives* I and II (2006, 2008), *Faces of America* (2010), and *Finding Your Roots* (2012–). Historical Research and genealogy have become intertwined in the U.S popular culture. All of Gates' series make interesting use of DNA analysis to track ethnicity and to link to historical, social, and migratory patterns.

The use of genealogy today is more widespread, varied, and sophisticated than ever before. Increasingly historians are not only using genealogical research techniques in their own research, but desire to include these techniques in their classes. However, regular credit courses focusing on genealogy are rare in academia. One example of a particular course is described below. It is taught by a librarian within the general education curriculum at Whitworth University, a medium-sized liberal arts school in Spokane, Washington.

Details of an Academic Genealogy Course

Before creating the genealogy course in 2010, a substantial search was executed looking for existing courses in any type of academic institution nationwide. Outside of the universities affiliated with the Church of Jesus Christ of Latter-day Saints there were just a handful of courses taught in general undergraduate curriculum. A recent search has turned up just as few courses.

There are some courses in graduate programs in Library and Information Science to aid future librarians in answering the needs of genealogy patrons. The History Section of the American Library Association/Reference and User Services Division maintains guidelines on the subject "Guidelines for a Unit or Course of Instruction in Genealogical Research at Schools of Library and Information Science" (Guidelines 2007) on what types of content should be included for preparing librarians for frontline genealogy.

There are also a number of non-credit genealogy courses. These are offered at community colleges and through for-profit or nonprofit organizations. Some universities offer these non-credit courses as well but few offer a course in the general curriculum. Increasingly, history librarians are seeing genealogy projects within a variety of courses encompassing a wide range of disciplines. Librarians have reported seeing genealogy projects on syllabuses of courses in the fields of History, Anthropology, Sociology, Psychology, and Theology.

Interdisciplinary Studies 201 Genealogy in Cultural Context

Genealogy in Cultural Context was first offered in spring of 2011 as a two-credit interdisciplinary studies course with American Diversity credit. The course description on the syllabus reads:

> This course introduces students to genealogical research in the context of cultural diversity. Students will learn genealogical research skills as well as historical research skills and theory. Emphasis is on placing genealogical study in context with regional, national, and international events. Students will learn about diverse viewpoints within American society and will synthesize this knowledge with their own family history. Students will analyze the cultural diversity of their family history; with particular attention to placing their family in historical context. (How was their family typical or atypical of their time, place and culture?) Students will be required to reflect on their research practice by understanding how larger events or institutional contexts allow them to better understand where to find information [Bunker, 2015].

The textbook for the class is *The Source: A Guidebook to American Genealogy* (2006), 3rd edition, edited by Loretto Dennis Szucs and Sandra Hargreaves Luebking. Although the book is available on paper, many of the students used the free online version. Ancestry, which hosts the book, breaks the text down into segments making assigned chapters directly and easily linkable into the course management system. No other textbook or genealogy software was required. Several students admitted that they took the class because there was no textbook to buy.

The first two semesters the class was taught, it was held in regular classrooms. Thereafter, it has been taught in a computer lab, which is highly recommended. If the lecture or presentations concluded early, the remainder of class time could be effectively filled with individual students' research questions while others searched for some additional sources or practiced the newly taught methodologies.

The first month of class consists of mostly lectures covering the basics of genealogy and cultural context; introduction to genealogy; how genealogy is similar and different from history as they learned in school; computer databases for genealogy research; beginning vital records and immigration records research. Within the first few weeks, a lecture on the problems of gender and names in genealogical (and historical) research is incorporated. Outside of class, the students are asked to gather family information by compiling what they know about their families and then selecting a branch of the family to look at in depth. At the beginning of the second month, the students are asked to select a branch and propose research topics for their final project.

The final project, introduced in the first month, involves compiling a branch of the tree going back at least five generations and providing documentation for at least nine people. At least thirty sources are required that document birth, marriage and/or death of their ancestors. Documentation could be birth certificates, marriage certificates, death certificates, photographs, newspaper articles, court documents, letters or other manuscript materials that prove the individuals were born, married, or died at a specific time and in a specific place. In addition, the students select three people of different generations to research in depth and then write a biographical sketch that places those individuals in cultural context. The final project also includes a cultural context analysis of the entire branch of the family, evaluating how the experiences of their ancestors influenced their family historically and currently. A third section requires a historical timeline of the major events in the lives of their family. The final project is due on the first day of finals week.

The proposal for the final project is due at the start of the second month of class. This involves both a written document for the professor, and an oral presentation (5–7 minutes) to the entire class. Students propose which branch of the family tree they will pursue and name the three people they plan to spotlight in their final project. Often this changes as the semester progresses and they uncover more information about interesting ancestors.

From the third week, students are asked to turn in, electronically, copies of the research and documents that they found. "Source Portfolios" are due each week and consist of three sources with appropriate citations. The students also need to identify the source type of the document, and whether it is primary or secondary resource. This task, which was assumed they would easily grasp, became a serious challenge for some students. The "Source Analysis" requires that one of those sources is discussed in detail explaining what it is, what it told them, and how it is helpful or not to their research. At the end of 10 weeks, the students would have turned in 30 sources, which they may include in their final project.

Additionally, the second month is occupied with further readings, classroom lectures and videos on more specific issues in genealogy and record types. These records include oral history; land, military, religious, social organizational, court, and newspaper records; and directories. Students usually move from searching for general vital records to searching for the additional record types as they are studied in class. This allows them to broaden their Source Portfolios and Source Analysis entries.

As the semester progresses, students often need to change the branch of their family tree to be researched or the individuals that they have selected to do the biographical sketches because they hit a brick wall and are unable to go back five generations. In that instance, an alternative research plan can be devised with instructor's approval and would be totally personalized to the student's research needs at that point. For example, profiling a family member not in a direct line or in another branch of the tree might be substituted for one on whom information is not available. After mid-semester break, the focus of the class changes from primarily readings and lectures on genealogy resources to setting the cultural context. The research question shifts to exploring the family story within the time and place and connecting the family to the general historical landscape.

Historical periods of the ancestors' lives are examined for intersections with the family history. For example, one great-great-great-great-grandfather might be profiled as a soldier in the Civil War. The life of a family of their means, and their location would be examined during that period, as well as regimental history for the soldier. A second profile might be of a great-great-grandmother who immigrated in 1900 and moved west. A third profile might be of a great-grandfather farming in the depression era of the 1930s. Other students who may not be able to trace their family back that many years will discuss issues of the 1950s, 1960s or 1970s. Several students tackled profiling family in Europe prior to moving to America, a task made easier every year as more international genealogy and historical resources are uploaded.

The general assumption of the American experience is that it has been more homogenous than history actually shows. The diversity in American culture goes back to the earliest settlement of the first nations. It was not certain racial or ethnic groups that had experiences outside the norm. In truth, no norms existed. Each of the students' families has different experiences based on their origin, place of settlement, occupation, gender, and faith. By examining their own families' experiences and understanding what it meant to be a small farmer during the dustbowl, a watchmaker in a borough of New York, a saloon keeper in the midst of prohibition, or a cavalry soldier on the great plains, students understand more about how history and their own families are intertwined.

Throughout the course, as the students learn about their own families, they are asked to share with the entire class. This also brings out the diversity of experiences in backgrounds that appear to be similar and provides student to student assistance in pursuing their research. In a perfect world, a class would represent a wide range of ethnic and cultural backgrounds. Sharing with classmates would be sufficient for everyone to learn about a wide variety of American experiences. Class makeup is seldom optimal with some cultures, classes, or experiences not represented.

As the course fulfills an American Diversity General Education requirement, the students are also asked to research a major ethnic group of which they may or may not be a part. The first time the course was offered, lectures, films, and guest speakers covered the diversity of Native Americans, African Americans, Asian Americans, Hispanic Americans, and European Americans. Some of the students were not appreciative of "wasting their time learning about other ethnic groups when it did not apply to their family." The second time the class was taught the major diversity groups exercise became student-led projects. Groups of 3–5 students were assigned to research one of the groups and present their findings to the class incorporating audiovisual, lecture and/or class activities. The response of the students to their peers teaching them about the same subjects and showing the same type of videos was very different. Having a student stand in front of his/her peers and saying "I had never heard of Angel Island but you really should learn about it" bred enthusiasm for the subject. At the end of the group presentations discussion is used to examine the subject in more detail, bring up information that might have been omitted, or sometimes, incorrectly stated.

The course is designed to frontload the readings and instruction to give the students opportunity to use what they learned. The second part of the class requires building and writing the final project; it is worth 250 points. The research topic proposal and presentation is worth 150 points; groups are awarded 40 points for presentations on ethnic groups. Source Portfolios and Source Analysis are worth 300 points. The final project presentation is worth 100 points, peer evaluations of the presentations (they have to listen to each other) and group interactions are also worth 50 points. The remaining points include quizzes (to encourage reading assigned articles) and progress meetings with the instructors. Progress meetings, which are essential when the class is taught in a classroom, are less beneficial with the lab classes since the professors can keep abreast of the students' progress on a weekly basis.

Adaptations and Assignments

While this is an example of a complete course, other potential projects could result. Instead of individual genealogy histories, students could look at a block or section of a city, or of a small town and look at changes over time or changes between decades. Students can examine location-related questions. What businesses were there? What type of transportation? What was the ethnic makeup of the community? Where did residents live, work, shop, worship and recreate? What were the wages? How, when, and why did these things change? While this approach is less personal, it can also give students a sense of the place in which they live. Similar to the online collection, *Valley of the Shadow* (http://valley.lib.virginia.edu/), students could look comparatively at neighboring communities (but on a much smaller scale than this project). Students could also compare the histories of two houses and their residents from two contrasting neighborhoods.

These types of assignments are increasing in a variety of classes across the curriculum. These assignments show the students another side of history. History did not happen to our ancestors; they were integral in making it happen. The choices they made to immigrate, to settle in a certain area, the education they received, the occupation they chose, and even the person they married, all that influenced where their families are today. Lives seldom exist in a vacuum. Placing our ancestors or even those who inhabited our neighborhoods in the cultural context of their times allows us to view history as it was meant to be viewed.

Conclusion

Genealogy has entered mainstream historical research. In many ways, genealogists have embraced historical methodologies at a faster rate than historians have sought out the genealogical sources. However, it is history's loss, for the genealogy resources are now based in strong historical documentation that is not available to historians anywhere else. Divisions between historians and genealogists are slowly blurring, as each adopts the techniques and skills of the other. Separate courses as well as an integration of genealogical style research into regular curriculum is needed, not just for history students but for many other disciplines as well. Librarians are well positioned to bring genealogists, historians, and other academics together in today's college education.

Works Cited

Bunker, Nancy A., and Judy Dehle. 2015. "Genealogy in Cultural Context," Syllabus. Whitworth University, Spokane, WA.
Family Search Wiki. s.v. "Elizabeth Shown Mills." 16, Feb. 2016. https://familysearch.org/wiki/en/Elizabeth_Shown_Mills.
Guidelines for a Unit or Course of Instruction in Genealogical Research at Schools of Library and Information Science. 2007. http://www.ala.org/rusa/resources/guidelines/guidelinesunit.
Howe, Neil, and William Strauss. 2000. *Millennials Rising: The Next Great Generation*. New York: Random House/Vintage Books.
O'Hare, Sheila. 2002. "Genealogy and History." *Common-Place* 2. Part I. http://www.common-place-archives.org/vol-02/no-03/ohare/
Szucs, Loretto Dennis, and Sandra Hargreaves Luebking. (2006). *The Source: A Guidebook to American Genealogy*, 3rd edition. Provo, UT: Ancestry Publishing.
Valley of the Shadow. http://valley.lib.virginia.edu/
Weil, François. 2013. *Family Trees: A History of Genealogy in America*. Cambridge, MA: Harvard University Press.

The Butler County Obituary and Newspaper Index
An Example of Genealogy Database Creation and Ongoing Management

MARGARET E. HEWITT

Newspapers are a valuable and frequently overlooked genealogy research tool. While obituaries are the most obvious source of family information within their pages, a host of articles can yield connections to missing relatives, complete gaps in timelines, and produce clues that flesh out the personalities of those long-dead. Birthplace, residence, occupation, civic involvement, date of death, cause of death, character, relatives, friends, and funeral arrangements can all be gleaned from one small obituary, leading researchers to other avenues of exploration (Morgan and Smith, 2014, 30–32).

In all genealogical research, no single source should be taken as fact unless it can be corroborated by other documentation. On census records, death certificates, and marriage licenses, informants can be unintentionally wrong or willfully misleading in the information they provide—ages can be wrong, relatives' names can be omitted, and spellings can vary wildly. Newspaper articles are accessible additional documents that can be compared to historic sources to build or disprove a genealogical case (Breland, 2014, 29). Although a newspaper article may also have omissions and errors, their supplemental research value is immense.

Historic newspapers can also stand in for missing documentation when absolutely necessary. In Pennsylvania, counties were not required to collect marriage licenses until 1885 (Humphrey, 2006). Notice of a marriage in a 19th century newspaper's social columns may be the only surviving proof that a marriage took place—and for lineage organizations like the Daughters of the American Revolution that require documentation of marriages, the article might be essential. Similarly, birth and death records were not collected in Pennsylvania with any consistency until after 1893 (Humphrey, 2006, iv). Early newspaper accounts of these events are again likely the only proof available to a genealogist.

Knowing the value potentially hidden in historic newspapers, researchers still too often pass them up because the process of browsing microfilm collections can be prohibitively time consuming. Historic communication delays could bury the announcement of a marriage or death in an issue published weeks after the actual event date. Most historic papers also lack modern front page indexes and standardized layouts, shoehorning obituaries, personal notices, and court events in wherever they fit amid ads and national news. If faced with limited time, how does one know when to quit looking because an article does not exist, when it might be hiding a few pages away? Furthermore, if a researcher does not have any evidence to know that a marriage, death, or trial record even exists, how can they begin to search for it? In these instances, an indexed directory can revolutionize genealogy research.

Origins of the Obituary Index

The Butler Area Public Library houses a newspaper collection of more than 950 reels of microfilm. The collection spans issues of multiple, sometimes concurrently published, newspapers from 1818 to 2016 and continues to grow. Many rare Butler County papers were collected and microfilmed by the library in the 1990s and early 2000s, first in collaboration with the county historical society and later as part of the Penn State University Pennsylvania Newspaper Project, which was sponsored by the National Endowment for the Humanities (Ruch, 1999; Andrasovsky, 2006). For eleven years, a library-administered online Obituary and Newspaper Index has been paired with this microfilm collection, enhancing patron access to the material and improving genealogical research in Butler County.

The Butler Area Public Library genealogy department began an obituary index on 3 × 5 paper cards in 1990. Volunteers recorded current death notices in the paper as they were published, while indexing past obituaries, starting with the earliest microfilmed papers from 1824. (At the time, the microfilmed newspaper collection was approximately 650 reels.) By 1999, the collection had grown to more than 70,000 cards, spanning 1824–1968 and 1990–1999, and was becoming unmanageable (Rittmeyer, 2000). As the index grew, it took up increasing physical space in the genealogy department, and it became more difficult to keep the cards alphabetized and tidy. The flimsy cards were also at risk of damage during use or theft.

The decision was made to convert the system over to a searchable database; the project was the brainchild of then-genealogist Luanne Eisler and volunteer Louis Heitlinger. The database would not only be a searchable list of names to provide faster access to the known obituaries in Butler County newspapers, it would allow patrons to use additional search parameters to help break through brick walls. Volunteers simultaneously began indexing obituaries from microfilm to fill the 22-year gap in the card collection, while also typing information from existing cards into a database. Heitlinger and Eisler recruited undergraduate computer science students from Slippery Rock University to build the website as a cost-saving measure. Six years later, the Obituary Index website officially launched on January 28, 2006, with a Grim Reaper–themed party for local genealogists (Rittmeyer, 2000). At launch, the typing project was only through surnames beginning with "R," but was soon completed. The index would hit the 100,000 name entry mark in 2007, and has grown at a pace of approximately 30,000 new entries per year.

The Current Record Creation Process

The initial index database was populated from the information written on the paper index card collection. Generally, a name, date of obituary publication, and name of newspaper were all that was provided, though some cards occasionally had the name of a relative. Once the process of documenting and inputting deaths was largely complete, the focus of the project turned to expanding the index. The Index now cites articles on marriages, divorces, family reunions, major accidents, significant court proceedings, anniversaries, and family reunions. While more content is available that is of interest—local papers were filled with the comings and goings of relatives, vacation plans, hospitalizations, parties, and business dealings—limited parameters were necessary to keep the database size manageable and encourage wider coverage of the collection. Indexing volunteers continue working from the oldest issues toward the present. Even with these limitations in place, the Index has grown to over 429,800 entries at the time of this writing. Non-obituary coverage is still largely limited to dates before the early 20th century, indicating room for further exponential growth.

New entries to the now-renamed Obituary and Newspaper Index are more detailed than the initial cards to provide a more complete citation. The creation process is broken down into three main phases: extraction, data entry, and proofreading. A lead genealogy volunteer coordinates much of the process, freeing up library staff. In the first phase, extraction volunteers read page-by-page through the newspaper, pulling information from the microfilm and entering it into a standardized Excel spreadsheet. One Excel file is created per reel of microfilm. This step must be completed at the library at stations set up for this process. A computer and microfilm reader are paired together at a desk, enabling volunteers to transcribe information while looking at the microfilm images on a separate screen. It is also the slowest phase of the process.

Extracted article information will include newspaper, date of publication, page number, article type, and reel number. Extracted personal information can include: surname, given name, title (Dr., Miss, Capt.), extension (Jr., III), nickname, age, location, and name of immediate relative. Not all personally identifying categories are present in all article types—marriage license notices do not include ages; an obituary may only list "the widow" as a survivor—but those facts directing researchers to the specific reel, issue, date, and page are always recorded. A column for comments is also included, where more information can be logged if necessary. The comment field can be used to specify a column or article heading if the information is not easily found on the page, indicate a city or state outside the Butler area, or add context to a court report.

In instances where a name is incomplete in the article, a standardized system of placeholders is used. Using context from the article, phrases like Unknown Adult Female, Unknown Adult Male, Unknown Male Infant, or simply Unknown complete the First Name field. For example, in 19th- and early 20th-century obituaries it is common to find women referred to only under their husbands' names, such as "Mrs. Albert McCandless." In the index, this individual would be entered as Unknown Adult Female McCandless, with Albert McCandless recorded as husband in the Relation field. Men could also fall victim to truncated reporting, appearing only as Mr. Jones or Dr. Graham. Extracting volunteers are encouraged not to correct the newspaper articles unless absolutely obvious that something is an error. Spellings, especially in names of individuals from Butler's early Eastern European immigrant community, could be mangled by newspaper reports and even differ in spelling within the same article, so it was decided from the outset not to editorialize names but record them as printed.

In the second phase, the volunteer coordinator prints smaller data entry packets of 250–300 lines of extracted articles from the full extraction spreadsheets. Each packet is assigned a number used on the indexing site. Data entry volunteers pick up new packets at their convenience, and most prefer to take their packets home to input into the Obituary and Newspaper Index website. The online input system has been beneficial as it opened up volunteer opportunities to individuals who may not have otherwise been able to contribute to the project, such as those working full-time who cannot spend several hours during weekday hours at the library. The online-based process is also helpful because it keeps workspace in the genealogy department open for researchers. The website is password protected, and data entry volunteers log in to begin their work. Information from the data entry packets is input into corresponding fields exactly as it appears in the excel sheets. If something looks amiss or raises questions, such as the spelling of a name or a page number, the data entry volunteer can refer to the microfilm to confirm or correct the information.

In the third phase, the work of the data entry volunteers is proofread. In a separate section of the index website, proofreaders log in and view completed data entry packets. These volunteers check the submitted list of entries for any obvious errors or inconsistencies in formatting, and any omissions from the printed data entry packet. At this stage, volunteers are again encouraged to refer to the microfilm in cases of uncertainty. Many data entry volunteers also do proofreading, but they will never be assigned the same packets they initially input into the website to ensure a second set of eyes checks the information. When the proofreaders feel the information is accurate and formatted according to the library style guide, they submit the packets and the information goes live on the Obituary and Newspaper Index website.

Once entries are active on the Index website, they can still be modified. An Editor Index section of the site exists for single-record changes. When errors or omissions that have slipped by the proofreading process are found during day-to-day research, the information can be fixed quickly by the Special Collections Librarian. The most common corrections in this stage are roll and page numbers left blank on entries created from the physical index cards during the initial site creation.

Searching the Obituary and Newspaper Index Database

The Obituary Index link is prominently featured on the Butler Library's Genealogy webpage. The Index has basic and advanced search options. On the basic search page, users are given three search fields: Last Name, First Name, and Article Year. All three can be used, or any combination of one or more fields. On both the basic and advanced search pages, a pull down menu allows the user to choose between 10, 15, or 20 results returned per page.

The advanced search page provides greater modification, with options designed to help overcome typical genealogy pitfalls like irregular spelling and unknown event years. Last Name, First Name, Middle Name, Maiden Name, Nickname, and Title are all available as options for names. Two year options—Year of Death and Year of Birth, for obituaries that have full birthdates extracted—replace the Article Year field from the basic search, though the Year of Death field continues to function more broadly as a general article year. Users can again use any combination of these fields when searching. In some instances, ignoring a surname altogether and focusing on first names, maiden names, or dates alone can produce results missed in a traditional search (Osborn, 2012, 56).

More advanced search alternatives can be returned with the use of built-in pull down menus next to each field. The default mode for all menus is an exact match. The First and Middle name fields can be searched with Begins With, which will yield all matches starting with any number of characters provided. If one were searching for a relative who alternated between the formal given name Joshua and more casual Josh, choosing Begins With and typing only "Josh" in the First Name field would deliver all records for both forms of the name. The index's algorithms provide even greater options for surnames. In both the Last Name and Maiden Name fields, Partial Match, Soundex, and Wild Card menu options are available. A Partial Match will find an exact string of characters anywhere in the name—a partial match of "Worth" will match surnames like Airworth, Woodworth, Worthen, and Worthington. Soundex searches return phonetic algorithm matches of a surname, and most closely match the type of result variance seen on genealogy websites like Ancestry and FamilySearch. A Soundex search of the name Meyer in the Obituary Index provides variations like Maher, Maier, Mayer, Meier, Mohr, and Moyer. Finally, Wild Card searches allow users to substitute an asterisk for a possible single letter or string of characters. A Wild Card search for "B*ard" finds surnames in the index ranging from Ballard and Beard to Buzard.

Advanced year fields can also be modified to return a wider range of results. Like the name fields, the default option is an exact match. Choosing "+/- 1" will provide records that deviate one year in either direction; this modification of a search on 1975 will provide all matches between 1974 and 1976. The Decade option returns all records in the same decade of a searched year. For instances where an ancestor disappears between federal census years, the Decade search function can quickly produce a lead on a date of death.

Whatever the search parameters used, results are returned as an alphabetical name list, displayed in "Surname, Given Name" format, with the publication date shown to the right of each name. Clicking any displayed name opens a pop-up window with full citation details; the library refers to this full page as a Record Sheet. This printable Record Sheet is a ready-made source citation to ensure researchers have all information on an article.

Using the Collection In-House

At the Butler Area Public Library, the microfilm collection is considered an open stack, and patrons are able to use microfilm during all library operating hours. Those doing research in-person can make prints from microfilm readers for 25 cents/page, or save image captures to a USB drive via one digital microfilm reader. Two computer stations are available in the genealogy department for patron use of the Newspaper Index and other genealogy-specific research. Patrons may quickly look up an ancestor's name, pull the correct reel of film, and view the article. The Special Collections Librarian can provide look-up assistance, and the reference department staff are also able to provide citations from the site and guidance on the reader equipment.

For patrons visiting from outside the area with limited time to research, viewing the online index ahead of time can greatly improve a trip's efficiency. Rather than browse issue by issue of the paper, skimming for death notices or the marriage columns, patrons can navigate directly to the specific page they need, capture an image of the article, and move on to the next record. Many visitors will bring a stack of printouts of individual Record Sheets, and those who are extra-prepared have even arrived armed with Excel spreadsheets of citations gleaned from the index, sorted by date or priority family lines.

Research Requesting Process

For those unable to visit the library for in-person research, the library will provide paper or digital copies of articles. A small fee is charged to cover materials, postage, and time: $5.00 for a single article search, or a flat $10.00 for a batch of up to five articles. Researchers interested in having the library perform newspaper research must submit a request form found on the library website. The request form details full contact information for the researcher and payment method. This form is submitted to the genealogy department (either via conventional mail or as an email attachment) along with payment and the Record Sheet for each article desired.

The library currently recommends that patrons limit research requests to groupings of five articles at one time. This guideline serves two purposes: preventing outsized research requests from overwhelming library personnel time, and automatically creating manageable work parcels for volunteer workers who process orders. Occasional exceptions are made for larger batch requests that are subdivided in-house, when the patron understands that turnaround time may be greater and dependent upon staff and volunteer availability.

When a request arrives, it is logged by the Special Collections Librarian in a request spreadsheet that records patron contact information, request type, payment amount, arrival date, and return date of finished materials. For data-tracking purposes, each unique contact from a patron is considered a single research request, whether that request is for a single article or the maximum number allowed. The submitted Record Sheets are placed in a folder labeled with the researcher's name and arrival date, and are then considered ready to be processed. These requests are handled by the Special Collections Librarian and genealogy volunteers on a first-in, first-out basis.

Three volunteers come to the library weekly to search for and print article requests. As the printed Record Sheets provide a full citation of each article, volunteers are able to work independently on their own schedule. Additional citation information is written on the Record Sheet as needed, correcting any errors in the index, adding a page number or roll number if it was omitted online, or adding a comment for context if necessary. Finished files are initialed and dated by volunteers and placed in a bin for review by the Special Collections Librarian. The librarian makes any noted corrections to the online index before mailing the completed material. This system allows the department to return files to researchers within a week to ten days of their arrival, though they are typically out the door even sooner.

Benefits for Library

Streamlining the request process greatly minimizes library staff time spent browsing the microfilm searching for an article. Volunteers are able to process more article requests via the library's Index, and in less time than a manual search based on a known or presumed date supplied by the researcher. Delegating basic newspaper search and copy tasks to genealogy department volunteers also allows library staff to take on more complex research requests.

Before the Index went online, the genealogy department received no more than ten requests for specific newspaper information in a month. The digital conversion made an immediate difference: in the weeks between Thanksgiving 2005 and the official launch party for the website at the end of January 2006, the library received more than 100 request letters (Izzo, 2006). The index had an immediate impact of increasing average monthly research requests to approximately 85 per month. In 2011, the Index was picked up by Ancestry as part of the Ancestry WebSearch collection. WebSearch results on Ancestry include shortened results from the library's database, with a link out to the Index for researchers to search for full records and contact the library directly for information. Discovery via Ancestry led to another spike in research requests, and in 2012 the library hit a peak year average of 106 patron requests per month. That pace has since settled back into an average of 72–80 patron requests a month in recent years, with requests coming from all corners of the United States, Canada, Europe, and even Asia. In addition to amateur family historians, the index has been utilized by professional genealogists, law firms, oil and gas rights researchers, and professors. Overall, the online Index has brought steady attention to the library's collection, sustaining the genealogy department with a steady source of supplemental funding to microfilm more newspapers, repair and reproduce microfilm, replace equipment, and expand the general genealogy reference collection.

Indexing vs. Digitization

Patrons occasionally request that the microfilm collection be digitized so users can use a keyword search to find articles. But digitization is not without its own hurdles: the cost of converting microfilm to digital, especially a collection the size of the Butler Library's, would be prohibitive without a specialized fundraising campaign. The ongoing costs of hosting the large number of images and making them available to the public would also pose continued expenses after digitization. Copyright can be another issue. While the library holds more than 200 reels of microfilmed newspapers published before 1922 that are thus considered in the public domain, the bulk of the reels in the collection are subject to copyright.

Questions of copyright, hosting, and maintenance aside, many of the earliest newspapers that would be most desirable for digitization from the Butler Library collection are also the least likely to provide quality results. While readable to the careful human eye, faint lettering, small typefaces, and dark gutter shadows from heavily creased original paper copies all greatly reduce the potential accuracy of optical character recognition (OCR) software. This is not a hard and fast rule—some microfilmed issues of the *Whig* from the 1850s are of better quality than issues of the *Butler Eagle* from the 1920s—but generally one can assume that older collections will be less OCR-friendly. At this stage and with current resources, library staff is of the opinion that the genealogy department can better serve patrons by maintaining and improving the current database of citations.

Outlook

As the Obituary and Newspaper Index continues to grow, the library must anticipate the future of the project and rebuild portions of the website. The database's main strength, its growing size, becomes a hindrance for common regional surnames like Graham and McCandless that yield high numbers of record matches. As more articles are added, it would be ideal if search results could be manipulated by patrons. Possibilities include filtering matches by article type, and the ability to sort records chronologically rather than just alphabetically by surname.

The Obituary and Newspaper Index project has been more than a decade in the making, with no completion date in sight. Even so, the benefit to researchers and local historical knowledge has been immense. The value of library volunteers when attempting a project of this type can never be overstated, especially for an organization with limited full-time staff. Overall, the time and resources put into developing and maintaining an index of this size benefited the library and could be successfully duplicated by other institutions.

WORKS CITED

Andrasovsky, Jeff. 2006. "Preserving Old Newspapers," *Butler Eagle*, October 13, p. 15.
Breland, Claudia. 2014. *Searching for Your Ancestors in Historic Newspapers*, Gig Harbor, WA: CreateSpace Independent Publishing Platform (Genealogy and Online Research).
Humphrey, John T. 2006. *Pennsylvania Research: County and Township Records*, Washington, D.C.: PA Genealogy Books.
Izzo, Madeline. 2006. "Old Obits Enter Cyberspace at Library," *Pittsburgh Post-Gazette*, January 26, sec. A.
Morgan, George G., and Drew Smith. 2014. *Advanced Genealogy Research Techniques*, New York: McGraw-Hill Education.
Osborn, Helen. 2012. *Genealogy: Essential Research Methods*, London: Robert Hale Limited.
Rittmeyer, Brian C. 2000. "Obits Are Lifeline of Information," *Butler Eagle*, January 11, p. 15.
Ruch, Shelby. 1999. "Historians Preserve Early Papers," *Butler Eagle*, April 7, p. 19.

Digitize Your Old Media
A Self-Service Station for Public Library Patrons
Kirsten Canfield

Digitization of old media is a popular library service, especially among genealogists and local historians. Patrons of Arapahoe Libraries in Colorado have used our self-service digitization stations to create surrogates of old scrapbooks, make DVDs of old family tapes to share at reunions, digitize oral history collections, relive cherished memories, and pass on family history to the next generation.

In this essay, I will describe the digitization stations of Arapahoe Libraries; the popularity, costs, maintenance, and specifications of each format; teaching the tools to patrons; teaching the tools to staff; and promoting this service to the public.

What Are Digitization Tools?

Old media—including such formats as VHS tapes, audiocassette tapes, and 35mm slides are at risk. Age and less-than-ideal storage conditions contribute to their deterioration. Due to their obsolescence and the scarcity of players and viewers, these formats' information is less accessible. People who inherit old media upon a family member's passing lament the amount of space they take up and their inability to view, watch, or listen to them, and may end up throwing them away.

Digitization tools allow patrons to bring old media formats to the library to copy information from obsolete media to current digital media. The digital surrogates can be easily accessed, widely shared, and take up less space than physical media. I recommend that patrons retain the originals if they care deeply about them, and I suggest that patrons consult historical societies and other repositories to gauge interest in donations of originals they do not wish to keep.

What Media Can We Digitize?

The self-service digitization stations at Arapahoe Libraries allow patrons to digitize VHS tapes, vinyl records, audiocassette tapes, old photos and documents, 35mm slides, and negatives. Extra equipment supplied by a patron can allow for the digitization of more formats.

What Is the Setup?

There are two digitization stations at Arapahoe Libraries; one is located at the Southglenn Library and one is located at the Smoky Hill Library. Both stations are free for any member of the public to use. A library card is not required.

Figure 1. Digitization station at Southglenn Library (photograph by Kirsten Canfield).

At our Southglenn Library, the tools are kept in an audiovisual creative space called the Green Room. They are situated on a shelf, perpetually plugged into power, and are connected to a computer. Patrons can reserve the room to use the tools, or they can walk in to use the room if it is not booked.

The tools at the Southglenn Library digitization station were purchased between April 2014 and February 2015. They were scattered between two rooms until August 2015 when they were consolidated in the Green Room on a custom-built shelf and hooked up to one computer, simplifying their use for patrons.

At our Smoky Hill Library, the tools are kept on a cart in an audiovisual creative space called the Recording Studio. When patrons wish to use the tools, they wheel the cart to the computer and plug the tools in to power and to the computer at the beginning of each session. Patrons must reserve the room to use the tools, and must specifically ask for the VHS converter and audio cassette converter which are kept at the circulation desk. All the tools for the Smoky Hill Library digitization station were purchased together in December 2015.

Figure 2. Digitization station on a cart at Smoky Hill Library (photograph by Kirsten Canfield).

Tool Costs and Popularity

Altogether, it costs between $429 and $647 to set up a digitization station like the ones at Arapahoe Libraries, not including a computer. Below the tools are listed by popularity so libraries planning a similar station can prioritize based on their budget. Popularity is based on number of appointment requests for each type of media, and does not reflect walk-ins or patrons who do not need staff assistance.

The digitization tools require a computer to run the software. One computer is sufficient to run all the tools. The digitization stations at Arapahoe Libraries use iMacs with 3.4 GHz processors and 8 GB RAM. I suggest getting a computer with at least a 2.0 GHz processor and 4 GB of RAM. The scanner is the only tool that requires much computing power; the faster a computer you get, the faster the scanning process will be. All the digitization tools described below will work on either a PC or a Mac.

VHS Tapes

VHS tapes are the most popular format to digitize, overall and at both individual libraries. We use Elgato Video Capture ($82.99 on Amazon) connected to a VCR ($80 to $200). If the VCR does not include RCA cables, you will need to purchase those additionally. VHS tapes convert in real time.

Elgato Video Capture allows for versatility, so if a patron wishes to digitize another type of audiovisual media, and has a player for that media that hooks up via RCA or S-Video cable, they can bring in their media, player, and cables to connect to Elgato Video Capture, and will be able to digitize it. For instance, one of our patrons brought in a Sony 120 MP 8mm video cassette tape and a Sony Digital8 Camcorder with which to play it. We connected the camcorder to Elgato Video Capture with RCA cables and from there could digitize it the same way we would a VHS tape. If a patron has VHS-C tapes and an accompanying VHS adapter, they can digitize those with the Elgato setup as well.

The VHS player has required no maintenance in our experience, possibly because we purchased it new. We have a VHS cleaner tape on hand, but we have not yet needed it. Most quality issues involved in VHS tape digitization are caused by the degradation of the tape itself.

35mm Slides, Negatives, Photos and Documents

The transparency-enabled scanner is the second most popular tool, overall and at both individual libraries. We use an Epson Perfection V550 Photo Color Scanner ($165.99 on Amazon). This scanner includes transparency adapters for 35mm slides and various sizes of negatives. Of the formats the scanner can accommodate, the most popular is 35mm slides, followed by old photos/documents, followed by negatives.

Occasionally patrons bring in negatives larger than the adapters accommodate. In these cases, we lay the negative shiny side down on the bed and place a sheet of glass over the negative to hold it in place. We keep a 5 × 7" sheet of glass from a photo frame with the tools for these occasions. Because the transparency scanning area is smaller than the scan bed, large negatives may need to be scanned in multiple iterations and stitched together in photo editing software.

The resolution (dpi) at which images are scanned determines the size and quality of the image. The higher the resolution, the bigger and higher quality the image will be, and the slower it will scan. I recommend scanning images as TIFFs with the following settings:

- 35mm slides: 4800 dpi, 48-bit Color
- Small negatives: 4800 dpi, 48-bit Color
- Large negatives: 2400 dpi, 48-bit Color
- Photographs: 1200 dpi, 48-bit Color

These settings produce large, high-quality images which can be printed at a small poster size. They are larger than most people will realistically need, but scanning at these sizes reduces the chance of needing to rescan images later. Patrons who wish to cut down on scan time can experiment with lower dpi to find the image quality and scan speed that works for them.

The scanner requires little maintenance; you may need to clean the glass occasionally. We use a microfiber cloth, though any soft dry cloth should work well.

Audio Cassette Tapes

Audio cassette tapes are the third most popular format to digitize, overall and at both individual libraries. We use an ION Tape Express Plus ($32.95 on Amazon). Audio cassette tapes convert in real time. This device has never required maintenance in our experience, but we suggest having a spare mini USB cable on hand in case the device's cable is lost.

Vinyl Records

Vinyl records are the fourth most popular media to digitize, overall and at both individual libraries. At our Southglenn Library we use an ION TTUSB10 USB Turntable and at the Smoky Hill Library we use a Numark TTUSB USB Turntable. They work almost identically. Both models have been discontinued, but comparable models range from $55 to $150 on Amazon. Vinyl records convert in real time.

The turntables can digitize 33 1/3 and 45 rpm records, and can do 78 rpm records with a bit of processing in the software Audacity.

The vinyl record converter requires the most maintenance of the digitization tools. Based on our experiences at Arapahoe Libraries, concerns include the following:

- Turntables present a temptation for younger patrons, resulting in damage, particularly to the needle.
- Plastic dust covers (with which some turntables are sold) help prevent patrons from playing with the turntable.
- Turntable needles cost between $10 and $20 each. We recommend having at least two backup needles. Keeping the plastic cover on the needle—or keeping needles in a separate area and requiring their installation at the beginning of each session—can help prevent broken needles.
- Plastic turntable platters occasionally warp and need to be replaced. Platters made of a sturdier material may fare better.

Betamax Tapes

A patron donated a Betamax player to our Southglenn Library, which we connected to Elgato Video Capture. After very few uses, it broke. Because of low patron demand, the scarcity of working Betamax players, and proximity to local vendors who digitize Betamax tapes, we have not replaced it.

Floppy Discs

At several of our library branches, we have USB floppy disc drives for patron use. These cost between $12 and $15 on Amazon. At our Southglenn Library, one of these drives is kept with the digitization tools for patrons who wish to migrate data to newer formats. We rarely get appointments for this tool, but it is used occasionally on a walk-in basis.

Requests for Other Formats

Patrons occasionally ask if we have the means to digitize other formats. Requests have included Hi8, Super 8, 8mm, Kodachrome movie reels, and reel to reel audio. Due to the infrequency of these requests, the expense involved in obtaining and maintaining the machinery and training staff (especially for movie reels), and the presence of multiple vendors who digitize these formats within half an hour's drive of both libraries, we have not yet taken steps to include these media in our stations.

Retouching Old Photos

Patrons who scan their old photos and 35mm slides are often interested in retouching the scans by removing dust, fixing scratches, stitching ripped parts of photographs together, adjusting colors, and rotating and cropping photos. At both our Southglenn Library and Smoky Hill Library, we have Photoshop available for patron use, and staff are available to teach patrons how to retouch their old photos.

Demographics

While we do not have data on the ages of patrons who use the digitization stations at Arapahoe Libraries, according to our observations they are overwhelmingly adults over the age of 40.

Patron Instruction

Patrons are primarily taught to use the digitization stations through our Book-a-Librarian service, through which a patron meets one-on-one with a Librarian. The Librarian and patron determine a time that works for both, and the Librarian books the space where the tools reside. During the appointment, the Librarian guides the patron in the use of the tools, letting the patron "drive."

Some patrons use the service on a walk-in basis, and consult a Technology Specialist when they require help using the tools or want to learn more about them. The Technology Specialists are on-floor staff who provide free technology help to the public, and are stationed near the rooms containing the digitization stations. The Librarians mostly handle appointments, while the Technology Specialists mostly handle walk-ins.

Tutorials are available for the scanner (one for 35mm slides and one for historic photos), since its software is less guided than that of the other tools. These tutorials are kept in a notebook in the spaces with the digitization stations, and they include pictures for every step from plugging in the device to choosing settings. Patrons use these tutorials as a refresher after receiving staff guidance, or to learn the tools on their own.

Staff Training

The Librarians and Technology Specialists are the primary staff members who train patrons in the use of the digitization tools, so they also train the rest of the library staff in the use of the tools. The goals for this training are to ensure that library staff members are aware of the services available to patrons, and to ensure that they can help patrons with the tools in the absence of a Librarian or Technology Specialist.

Staff training is primarily done through small-group demonstrations of each of the tools. Additional one-on-one guidance is available for staff who request it.

Promotion

Our digitization stations generate excitement inside and outside the library. The tools have been promoted in a variety of ways, with varying levels of success.

The effort that created the largest and most immediate influx of appointment requests was the debut issue of the Arapahoe Libraries technology e-newsletter that featured the digitization tools. This newsletter was distributed to more than 30,000 subscribers.

Outreach visits to local historical societies are conducted approximately once per year to present about our digitization stations, and these are usually followed by an influx of appointments. Historical societies always ask multitudes of questions about this service and are especially engaged and interested. This has been our second most effective method of promotion.

We have written newsletter articles about our digitization stations for two local historical societies. These bring people in gradually; patrons referred by the newsletters tell us they kept the article for reference and scheduled an appointment when time permitted.

Arapahoe Libraries created a successful social media post about our digitization stations. A patron digitized a vinyl record of her grandparents' wedding; it was the first time she had heard her grandfather's voice in 20 years. She allowed us to take a photo of the record, and sent us an old photo from the wedding. With the patron's permission, we posted these photos to Facebook (54 likes—well above our average) and Instagram (25 likes—about average). This promotion resulted in another influx of appointment requests.

Occasionally we promote our digitization stations at events hosted by Arapahoe Libraries. The most successful of these was an author event attended by over 200 people. At large events such as this, the library sets up tables to feature our offerings such as technology and upcoming programs. We brought one of our turntables as a talking piece, and before the event began, patrons visited the table to learn about the digitization stations. Throughout the following year, patrons cited that event as the way they first heard about the digitization stations.

Library programs are held a few times a year at the branches which have digitization stations to provide patrons with an introduction to and demonstration of digitization. Each program typically draws between five and ten attendees, and those patrons often book appointments or schedule self-service sessions following these programs.

For a short while, the Technology Specialist staff conducted drop-in demos, during which the staff member would make an announcement in the library encouraging people to attend a short technology demonstration. A few of these demos centered around the digitization tools. The drop-in demos, including the digitization demos, were not very successful and the attempt was eventually abandoned.

Next Steps

One plan for the digitization stations is to create a page on our website about them. We believe that having a dedicated page about the tools will help direct patrons to us if they are searching for this type of service in our area, making the tools more easily discoverable.

Another future step is to move the digitization station at our Smoky Hill Library to a new area outside of the Recording Studio to simplify the setup process for patrons, to accommodate the growing demand for both the digitization tools and the Recording Studio, and to make the tools more visible.

We also plan to write tutorials for all the digitization tools, like the ones we have for the scanner, in the hopes that this will increase patron autonomy and staff ability to help patrons.

How Your Library Can Implement This Service

Your library can take the following steps to create a media digitization station:

- Find a computer with at least 4 GB of RAM (preferably 8 GB of RAM) and at least 2.0 GHz processor (preferably 3.4 GHz processor). All the tools will work on either a PC or a Mac.
- From the above list of popularity, choose which tools fit your budget the best.
- Research digitization services in your area so you can direct patrons to appropriate resources if you do not have the tools they are seeking, or if they decide after trying the process that they would rather outsource it.
- Build a station for the tools. Arapahoe Libraries had shelves custom built for our digitization stations. The ideal station allows all tools to be plugged in and set up for use at all times, and has a sign indicating what the station is.
- Train staff in the use of the tools so they can provide patron support. Most of the tools require little maintenance and their use is straightforward.
- Write tutorials on the operation of the tools for patrons and staff to use as reference.
- Since digitization can be a lengthy process, allow or require patrons to reserve the tools to avoid conflicts. The tools at Arapahoe Libraries are kept in bookable rooms with a three-hour-per-day time limit.
- Promote the tools to the community. Email blasts, outreach events and newsletter articles for historical societies, social media posts, promotion during other library events, and programs on how to use the tools have been successful for promoting the tools at Arapahoe Libraries.

Conclusion

Patrons of Arapahoe Libraries have enjoyed this service immensely. Helping people digitize their old media can be a way to build personal relationships with your patrons. They enjoy reliving old memories, and they often have stories to tell about the people and places they rediscover in the process.

Crowdsourcing Genealogy

Evaluating Sources in the Age of Ancestry.com

KATHRINE C. AYDELOTT

There is no doubt that bad online genealogy abounds: women give birth years after their deaths, siblings are born centuries apart, dates are listed merely as ranges spanning decades, and with many trees and database results homogenized to look the same, it is often difficult to know when information is complete and when more information exists that a researcher simply hasn't traced. At the same time, one cannot simply dismiss the work of tens of thousands of avid hobbyists, staunch enthusiasts, and diligent researchers who have shared their genealogical work in any number of online venues.

For some, the proliferation of Internet subscription sites, free websites, and online family trees presents a supplemental if not an alternative way to pursue genealogy. Once reliant solely upon the painstaking acquisition of primary source documents, and informed by carefully evaluated secondary sources, much genealogical work today can be done simply by using a Web browser. While not as rigorous as traditional or professional genealogy, for some goals, the ability to access online genealogies has allowed many to build trees and trace roots with less travel and effort than ever before. But it is also fraught with danger, including bad sourcing and proliferating error. How can librarians best help patrons with such a vast and growing ecosystem of genealogical information? The challenge is to use the wisdom of the crowd to siphon off the best information, the same way a librarian searches out and evaluates any other source.

Although "crowdsource," a combination of "crowd" and "outsource" is a recent term (Howe 2006), using the public to solve problems is centuries old. Both on and offline examples are legion, from the eighteenth-century effort to find a ship's longitudinal position, to nineteenth-century architectural design contests, to twenty-first-century asteroid hunts, using the public for labor has long demonstrated their wealth of intelligence, innovation, and expertise to solve problems. Crowdsourcing today functions, typically, as a large body of networked individuals, and the Internet has provided a way for people with interest and skills in discreet areas of knowledge to collaborate anonymously and powerfully. Wikipedia is one of the best known and widely used crowdsourced entities with thousands of editors collectively vested in making the site as accurate as possible. Librarians and teachers used to forbid the use of Wikipedia; now, many of us rely on it as a key resource, and well known studies have shown that the currency and accuracy of Wikipedia can be as high as the most respected vetted encyclopedias (Giles 2005). We less forbid the use of Wikipedia today than expect people to use it as they would any other reference source, as a starting place, and one that should be corroborated by other sources.

To crowdsource genealogy is to recognize the power of the myriad of researchers—of all skill levels—motivated to post their family histories and research online. These contributors comprise the genealogy "crowd," a vested subset of the public at large. It's easier than ever before to enter the conversation of the crowd; genealogical inquiry is ubiquitous: blogs, websites, subscription services, social media, all can tap into the experience and provisional authority of others. The librarian's goal when helping genealogists is to carefully tap into this crowd's wisdom just as one would if working with a single researcher: by thinking critically, sourcing carefully, and exercising the mindful skepticism of the scientist. By accessing publicly available genealogical information, crowdsourcing can provide a wealth of information that would take years to assemble independently. Utilizing that information can help researchers make progress, feel a sense of accomplishment, and develop a roadmap for where to go next in the search for documentation. Crowdsourcing may even help solve mysteries and break down brick walls. Indeed, many hobbyists can be satisfied with research found online if it produces logical and reasoned results.

But how do we know that the crowd is smart? James Surowiecki, in *The Wisdom of Crowds*, argues that three conditions need to be met for a crowd to be wise: "diversity, independence, and a particular kind of decentralization" (2004, xviii). He cites, as many others do, the "ask the audience" option in the television game show *Who Wants to Be a Millionaire*, where the collective wisdom of the studio audience answered questions correctly 91 percent of the time (2004, 4). Jeff Howe, the founding father of crowdsourcing, explains that the reason for this phenomenon is "just a function of simplest arithmetic, an illustration that if even a tiny number of individuals possess the correct answer, the group itself will predict accurately" by boosting the correct answer above the collection of other random guesses (*Crowdsourcing* 2009, 144).

The conditions for crowd wisdom are well mirrored in the genealogical community, diverse in geography, culture, education, and resources; independent in their motivation to pursue genealogical work, and often working on their own; and decentralized in that there is no top-down directive governing their direction of research: they each trace generations back from their own starting point. In this regard, the genealogical crowd should be as wise as any other large group with a common interest.

One of the reasons RootsWeb's WorldConnect Project is a great crowdsourcing resource, for example, is that it is so large: more than 6 million names in over 400,000 user-submitted databases (WorldConnect). Not all of the information in these databases is correct, and much is unsourced, but in this case the "crowd," in its size, can still be wise. Surowiecki states that

> the crowd becomes more influential as it becomes bigger: every additional person is proof that something important is happening [*Wisdom*, 2004, 43–44]. The genealogy crowd is also independent and decentralized: no one is directing anyone's genealogical pursuits; indeed, best practice dictates that genealogical research begins with oneself and work backwards into the past. Making connections to previous generations is done by independent scholars pursuing their own ends. Surowiecki echoes, "Ultimately, diversity contributes not just by adding different perspectives to the group but also by making it easier for individuals to say what they really think [*Wisdom*, 2004, 39].

Thus, as long as the crowd is independent and diverse, researchers can share their knowledge and genealogists can crowdsource by finding the best answers from within the group.

Some argue that crowdsourcing genealogy is akin to swimming in muddy water: the assumption being that there are too many amateurs who post work online and amateur work is full of errors. But expertise is not only held by professionals. Noting that amateurs have turned around even academic fields such as ornithology (*Crowdsourcing* 2009, 30–31), Howe explains that "amateurs are competing successfully with professionals in fields ranging from computer programming to journalism to the sciences. The energy and devotion of the amateur comprises the fuel for the crowdsourcing engine" (*Crowdsourcing* 2009, 23). The new information that amateurs bring is valuable to the crowd: Surowiecki states that "Bringing new members into the organization, even if they're less experienced and less capable, actually makes the group smarter simply because what little the new members do know is not redundant with what everyone else knows"; he further insists that "The gains come from [the amateurs'] diversity" (*Wisdom*, 2004, 31).

Even single outliers can move consensus beyond mere duplication toward providing additional information. New family trees, for example, provide information about more contemporary family connections: if these trees connect to more established, better-researched trees, this new knowledge provides more information than what the collective has had before. It seems counterintuitive, but a group of family trees, even if much is copied or otherwise prone to error, may still include hints, paths, connections, ideas, leads, or might otherwise flesh out information about a researcher's families.

It is important to recognize that in the end, the crowd doesn't make the decisions to add information to family trees, the individual researcher does. Lior Zoref, in *Mindsharing; The Art of Crowdsourcing Everything*, argues, "Leveraging crowd wisdom through Mindsharing doesn't mean following the herd. It doesn't mean giving up our autonomy or independence. The crowd isn't making the decision, we are. But through the process of Mindsharing we gain access to information, insights, and knowledge that will improve our thinking" (*Mindsharing*, 2015, 5).

Having the crowd weigh in on a genealogical problem will often provide a wide variety of crowdsourced answers: names repeat, husbands may show up with only one of their several wives, and dates may be missing or may vary by a year or two depending on how researchers handle the Gregorian calendar shift (FamilySearch Wiki). But the value of crowdsourcing is the ability to find what is the most likely answer or the most given answer. This is unlike groupthink, which is when there is social pressure to go along with the crowd, or where humiliation and shunning is the price for independent thinking. Zoref states this principle this way: "Successful Mindsharing depends on people thinking together, not being coerced into thinking alike" (*Mindsharing* 2015, 106). Some criticize crowdsourcing as merely looking for consensus. But, if in asking a genealogical question to the crowd, we are looking to determine who else has done work on this family, and what, if anything at all, is the most likely answer to the question as to dates, or parents, or children, consensus may be the aim: we want the most common answer people are giving.

The danger, of course, is that if genealogical information is merely copied by researcher after researcher, the crowd becomes less intelligent. Surowiecki notes, "We are autonomous beings, but we are also social beings. We want to learn from each other, and learning is a social process" (*Wisdom*, 2004, 42). Researchers and librarians might see this "dumbing down" of the crowd when we start to notice many—often unsourced—duplicates of the same genealogical information. Crowds can be dumb, and crowds can fail, which is why independence is one of crowdsourcing's key components. In the age of the Internet, independence comes from the amateur enthusiasts who are now able to connect to, communicate with, and learn from the professionals.

To continue from the earlier example, a further benefit of Rootsweb's WorldConnect Project is that the advanced search allows for filtering to just those results that have more information, such as those records that include descendants, notes, or sources. Selecting one or more of these options has the effect of making the set of search results smaller by identifying results from just those records that contain more information, effectively making the intelligence of the already select "crowd" even smarter. In these cases, crowdsourcing means to look beyond consensus for individuality and uniqueness often in the form of better sourcing, or more specific information, such as more complete dates or lists of children. Howe argues that "When uniqueness persists in large groups we call it diversity ... [s]cholars and entrepreneurs are discovering that the sum of our differences constitutes an immensely powerful force" (*Crowdsourcing* 2009, 135). If we cross-reference results in WorldConnect with Ancestry.com, FindAGrave.com, FamilySearch.org, and any number of other sites, for example, we can compound forces and start to understand both the large size of the crowd and how careful manipulation of search strategies can make a wise crowd even smarter.

The crowd can help us make decisions when having a stake in the outcome could cloud our thinking. Zoref argues,

> When we reach out to the crowd for wisdom, we are able to access decision-making skills that are free of our own emotion. We are able to seek out the solutions to our problems and weigh our choices free of the bias intrinsic to unilateral decision making. If we learn to rely on and trust the wisdom of the crowd, our decisions will be better, quicker, and easier [2015, 4].

Making these emotion-free research decisions is common in other areas of academe and librarianship (think: collection development), and we must maintain this sense of neutrality when helping with genealogical work as well, as little can be more emotionally entangling than genealogical investigations.

Having a scientific mindset can help mitigate these challenges. The scientific method allows for something to be a theory to the point where it no longer supports the hypothesis; then, a new hypothesis is demanded and a new theory is formed. Naomi Oreskes argues that scientists form a kind of "jury," a focused community of practice, "except it's a very special kind of jury. It's not a jury of your peers, it's a jury of geeks" (Oreskes 2014). Oreskes is identifying the scientists as a subset of the public, their own "crowd," with specialized knowledge. And the reason we should believe geeky scientists is not simply an appeal to authority: "Science is the appeal to authority, but it's not the authority of the individual ... it's the authority of the collective community" (Oreskes 2014). A specifically oriented community looking for the consensus of the collective, the genealogy "crowd" works the same way. The difference between the scientific community and the genealogical community is that the scientists become authorities through years of education and practice in structured environments; genealogists become authorities in less structured, often independent ways, when they extend tree tops, continue known lines closer to the present day, and correct errors. But today, besides experts who pursue genealogical education, or professional practice, many amateurs can practice genealogy from the comfort of their couches; that places a special burden on us as researchers and librarians to walk the line between seeking consensus, being alert to error, and evaluating the outliers for authoritative claims. Like scientists using the scientific method, genealogists must look for where the theory of a family connection fails, or where the information doesn't support the genealogical conclusion.

Some will argue that this isn't genealogy work at all, that it's name collecting, a lesser activity that has little to do with finding the truth than with extending a web of connection. But professional genealogists understand that in many cases genealogy research is more "truthy" in the Stephen Colbert sense (Wikipedia 2017b) than truth that approaches some kind of Platonic Ideal: documents themselves contain error, information on multiple documents can conflict, and genealogical claims are proven with educated guesses when documentation no longer exists. Researchers can often only approach the truth by assembling the best case using the documents available. The Genealogical Proof Standard (Wikipedia 2017a) acknowledges that claims can still be proven using a careful assessment of the available facts and careful extrapolation with regard to the range of possible family connections.

Indeed, tapping into crowdsourced genealogical information can allow for significant development and expansion of family trees, particularly if the principles of information literacy are reliably and carefully followed. Recognizing that genealogy is a research project like any other, librarians can apply the ACRL Framework for Information Literacy for Higher Education (ACRL 2016) to genealogical research in a variety of ways:

Scholarship as Conversation: Ideas and understandings grow and evolve over time, and the same can be true for genealogical "facts." As researchers refine their understanding of an individual's life, legacy, and death, details, including dates and relationships, may shift and change from an earlier understanding to a new, fuller one. Older materials understood as "standard genealogical sources," but containing errors unrecognized at the time, will be reexamined and the errors corrected or better understood.

Authority Is Constructed and Contextual: Authors of "standard" print genealogies are authoritative and are the source for much consensus online; books that undergo revision into editions are more authoritative as new editions correct errors and extend the research. Today, anyone can become an authority if an aspect of genealogical research is newly developed and placed in the world for consideration. Social media and informal sources can be authoritative under certain circumstances. Evaluate everything accordingly.

Research as Inquiry: Approach genealogical research with an open, enquiring mind: follow leads, revisit overlooked sources, ask questions; take little at face value.

Information Creation as a Process: Beginning researchers may stick to commonly recognized sources, such as standard print genealogies and Ancestry.com. But genealogists know that not everything has been digitized and much can still be gained from visiting archives, museums, court houses, and town offices for less accessible information sources, including maps, deeds, probate records and wills, custody agreements, and other primary sources.

Information Has Value: Different sites may have different financial or cultural objectives for offering information for free or by paid subscription. Make responsible choices when paying for information, and it is essential to cite all sources to both help other researchers and to credit the research of others.

Searching as Strategic Exploration: determine the scope of the project; match information needs to appropriate search tools; be iterative, flexible, and creative; seek guidance from experts—we don't have all the answers (or the resources); recognize the value of serendipity.

Clearly, crowdsourcing genealogy isn't appropriate for all genealogical tasks, and primary source research will always be required when working on difficult family lines and when trying to establish a yet unproved connection. Nevertheless, it pays to tap the wisdom of the crowd in these cases as well. Cluster genealogy is widely used to broaden a search to extended family, neighbors, and other community members to see whether there are affiliated family connections. The crowd is handy for this task in particular, and the crowd's wisdom may well allow a researcher to make the case for a connection based on what the crowd shows to be *not* the answer.

Crowdsourcing genealogy will still be controversial to some. Professional genealogists rely on their ability to find and use documentation that others can't find, access, or afford. And it's all about the documentation. But our patrons have a variety of genealogical goals, and unless intending to apply for membership in a genealogical heritage society, most just want to know whether Aunt Frances's hunch about having Swedish ancestry, or Aunt Edna's stories of a royal connection are correct. Most of us are hobbyists. We might want "the truth" but we'll settle for a good enough version if it seems reasonable and doesn't take decades to come to light. Crowdsourcing can take us quite far down this road.

There are multitudes of caveats. Crowdsourcing won't solve all problems—or even most of them. It can be as notoriously unreliable as "fake news" and as challenging to discern. Recent failures of crowdsourcing include the Google Flu Tracker project (Lazer and Kennedy, *Wired* 2015) and political polling from the past several elections. But done carefully, using the best tools and strategies, librarians can help patrons get launched on their genealogical adventures with direction, and, to some degree, confidence. No one is perfect and no crowd is perfect. That's why genealogy is a research project. As Lior Zoref states, "We are more intelligent together, and in the future, perhaps our intelligence will be measured more by our connections to one another than by our intelligence as individuals" (Mindsharing 2015, 224). If this is true, then crowdsourcing and genealogy go hand in hand. The connections you make may well be family.

Works Cited

ACRL. 2016. "Information Literacy Framework for Higher Education." Association of College and Research Libraries. http://www.ala.org/acrl/sites/ala.org.acrl/files/content/issues/infolit/Framework_ILHE.pdf. Last accessed 14 Apr 2017.
FamilySearch Wiki contributors, "Julian and Gregorian Calendars," *FamilySearch Wiki*. https://familysearch.org/wiki/en/index.php?title=Julian_and_Gregorian_Calendars&oldid=2686765 Last accessed April 9, 2017.
Giles, Jim. 2005. "Internet Encyclopedias Go Head to Head: Jimmy Wales' Wikipedia Comes Close to Britannia in Terms of the Accuracy of Its Science Entries." *Nature*. 438 (7070): 900–1. doi:10.1038/438900a
Howe, Jeff. June 2, 2006. "Crowdsourcing: A Definition." *Crowdsourcing Blog*. http://crowdsourcing.typepad.com/cs/2006/06/crowdsourcing_a.html. Last accessed 16 Mar 2017.
Howe, Jeff. 2009. *Crowdsourcing: Why the Power of the Crowd Is Driving the Future of Business*. New York: Three Rivers Press.
Howe, Jeff. 2006. "The Rise of Crowdsourcing." *Wired*. https://www.wired.com/2006/06/crowds/. Last accessed 16 Mar 2017.
Lazer, David, and Ryan Kennedy. October 1, 2015. "What We Can Learn from the Epic Failure of Google Flu Trends." *Wired*. https://www.wired.com/2015/10/can-learn-epic-failure-google-flu-trends/ Last accessed 10 April 2017.
Oreskes, Naomi. 2014. "Why We Should Trust Scientists." *TED*. https://www.ted.com/talks/naomi_oreskes_why_we_should_believe_in_science. Last accessed 16 March 2017.
RootsWeb WorldConnect Project Global Search. *Ancestry.com*. http://wc.rootsweb.ancestry.com/cgi-bin/igm.cgi. Last accessed 10 April 2017.
Surowiecki, James. 2004. *The Wisdom of Crowds: Why the Many Are Smarter Than the Few and How Collective Wisdom Shapes Business, Economies, Societies, and Nations*. New York: Doubleday.
Wikipedia contributors. 2017a. "Genealogical Proof Standard," *Wikipedia*. https://en.wikipedia.org/w/index.php?title=Genealogical_Proof_Standard&oldid=715773751 Last accessed April 9, 2017.
Wikipedia contributors. 2017b. "Truthiness," *Wikipedia*. https://en.wikipedia.org/w/index.php?title=Truthiness&oldid=766466367. Last accessed April 9, 2017.
Zoref, Lior. 2015. *Mindsharing: The Art of Crowdsourcing Everything*. New York: Penguin.

Doing Your Data Digitally—Why and How

Larry Naukam

The first, and perhaps most important, reason to digitize items in your genealogy and local history collection is because it's an excellent way to keep delicate originals from further degradation from being handled. In archives, there are standard policies and practices that can be promulgated and enforced. It is almost impossible to consistently follow solid archival practice in a public library setting. Each use of a fragile item does some damage, however slight, and by requiring that researchers use a digital surrogate of the original item, the original can be kept in safe storage, and the opportunity for abuse or theft is decreased. In a non-archival setting, there is always the potential for further damage. Even if there is thorough support from management, there is still the cost of archival materials such as gloves, security cameras and film, and personnel to set these items up and to monitor them. If the overarching idea is to make items available for research, and to not put originals at risk, then digitizing is a solid choice for solving this quandary. You can increase access and help preserve the original materials without having to impose access restrictions.

Digitization takes an investment of time and money. Before undergoing either of these investments, it's important to have a clear understanding of what digitization will do for the library and for patrons accessing the collection. Here are a few more reasons to digitize some of your collection's materials:

1. Increase the use of materials, especially old and fragile ones. Doing a digitizing project allows to grow the use of the library's materials without requiring an increase in funding and staffing.

2. Give access to more facets of a collection. You put the materials on a web server, and users will come to you, 24/7. The actual display area is a computer screen, not an entire room requiring specific environmental conditions. The security of the material is ensured because even if someone hacks into the computer files and destroys or alters the digital image found there, a copy of the digital file could simply be reloaded onto the server.

3. Preserve old and fragile materials. Digitization allows the public to view rare, fragile items that may otherwise be inaccessible. Although concerns about conservation and preservation of the original items remain, users can have access to a

digital surrogate. There is little sense in building a collection and denying access to it. Your library can make sure that even the most delicate and rare items are always available for researchers' use by providing a digital format.

    4. Help build a digital learning community. A digital project can make a point or tell a story in addition to providing facts. Remote digital access to collections lets a researcher know if the trip is worth it. Digitization actually can enhance the experience of viewing the collection. A photo can be digitally enhanced to show items hidden in the shadows in the original.

People these days respond more quickly to images than to words in print. People seem to think that "everything is on the web," free and whenever they want it. By completing a digitization project, the library can raise its profile and the profile of its collections in the community. The organization and its collection are perceived as being valuable and integral to a community. The library is perceived as being the place to go to find information, and as a place where items of historical and genealogical import can be placed to ensure their availability to the widest audience in the future. The library is seen as being an important information source. Even making copies is easier, because the output of a digital image can be directed to a paper printer, a flash drive, or an optical drive per the researcher's preference. There is little degradation in making many copies. Materials don't risk further damage in the duplication process.

Access and preservation are not always compatible. Digitizing allows achieving some compatibility. There are preservation projects that contain a great deal of information about the original item, and have a longer expected life span of use. They are more expensive to create since they require better equipment and longer setup and production times. Larger files require more storage. For example, a quality TIFF file is usually 3 or 4 megabytes in size; a TIFF of a newspaper page or a map can be 50 to several hundred megabytes in size. A JPEG of the same item is likely to be 1 percent of the size, because it contains less information in a smaller image file.

Files created for simple access to an item are cheaper to produce because they do not require as much equipment horsepower, can have a faster production schedule, and more of them can be stored on any given storage media. On the other hand, digital images require technology to use.

Finally, digitization helps build a digital learning community. By using items in your digital collection as a way of reaching out to teachers and students, you are not only providing a service to those users, you're keeping the library and its collection in a place of respect and use by the community. Students of all ages can benefit by participating in a digital learning community that is available 24/7 and contains different ways of looking at materials. Include lesson plans written by teachers. If they use the library collection to write the lesson plans, then they are partners in production and have a vested interest in the project turning out well and getting to be known and valued.

Just as there are good reasons to digitize, there are poor ones as well. For example, there is a mistaken belief that digitization saves money. It actually costs money to render something into a digital format, and to keep refreshing the media that it is stored on. You cannot throw away or discard the original materials after you scan them to save space and storage, because you may need to refer back to them. If you make something available digitally and do not think through how you will allow use and provide copies, then you run the risk of frustrating users. You should do due diligence and not select to digitize something that has already been done by someone else. And lastly, showing off for the director or the board of trustees isn't a good justification for digitizing either. You want to add to the sum total of knowledge and not do computer tricks for the sake of doing them. Only do something if you have reason to believe that it adds value and aids in usefulness and comprehension of what you are trying to show. If your unit has a large and significant collection of regional history material, it is an important resource for students, educators, historians and genealogists.

If there is a heavily utilized non-digital collection in fragile condition, portions could be in danger of being damaged beyond recovery. As anyone who works with historical materials can tell you, each handling of the original item has a cumulatively degrading effect on it. No matter how good a sleeve you use and how good is a protective box in a carefully controlled environment that you have, when the originals are brought out and given to the public to handle, there are problems—the actual touch of human hands on an original, the security of the collection, and making sure that proper practices are followed. In a public library (as opposed to a formal archive) it is highly unlikely that you will have the time and staff to follow these good practices. When you decide to have a digitization project, make sure that you have dedicated staff for it.

Collaborate with other collections to have a joint digital collection. It should be well thought out and interestingly presented. This might include all the city/area directories that are free from copyright; letters from locally recognized historic figures; or Civil War or World War I collections. If you are partnering with other groups, chances are better of getting funding from outside sources. If you decide to sell copies, it's another revenue stream. Make sure that all relevant possibilities are described in writing for a clear understanding of responsibilities.

Use good equipment, not a simple copier. Use a real document imaging system, or automatic book scanner. These should be excellent at doing automated image acquisition, enhancement (using software tools that are part of the package), and be able to apply optical character recognition (OCR) software to turn a graphic image of words into editable and searchable text. Indexing software can be used with such text. Make sure that you know about any required software or hardware upgrades. Look for a turnkey training process to make implementation of the scanner quick and easy, covering operation instructions, usage, and basic troubleshooting. Do price comparison to determine if it might be cheaper to hire an outside organization, or to have your own equipment. The ease of training and ease of use of the software is an important part in doing any project.

Do's and Don'ts for Digitizing

Do

- Have an organized committee to meet regularly and discuss progress and tasks. In a smaller library, or on a smaller project, have one or two specific people to do this.
- Apply for a grant; include an amount not only for equipment but also for live people to operate it. You may be able to use current employees if they have an interest and capabilities, but you should not add a project of any size onto current responsibilities.

- Have a written agenda for who does what when, and set definite time goals for getting things done. Adhere to them if at all possible.
- Keep track in writing of who did what when and how long it took them. If you have a grant, this may be required. If you have a current operating budget, a manager or auditing unit will want to see how people spend their time and the library's money.
- Seek grants and other funding that will help you tell a story as well as preserve delicate items.
- Provide adequate cataloging and description to meet generally accepted standards. Make items searchable in the library's catalog.

Don't

- Assign digitizing tasks in addition to current duties. You cannot set camera settings and calibrate machines while you are at the reference desk.
- Go chasing grants etc. just to get money; then realize that you are in way over your head in technical expectations and deadlines.
- Skimp on machines to get more people-hours. It should be a given that you get the best camera (that you can afford), the best and most powerful computer equipment (ditto), and figure out ahead of time what it costs to get excellent output. This may mean paying a professional photographer rather than taking a chance on an amateur's guesses.
- Let work be done out of the building or organization unless there are adequate safeguards, such as storage, transportation, handling, etc.

What Should You Digitize?

Here are some "rules of thumb" for choosing what to digitize. What do you have to tell a story? Is that story worth telling? Are there items in your collection that should be used more, but in your judgment could not stand the actual physical handling?

Those are the ones that are most important. If there are some fragile but very useful historical items which could not stand the actual physical handling of them, then that is a good reason to digitize them. An example includes the letters of Susan B. Anthony, the famous woman activist of the 19th century who lived in Rochester. Her letters were in the collection, but in fragile condition. Also, some things are worth a fair amount of money (just because something is old doesn't mean that it is worth a lot, but if there is a connection with an important figure, that ups the ante). The case was that the letters existed, were fragile and valuable, and were not being used. By digitizing them, a perfect copy was made which allows various kinds of examination, and permits the actual originals to be kept in a safe preservation location. This way the items have the widest possible audience that can find the letters online.

If you have a great deal of materials that illustrate a historical or economic fact that is important to the history and development of your area, digitize them. This allows the items to be used and copied much more easily than if they were lying loose. If they are digital, creative people like teachers can use them to tell their own stories to classes.

The fact is that digitizing facilitates the preservation of items by providing an accurate surrogate of the original, and allows you and other users examine facts and items in ways that might not be possible in hard copy. Examples include cross-year analysis of occupations, comparison of population from various times, ethnic makeup of an area, the history and publications and pictures of ethnic groups that are in people's attics or social clubs. By having them available in a digital format, users can access them at any time, print out if need be, etc. This is a way to collect, preserve, and teach that was not possible just a few years ago.

And if you are able to put them online, it makes them always available. That is one of the great satisfactions of doing a digital project, to create something that people in many places will be able to see and enjoy and learn from. It helps break down the divisions that time and distance place between the humans on the globe.

The American Library Association has created a list of "Principles for Digitized Content." This list contains good discussions and links to books. Included in the list of nine principles are statements that digital libraries are libraries just like their brick and mortar counterparts. Contents can be given consideration for collection development. Projects can require collaboration to be successful; they address an international audience; they should be the object of appropriate preservation techniques; they should meet standards that ensure sustainability. Digitizing enables looking outward to enhance usage, versus looking inward and saying "this is ours and you must come to us for access."

When deciding how and what to digitize, or what to digitize first, it might be helpful to think in the following terms. Do you have any items that run the risk of further degradation due to handling? Would digitization of certain items make life easier for staff by making the provision of them less nerve-wracking? In general, when deciding what to digitize, look for items that are unique and not generally available (and also rare and fragile). Examples of these kinds of materials are rare old books of county histories, pictures from decades ago, maps that are in dilapidated condition, old broadsides of events, city directories, yearbooks, or letters from the famous and the common. Any of these can tell a story and make the collection more used.

Consider directories. Frequent use causes a serious state of degradation. Staff and the public use them heavily, and they have to be used on site in the library during the building's open hours. If the library is closed, the directories are not available. If the library is open, there is an ongoing problem of not just use, but of providing copies from the pages of the books. If there are a microfiche and a microfilm version, they require a microfilm reader-printer, paper, and toner. Staff time is taken up by doing the setup of the machines, replacing the paper, replacing toner (which always seems to fail at the most inopportune moment), and time also is taken to help adjust focus, magnification etc. Another tedious way to save information is to write it out longhand, or to make a copy from the microfilm and hope that it is legible.

In short, because of the heavy use of these books, and the real risk of degradation, it makes sense to make them a priority for a digitization process. There are things that can be done electronically that could not be done by microfilm. A watermark of the library's ownership and the year of the directory should be overlaid on every single page of the directories. That way, when they are printed out, the information appears on each page and the user does not have to guess what year it was and which collection the books came from.

Find partners for your efforts. For the most part, they can be local historians or museums that have significant collections of value and want them to be more available for usage and copying. Find these people and organizations by knowing them from conferences, having had interactions with them in the past, and so on. People get to know you and your work and feel that they can reliably work with you. If an item is in a professionally maintained collection, there is a clear chain of ownership, professional decisions about origin and style, and a lesser chance of perhaps coming upon something that has legal restrictions on it.

Reach out by calling and informing the partners that you are applying for a grant or have gotten one which would be beneficial to the partners, and offer to actually do the digitization, scanning, and cataloging plus hosting the actual products. It's a practical truth that libraries do not operate in a vacuum. Perhaps the library may be a small one and the nearest educational institution is some distance away, but almost every place has a grade school and perhaps a high school. Getting involved with teachers is a good way to make contacts. Also, every place has some sort of political governance, and so there may be collections of items already housed and owned by a government entity than can be used for a project.

When your partners find out that you have scanning machines and the super camera for book scanning, they ask questions. Give tours and answer questions for interested prospective partners. They all may not work out, but partners may be impressed with what they see and offer their items to be included. For example, partners in the Rochester Images database contributed various items, and they were scanned and cataloged. More than 20,000 pictures now are included in that product; they are available at all times to be downloaded for individual scholarly use and there are ways of selling production quality images to be used for more commercial ventures.

The partners who contributed images did not charge the library for their use, but rather lent the items for copying and digitizing, and the result is hosted on the library web servers. Further example: The Rochester, NY, City Hall Photo Lab Contemporary collection contains 1,600 images depicting official City events and programs and documenting public works services and projects in Rochester during the past 25 years. The images were selected from 20,000 slides and negatives taken by Rochester City photographers, so less than 10 percent of that collection is available online at the time of writing. Images include many aspects of City government through the years, plus general views of Rochester from the 1760s through the 1960s. But it needs to exist, and having 10 percent of a great collection is much better than having no percent.

The Dollars and Cents: How to Fund Your Digitization Project

Fortunately, there are grants and gifts available that allow for much of this work to be done. There are several options for libraries that looking for special project funding—through the Library Services and Technology Act (LSTA). These grants are usually disbursed at the state level. LSTA web pages are available for individual states, describing each state's requirements and procedure for applying and reporting. One example is the New York State page (http://www.nysl.nysed.gov/libdev/lsta/), which is a subset of the State Library's Division of Library Development. These federal funds can be used to match state and local funds, to help deliver high quality electronic resources.

The LSTA is the successor to older programs dating from the 1950s, which awards local assistance grants to locally initiated proposals. These must meet the purposes of the Act, which includes technology-related items.

There generally is a letter of intent that must be filed by a fixed deadline, and specific forms to use. The types of grants include automated system's grants (allowing purchase of hardware or software for a project); innovation and demonstration grants (to try a project an see if it was successful or not); Internet Infrastructure Improvement Grants, which allow improvement and upgrading to the technical infrastructure; Library Outreach Services Grants, which allow creating inviting and accessible programs with innovative approaches; and of course digitization grants to broaden access to unique collections housed in libraries in a region. There may also be related materials such as CIPA certification, and financial factors to consider (how much the library can actually contribute of its own funds or by in-kind contributions of staff time etc.).

To summarize, here are the potential and realized payoffs of digitization projects:

1. Your collections are much better known and accessible.
2. They can be marketed and sold.
3. You have the chance to be transformative—providing illustrations and historical context for the power of people, places and ideas.
4. You can create great examples of your work. In 2008, we created nicely illustrated CD of PowerPoint presentations that contained the projects we completed and demonstrated ways to access the digital collection. This was for the American Association of State and Local History national convention.
5. If you digitize or partner with a group that digitizes local historical materials, you reap the benefit of being able to use them. I am associated with a group that has done over 250,000 pages of local materials, and has received an award from the National Genealogical Society for this work. They have over 180,000 names indexed by volunteers.
6. Besides the satisfaction of getting some items up online and useable, with over 100,000 hits in a year, that project engendered a $10,000 donation to continue the work.
7. Several of the projects that I worked on have been allowed to use the National Park Service logo as recommended research sites [Erie Canal and Underground Railroad].

Digitization projects require thoughtful advanced planning, secure funding, adequate staffing, but the benefits for libraries, local individual researchers, societies, and educators are invaluable. With local support and dedication, the projects can be successfully accomplished and pay for themselves in the long run.

PART IX: FINANCES

Grants
Finding, Writing and Following Through

NATALIE BAZAN STAROSTA

Grant funding can enhance your genealogy budget. The right grants can take you from no programming budget to the whole world in just one application. And let's not forget those grants that can make your genealogical society or collection accessible through new technology, building updates, a new signage, and so much more! But there is that little problem ... where to find 'em and how to catch 'em!

Yes, finding and securing grants does have something in common with Pokémon hunting. Some of them are easy to find and plentiful (like the wonderful businesses that provide grants, for example, Dollar General and Walmart/Sam's Club among others); almost anyone can apply for them. And then there are the rare grants, which only a few libraries nationwide have received (for example Califa Foundation's grants or maybe Best Buy's teen technology grant). But there is hope and help for everyone out there (yes, you can catch ... I mean apply for 'em all!).

Let's start with a basic "how to find them." With limited time and even more limited resources, librarians and genealogists are like teachers; stretched thin and providing more than most people will ever understand. So, how about we look at a few websites and groups where you can find grants for libraries in just a minute. However, there is something we have to do even before we start looking for that "free" money out there. You need to decide on what you want to do. Maybe you are a tiny library trying to update your collection; maybe you want to be able to offer some new programs to attract new patrons, or you are looking at a library renovation, expansion, or overhauling your technology? I suggest you make a list of the things you would like to do with grant funding and be sure to include:

1. Motive:
    a. What makes you interested in that topic, program, update? Why are you willing to put time and effort into this project? Does this topic fit into your strategic plan and library or genealogical society's mission statement?
2. Means:
    a. What do you have to put forward? Do you have volunteers who would love to work on this project (like, say, collaborating with a local school to

create a weekly program for parents and children with funding from the Primetime Story Time grants).
   3. Opportunity:
      a. What will this allow you to do in your community? How will it make an impact for your patrons? Will you be able to offer free financial or digital literacy classes? Teach self-defense classes to kids going off on mission trips? Or maybe add an accessible computer terminal with text to talk for vision-impaired?
   4. Special notes:
      a. Are you a 501(c)3 organization? Is your Friends group? Would they be willing to apply for these grants for you or with you?

Ok, now you have your list and you know just what you are looking for, right? That's great! You are ready for grant hunting for years to come! All right, maybe I was just being optimistic, but you are ready to start hunting for grant opportunities. Or ... maybe not quite yet. Let's take a look at you. What kind of budget do you have to possibly match a grant? And yes, that might be none, and that's ok, but you need to know what resources you can put toward any grant before you apply. So let's look into your documents for a minute before we start searching the world for the best grants for your goals and institution.

I asked earlier, are you a non-profit with a valid 501(c)3 status with the IRS? This may seem like it should not be a problem, we are libraries, historical societies and genealogists after all, but not all libraries are founded under laws that will allow for non-profit status. If you are not a non-profit, do you have a Friends group, other community group that is? Or would you like to start one? There are many benefits to you and your donors if you are a non-profit when it comes to tax time, but that's for another essay! There are many grant opportunities that are only open to those who hold a 501(c)3 status so keep those documents handy.

Next are the basics, what do you know about your institution and your area? Well, now is the time to learn! You should have access to your Federal Employment Identification Number (FEIN or EIN number), be sure you know how to find your DUNS number (you can look this up at a number of DUNS look-up websites), and most importantly, have a copy of your most recent financial statement and audit report. Many grants will require at least the most current audit report if not several to be sure that you are indeed in good financial standing and will be able to carry through any obligations that you may have agreed to in the grant process (especially important if you have a matching grant or donation).

On to your area. This is where you get your first chance to explain to the grant administrators why your area needs this grant. You only get a few chances in a grant application to connect the grant readers and decision makers with your area and your people. Remember that everyone applying for that grant has difficult situations; what makes your area special, unique, exciting? Let them know what makes you ... well, YOU! You can do this!

Ok, you've got this! You know what you are looking for, you have your documents all lined up and ready to go, so let's go and get some grants! Don't get me wrong, I love looking at and applying for those big nationwide grants, and we'll get to that, but let's not forget your local grants. Groups and organizations that you might not think about.

Below is a list of several places you might want to check to get you started in your grant hunting!

- Your State Library Organizations:
    - Have you looked? Seen the emails come through but thought that couldn't work for you? Well, you are wrong. The only grants you regret are the ones you didn't apply for.
- Community Foundations:
    - Often local community foundations will offer grants to local organizations. Just because libraries and historical societies haven't applied or been granted any before is not a good reason not to apply! Give them a call and let them know what you are thinking about doing to see if it is something that they might have an interest in funding.
- Schools:
    - Yup, I know. They often have even more funding problems than we do but I know that our local schools have educational groups that give funding to local organizations that provide community educational programming.
- Health and Youth organizations:
    - It's surprising how many mental health and youth organizations give grants for suicide prevention which could be funding used for anything from programs to creating a website or blog and much more! Unfortunately, not all places have funding available (my county didn't, sadly) but it doesn't hurt to look.
- Local Corporations:
    - Many corporations have a giving policy which includes grants. Check them out!
- Other Non-Profits:
    - Many other groups might be willing to give grants to you depending on what you are planning to do.

You've checked out your local grant opportunities and now you're looking for something different, something bigger, something new! There are many national grants that are open to small, medium and large libraries and historical societies. Just because you are a one-librarian library and do-it-all genealogist doesn't mean that you can't look at national grants. Just like if you are a hundred-plus-employee library, you can still apply for local grants to provide for your patrons or customers. So, let's check these out!

- IMLS Grants page
    - You will find some amazing grant opportunities here. Be aware that they are federal grants for the most part and will require a great deal of paperwork. Be sure that you are prepared to follow through if you receive one of these. Also many of these grants are not library specific so you may be competing against other types of organizations. Don't let this get you down, libraries are awesome in so many ways and you can do this!
- ALA's Awards and Grants page
    - ALA is a great source for grants, scholarships, and awards. They will all be library related but may be for other types of libraries or other specializations;

read carefully before you apply. Also, beware of historical grants which are no longer offered, but are still listed there.
- Scholastic Librarian Grants page
    - Scholastic's page is a great resource. They have collected grants from all over the web for libraries. Make sure that if you are applying for school library grants, you don't click on those for public or academic libraries. Also be aware that some of these grants are from corporations and require you to have a 501(c)3 non-profit designation.
- Library Grants BlogSpot
    - New grants are listed here every month or so; you have the ability to scroll through old grants to see what might be coming up again; you can check organizations for donations or grants that they might offer in addition to the ones on the site.
- Library Works website Grants & Funding page
    - Wide variety of grants here and again all focused on libraries.

There are also numerous books and programs published with grant listings for non-profits. I recommend starting with:

- Rossman, Edmund A. 2016. *40+ New Revenue Sources for Libraries and Non-Profits.* Chicago: ALA Editions.
- Grant Station is a database program focused on non-profits. It is a subscription service (check on Tech Soup for deals each year), however, it is up to date and has the latest grants searchable by geographical area, keywords, and more.

You've done all the prep work and now you are wondering how in the world to write up a grant application that sounds good and will be picked as the ONE, the winning one? There are lots of strategies; everyone you talk to will tell you something slightly different but one thing always remains constant, be sincere and be personable. Make sure you leave an impact; let the people reading and evaluating your grant know who you are and why you matter. Most of the time you will have limited space, character or page limits, and often limited time, because who really has all the time in the world to think about what they are going to write? Just because you have limits doesn't mean that you can't create an amazing application. Below I will recommend several great resources for you to check out for hints and tips; here are some things that I look for when evaluating a grant application or when I am writing one:

- Be concise. Don't use 4 words when 1 will do. Practice telling a story or imparting a feeling in 5 words. It's not easy, but if you do it, it will make you a better writer.
- Be convincing. Everyone who applies for a grant wants it. Most of them need it for one reason or another. Why are you special? Make a list of why your project is special and why you are excited about it. Be sure to include those things. In addition to the project timeline show how much you are excited. An example of the language can be: "April 1st Team with Humane Society to offer Library Cat Café—first in the nation @ your library!"

Resources to check out for grant writing hints and tips:

- ALA workshops: In 2016 the American Library Association offered a two-part workshop called "The Basics of Federal Grant Writing." They offer several workshops along with the Public Library Association and other library organizations. Check their websites and find the ones that work for you. Some are free and others are offered at low cost to members and non-members.
    ◦ For example, ALSC has an archived grant talk that you can purchase called: "Be A Winner: Inspired Youth Grant Writing."
    ◦ Also, if you are considering ALA's Certified Public Library Administrator program, be sure to take the Grant Writing course; even if you are not in the program, it's a very worthwhile course to invest in.
- Perdue Owl Website—Introduction to Grant Writing. This is a great concise article with links to more information on various parts that may be asked for in a grant application.
- Gerding, Stephanie K, et al. 2017. *Winning Grants, Second Edition: A How-To-Do-It Manual for Librarians.* Chicago: ALA Editions.

Ok, you've found lots of grants, filled out the applications, created the narratives, and addressed all the other requirements. You got that email, letter, phone call and congratulations! You've done it! The money's rolling in and the reality hits you, you need to be getting ready to institute the first grant.

First things first. Write that "Thank You" note, get your board, boss, volunteers, anyone and everyone to sign it; remember that you should send your grantors pictures and a note at the end too. This does two things. First, it helps you announce to your community that you got the grant and gives you a chance to invite the community in, show off that timeline of events you created so that they know what's coming up, and advertise on behalf of your grantor. If your state library gave you money for that new building project, I am sure that they would love to have you tell everyone how the state is helping their local library. It also gives you an initial way to thank them for believing in you, your project and plan, and your community. You will again thank them when you send in your final report but it's always nice to connect with your grantors right away. Now let's start spending that money.

Got all your scheduling done? Now it is time to make sure that you record your statistics and track your budget, and also yet get the data that can help you prove your case for future grants. Statistics and budgeting are very important to your final reporting, letting your community know what is happening and your planning for the future. Here are a few suggestions for budgeting:

- Copy the receipts, all of the receipts, every little one! This may seem insignificant, but your auditors will want to check your spending, and the grantors may require you to send the receipts (or their copies) to them with your final report for final payment. Start a binder! In your binder include:
    ◦ your original grant applications
    ◦ grant agreement and award letter
    ◦ list of key dates (midterm report, final report, webinars, presentations, etc.)
    ◦ timeline/schedule
    ◦ copies of all receipts (if you can, scan these for your grantors)
    ◦ all publicity (newspaper reports, your announcements, links to or prints of advertisements, thank-you notes, etc.)

- list of any donations (items, funds, or time) by community members
- program signup sheets or attendance logs
- everything else the grant asks for
- Keep a running spreadsheet for your spending, its categories, and how much you are spending vs. how much was budgeted.
- Be sure to talk with your bookkeeper, accountant, and/or auditor to see if they need anything additional from you. Depending on your state, some grants may require you to have a single audit to account for funds from grants over a set amount.

Now that your bookkeeper and auditors are happy, on to the statistics! Who didn't love that class? Didn't take it? Neither did I, but I still do this part, so no worries there. Let's start with a few suggestions for programs you can use to help you keep track of statistics and compile them as you go.

- Excel. Easy to use; it is included in the Microsoft Office suite. Allows you to create charts from inputted data.
- Access. It is included in some Microsoft Office suite packages, so you may already have this. It allows you create databases of information.
- Google Forms. Free online tool. You can set up a Google form which will feed automatically into a Google sheet. This is great for web surveys for patrons, library staff keeping track of attendance statistics, however, it is harder to create charts from the data unless you download it.
- SQL and Oracle. Used for larger institutions to share data across multiple locations or people. You can put the information up on a web page. These can be cost prohibitive and do require extra training to use.
- PLA's Project Outcome. Free to use and user friendly. This will allow you to input program statistics and compile them, compare them to other libraries' data.

Now that you have lots of ways to keep track of your statistical data, let's talk about stories. We need to make these grant results personal. I want to hear about the grandchildren who are now so excited to be able to use their library's Skype terminal to talk to their grandparent about their family history. Introduce me to the homeschool mom who just moved to the area and is able to connect her kids to others with your collaborative projection service allowing people to call in and work together on a project. Get me excited with your story about the 20-something who just finished studying for an entrance exam in your new meeting room thanks to that renovation grant. In each survey, group discussion, or email, make sure that you include a way that people can tell you their story. Ask them! You might get very few people who tell you something special, but that special story touches hearts, keeps us all going, and is important to share with your patrons and your grantors. Show them all why this grant made all the difference in someone's life.

Before you know it, you've finished your whole project, collected and compiled all of your data, have all your photos ready, and can show how well (or how … not so well) your project went. Final report time! Arguably this can be the most important part of any grant. Completing the final report and doing it well (and on time) is one of the things that grantors will keep track of when they are considering renewing your grant or giving you another for later projects. Don't leave this till the last possible minute. Spend some time here. Here are the steps I usually follow when working on my final report:

- When you receive your grant paperwork, be sure to put any due dates (midterm reports, final reports, required webinars, etc.) in your calendar immediately. Don't wait on this because all of the dates they give you are hard deadlines!
- Keep on top of it! We've already discussed Project Outcome or other means you might use to collect data. Don't keep those surveys in a pile on your desk until 4 p.m. the night before your report is due. Imputing data throughout your project lets you see trends and understand what you're doing that is making the greatest impact as you go.
- Have all your budget information and receipts together so you aren't searching for your spending at the last minute.
- Make sure that you have all your photo and video release forms so that you can share those precious, fun, and sometimes crazy (don't ever let that kid paint walls again! … sorry, just reminiscing) photos.

Congratulations, you've finished all of your requirements, submitted all your data and given your all to your community by winning them and following through with that one special grant … let's do it all again sometimes!

Developing Materials and Instruction on a Budget for Local Patrons

Janet Curtiss

This essay will highlight how the St. Clair County Library System in Southeastern Michigan has developed methods of genealogical instruction to patrons and has increased awareness and usage of the materials in the historical collection. The first step I took was to reorganize and streamline the physical space and collection, then to actively market the collection to the public and develop a program of instruction in genealogical research. The collection itself was assessed, weeded, and enhanced, with some items digitized to improve accessibility.

My primary goal in delivering genealogical instruction to our patrons was to develop and implement a sustainable program on a limited budget, making optimum use of free or low-cost resources as well as the materials already in our collection. One core necessity was to develop staff knowledge and skills. Next, we planned a curriculum for an ongoing program, starting with basic procedures and creating a foundation on which to build a body of knowledge.

Creating a Space for Genealogy

Most of the local history and genealogy collection was housed in two separate areas of the basement: closed stacks and a browsing section in one small corner. It consisted of a core group of materials bequeathed decades ago to the library by a local historian, William Jenks. Over the years, donated and purchased books, indexes, and self-published family histories have increased the size and scope of the collection now known as the Michigan Room. The physical layout included the map case, shelving, filing cabinets with pamphlet files, two tables, and a large, L-shaped staff desk. This cramped area did not comply with the Americans with Disabilities Act. The area adjacent to the Michigan Room combined staff desks, Friends of the Library workspace and storage, and a general storage area of cast-off furniture. Other non-circulating genealogical materials were located in several different areas on the main floor, which was inconvenient for patrons and staff. Some items were in the Reference section, and others were in the Ready Reference shelves behind the Reference desk. The microfilm reels of the local historical newspapers and the microfilm readers sat on the main floor next to the patron computers. These items needed to be consolidated into one central space.

We reconfigured the area to expand the Michigan Room. We relocated the staff desks to the opposite side of the basement, and pushed back the Friends area along the wall, which provided them with added shelving and a more defined space. The pamphlet file cabinets serve as a partition between the Friends area and the Michigan Room. The furniture and extra storage cabinets were sorted and either discarded or removed. This doubled the footprint of the Michigan Room and allowed space for the microfilm materials to be relocated to the local history collection. The new layout is less crowded and more accessible.

Except for circulating materials, all of the local history and genealogy materials are now together in the basement. While this limits the accessibility after 5:00 p.m. due to minimal staffing for evening hours, the reconfiguration is overall more convenient for researchers and staff alike. The Michigan Room now includes a new printer/scanner/copier and six computers which are reserved for research purposes only.

Staff Development

When I was assigned to the special collections, I made a goal to start a monthly genealogy club. I had dabbled in researching my family history for several years, so the first thing I needed to do was sharpen my skills to ensure I had a firm understanding of the basic tenets of genealogical research. Luckily, a skilled genealogist works as a library assistant in our library system; administration took advantage of her knowledge and supported me in my work by assigning her to my department. She shared her knowledge with me, taught me about available resources, and provided valuable research tips.

I checked local and nearby genealogical and historical societies for upcoming opportunities and attended several workshops, namely the spring seminar of the Genealogical Society of Monroe County (Michigan), the History Skills workshop series through the Historical Society of Michigan, and the Abrams Foundation Family History Seminar hosted by the Archives of Michigan and the Michigan Genealogical Council. I found countless professional development tools on websites such as YouTube, Legacy Family Tree Webinars, American Ancestors by New England Historic Genealogical Society, and wikis on Family Search and Ancestry. These resources provided a good working knowledge of genealogical research methods.

Program Development

My colleague and I developed an ongoing program named the "Plant a Family Tree Genealogy Club." We decided to meet monthly, at the same time each month. This consistency allowed patrons to find it easier to remember when the meetings were scheduled. Meetings last two hours, with the exception of our fall seminar which is planned as an all-day event. We have several spaces available for programming: the meeting room, the Michigan Room, the computer lab, and the county auditorium which is off-site but just across the street from the library. We have used each of these spaces depending on availability and our needs for specific programs. The computer lab works well for teaching about databases such as Ancestry Library Edition (available onsite only) and Family Search (a free database offered by the Latter Day Saints church) because each person has access to a computer. It also has a projector and screen for streaming webinars or presentations that use PowerPoint or a slideshow of images. The Michigan Room space is used for working and planning meetings as well as discussions on various genealogy topics. The auditorium at our county administration building offers capacity for a larger number of people; we booked this venue for our annual seminar.

Methods and Topics of Instruction

For our first meeting, around twenty-five people attended. This number has held steady for most of our monthly meetings. We talked about why genealogy is important and why people are interested in learning about their ancestors. These reasons range from mere curiosity to historical research to family medical information. We shared personal and professional experiences with our own genealogical research, including successes and challenges encountered along the way. We defined the differences between primary and secondary sources, and emphasized the importance of always recording the sources we use. Then we discussed some of the basic forms genealogists use when conducting research and recording information:

- Ancestral or pedigree chart: used to show a direct line of ancestors
- Family group sheet: filled out for each family unit consisting of a couple (married or not) and their children
- Research log or calendar: a record of every source searched by a genealogist, including the results of the search; keeps track of research

We demonstrated proper formatting:

- Dates: DD/MM/YYYY
- Names: Last name (always use the maiden name for females), first name
- Geographic locations: smallest division to largest division—City/village/town/township, County, State/District, Country

In genealogy, the first step is to start with what you know. We passed out blank forms and pencils to each attendee, recommending the use of pencil rather than pen until names and dates are verified with official records. Using the ancestral charts, we asked them to fill in everything they already knew, beginning with vital facts about themselves and then moving to parents and grandparents. If they had information on both birth and adoptive families, they chose which line to record. The same procedure was used for step-families, although there are forms specifically used for a blend of families and step families. Writing down names, dates, and locations in the specified formats, attendees gained practical experience with proper format of vital information.

The next step directed them to return to their homes after the program and search for any information they may have there: family Bibles, marriage certificates, death records, birth records, and baptism, christening, or confirmation records. We then discussed the process of finding vital records at county clerk offices. For instance, while some offices have online ordering options for records, others may require in-person or mailed payments.

Subsequent meetings covered various topics such as:

- information found in census records and how the census changed over time regarding what information was collected
- how to locate military records and methods for requesting these records
- the history of immigration and naturalization and which records are available in our own collection and at the state or national archives
- gravestone symbolism and proper etiquette when visiting cemeteries
- deciphering difficult-to-read handwriting in old documents
- organizing genealogical research in both digital and analog formats

We keep a file of the handouts for each month's meeting for regular members of the club or for any patrons who visit the Michigan Room and have questions about topics we have covered in the past. When new attendees join the club, they have access to previous materials. It also helps me keep track of program topics. To make genealogical research more user-friendly, we also provide various research forms for patrons, including ancestor charts, family group sheets, blank census forms, research calendars, research checklists, and source summaries.

After several months of learning about the basics of genealogy and the various resources and research methods, we scheduled a few programs we called "working meetings" where people bounced ideas off each other, asked questions, shared stories, and worked on their family trees. We offered one-on-one assistance at these times as well. The working meetings were good alternatives for busy months like summer months and December. This takes pressure off people who cannot attend programs during these times. They do not feel like they are missing out on learning something new from a presentation. For working meetings, we use the Michigan Room. Using this space also provides easy access to the local history collection and helps patrons become more familiar and comfortable with the environment.

We have also had meetings that simply consisted of watching a webinar available online for free from Legacy Family Tree Webinars. The webinars generally lasted 45 minutes to an hour. This gave us time to discuss what we learned, ask questions, and propose practical applications to use in our individual genealogical research projects. There are a variety of free or low cost webinars available on this site, some of which have a syllabus that can be used as a handout.

We continue to plan and develop future programs with input and suggestions from the patrons who attend our genealogy programs. Topics of interest include the following:

- how to verify family lore;
- ways to develop and publish family history writing projects;
- methods of working around adoption records to find biological ancestors;
- opportunities to give back to the genealogy world through volunteer work on indexing, transcribing, tagging, or scanning records;
- requirements to obtain membership in societies such as the DAR;
- continue an annual all-day seminar with special presenters;
- tour of a local cemetery with anecdotes of notable historical persons from this area

Our budget is small; we share funds with the adult programming staff. This challenge is met through creative use of free and low-cost resources. Generous donations from grateful patrons also provide additional aid for programming and guest speakers. Often libraries are under tight budget constraints. We have learned how to provide top-notch instruction without spending a large amount of money. We generally plan several months ahead in order to line up any guest speakers and to give our marketing department enough time to create effective promotional materials. The Plant a Family Tree Genealogy Club is considered a success due to the continued interest and steady or increasing attendance at programs.

Some of the challenges in providing instruction to patrons include overcoming the following myths:

- everything is available online
- everything online is accurate
- everything in print is accurate
- spelling mattered in previous centuries

These challenges were met by our gentle but firm repetition to take everything with a grain of salt and to read all historical records with an open mind and an understanding of the historical context and purpose of their creation. Most programs include some form of historical lesson to provide a basic understanding of the thought processes behind the records we study.

Annual All-Day Seminar

Seven months after we began promoting our genealogical services, we held an all-day seminar featuring professional genealogists and guest speakers from our state archives. They presented topics such as historic newspapers, immigration, secret societies and fraternities, and how to overcome brick walls. We partnered with the St. Clair County Family History Group (SCCFHG) and local chapter of the Daughters of the American Revolution (DAR). The SCCFHG provided drinks for attendees, and the DAR offered one-on-one research assistance during the lunch break. The seminar provided professional guidance at a relatively low cost to the library of around $350. We did not charge patrons for attending the seminar.

Marketing and Outreach

We have a small but effective marketing department that does a fantastic job promoting our programs through printed materials, the library website, and social media. Posting things on the library Facebook page allows staff members to share it with their friends and followers, increasing exposure and awareness of programs. Printed flyers posted around the library on bulletin boards and smaller postcards left near the reference and circulations desks added exposure to our events to anyone walking through the front doors. Our website contains a calendar with library events, where patrons can register for events using their name and either a phone number or an email address.

I have provided outreach by speaking at programs presented by the local family history group at two of our library system branches. I gave a brief overview of the local history collection in the Michigan Room at the Main Library and encouraged them to visit and explore our print resources. I send out a monthly email to everyone who has attended one of our meetings or programs to remind them of upcoming presentations, new materials available, local or nearby conferences and seminars, and tips and tricks that we have learned or that have been shared with us.

Collection Development

In addition to redesigning the space in the basement, we also assessed the genealogy materials in the nonfiction circulating collection on the main floor. Several titles were weeded due to outdated information on online resources, websites, software, and technology. New information on genetic genealogy and DNA testing continues to be developed, resulting in newer, more relevant resources. These materials are assessed annually and removed or replaced as new material is published. Recent additions to our circulating collection are listed at the end of this essay.

While we strive to offer the best collection we can, we also track items available through other libraries that our patrons can borrow through interlibrary loan agreements. Some out-of-print items may be available digitally through collections such as HathiTrust, so providing a list of such sources on our website or even printing out a brochure can help patrons access those difficult-to-find materials. Our partnerships with the SCCFHG and the DAR result in these groups generously donating new print materials for our collection. The SCCFHG also has a long history of creating indexes of local records, making these records usable to researchers in the library. The DAR, at the time of this writing, is transcribing the family Bibles in the library's collection. Both groups continue to support the Michigan Room collection and programming.

Many of the historical materials in the Michigan Room require careful consideration of preservation practices. One way we help preserve these valuable items is to provide digital access, which reduces the handling of the physical item. Several titles, such as county histories, biographical histories, plat maps, and city directories, currently exist in digital format and are available on the library website. Other items like yearbooks may only be available in print format. We recently completed a yearbook digitization project in an attempt to offer digital access to yearbooks from St. Clair County high schools. Altogether more than three hundred yearbooks from thirteen different schools were digitized and are now available on our website. More digitization projects are being planned to increase accessibility to useful genealogical materials.

Results

The changes implemented in the layout of the Michigan Room, the relocation of materials, and the development of instructional programs have resulted in a large increase in the use of the collection. We have acquired a reputation for helpfulness and for offering a welcoming environment with resources relevant for genealogical research. This has led to more requests for one-on-one instruction, which we offer by appointment or walk-in. Many patrons who have visited the Michigan Room recently have expressed surprise at the physical changes and improvements, but they also seem delighted with the heightened level of customer service they now receive along with an updated and relevant collection of materials. As word spreads throughout the local genealogy community, we will continue to improve and develop our methods of providing genealogical instruction to our patrons.

Resources Added During Collection Development

Anbinder, Tyler. 2016. *City of Dreams: The 400 Year Epic History of Immigrant New York*. Boston: Houghton Mifflin Harcourt.

Bettinger, Blaine T. 2016. *The Family Tree Guide to DNA Testing and Genetic Genealogy*. Cincinnati: Family Tree Books.

Blanchard, Gil. 2014. *Writing Your Family History: A Guide for Family Historians*. Barnsley, South Yorkshire, England: Pen & Sword Family History.

Dolan, Allison, ed. 2017. *The Family Tree Historical Atlas of American Cities*. F & W Media Inc.

Heine, Steven J. 2017. *DNA Is Not Destiny: The Remarkable, Completely Misunderstood Relationship Between You and Your Genes*. New York: W.W. Norton.

McCarthy, Andrew. 2015. *Journeys Home: Inspiring Stories, Plus Tips and Strategies to Find Your Family History*. Washington, D.C.: National Geographic.

Oates, Jonathan. 2016. *Tracing Your Ancestors Through Local History Records*. Barnsley, South Yorkshire, England: Pen & Sword Family History.

Quillen, W. Daniel. 2015. *Mastering Immigration and Naturalization Records*. Cold Spring Harbor, NY: Cold Spring Press.

Raymond, Stuart A. 2016. *Tracing Your Ancestors in County Records: A Guide for Family and Local Historians*. Barnsley, South Yorkshire, England: Pen & Sword Family History.

Scott, Jonathan. 2016. *Tracing Your British and Irish Ancestors: A Guide for Family Historians*. Barnsley, South Yorkshire, England: Pen & Sword Family History.

Smith, Drew. 2016. *Organize Your Genealogy: Strategies and Solutions for Every Researcher*. Cincinnati: Family Tree Books.

About the Contributors

Kathrine C. **Aydelott** is the instruction librarian at Dimond Library at the University of New Hampshire. She earned a doctorate in English from the University of Connecticut. Her research interests include information literacy, gamification and genealogy. She published newfound short stories by Sarah Orne Jewett and Mary Wilkins Freeman.

Roland **Barksdale-Hall** is the library director of the Mercer County Housing Authority's Quinby Street Resource Center in Sharon, Pennsylvania. He is the author of *Leadership Under Fire* and the former editor of the *Journal of the Afro-American Historical and Genealogical Society*. He received the 2015 Black Caucus of the American Library Association Leadership Award.

Joan M. **Barnes** is the community engagement librarian at the University of Nebraska–Lincoln libraries and earned her MLIS from the University of Rhode Island. She promotes library services to students, faculty and community members and coordinates the peer guide program, employing students to assist with student-to-student marketing via social media and events.

Debra Carrier **Bloom** is the Richland Library Walker Local and Family History Center manager in Columbia, South Carolina. She earned her MLIS from the University of South Carolina. She has written for *Carologue* and *Auntie Bellum* as well as *Proceedings of the South Carolina Historical Association*. Her book, *Women Diaries and Letters of the South*, is forthcoming.

Wendy Lombard **Bossie** is an educator and librarian and earned her MLIS from the University of Maine. She is an acting archivist for the Caribou Public Library in Caribou, Maine, and is also on the Caribou Public Library board of trustees.

Brenda Jackson **Bourgoine** is a genealogist and a charter member of the Aroostook County Genealogical Society. She has served as past president of the Nylander Museum of Natural History in Caribou, Maine, and as past vice president of the Caribou Public Library Board of Trustees.

Nancy A. **Bunker** is the head of public services at the Whitworth University Library in Spokane, Washington. She earned her MLS from the University of Denver and has taught a course entitled "Genealogy in Cultural Context" at the university for several years. She is the author of *Primary Source Collections in the Pacific Northwest*.

Kirsten **Canfield** is the multimedia librarian for Arapahoe Libraries in Arapahoe County, Colorado. She earned her MLIS from Rutgers University. She specializes in helping patrons digitize their old media, create audiovisual projects and use technology.

Tracy **Carr** is the library services director at the Mississippi Library Commission in Jackson, Mississippi, where she also serves at the Mississippi Center. She earned her MLIS from the University of Alabama. She is a contributor to *The Mississippi Encyclopedia* and is a reviewer for *Reference and User Services Quarterly*.

Hong **Cheng** is a librarian at the University of California, Los Angeles (UCLA), where he also earned his MLIS. He also worked as the library director at the Art Institute of California, Los

Angeles. He has published on modern and contemporary Chinese history, Chinese local gazetteers and genealogies, historical theory and library science.

Rhonda L. **Clark** is an associate professor of information and library science at Clarion University of Pennsylvania and oversees the MSLS concentration in local and archival studies. She earned her MLIS from the University of Pittsburgh. She volunteers at the community level in local studies and genealogy programming, indexing and digital access.

Janet **Curtiss** is the special collections librarian for the St. Clair County Library System in Port Huron, Michigan. She earned her MLIS at Wayne State University in Detroit and has experience in both public and academic libraries, and as a freelance indexer.

Cheri J. **Daniels** is head of reference services at the Kentucky Historical Society in Frankfort, Kentucky, and also serves as the editor for *Kentucky Ancestors*, KHS' genealogy publication. She earned her MSLS from the University of Kentucky and lectures frequently at national genealogical conferences, also advising on genealogical subjects on local and national television.

Renée L. **DesRoberts** is the special collections librarian at the McArthur Public Library in Biddeford, Maine. She holds an MLIS from Simmons College in Boston. She was a founding member of both the Society of American Archivists' Public Library Archives + Special Collections and New England Archivist's Local History roundtables.

Chelsea S. **Dinsmore** is the chair of digital support services and associate university librarian at the George A. Smathers Libraries at the University of Florida. She holds an MLIS from the University of Texas at Austin and conducts research to improve the accessibility of UF's digital collections.

Charlene **Garcia Simms** is a genealogy and special collections librarian at Pueblo City-County Library District in Colorado and has an MLIS from the University of Arizona. She was a part of the Knowledge River program that encourages Hispanics and Native Americans to pursue library science. She has published on genealogy and the regional history of Colorado and New Mexico.

Vera **Gubnitskaia** is a reference librarian at Valencia College in Winter Park, Florida, and has library degrees from the Moscow Institute of Culture in Russia and Florida State University. She has published essays in numerous anthologies, coedited multiple essay collections, written indexes, authored book reviews, and presented at conferences.

Barbara J. **Hampton** is an academic reference librarian and earned her MLIS from Southern Connecticut State University. She specializes in social sciences, particularly patents, trademarks, and copyright. She has served as representative to the United States Patent and Trademark Office's Patent and Trademark Resource Center (PTRC) program.

Andrew **Hart** is a reference librarian and earned an MSLS from Clarion University and an MSS from Ohio University. He is a member of the American Library Association, the Ohio Library Council and the Correctional Education Association. He is a contributor to Public Libraries Online and writes monthly articles on library ethics, outreach services and programming.

Margaret E. **Hewitt** is a special collections librarian for the Butler Area Public Library, in Butler, Pennsylvania. She received her MA in public history at Duquesne University. She is a member of the Society of American Archivists, the Pennsylvania Library Association and the Stone House Center for Public Humanities' community advisory board.

Jessica **Holden** manages archival reference services in the Joseph P. Healey Library at the University of Massachusetts in Boston. She holds an MLIS from Simmons College. She has processed manuscript collections at the Boston Public Library and The History Project, an LGBTQ community archive in Boston.

Anna J. **Kephart** is the coordinator of the Southern Maryland Studies Center, a local history collection at the College of Southern Maryland. She earned an MSLS with a concentration in archives and records management from the University of North Carolina at Chapel Hill. She serves on the advisory board for the Historic Maryland Newspapers Project.

Noah **Lenstra** is an assistant professor of library and information studies at the University of North Carolina at Greensboro, where he teaches on archives and special collections. His work on the history of genealogy in public libraries was included in *Encounters with Popular Pasts*.

Douglas **McElrath** is the director of special collections and university archives at the University of Maryland Libraries. He is the co-principal investigator of the Historic Maryland Newspapers Project and teaches courses in the College of Information Studies and the School of Architecture, Planning, and Preservation.

Thomas **McFarland** is the staff development program officer and a member of the User Experience Team for the University of Nebraska–Lincoln Libraries. He earned his MLS from Emporia State University in Kansas. He is a member of the Association of Professional Genealogists and president of the Great Plains Chapter.

Rosemary L. **Meszaros** is a professor and coordinator of government information/law at Western Kentucky University. She is the author of *Rising Through the Ranks* and has contributed to the *Encyclopedia of American Law and Criminal Justice* and the *Encyclopedia of Military Science*. She serves on the editorial board of the *Journal of Academic Librarianship*.

Larry **Naukam** is the retired historical services consultant for the Central Library of Rochester and Monroe County in New York. He was the head of the local history, genealogy, and digitizing departments and received his MLS from the State University of New York at Buffalo. He volunteers as a scanner and cataloger and is president of the Rochester Genealogical Society.

Carmen **Nigro** provides genealogy instruction for the Irma and Paul Milstein Division of United States History, Local History and Genealogy at the New York Public Library. She holds an MLIS from San Jose State University and a Certificate of Genealogical Research from Boston University.

Lisa A. **Oberg** received her MLS from the University of Washington (UW), where she is the associate director and history of science and medicine curator for special collections in the UW Libraries. She serves on the advisory board for UW's genealogy and family history certificate program and gives genealogy lectures at UW and the Seattle Genealogical Society.

Katherine **Pennavaria** is a professor and coordinator of the Visual and Performing Arts Library at Western Kentucky University. She is the author of *Genealogy* and *Providing Reference Services*, as well as numerous columns on genealogy in *Kentucky Libraries*. She has given state and national presentations on genealogy and published articles in various scholarly journals.

Robin C. **Pike** is the manager of digital conversion and media reformatting at the University of Maryland. She received her MLIS from the University of Pittsburgh, specializing in archives and records management. She is co-principal investigator on the Historic Maryland Newspapers Project.

Jenny L. **Presnell** is a humanities/social sciences librarian at the Miami University Libraries and obtained her MLS from Indiana University. She has taught courses on the history of information and historical research, and is the author of *The Information-Literate Historian*. Her research interests include first generation college students and historical newspaper preservation.

Nancy **Richey** is the reading room coordinator and visual resources librarian for the Department of Library Special Collections at Western Kentucky University. She received her degree in Information Science from the University of Kentucky. She provides research assistance, preservation classes and library research instruction to individuals and university classes.

Joanne M. **Riley** is interim dean of libraries at the University of Massachusetts Boston, where she has led several community archives projects, including the "Mass. Memories Road Show" and the "1919 Boston Police Strike Project." She holds an MLIS degree from the University of Alabama.

About the Contributors

Carol **Smallwood** received her MLS from Western Michigan University. She has edited the essay collections *Librarians as Community Partners, Bringing the Arts into the Library, Creative Management of Small Public Libraries in the 21st Century*, and *The Library's Role in Supporting Financial Literacy for Patrons*, and others. She has worked in school, public, academic and special libraries.

Beth **Stahr** is the head of reference and instruction at Southeastern Louisiana University in Hammond, Louisiana. She earned her MLS from Syracuse University. She is a Certified Genealogist (SM), a frequent lecturer at genealogy conferences and was named Outstanding Academic Librarian by the Louisiana Library Association in 2012.

Natalie Bazan **Starosta** earned her MLIS from the University of Illinois. She is a member of the American Library Association and serves on the LearningRT board. She was a 2016 ALA Emerging Leader. She received the 2016 Citizen of the Year Award from the Dorr Lions Club and volunteers for many organizations.

Susan **Steele** is co-president of TIARA—The Irish Ancestral Research Association. She served as director of TIARA's Foresters Project, has given numerous Foresters Project presentations and continues to supervise volunteers. She holds an MS in human services from the University of Massachusetts Boston.

Barry L. **Stiefel** is an associate professor of art and architectural history at the College of Charleston in South Carolina. He earned his Ph.D. from Tulane University in Louisiana and teaches a seminar where students conduct in-depth research on preservation of heritage sites, material objects, or traditions associated with their family's history.

Leslie A. **Wagner** is an Associate Archivist at the University of Texas at Arlington, where she received her MA in history. She is chair of the American Library Association's Mapping and Geospatial Information Round Table (MAGIRT), coeditor of *Spoken Memories* and author of several LibGuides on Genealogy, Texas, and local history resources.

Ben **Walker** is the associate dean for discovery, digital services and shared collections and associate university librarian at the George A. Smathers Libraries at the University of Florida. He received his MS in library studies from Florida State University and has published on storage facilities, collection development, and leadership.

Anastasia Varnalis **Weigle** is a Ph.D. student at Simmons College in Boston and director of the Caribou Public Library in Maine. Her research interests include user's experience with physical objects, materials literacy, and materials experience of the studio artist. She is part-time faculty at the University of Maine at Augusta, teaching archives management and digital preservation.

Index

abstracting 22, 23–24
academic instruction 16–17
academic libraries 52–59; Chinese genealogy 104–111; outreach 85–93
accuracy 10, 242, 258–263
ACRL Framework for Information Literacy 262
addresses 195
advertising *see* publicity and marketing
advocacy 73, 74
African American genealogy 115
African American Lives 237
African American photographs 224
Afro-American Historical and Genealogical Society 61
agreements, partnerships 72–74
aircraft, historic 158
albumen prints 152
altered books 36–43
amateur cemetery catalogers 141–142
The American Guide Series 33
American Library Association 268; awards and grants 273–274; workshops 275
American Life Histories 34
analysis 38–39, 179
Ancestor Chart 151
Ancestry.com 98, 167–168, 176, 179, 238
annotation 21
answers, crowdsourced 259, 260–261; *see also* "Crowdsourcing" titles
Arapahoe Libraries, Colorado 250–257
architecture 16–17
Archive.org 231
archives 17–19, 36–43, 112; digitization of 45–51; Irish records 52–59; mission and goals 72; policies 71, 72–74; public libraries 71–72, 73; research sources instruction 80; *see also* collections
Arlington, Texas (case study) 30–31
army discharge records 98

Aroostook County, Maine 69–76
art 36–43
assessment, historic places 160
assessment, program *see* evaluation
assisting patrons 146–155; *see also* patrons; reference interview; reference service
Association for Documentary Editing 27
Association of the Chinese Genealogy 109
at-risk records 52–59
attributes, information 38–39
audiocassette tapes 253–254
authority control 109–110
autopsy reports 166

behavior, research 9–11; *see also* research
Betamax tapes 254
bibliographic references 102, 110, 129
biographical research 58
births 140; *see also* vital records
blogs *see* social media
Bloom's taxonomy 134
Board for Certification of Genealogists 129
Boston Police Department 58
brochures, informational 14, 74
budgets 271; 278–284; *see also* finances; funding
buffered enclosures 153
buildings 159–161; preservation 16–17
burials 141–142, 166
Butler Area Public Library, Pennsylvania 242–249

Caribou Public Library, Maine 69–76
cataloging 267
Catholic Association of Foresters (CAF) 52–59
cemeteries 141–142, 167, 169–171
census 79–80, 195; military information 98
Champaign County Historical Archives 112
Champaign Public Library 112

Charles Revson Foundation 131
charts 115, 135, 151; ancestral 280
Chinese genealogy 104–111
Chronicling America 12–20, 32, 33, 169; *see also* newspapers
Church of Jesus Christ of the Latter-day Saints 140–141, 237
citations, bibliographic 102, 110, 129
citizenship 184
city directories 195
civil court records 99–100
Civil War Soldiers and Sailors Database 99
Clarion University, Pennsylvania 227–234
classes *see* instruction
collaboration *see* partnerships
collaborative learning 130–131; *see also* "Crowdsourcing" titles
collaborative web presence 230–231
collection development 21–28, 283; graduate courses in 83
collections 36–43; budgets 278–284; digitized 231–232, 264–270; microfilm 246–247; ownership 74; programs based on 221–224; promotion of 210–217; sharing 74; types of 148–149; value of 104–111; *see also* archives
collective wisdom 259, 260–261; *see also* "Crowdsourcing" titles
College of Southern Maryland 17–19
colleges 17–19, 77–84, 211, 227–234
Columbia City Council Minutes Project 25–26
community foundations 273
community records 183–192
competency standards 173
compiled service records 97
concentration, academic 227–234; *see also* instruction; MLIS
Confucius Family Genealogy 106
context, historical 31–32
continuing education 120–127, 177; *see also* instruction
controlled vocabulary 232; *see also* authority control

289

coordinates, geographic 196–200
copyright 191, 232
coroner's autopsy reports 166
corporations 273
costs, digitization 252
courses, college 227–234, 235–241; MLIS 77–84; *see also* instruction
court records 99–102
craft, historic 158
creativity 36–43
credibility 129, 130, 242, 258–263
crew, ship 142–143
criminal court records 100
critical evaluation 10
crowd wisdom 259, 260–261; *see also* "Crowdsourcing" titles
cultural context 238–240
cultural heritage 157, 159, 161–162
customs 157, 161–162
cyanotype 152
Cyndi's List 27, 143

daguerreotype 152
DAR (Daughters of American Revolution) 17–19
data, digital 264–270
data entry 243–245
data gathering 38–39
data profiles 144
data verification 258–263
databases 12–20, 21–28, 91; Chronicling America 12–20; death records 167–170; FamilySearch 45–51; free 139–144; instruction 87–88; Internet Archive 45–51; newspapers 169, 242–249; obituaries 242–249; patent 185–190
Daughters of American Revolution (DAR) 17–19
death records 139, 140, 164–172; *see also* vital records
decentralization, Chinese 105
decisions, research 261
digital content management 21–28
digital family maps 193–201
digital learning community 265
Digital Public Library of America (DPLA) 231
digital services 227–234
digitization 7, 32–33, 110, 140, 142–143, 154, 168, 176; archives 45–51; graduate courses 82–83; vs. indexing 248; newspaper 12–20; reasons and methods 264–270; obituaries 242–249; self-service stations 250–257
directories 268
displays, library 212–213
DNA testing 6, 8–9, 88, 124–125
docents 214
documentary editing 21–28
documents 151–154, 253; *see also* records
donors 272–273; *see also* finances
draft registrations 96

economy 106
editing, documentary 21–28

education 120–127; *see also* instruction; MLIS
elementary school students 62–63
Ellis Island 142
emotions 37
employment 60
enclosures, storage 153; *see also* preservation
enlistment records 96
ephemera 42
equipment: digitization 250–257, 266, 267; oral history interviews 117; scanning 45–51
errors, research 10
ethical issues 11
ethnic groups 7–8, 186, 236–237, 240; *see also* under specific groups and nationalities
evaluation 217; program 67, 92–93; search 179; of sources 258–263
events *see* programs
evidence 179
evidence-based writing 133–134
Excel, Microsoft 196
experiences, user 38–39
external information attributes 38–39

Facebook *see* social media
Faces of America 237
fact evaluation 10
Family Group Sheet 151
family heritage 156–163
family history 146–155
Family History Library (Salt Lake City) 168
family records 99, 183–192
family stories 113–114
family tree software 144
FamilySearch.org 45–51, 61, 140–141, 168, 231
federal records 101
Federal Writers' Project 33, 34
Federation of Genealogical Societies (FGS) 6, 9
FGS (Federation of Genealogical Societies) 6, 9
filiation genealogists 146
film-based photographic materials 153
finances 271–277, 278–284; *see also* funding
Find a Grave 141–142, 169–170
Finding Your Roots 6, 114, 146, 237
fire insurance maps 29–31
floppy discs 254
Fold3.com 98
Folklore Project 34
formats, digitized 252–255
foundations 131, 142, 273
fragile materials 154, 264, 265–266; *see also* preservation
free resources 138–145
Freedmen's Bureau Records 61
friends records 183–192
funding 74–75; digitization 266–267, 269–270; grants 271–277
funeral documents 139, 165, 166

Gates, Henry Lewis 6
gelatin silver print 153
Genealogical Proof Standard 173, 178, 179, 180
genealogists *see* patrons
Genealogy and Family History Day program 85, 89–91
Genealogy in Cultural Context course 238–240
Genealogy Library Services graduate course 77–84
Genealogy Over Lunch program 85, 86–89
Genealogy Proof Standard 129
Genealogy Roadshow 114
Genealogy Tea and Sympathy program 218–221
genetic genealogy 124–125; *see also* DNA testing
geographic coordinates 196–200
geographic name authority 109
German population 8
glass plate negatives 152
goals: information literacy 180–181; research 9–10, 157
Google 138–139; maps 195, 196; patent search 187–190
government records 95–103
government regulations 159
graduate degrees 77–84; *see also* courses, college; education; instruction
graphic design 89–90
graphic organizers 135
graves 141–142, 167, 169–170
group-based problem solving 131; *see also* crowdsourcing
groups 210, 214

Haley, Alex 6, 114
health organizations 273
heirlooms 158
heritage, family 156–163
heritage documentation project 160–161
high school students 63–64
Hispanic population 8
Historic Maryland Newspaper Project 13–19
historic places 159–161
historic registry designation 159–161
historical literature 104
historical records 21–28; court 99–102; military 95–99; research instruction 81
historical resources 29–35
historical societies 48, 85–86, 218–226, 228–229
historical timelines 31–32
history, family 146–155
history and genealogy 235–241
History Section Genealogy Committee (RUSA) 122–123, 124
Hughes, Carl 203–209

identification storage labels 153
identity theft 10–11
immoveable objects 157, 159–161

impact *see* evaluation
indexing 22, 23–25, 55, 56, 57, 140, 142–143, 210; newspapers 242–249; obituaries 242–249; volunteers 243–245; *vs.* digitization 248
Indianapolis, Indiana 32–33
information, forms of 38–39
information literacy 134–135; standards 173–181, 262
innovation 60–68
The Innovation Project 131
inquest proceedings 166
Instagram *see* social media
Institute of Museum and Library Services (IMLS) 273
instruction 7, 8, 9–10, 14, 60–61, 64–66; archival 58; art 37–38; budgets 278–284; crowdsourcing 218–226; Daughters of American Revolution 17–19; death records 164–172; digitization 255; grant-writing 271–272; methods and topics 87–88, 129–137, 280; outreach 210–211; preservation 151–154, 156–163
instruction, college 16–17, 211, 227–234, 235–241; MLIS 77–84
instruction, free online resources 138–145
instruction, information literacy 173–181
instruction, reference 77–84
insurance maps 29–31
intangible heritage 157, 161–162
intellectual property 191, 232
interactive family tree 144
interdisciplinary studies 238–240
interest in genealogy 45–46
internal information attributes 38–39, 40
international (non-U.S.) records 168
International Society of Genetic Genealogy 124
internet resources 45–51, 175–176
interns 213, 227, 230
interviews 7, 62–63; oral history 112–119
introduction to genealogy 79
inventions 183–192
The Irish Ancestral Research Association (TIARA) 52–59
Irish genealogy 52–59

Kentucky Historical Society 218–226
keywords 178, 187–188; *see also* search

labels, storage 153
learning, collaborative 130–131
learning community 265
legal cases 101–102
legal issues 11, 57, 184
LibCal 90
Liberty Ellis Foundation 142–143
Library Grants Blogspot 274

Library of Congress 13, 14, 29–30, 32, 34, 115, 160–161
Library Works Website Grants and Funding page 274
life events 140
lineage societies 177
linked data 233
literacy, information 173–181
local digital services 227–234
local donors 272–273
local history and sources 60–68, 101, 125, 159, 215
locations 194–195

magazine gun 184
magazine indexing 24–25; *see also* indexing
management: digitization 266–267; grants 275–277
manifest records, ship 142–143
Mannix, Mary 15–16
maps 29–31, 136, 193–201
marketing *see* publicity and marketing
marriages 140
Maryland State Archives 12–20; *see also* archives
Master Degrees, Library and Information Science 77–84, 227–234
McArthur Public Library, Maine 37
media releases 89
memorial notices 166
memory issues 226
Mercer County, Pennsylvania 60–68
metadata 226, 232–233
methodologies, outreach 13–15; research 261–262; *see also* outreach; research
Michigan Room 278–279
middle school students 63
migration 8, 105–106, 193–201
military records 95–99
militia records 98
MLIS (Master of Library and Information Science) 77–84, 123, 227–234
models, patent 184–185; *see also* patent records
modernization 109
modules, course 79–84; *see also* instruction
Montgomery County, Mississippi 34–35
motivation for research 174–175; *see also* research
moveable objects 157, 158
movies and television 214, 237
museums 48
muster rolls 96
"Mystery quilt" 73

narratives 36–43, 179–180
National Archives and Records Administration 98
National Digital Newspaper Program 12–13

National Endowment for Humanities 12–20
National Park Service 99, 160–161
National Personnel Records Center 98
National Register of Historic Places 16, 159–160
National Trust for Historic Preservation 159
Native American genealogy 115
Nebraska State Historical Society 85–86
negatives, photography 153, 253
neighbors records 183–192
networking 110
new information, creation of 38–39, 41–42
New York Public Library 131; *see also* public libraries
Newspaper Title Directory 13
newspapers 12–20, 23–24; death records 169; digitizing historical 32–33; indexing 242–249
non-profit organizations 272

obituaries 165; indexing 23–24, 242–249
objectives: instructional 79–84; programs 92; *see also* instruction
OCR (optical character recognition) 188, 190
Ogden Photograph Collection program 223–224
Online Military Indexes and Records 99
online resources 138–145, 176, 258–263; *see also* databases
open house 73
optical character recognition (OCR) 188, 190
oral history 112–119
original sources 132–133
outcomes: grant reporting 276, 277; research 180
outreach 7, 13–15, 60–68, 73, 74, 282–283; academic libraries 85–93; archives 17–19; crowdsourcing 218–226; graduate courses 83; prison 203–209; programs 218–226; *see also* partnerships
ownership, collection 74

paper prints 152
paradigm shift 6
partnerships 7, 25–26, 52–59, 60–68, 69–76, 216; collections 231–232; colleges 211; digitization 268–269; with historians 235–241; policies 72–74; types of 73; web presence 230–231; *see also* outreach
passengers 142–143
patent records 183–192
patrilineal family lineage 105, 106
patrons 9–11, 15–16; death records search 164–172; instruction 138–145; patron types 146–147, 148–150, 176–177, 235–236;

performance indicators 180; preservation instruction 156–163
pedigrees 78, 151, 236
peer-to-peer learning 130–131
pension records 97
performance indicators 180
Personal Archiving: Preserving Your Digital Memories 115
personal name authority 109
personnel records 96
Pew Internet and American Life Study 15, 120
photographs 7, 152–154, 159, 253, 255
Piecing Together History 221–223
pinning location 195–196
Pinterest *see* social media
plastic storage 153
policies: archives 71, 72–74; reference service 150
political structure 105
popularity: of digitization 252; of genealogy 45–46
Port of New York 142
Port Tobacco, Maryland 17–18
portals, web 230–231
portfolio, genealogical 77, 78–79
preparation: patrons 151; staff 146–155; *see also* continuing education; instruction; staff development
presentations 211–212
preservation 7, 156–163; and digitization 264–265, 266, 267–268; environmental concerns 154; graduate courses 82–83; historic 16–17; immoveable objects 159–161; intangible heritage 161–162; moveable objects 158; newspaper 12–20; paper items 152–154; patron assistance 146–155; photographs 152–154; technology use 154
primary resources 21–28, 108, 132–133
"Principles for Digitized Content" (ALA) 268
prints 152–153
prison outreach 203–209
probate proceedings 166
problem-based learning 131–132
processing of records 52–59
professional development 177, 203–209; graduate courses 83; *see also* instruction; MLIS
professional genealogists 177
programs 60–68, 73, 279–280; academic libraries 85–93; graduate courses 83; objectives 92; oral history 112–119; outreach 218–226; tea party 218–221; topics 91, 220; *see also* instruction
promotion *see* publicity and marketing
pseudo collections 42
public housing residents 60–68
public libraries 37, 69–76, 112, 131, 242–249, 250–257, 278–284
public speaking 211

publications 74, 124
publicity and marketing 67, 88, 89–90, 210–217, 233, 282–283; digitization self-service 256–257
publishing 108, 109, 216
purpose of genealogy 236–237

queries, research 131–132, 147, 150, 151–154, 178
questionnaires 7, 120, 123; evaluations 92–93
quilts 73
Quinby Street Resource Center 60–68

racial heritage 186
record preservation *see* preservation
record processing 52–59
record years 140
recording results 144
records: death 164–172; historical 21–28; patents 183–192
reference, instruction 77–84; *see also* instruction
reference interview 124, 131–132, 178
reference service 15–16, 120, 146–155; archives 17–19; death records search 164–172; education 122–124; graduate courses 81–82; information literacy 173–181; obituaries and newspapers 247; policies 150; preservation 156–163; standards 177–178; virtual 229–230
registration, program 90
regulations, government 159
relationships 141
religion 105
repeating rifle 184
research: Chinese genealogy 101; decisions 261; examples 30–31, 32–33, 34–35; genealogy utilization 107–108; methods 38–39; military and court records 95–103; newspapers 242–249; obituaries 242–249; oral history 112–119; patent 185–190; process 79–84; researchers 9–11, 15–16; support 74–75; timelines 157; types 235–236
residence 140, 184, 194–196
resources: free online 138–145; historical 29–35; types of 148–149
responsibilities, librarians' 10–11
result verification 139
Richland Library (Columbus, South Carolina) 21–28
Robinson family letters program 224–225
Roots (movie) 6, 114, 237
Roots Tech 6, 9
RootsWeb 259, 261
RUSA 122–123, 124

St. Clair County Library, Michigan 278–284

salted paper 152
Sanborn Fire Insurance Maps 29–31
scaffolding, education 130
scanning 45–51, 154; *see also* digitization
Scholastic Librarian Grants page 274
scientific research method 261–262
search: Google 138–139; keywords 187–190; military and court records 95–103; newspapers 242–249; obituaries 242–249; strategies 164–172; tools 21–28, 108, 124; *see also* research
self-publishing 8, 109
self-reporting 38–39
self-service digitization stations 250–257
seminars 282
senior citizens 7, 9–10, 60, 67–68
settlement 193–201
shared collections 74, 231–232; *see also* collections; outreach; partnerships
Sharon, Pennsylvania 60–68
ship manifest records 142–143
ships, historic 158
skill levels, patron 146–147
slavery 64–65, 224–225
slides, 35 mm 253
Smoky Hill Library 251–252
social history 104–105, 237
social media 124, 177, 213, 228–229
Social Security Death Index 167–168
societies 214, 218–226; genealogical 69–76; historical 48, 52–59, 61, 85–86, 228–229; mission and goals 72; volunteers 230
socio-cultural information attributes 38–39, 40–41
software, mapping 200–201
Southglenn Library, Colorado 251
space 50, 278–279
speakers 215
special collections 36–43, 146–155; features of 147; local 229–231; *see also* archives; collections
Spencer, Christopher 184
spreadsheets 196
staff development 24, 26, 77–84, 278, 279; digitization 255–256; *see also* instruction; MLIS
staffing 49–50, 217
standards 109, 235; information literacy 173–181; instructional 129–130; terminology 109–110
state library organizations 273
states, U.S. 12–20; records 101
statistics 110, 276
The Statue of Liberty-Ellis Island Foundation, Inc. 142
status-related genealogy 236
storage 153
stories 36–43, 113–114
strategic initiatives 85

strategies, search 164–172; see also research; search
students: college 56, 63–64; elementary school 62–63; high school 63–64; middle school 63
surnames 8

T.T. Wendell Collection program 224
tagging 233
tangible heritage 157
taxonomy 134
tea parties 218–221; see also programs
techniques, educational 129–137; see also instruction
technology 6, 12–20, 176; information about 186–187; preservation issues 154
television and movies 237
textbooks 124, 126
themes 38–39
timelines 31–32, 157
tintypes 152
Titusville Historical Society, Pennsylvania 228–229
tools, information about 186–187; digitization 250–257
tours 216
Tracing Enslaved Ancestry presentation 64–65
trademarks 191
traditional Chinese genealogy 104–106
traditions 157, 161–162
training see instruction; staff development
transcription 21, 25–26, 27
tree, genealogy 135, 144; 156, 173–181, 260
trust issues 225–226
tutorials, video 14

U.S. Newspaper Program 12–20; see also newspapers
U.S. Patent and Trademark Office (USPTO) 183; see also patent records
universities, Chinese genealogy in 104–111
University of Florida 45–51
University of Illinois 112
University of Maryland 16–17
University of Massachusetts 52–59
University of Nebraska–Lincoln 85–93
University of New Hampshire 203–209
University of Washington 77–84
Urbana Free Library, Illinois 112
urbanization 105–106
usage and digitization 264
user experiences 38–39
utilization of genealogy 107–108

value, genealogy 104–111
vehicle, historic 158
vendors 216
verification 139, 242, 258–263
Vermont Digital Newspaper Project 14; see also newspapers
VHS tapes, digitization 252–253
Vicksburg, Mississippi 34–35
vinyl records 254
virtual reference 229–230; see also reference service

visual representation 193–201
vital records 165; see also births; death records
volunteers 48, 49, 54, 56, 58, 140, 141–142, 214, 230; indexing 243–245; research 247
Voter Registration Census (1868) 26–27

war records 99
wartime patents 187; see also patent records
washing machine 184
Watson family letters program 224–225
web presence 139–144, 228–231
webinars 281
Wendell, T.T. collection 224
Western genealogical research 104
White Frost Icebox 184
Who Do You Think You Are? 6, 114, 146, 237
Wisconsin 73
wisdom, crowd 259, 260–261; see also "Crowdsourcing" titles
women, resources about 186
Works Progress Administration 33–35
workshops see instruction
WorldConnect Project 259, 261
WPA County Files 33–35
writing grant applications 274–275

youth organizations 273

ZeeMaps (software) 199